PRAISE FOR
FIGHTING
FOR PEACE

"He aggressively and successfully waged war against the Washington Establishment....Few former secretaries of defense have been willing to explain why they did what they did while they were in the Pentagon. Caspar Weinberger has no such reservations."
—*Los Angeles Times*

❖

"His inside account of the Irangate episode is especially worth reading. His views may sound old-fashioned—just as Churchill's did 50 years ago—but events around the world confirm the view that strength, not weakness, is the surest path to peace."
—*Forbes*

❖

"A revealing and interesting account of the times."
—*Newark Star-Ledger*

❖

"Essential reading for those alarmed about the current trend in U.S. military cutbacks....In his familiar, no-nonsense style, Weinberger discusses the massive build-up of American arms during his tenure as secretary of defense, 1980-1988, and warns it is essential that the U.S. retain its present military strength."
—*Publishers Weekly*

❖

"An important, serious book. Weinberger's vantage point was unique; his remembrances are undistorted by self-aggrandizement."
—*Booklist*

❖

"An in-depth look at some of the major political and military challenges which faced the Reagan administration during Weinberger's tour of duty....Weinberger's memoirs—written in a clear, lively, and decidedly non-bureaucratic style—offer considerable insight in the kaleidoscopic array of historical events of the early and mid-1980s and the dynamic personalities who were the dominant players in that era. His multifaceted survey highlights developments across a wide spectrum of issues...*Fighting for Peace* is a 'must.'"
—*Sea Power*

❖

"Each chapter adds considerable detail to the public record, painting an overall picture of a coherent strategy: military strength on the U.S. side would have a direct political impact on the Soviet side."
—*Newsweek*

❖

Caspar Weinberger

FIGHTING FOR PEACE

Seven Critical Years in the Pentagon

WARNER BOOKS

A Time Warner Company

Warner Books, Inc., 666 Fifth Avenue, New York, NY 10103
W A Time Warner Company
Printed in the United States of America
First trade printing: April 1991
10 9 8 7 6 5 4 3 2 1

Library of Congress Cataloging-in-Publication Data

Weinberger, Caspar W.
  Fighting for peace: seven critical years in the Pentagon / by
Caspar W. Weinberger.
      p. cm.
    ISBN 0-446-39238-3
    1. United States—Military policy. 2. United States—Politics
and governrnent—1981-1989. 3. United States—History, Military—20th
century. 4. Weinberger, Caspar W. 5. Cabinet officers—United
States—Biography. I. Title.
UA23.W3697   1990
973.927—dc20   89-40462
                                                            CIP

Designed by Giorgetta Bell McRee
Cover designed by Tom Tafuri of One Plus One Studio
Cover photo by Burgess Blevins

CONTENTS

PREFACE

"*T*here is hereby established, as an Executive Department of the Government, the Department of Defense," in the words of the National Security Act of 1947, which consolidated the Departments of the Army, Navy and Air Force, "and the Secretary of Defense shall be the head thereof."

I was the Secretary of Defense from January 20, 1981, until November 23, 1987, and it is some of the major security and defense issues, events and activities of those years that I will attempt to record here.

There have, of course, been many other accounts written of those events. Some have come in the form of memoirs of people who served in President Reagan's Administration but had no responsibilities for defense matters. Most other accounts, articles appearing in daily newspapers and in periodicals, have been offered by writers who did not have the privilege of being present or personally involved in the issues about which they have written.

I have long wanted to set out the history and something of

the context of those near-seven years' events, as they appeared to me through my own participation in them.

It seems to me that it is appropriate, and indeed that it is my duty, to do so, because I was privileged to be a small part of that period. As one who has read and studied much history, I always prefer to read the accounts of those who themselves were there to take some part in the great events. Personal accounts—among the most notable, Winston Churchill's *World Crisis*, Dean Acheson's *Present at the Creation* and, available in eight volumes, *The Letters of Theodore Roosevelt*—always seem to me to be more vivid than others. No matter that their authors may be untrained as historians; personal accounts by participants have always given me a very much better sense of having been present than any second- or third-hand reports, no matter how well written and ornamental those research-based histories or sketches may be.

The writing of the full story—all the events of all of the days of those nearly seven years—will have to await a later day. It has seemed vital to me to record, as soon as possible, some of the highlights of those years as they appeared to a participant.

The process of writing this history of those several events, strung together on the thread of personal reminiscences, has served to remind me again of the debt I owe for the great privilege and honor that was mine in working with so many extraordinarily gifted and dedicated people. Their devotion to our country and to our freedom was the bond that united all their diverse talents.

First, of course, is President Reagan, whose leadership, political courage and vision enabled Americans to secure the benefits that come only with military strength: arms reduction, and increased stability. And my debt to him is all the greater because he gave me, with his confidence and trust, the matchless opportunity to share with him a part of this history.

And I must record my thanks to many others: to Will Taft[1],

---

1. Now our ambassador to NATO.

with whom I worked in great harmony and with great fun for all my years in the Federal Government, and who in a quiet way performed service the enormous value of which is only now coming to be known; and to Frank Carlucci, with whom I worked almost as long in various capacities, in all of which he displayed great loyalty, skill, and effectiveness.

General Colin Powell, Lieutenant General Carl Smith and Lieutenant General Gordon Fornell were my Senior Military Assistants, whose work in many ways made it possible for me to do whatever I was able to accomplish. They are all superb officers, and indeed they were nominated by their services because they were so skilled. They all went on from my office to other assignments of great responsibility, and have performed in them as they always would—with truly outstanding records. Colin I have known the longest—since he held a highly prized White House Fellowship in 1970, when I was in the Office of Management and Budget; and his appointment as Chairman of the Joint Chiefs of Staff, America's highest military position, enriches the Administration and our country beyond measure. Among my other excellent military assistants with whom I was proud to work were Admiral Don Jones and Marine Lieutenant Colonel Rich Higgins. In his eagerness to serve in all ways, Rich, in February 1988, had undertaken personal reconnaissance in the Beirut area as Commander of the unarmed U.N. Liaison Mission to Lebanon. While so engaged, he was taken hostage by some demented sect. His captors later killed him, in another of their regular displays of bestiality. Rich Higgins's service to his country was enormous, as was our loss upon his death.

So many others deserve special mention: Rich Armitage, whose great understanding and encyclopedic knowledge of Asia, the Middle East, and much else, helped beyond measure in significantly improving our relationships and friendships with those most vital countries.

And there were Richard Perle and, later, his Deputy, Frank

Gaffney, who were knowledgeable enough about arms control and arms reduction to know how wrong the conventional wisdom can be. They were particularly helpful, despite our occasional policy disagreements.

And of course, no account of the Defense Department would be complete without acknowledgment of the expertise, patience, diplomatic skills and judgment that have always characterized the work of my Executive Assistant, Kay Leisz, who joined our team during the transition between the Carter and Reagan administrations in 1980, and who still handles all manner of my schedule problems, travel, correspondence and speeches, to say nothing of knowing all the right (and wrong) generals, admirals, secretaries and diplomats. It is fair to say that without her extraordinary contributions, little could have been accomplished from day to day.

I want also to record the debt I owe to John Duncan for his highly valued work on speeches, this book, and generally fine help for many years.

I thank Eva Spencer and three members of her word processing staff at Rogers & Wells, Carol Eldridge, Vincent Shuler, and Socorro Vidanes, for their excellent typing support on this manuscript.

There are many more, including Thelma Stubbs Smith, who loyally, diligently and cheerfully served me as she has seven other Secretaries of Defense; and Joe Zaice and Bill Brown, who protected us all at home and abroad with great expertise.

There are also a few others, a very few, whose help and support and constant encouragement have been instrumental and are deeply appreciated. They will know that I mean them, and that I know they would prefer to be thanked—if at all—in this way.

And then there are the millions of those who served in the armed forces, for all of whom I felt a deep kinship and an even deeper admiration and responsibility. General Jack Vessey, who began, as I did, as an infantry private and who became Chairman of the Joint Chiefs of Staff, epitomized all the best of the American military. He and I worked closely and in full harmony all the time he was Chairman, and I have the greatest admiration for him. Admiral William Crowe, his successor, is another superb officer with whom I worked exceptionally well all the years of his incumbency. And my thanks too go to the hundreds of thousands of civilians who backed and helped us all so skillfully, and who daily gave the lie to the ignorant who delighted in attacking "the bureaucrats."

And then there is Jane, my wife, who was there at the beginning when we were both in the Army, and who was at the next beginning running my first campaign for the California Legislature, and who is always a constant source of the support and inspiration we all need, and a constant example of the courage we all should have—and it is to her I dedicate this book.

ABBREVIATIONS

ADF　　　　　Arab Deterrent Force (Syrian)

AWACS　　　Airborne Warning and Control System

CBU　　　　　cluster bomb unit

CINCLANT　Commander in Chief, Atlantic Forces

DIA　　　　　Defense Intelligence Agency (of the DOD)

DOD　　　　　Department of Defense

FEMA　　　　Federal Emergency Management
　　　　　　　　Administration

IDF　　　　　Israeli Defense Force

INF　　　　　intermediate-range nuclear forces

IRGC　　　　Islamic Revolutionary Guard Corps (Iranian)

IRIN　　　　Islamic Republic Iranian Navy

JCS	Joint Chiefs of Staff
JDA	Japan Defense Agency
MNF	Multinational Force (peacekeeping units from the United States, Italy, France and Britain in Lebanon; not United Nations controlled)
NPG	Nuclear Planning Group (of NATO)
NSC	National Security Council (President's)
NSDD	National Security Decision Directive
NSPG	National Security Planning Group (of NSC)
OECS	Organization of Eastern Caribbean States
OMB	Office of Management and Budget
PRC	People's Republic of China
SDIO	Strategic Defense Initiative Organization
SEALs	Sea, Air, Land (special Navy personnel)
START	Strategic Arms Reduction Talks
UAE	United Arab Emirates

FIGHTING
FOR PEACE

INTRODUCTION

*T*his history begins for me on the November day in 1980 when the President-elect called to ask me to become Secretary of Defense. But in a larger sense it began many years before that, when my latent interest in history and government was brought to the fore by my father. He used a bedtime story period to tell my brother and me a story of his own creation—the story of the drafting of the Constitution and of the various disputes and agreements in the Constitutional Convention that ultimately made possible the foundation of our country. The story went on for, I believe, several weeks, and was told in such an entertaining and dramatic fashion that my brother and I looked forward eagerly each night to the succeeding chapters. It takes a skilled storyteller to impart to subteenage children a sense of excitement in the story of how the authority and structure of the Senate and the House of Representatives were crafted by the members of the Constitutional Convention. But my father was both a skilled storyteller and an extraordinarily understanding and effective parent, as was my mother, a highly talented violinist who gladly gave up her career, because she believed that her proper role was to spend all of her time with her children. She did that; and it is from her that I derived my great interest in music and in the arts in general.

My father, it seemed to me, had always been vitally interested in politics and government. That began, I suppose, with his very active role in campus politics at the University of Colorado, and was fueled when he served briefly as a clerk to a Colorado legislative committee the summer after he graduated from law school in 1910.

My father continued to nurture and support my very early interest in politics and government. He encouraged me, when I was seven years old, to listen, on a quite primitive radio, to some of the proceedings of the 1924 Democratic National Convention in New York. That convention, in which the Democrats required 102 ballots to agree on a nominee, made an indelible impression on me. By the time I reached high school, not only had that basic interest never flagged; it had been spurred further by the advent of Franklin Roosevelt's New Deal in 1933. My excited and indeed insatiable quest for knowledge about politics and government now became even stronger. I had of course followed the 1932 campaign with great interest and had kept scrapbooks of the two conventions that year. I was a strong partisan of Herbert Hoover—a seemingly unlikely person to inspire a fifteen-year-old sophomore in high school, but I had always admired and been interested in him.

At the age of eleven, I had been taken by my father to a reception for Hoover in one of the San Francisco hotels during the 1928 campaign; and on election day in 1932 I had gone down to the San Francisco City Hall with several hundred school pupils to greet him, after his long and unsuccessful campaign for re-election. I have never forgotten the look of absolute weariness and total discouragement on Hoover's face as he stepped out on the balcony from one of the windows of the San Francisco City Hall, just above the statue of Lincoln, and greeted the school children who had been brought down to see the President of the United States. As the campaign was over and people had voted that morning (I had gone with my father into the curtained booth of the election machines near our home and seen him vote for Hoover), it was presumably considered proper then for the non-partisan school system to let the children see their President.

At home, of course, we followed the 1932 election returns very closely on the radio, as we had in 1928. The contrast was marked. In 1928 the evening radio broadcasts were made from the home of the President-elect on the campus of Stanford University, and there were various student groups serenading him and general signs of jubilation. A single less festive note was added by one of the students who got access to the radio and said that part of the joy at the election of Hoover came from the certain belief that he would move the then president of Stanford, Ray Lyman Wilbur, back to his cabinet, which indeed happened. In 1932, however, all the returns went the other way. Seeing how rapidly the fortunes of governments, politicians and indeed countries, could change was another valuable lesson for me.

Shortly after the inauguration of Roosevelt, the New Deal began in earnest and the papers were filled with references, puzzling to me because they were so incomplete, of many of the proposals and plans and the excited rhetoric of the early days of the New Deal. I felt that I was unable to get anything like the complete picture by reading merely the papers, and so I wrote to a California congressman and asked him to send me the *Congressional Record*. It duly arrived (normally about 7 or 8 days after the date of issue) and I read it assiduously, even including the "remarks extended in the Record," meaning the speeches never actually delivered.

Through it I gained an invaluable familiarity with congressional procedures, as well as a considerable insight into the nature of the legislation being sponsored. Most of that legislation filled me with apprehension. I thought that it imitated systems in other countries in trying to provide detailed planning and tight regulation of the actions of the individual, and that such regulation would fundamentally threaten our country's great opportunities for exercise of individual freedom—opportunities that had created so many new industries and brought such a high standard of living for so many. I had read some of Adam Smith and generally agreed with laissez-faire economic theory. I had also followed Hoover's 1932 campaign and liked his heavy reliance on individualism. I felt the country had prospered and progressed as far and as quickly as it had largely because everyone had a very great degree of individual freedom. I believed then, and believe now, that the greatest good for the greatest number is secured with a system that permits each person to choose his own path, or ladder, to rise as far and as fast as his abilities will take him, so long as he does not interfere with or harm others.

I understood or thought I understood that international factors had led to, or really caused, the depression we faced in 1933, but I was confident that we could get out of it by waiting for many of those conditions that caused it to abate, rather than by adopting the vigorous (and admittedly more exciting) actions the new Administration was taking every day. However, of this there will perhaps be more in later volumes, for it is my intention in this history to concentrate on some of the main actions that the United States Government took between the years 1981 and 1987 to improve and assure our own security and safety and that of our allies. I mention memories of childhood here only to bring into perspective the keen, deep and continuing interest I have always taken in virtually all governmental and political matters.

In 1934 I entered Harvard College, and after spending most of the first year struggling through and finally passing courses to satisfy the foreign language requirements Harvard then imposed on its undergraduates (to my lasting regret, I have never been very good at foreign languages), I enrolled primarily in government and English history courses. I continued to believe in and expound Adam Smith economics and the doctrine of individual freedom, and the danger, as I saw it, in collective, centralized, planned economies. I was, during much of that time, more or less the spokesman for what were then labeled conservative, anti-New Deal arguments on the issues of the day. I recall that Professor Arthur Holcomb, one of Harvard's leading teachers of government, would sometimes stop the discussion in his classes about five minutes before the end to say, "Let's hear what our conservative has to say about this," and then call on me.

Many of my views also found outlet in editorials in the Harvard *Crimson*, where I spent most of my undergraduate time. The *Crimson* was, and remains, a very independent, daily college newspaper. I believe now that my work there was instrumental in my learning to express, both orally and in writing, my pronounced views on both domestic and foreign matters. I did so often to the amusement of other students, who either were less engaged and more casual about their opinions, or felt as strongly as I did but in the opposite direction. The New Deal was very exciting then to many, and excitement breeds enthusiasm.

Over the years I have softened somewhat the intensity with which I express my views: Not Harvard indifference, but Harvard's "healthy skepticism" has modulated the vigor of my expression.

As events in Europe drew closer to war, my interest turned more from castigations of the New Deal to worries about another German attempt to dominate Europe, in what I felt appeared to be in many ways a repeat of the days before World War I. I felt a growing concern over the lack of preparedness in Britain that Winston Churchill was exposing in exciting and masterful speeches. I was also deeply unhappy with the isolationist and pacifist tendencies of the United States, which seemed designed primarily to keep us out of any war no matter what the cause and to ignore the fact, as I saw it, that our allies were right and the Germans and their allies were wrong. Neutrality never did appeal to me. I always felt that there was basically a right side and a wrong side and that it was important to enlist on the side of the right. But it was not enough just to enlist. Participation to me meant vigorous advocacy.

I greatly admired Theodore Roosevelt, not for all of his views, but for his passionate engagement and his scorn for those whose only role was that of spectator. I shared his feeling that the only noble course was to be in the dusty arena, striving valiantly.

> Service is rendered . . . by the man who . . . is actually in the arena, whose face is marred by dust and sweat and blood; who strives valiantly; who errs, and comes short again and again, because there is no effort without error and shortcomings; but who does actually strive to do the deeds; who knows the great enthusiasms, the great devotions; who spends himself in a worthy cause; who at the best knows in the end the triumph of high achievement and who, at the worst, if he fails, at least fails while daring greatly, so that his place shall never be with those cold and timid souls who know neither victory nor defeat.[1]

I did heed my father's wishes to complete Harvard Law School before going into the military; but as soon as I had graduated, I decided I had to enlist and that it had to be the infantry. To a considerable extent, my decision was influenced by reading I had done at Harvard, notably two of Siegfried Sassoon's novels, *Memoirs of a Foxhunting Man* and *Memoirs of an Infantry Officer*. As

---

1. Quoted in *The Free Citizen*, selections from the writings of Theodore Roosevelt, edited by Herman Hegedorn (New York: The Macmillan Company, 1956), pp. 91–92.

other readers of those books will know, any influence they worked would not derive from any glamour or excitement attached to the tasks of an infantry officer. I was simply struck with the belief that the way of the infantry was the only right and honorable way to serve. My mother's New England ancestry probably reinforced that attitude. In the days of her parents, it seemed, New England philosophy was based on the general idea that only the most disagreeable and uncomfortable course was honorable and that anything one enjoyed must be wrong! (I must confess that after I did enlist in the Army in San Francisco in September 1941 and found myself at the Presidio of Monterey, California, my first post, assigned for several weeks almost exclusively to kitchen police and latrine duty, my crusading fervor burned a bit low.)

What struck me most, however, was our total lack of preparedness for war itself. It showed in the attitudes of our instructors, officers and my colleagues, most of whom had been drafted rather than volunteering. It was also evident from the equipment we were issued, at Monterey and later at Camp Roberts, California. For some time it consisted of wooden replicas of rifles, small wooden blocks labeled "Hand Grenade," a few World War I bayonets and some clearly pre–1914 and extremely temperamental machine guns.

I had never fired a rifle, or indeed any weapon before. But in a very short time I appeared to be hitting bull's-eyes simply by doing what I was told; so despite my strong doubts about our general readiness for war, I felt that the Army training was basically good. Most of my colleagues, many of whom had had extensive hunting experience, were outraged by the positions the Army drill instructors insisted on for firing and, despite being veteran hunters, had great difficulty hitting anything.

Our lack of training and preparation became even more evident when the unit to which I was assigned after training, the 41st

Infantry Division, was sent to New Guinea. None of us, officers or men, had seen a jungle before or had the faintest idea how to deal with the tropical climate or the jungle environment.

Our Japanese opponents, on the other hand, had been well trained in jungle warfare and seemed little troubled by malaria or other hazards of the jungle environment. They were also extraordinarily good at concealment. Once, I recall, they managed to haul a reasonably large naval gun up into the thick coconut trees bordering the Buna airstrip, thus rendering the airstrip inoperable for several days. They would also tie a rifleman high up in jungle trees, and his unseen presence added unexpected hazards to our jungle patrols. (Now, fortunately, we have an excellent jungle training school in Panama, where the realistic training I saw as Secretary of Defense included even the surprise introduction into the curriculum of large snakes.)

I am sure that such early wartime experiences, coupled with my awareness of the problems Britain had had, caused by its unpreparedness, since the war began for it in 1939, impressed upon me the simple truth I have believed ever since: It is an extremely risky and dangerous business for any country to allow itself to become unarmed and unready for war.

Many years later, my reactions to our policy in Korea were that it was right for us to try to prevent Communist North Korea from overrunning the South, but seriously wrong for the Truman Administration to place so many restrictions, geographical and otherwise, upon our actions. I likened the effect of those constraints to trying to fight a war inside a football stadium. My personal experiences and those I had read about told me that if you had to go to war, you vitally needed enough freedom of maneuver to allow for flanking and behind-the-lines operations. I was particularly unhappy with the moves to limit General Douglas MacArthur's freedom of movement in Korea and the reprimands that were administered to him for going too far.

The war in Vietnam, with our "limited objectives" and yet our unlimited willingness to commit troops, reinforced my belief, which I expressed many times when I was the Secretary of Defense, that it was a very terrible mistake for a government to commit soldiers to battle without any intention of supporting them sufficiently to enable them to win, and indeed without any intention to win.[2]

Thus, it was not to an uninterested person that President Reagan had extended his invitation to serve him as his Secretary of Defense. Nor was the President-elect an unknown quantity to me.

I first met Ronald Reagan in 1965, when he had pretty well made up his mind that he would run for Governor of California. I had served in the California Legislature for six years, and had been quite active in San Francisco and California Republican Party affairs. Mr. Reagan was scheduled to attend a meeting in San Francisco of people who, for the most part, had been pledged to support the candidacy of George Christopher, who had been Mayor of San Francisco and was running for Governor after a prior candidacy for Lieutenant Governor. His supporters were gathered in one of the smaller private dining rooms of the Hotel Sir Francis Drake, waiting to meet and hear from Ronald Reagan. There had been some preliminary discussion, the gist of which was that it would be unfortunate to have a primary fight in California within the Republican Party, since we were a smaller party than the Democrats. Many held that Mayor Christopher, having been long associated with the party and having run for statewide office before, was entitled to more party support than someone such as Ronald Reagan, who had not run for office before.

Yet when Mr. Reagan entered that room and I met him for

---

2. I believe the first time I spoke publicly about that matter was to a Senate committee hearing, which reacted rather stoically. Later I spoke of it at a Veterans Day ceremony at Arlington National Cemetery, where the reaction was one of unrestrained approval.

the first time, it seemed to me that a totally new atmosphere entered with him and that all other concerns and considerations were set aside while collective attention focused on him, and indeed, followed him wherever he went in the room. He moved about quickly, with an evident but attractive shyness. I felt it as a kind of diffidence conveying that he felt he was probably interrupting something important, but he appreciated the opportunity to meet these people.

This was also the first time I had ever seen the electric and electrifying nature of the President's smile. It is difficult to describe, but easy to experience. The President's smile has always seemed to me to have the effect not only of physically lighting the entire room, but even of changing for the better the atmosphere, the discussion, the debate, or whatever else is happening at the moment of the President's entrance upon the scene. Over the years, when seeing him walk onto a stage, take the rostrum at a national convention, walk into a Cabinet meeting or enter a room filled with his legislative opponents, I have never failed to see that magic at work. And I have never failed to be reminded of that first time I met Ronald Reagan, when he entered a drab hotel room in San Francisco filled with people most of whom, he knew, were opposed to his candidacy.

I had the opportunity to work with him when he was Governor of California, and even before that, during his campaign in 1966 and in the transition period before January 1967, when he took office. During that period, Bill Clark and I and a few others, including Bud Kenny, then Vice President of Pacific Telephone and a specialist in the management of large organizations, worked out a new administrative structure for the Executive Branch of the Government of California.

It was essentially a plan to apply business organizational principles to government, and to fold the one hundred fifty or so state agencies, theoretically reporting to the Governor, into five groups, each under the equivalent of a corporate group vice president. Those five people, with one or two others, then constituted the Governor's Cabinet, with whom he met regularly after he took office and put our plan into effect.

The various myths about President Reagan and his "detached, unengaged style," his "lack of knowledge or direction"—those and similar criticisms spawned mainly by people who did not know him and who had not worked with him—differ grossly from the facts as I have long known them.

Governor Reagan took office as Governor without extensive knowledge of state government. But he had a good general knowledge of government and, far more important, a philosophy that informed, a philosophical rudder that guided him in deciding the vast number of issues large and small that came before him.

He read voluminously and quickly; he knew what he wanted to accomplish and he moved steadily and skillfully to reach his goals. Those goals were, essentially, to reduce the size and cost of state government, to give more freedom to the individual and in general to acknowledge the limitations on government's ability to solve problems. At home and abroad, due largely to the leadership of Governor Reagan, those ideas are far more widely accepted now than they were when he first took office.

He was easy to brief and his memory was phenomenal. His success at press conferences and on television and political platforms did not depend on memory alone, but on his marvelous ability to communicate and identify with his audiences. He has a genuine and deep interest in people, and he is a warm, decent and exceedingly friendly man, with whom it is a delight to work.

He had many ideas of his own; and while he did not waste time working out all the details in each case, his leadership qualities produced some extremely creative and imaginative proposals. Two of these that come to mind immediately were his plans to secure a balanced budget in California and to reduce the reach of state government by limiting the amount of resources the State could collect, and the Strategic Defense Initiative, about which more later.

He never feared to challenge the conventional wisdom, and that is one of the reasons why he was so successful in changing the political agenda of California and then the nation.

One of my tasks after the Governor appointed me Director of Finance in February 1968 was to recommend signature or veto on legislative bills affecting State finances. That meant that I went over a vast number of bills with him. He was consistent—but not rigidly so. He would sign a bill of great interest to nuns who ran a Catholic hospital in San Francisco, even though it entailed some cost. He would block a teachers' pay raise even though some political advisers had told him, "Governor, you'll never get re-elected if you veto that." He replied mildly, "But I did not come up here to get re-elected." On that occasion, he was impressed with the point that the teachers' performance had been criticized, and he did not feel that paying them more money would make them better teachers.

The Governor's strong preference, and mine, for austerity in State spending, derived from two factors. First, the more revenue a government has, the more it is likely to expand its activities and thus narrow the freedom of the individual; and second (and in 1967 of immediate and major concern), the Governor had inherited a large deficit from his predecessor, Governor Edmund G. Brown. Deficits were not permitted under the California Constitution, so Governor Reagan, much against his will, had been forced to call for a tax increase.

A year after I took office as Director of Finance, and when our state finances had improved and costs had been cut, I told him that shortly we would be reporting a small surplus, and I asked if he had any special projects he favored. "Yes," he said. "Let's give it back." Thus was created one of the first tax refunds in the state's history.

He was also perfectly willing to listen to others' ideas, and also to change his mind. When I became convinced that the University of California and the state colleges had been pinched a bit too much in earlier budgets, he was quite willing to agree to some increases.

With all of this, his personality was so open and friendly, and he was so funny, that he always succeeded in making people around him laugh and feel comfortable and happy at the same time he was inspiring great loyalty. I suppose that fewer assistants or advisors left his teams over the years because they were unhappy with him than was the case with most other political leaders.

He has never really changed personally in all the years I have known him, nor does he have any hidden or devious agendas.

Of the many incidents involving the Governor Reagan that I knew, one stands out particularly in my mind. He was giving a spring party for the Sacramento press corps and had urged the press to bring their families—and all did.

In the middle of the afternoon, a small child playing too close to the edge of the swimming pool fell in. The Governor ran across the lawn and into the pool, fully clothed, and he was out with the child so rapidly that unless you'd happened to be watching him when the accident happened, you would probably not have seen the action. After he had delivered the child to its frightened parents, he turned to the reporters and said: "I really hope none of you will write anything about this." Most did not.

Working with him was a constant delight and when you couple that with a political philosophy that I strongly shared, it is easier to see why I and many others were so willing to accept his summons back to government service when it came after his election to the Presidency.

I had experienced the great privilege of working with Mr. Reagan when he was Governor, for two years of his first gubernatorial term as his Director of Finance, and I had seen him in a variety of situations, conducting the State Cabinet meetings, preparing for and holding press conferences, making speeches, dealing with students who began most gatherings with the utmost hostility to him, and in many other situations and places. All through those years I never failed to be refreshed and inspired by the opportunity to work with this very remarkable man.

So the President-elect was not an unknown quantity to me. Had he been, I might have been tempted to decline the invitation and stay in the private sector, despite even my deep interest in governmental matters. I had already had a fair amount of Federal Government experience between the years 1970 and 1975, when I served in a number of capacities in the Nixon Administration and later under President Ford. I had returned to the private sector in 1975, and that private sector had a number of extremely attractive aspects.

I was General Counsel and a member of the Board of the Bechtel Group of companies, one of the largest construction companies in the world, with worldwide tasks that enabled me to see in action in all parts of the world the very best that American skills and technology could offer. I had been with Bechtel for five years, and in addition I served as a member of the Board of Directors of two other American companies and one English company. I had also recently completed extensive remodeling on a large old house my wife and I had acquired in Hillsborough on the San Francisco Peninsula.

The President-elect summed it up when he called in November 1980 to ask me to come back to Washington: "I know that you have a full, a very exciting, and a very rich life. I know all of the rewards that there are there for you, and now I want to spoil the whole thing by asking you to serve as Secretary of Defense." He emphasized briefly many of the points he had made during the campaign and at the convention (which I had attended) that had nominated him in Detroit.

Those points were, of course, the lamentable state to which

our armed forces had sunk as a result of neglect, while at the same time the Soviets were expanding and rapidly increasing their own military capabilities, despite earlier hopeful expressions to the contrary by various members of the outgoing Administration.

The President also emphasized matters that I had previously discussed with him, namely the great alarm that our policies and our lack of strength had occasioned among our allies; the growing belief, among both our allies and other nations with whom we should be friendly, that the United States was a very unreliable ally, not a good partner and certainly not a country that was militarily strong, at least compared to the Soviet Union. Furthermore, they felt that the United States lacked the will to regain the military strength necessary to have any hope of its policies succeeding. I had experienced that reaction myself many times on my trips abroad for Bechtel and other companies between 1975 and 1980, in the Middle East, in Europe and in England.

The President, as always, was enormously persuasive, understanding and effective in our conversation. I told him that I would let him know very shortly; but I knew then, as I am sure he did, that I had no real option. I had strongly urged all of those things he had in his election campaign. I knew it was absolutely necessary for America to change course drastically to regain our military strength—and to regain also the respect and support of allies, without whom we could not expect to keep our freedom.

I called my wife to apprise her of this offer and of the imminence of the changes that would now affect our lives. Referring to her status as a lieutenant in the United States Army Nurse Corps during World War II, and to her having outranked me then—her commission had antedated mine by a few months—I began by saying, "Lieutenant Dalton, now *you* may salute."

The President delighted to repeat that story, but I did not report to him any of the forebodings and concerns my wife expressed at the nature of the drastic changes that were about to occur in our lives. On the other hand, she too recognized that there was really little choice, if we believed in any of the things we had been doing since I first ran for the California Legislature in 1952. We could not reject his request to assist him as he began the task of both changing the agenda of the nation and reviving our military strength.

The appointment was announced on December 1, 1980, the day that would have been my father's ninety-fourth birthday had he still lived. From then on I became almost totally immersed in defense and security issues, and would remain so with an intensity and single-mindedness that permitted thought about virtually nothing else, night and day, every day until the end of November 1987.

It is the history of that period that I write in these pages. Obviously it is the history that I found and in which, to some extent, I took part. It is the story of some of the major decisions and actions that the Administration and I took; of the activities and problems of that period; of my reactions; and, of course, of the people with whom I served.

Because this history is shaped by my own beliefs, experiences, and training, sometimes it will differ from accounts by others. It certainly differs from many of the partial accounts that have appeared in newspaper and television reporting of the events of those days. And it will differ, of course, from some of the many editorials, columns, books, and comments on those same activities, most of which are inevitably secondhand accounts. Many of them derived from the imperatives of editors' directions, or from the writers' own anxiety to hold the attention of their public, or from the distorted and usually incorrect information fed to the media from partial "sources." I frequently said, only half facetiously, that I had to read the *Washington Post* or the *New York Times* to find out what I was thinking.

My account will differ primarily from those other versions of the events recounted here because of one major difference in addition to all the other differences of heritage, viewpoint, and training: I was there.

This is not to say that the book will be an apologia or a defense of everything that the Administration and the President I served, or I, did or planned. On the contrary, it will, I hope, be true history; but every true history is of course the unique product of each historian. Thus, while I trust the book will not be merely a collection of biases, it will of course have the unique focus and dimensions that reflect the writer's viewpoint.

This history will not, however, consider everything that happened on a day-to-day basis during the seven-year period in which I had the honor and the responsibility of directing our armed forces under the President. That, I hope, will come later. I have felt that the best way now to present part of the history of that period would be to concentrate on about twelve of the major national security and foreign policy issues with which President Reagan's Administration dealt during the period when I was Secretary of Defense.

I should record here one other influence that has been a major factor in my thinking and actions. I have always been an avid and rapid reader, and as I grew up I was fortunate to have had a number of books available in my family's library. Also, we were members of the Mechanics Institute in San Francisco, an early, private, philanthropic organization formed about the time of the Gold Rush in California to aid, in the words of its charter, in the "education of indigent mechanics." It had evolved over the years into a private library; I much preferred it to the public library because its open shelving allowed you to hunt for books you wanted, or to browse as in a bookstore. Much later I became a trustee of the Mechanics Library and always tried to keep it the way I remembered and enjoyed it.

My family spent several summers, beginning in 1925, in a

garden apartment on the Stanford University campus, thirty miles south of San Francisco; and I used most of the summer days for long reading bouts, some sandlot baseball and—one summer when I was in high school—informally auditing political science courses in the University summer school. I read a good bit of Macaulay and was always much taken with his great round rolling phrases with their majestic cadences.

However, the summer I went to Stanford, when I was about twelve years old, with Volume I of Winston Churchill's *The World Crisis*, brought me the greatest pleasure and the most vivid memories. It was just before I entered high school, but I still recall the magnificence of the prose, the stately march of language that quickened and rose to sonorous heights like the finale of a great symphony as Churchill told the story of a battle, either with an enemy or with his political opponents. This was history, I thought (and still think) as it should be presented. My own imagination was reasonably vivid, and reading Churchill enabled me to exercise it to the full. World War I came alive for me. I understood it as I had never understood it before; and the desperate struggle of the British and the French against the German masses of infantry, the long deadly stalemate and, most of all, the magnificent descriptions of the naval battles, stayed fixed permanently in my mind. That Churchill was describing events in which he was a leading player added an immediacy to his unmatched descriptions. I had never enjoyed reading anything quite so much.

My admiration extended to the person of the author, and shortly I began to devour the (even then) formidable number of books by and about Churchill. I also followed his career in the 1930s with strong approval, until he supported Edward VIII far too long and too vigorously for my taste. I was a strong partisan and perhaps an even stronger opponent of many public figures of the time and I was most definitely not an admirer of either the King or Mrs. Simpson. Nothing that I have read about them since has altered that view.

Churchill reestablished himself in my estimation by his long series of eloquent speeches against appeasement and Britain's failure to arm. I had absorbed the lessons of *The World Crisis*: that the Royal Navy was ready, but the Army needed immense additions to its peacetime strength, and needed them very quickly if England was to fight and win a war.

By this time, I was in Harvard College and then in the Law School. I followed the unfolding drama of Churchill's lonely fight in the House of Commons for greater preparedness and his fury at the appeasement of Munich, the broken promises that he knew would follow and did, and England's declaration of war after their ultimatum expired on September 1, 1939. I was delighted by Churchill's return to power and thought it particularly fitting that it was to the Admiralty that he returned.

I followed all these events with the same deep sense of almost personal involvement, and with the passionate intensity that accompanied my interest in the domestic policies and politics of the United States.

Perhaps most vivid of all my recollections from this time was of a December day in 1941. By that time I had graduated from law school and enlisted as a private in our infantry, in September. I had tried in 1940 to persuade Royal Air Force recruiters in San Francisco that lack of depth perception in my eyes would not disqualify me from flying, but my effort was unsuccessful and was really made only because in 1940 the RAF seemed to offer the only immediate opportunity to get into the fray. In 1941 I returned to my original idea of the infantry, which did not worry much about the depth of anyone's perception.

Pearl Harbor had been bombed two weeks previously. I had returned to the barracks at Camp Roberts, California, after a long and muddy day on the rifle range and marching in the rolling scrub country around the camp. Most of my World War I equipment and my Springfield 1903 rifle needed cleaning, and I embarked upon that task before facing what I knew would be another grievously bad dinner. The barracks was nearly empty, but a small, tinny radio belonging to someone at the end of the quarters had been left on as usual. Instead of the normal dosages of what then passed for the "Top 40," roars of applause crackled out of the small speaker; Churchill had just been introduced to a Joint Session of Congress and the radio was rebroadcasting his talk.

I listened, enthralled, as he began with his joke about how he might have got there on his own; then he continued in his matchless prose, delivered with his sonorous, compelling and inspiring voice. The mud, the soaked equipment, the discouragement, were all forgotten as he continued; and literally from the moment he concluded, I no longer had any doubt that we would win in Europe and in the Pacific.

Thereafter, when I could, usually when at home on leave, I listened to everything Churchill broadcast and continued trying to find and read everything he wrote. (A note in the front of my one volume edition of *The World Crisis* reminds me that I bought it in Sydney, Australia, in 1943.) I always marveled at Churchill's ability to rally his own countrymen and their Allies, despite the most appalling reverses, and I never doubted that he would win, no matter how many black, wet days there would be and no matter how thick was the jungle.

Nor would I forget how vital it was to be prepared and ready to fight if we had to. And I would not forget how long it took us to get proper equipment, and how inexperienced we were, and how completely unready to fight in jungles against opponents who knew all about jungles and were remarkably well equipped and trained.

Thus, when forty years later I was placed in a position to have some ability to help influence events, and I saw what I believed then[3] to be the dangerous downward spiral of our military strength and our national will in the 1970s, I determined to do all I could to prevent America from continuing down that path of drift and self-disparagement and weakness that I was sure could lead to another war.

In short, I determined to apply all the lessons I had learned from the past and I determined to fight for peace—a peace that we could win, and keep, if we were strong.

Most of the events and issues chronicled here are interlinked. We cannot consider any one in isolation; each must be seen as part of the larger sphere of activities that reached back into previous years.

All of which is to say, that this history will not, and cannot, be a tidy account of several well-behaved crises and episodes each of which has a beginning, a middle and an end. The best way to think of them is as a series of overlapping concentric circles, continuously revolving and each requiring constant attention, with a bewildering array of ever-changing events, as the various bits and pieces of actions that went into and formed each of the circles, shifted and shimmered in much the same way that a kaleidoscopic pattern is never still, never the same. For one example, several years' efforts involving the American position in Lebanon came to a tragic climax with the terrorist bombing of the Marine barracks at the Beirut Airport—two days before we launched our rescue operations on Grenada.

But the best way to recount the history is to begin.

---

3. And sadly now. The budgets of 1987 through 1990 show actual declines each year in our Defense investment. Nothing in the world situation justifies four years of reductions. The Soviets, despite their soothing rhetoric and clever public relations activities, have continued the steady increases of their offensive military capabilities during these years, as indeed they have for the past two decades.

I

The Transition

*D*efense issues are not tidy nor are they subject to orderly packaging. Some will not even wait for a new President to be inaugurated, so that a history could properly begin, as one might like, on Inauguration Day.

The world was no more than normally turbulent in the fall of 1980. In October, a war had broken out between Iran and Iraq; and the fanatical Iranian government still held our hostages in the most barbarous fashion in the U.S. Embassy in Teheran, in violation of the most elementary rules of international law. We had more than our usual interest in that volatile region.

Much closer to home, it was becoming increasingly apparent in Nicaragua that the Sandinistas were little different from Somoza's recently overthrown regime. Free elections, elementary human and civil rights and liberties were apparently as repugnant to the new regime as to the old. All of this greatly attracted the Soviets, who saw this as their chance to gain a second base in the Caribbean. As a result, they were increasingly friendly and helpful to the Sandinistas. In El Salvador, Communist supported geurrillas threatened the legitimately elected incumbents. Afghanistan continued its seemingly helpless struggle against the Soviet invaders; and South Africa was in its familiar posture of turmoil within itself and with its neighbors, with the Soviets (and Cuban troops) helping their Marxist supporters in power in Angola.

In December 1980, then President-elect Reagan had announced most of his Cabinet and was still in the process of moving from California to Washington. We anticipated that one or more tests of the new President were being prepared in the Soviet Union. Soon it became clear that the first test involved the perennial problems of Poland.

Poland, with its long, tortured history and its nearly indefensible location in the midst of a great plain, highly suitable for tank warfare and attack by massed infantry, has been invaded many times and subjected to repeated conquest, occupation and partition. In Poland, however, the stirrings of liberty can never be completely quenched and its citizens will never cease trying to be as free as people in the West.

Their many brave efforts in the late 1970s included the emergence of a small, tentative thrust toward the establishment of a labor union, or unions, free of dominance by either the Polish government or the Soviet Union.

The Soviets have kept at least two infantry divisions in Poland since the end of War World II, and Poland was a member of the Warsaw Pact, but her people constituted something less than loyal and devoted allies of the Soviet Union.

The more the Polish government displayed independence from strict adherence to Soviet policies, and the more such Poles as Lech Walesa expressed the aspirations of the Polish people toward individual freedom, the more they were risking another of the invasions with which their history is replete; throttlings like the one the Soviets had administered to Czechoslovakians in 1968.

In late November and early December in 1980, after our presidential election, the faint stirrings toward freedom from some Polish people, under the puppet government of Premier Stanislaw Kania, began to set off alarm bells in the Soviet Union. Kania was "gradually" replaced by General Wojciech Jaruzelski, then Defense Minister of Poland, whom I always felt was no more than a Soviet General in a Polish uniform. Jaruzelski formally became Prime Minister the following February.[1]

Apparently believing that the transition period in the United States between the end of one presidential term and the beginning of another provided a suitable opportunity for stamping out any freedom in one of their possibly unreliable neighbors, the Soviets had embarked on various intimidating actions toward the Polish people. They seemed to feel there was little to fear from the United States and, therefore, little to fear from anyone else.

The President-elect correctly sensed that this was to be his first test and that a great deal would depend, for at least the next four years, on how he, and the nation, reacted to Soviet pressures on Poland.

There were, of course, other matters besides the Polish crisis to discuss, very much including the fate of our hostages who had been held prisoner in our Embassy in Iran for over 400 days. President Carter's State Department and his White House staff

---

1. In July 1989 he was chosen to fill the new post of President by a margin of one vote in the new, but still Communist Party dominated, Parliament. There is considerable evidence now that the Soviet government has decided it is politic and practical for them to allow more beginnings of self-rule in Poland and Hungary and their other satellite states than before. But it is still too early to tell whether this trend, with its welcome implications, will be allowed by the Soviets to continue if these satellite states should decide they no longer want to be in the Warsaw Pact Military Alliance. Indeed, the Soviet government said that while they will permit Poland to have a non-Communist government, Poland "of course must remain a member of the Warsaw Pact."

carried on the negotiations over claims against Iran and the Iranian funds that the Carter Administration had blocked in our country; but they did keep us generally advised of their progress. As we got closer to Inauguration Day and as the negotiators worked under Warren Christopher, President Carter's Under Secretary of State and a California friend, we were told by the negotiators and by others familiar with the negotiations that the Iranians were deliberately delaying release of the American hostages until sometime after President Carter left office.

All of those negotiations were actively carried out by the outgoing Administration, but to the best of my knowledge there was good cooperation between the outgoing and incoming Administration teams during those final negotiations. We all had one goal: to get our hostages back as soon as possible.

Recently, at a forum discussion that was part of the fiftieth reunion of my Harvard College class, I was asked why the "Reagan Administration deliberately delayed the return of the Iran hostages until after Inauguration Day." Of all the myths and outright lies I have encountered about events that took place during my service in Washington, that one must rank near the top for its absurdity. In the first place, the entire negotiations were controlled and conducted by the outgoing Carter Administration. Further, anyone with even the slightest acquaintance with the President-elect would know that he would do everything he could to get the hostages out as soon as possible. Finally, uninaugurated administrations have no authority or power to force Presidents in office to do anything.

But back to Poland. The Soviet pressures on that country were very real, including the massing on its borders of additional Soviet infantry divisions and some from other Warsaw Pact nations, making it clear that any day there could be another invasion of Poland. The President called a meeting of his security team at Blair House, where he was staying prior to the inauguration.

There in the upstairs sitting room, just off the Presidential bedroom, were gathered the new Secretary of State, Alexander Haig; the new National Security Advisor, Richard Allen; the author, as the new Secretary of Defense; and the President's co-Chiefs of Staff, Ed Meese and James A. Baker III. The new Director of Central Intelligence, William J. Casey, was there too.

Dick Allen is a cheerful man with a good sense of humor and an ability to deflate any showing of self-importance in others.

Ed Meese is well known to the American people through his many television appearances. He is affable, very well informed, and effective in argument—as is Jim Baker.

Bill Casey was a large, rumpled, highly intelligent veteran of many years of New York business and political experiences. His appearance and his voice (a gruff rumble that led some to feel he had a built-in scrambler to prevent anyone's hearing what he said) belied an original, searching and analytical mind. Bill Casey was much underestimated. He had many of the attributes of a historian, and indeed he did produce several credible works of American history, on our Revolutionary period. He was an omnivorous reader and could never pass a bookshop without buying (and then reading rapidly) several books in widely diverse categories. He was also a practical and persistent man and one who was very loyal to the President, having served as Chairman for the "Reagan for President" forces since 1979, when that cause seemed quite hopeless.

All present, except Al Haig, were well known to the President-elect; and two, Ed Meese and I, had been with him in various capacities since 1965. They all knew that the President enjoyed and benefited from quiet, civilized debates and discussions.

The meeting opened as almost all National Security Council meetings over the next few years were to open: with an intelligence assessment by Bill Casey. The upstairs sitting room at Blair

House, with its Victorian couches and easy chairs[2] had not been designed for meetings, but it made a most inviting setting for the early deliberations of the new Administration. Indeed I felt it happily symbolic that the people who were to constitute the National Security Council for the next Administration were convened in a solidly restored, richly historic setting, rather than formally drawn up about a sterile office table in some ordinary building.

The President has always preferred meetings of his advisors and friends in which their various viewpoints are presented comprehensively but concisely, and then argued out.

When he was Governor of California, Ronald Reagan had a small "Cabinet" consisting of the people who headed the major agencies of the state government. In Sacramento, in the formal setting of the Governor's small conference room, those five or six people usually met daily with him, guided by short outlines prepared by the Governor's Executive Secretary, William P. Clark, Jr. Those famous "one page summaries" each dealt with an issue to come before the Cabinet, and summarized the arguments and attached papers. They were most valuable in setting the stage for discussion. Everyone was free to bring up any points he wished, but the number of items on the agenda precluded lengthy speeches. It was clear the Governor liked the cut, thrust and parry of oral presentation and oral argument.

At Blair House, in the closing days of the Carter Administration, there were no such one page summaries for the President-elect; but there were detailed, reliable intelligence reports of Soviet capabilities and apparent Soviet intentions for Poland.

It seemed quite clear that if nothing at all was done, the Soviets would feel quite safe in adding several more divisions to the two

---

2. The entire Blair House, the official guest house of the United States, has been virtually rebuilt and restored. That work was completed in 1988. Major and successful attempts were made to be faithful to the original.

they already had in there;[3] and that that action alone, even with-out their putting those divisions into action against the Polish people (although that was clearly an option), would probably dry up the springs of liberty that were starting very slowly to flow in Poland.

There would be other meetings of the National Security Coun-cil, of course, in the days before inauguration—and a seemingly endless string of meetings thereafter, in which the positions of most of the participants on a great many issues could be predicted with reasonable accuracy as we got to know better one another's biases.

At this first meeting, in Blair House, the conversation ebbed and flowed with calm presentations of intelligence assessments, Soviet actions in Poland and Afghanistan, NATO worries, the Iranians' latest demands and the progress of our transition. We were told of the eagerness of Chancellor Helmut Schmidt of Germany to meet with America's new President and of the pro-posed visits of other leaders. With one exception, the participants put those and other matters before the President quietly and unemotionally.

The one exception, of course, was the Secretary of State-designate, Alexander Haig, who seemed to be constitutionally unable to present an argument without an enormous amount of passion and intensity, heavily overlaid with a deep suspicion of the competence and motives of anyone who did not share his opinions. At this meeting, however, there was little disagreement: Every one of us recognized the Soviets' tactic of testing a new President and the importance of their realizing that this new presidency would involve not just a change in name, but a change in policy. So out of the meeting emerged a clear feeling that the Soviets might very well simply keep adding more and more troops

---

3. Later I called this a process of "invasion by osmosis."

to the two divisions they already had inside Poland—if they believed the cost to them was negligible.

We did not discuss in any depth the problems of our own military capability. Others had been receiving the same briefings I had and, while we were not entirely over our shock at the weaknesses in our own military capability and the condition of our forces, we knew that we would be strengthening that capability very substantially in the years ahead. But we also knew that the effort would take a long time and continued support from Congress, and that our task would be made infinitely more difficult if the signal went to the Soviet Union that at this point America was neither ready nor resolved to do anything.

Carefully crafted messages and signals were therefore agreed upon to let the Soviet Union know that we simply would not sit idly by after the inauguration if they used their usual methods of trying to quench the beginnings of liberty in Poland; that the United States was prepared both mentally and militarily to take action that would make it clear to the Soviets that they would not have an easy time in such a pursuit; and that indeed there would be a cost to them if they moved again to stamp out the beginnings of efforts to secure some freedom in their neighborhood, as they had years before in Czechoslovakia.

That "settled," we were about to break up and go to our next meetings. In my case that meant to return to the depressing military briefings I had been receiving. But suddenly it appeared that this meeting was still going on. Al Haig, with perhaps more passionate intensity than usual, was telling the President that Poland was one thing, but that the real problem we were facing, and would all have to confront, was the increasing Communist inroads into and attempts to dominate our Caribbean and Central American neighbors.

He spoke with increasing intensity about Cuba and the risks it presented to us. He continued along that line for some time, and attached to it the problems that we would have to face in

El Salvador, where Communist insurgency was demonstrating the weakness of the legitimate government of El Salvador. He also mentioned the increasingly worrisome signs of the leftist tendencies of the Sandinista regime in Nicaragua. But the thrust of his argument and the principal target of his emotion was clearly Cuba. After some time, I broke in to inquire quietly where all of this was leading and what it was we should be doing. Al, who has never liked to be interrupted, stopped in mid-flight, turned one of his withering command glares in my direction and said that it was quite clear we would have to invade Cuba and, one way or another, put an end to the Castro regime.

I told the President that one of his predecessors had already tried that in a halfhearted way and that if we were to follow Al Haig's advice and if all went well, we *might* have a satisfactory result. But, I added, one of the principal lessons I had learned from the Vietnam experience was that we could not suddenly explode upon the American people a full-fledged war and expect to have their support. American public opinion would have to support such an action, and would therefore have to be convinced that our national interests required, indeed demanded, that we go to war. Furthermore, if we did go to war, this time we would have to do so with all necessary resources and an unshakable will to win, instead of entering the war as we did in Vietnam: without any intention or plan to win.

I said that while all agreed upon the nature of the Cuban regime and upon the basic risks it posed to us in view of Cuba's geographical position—its ability to interrupt our normal maritime trade, to interfere with any NATO reinforcement convoys that would have to pass close by Cuba, and to give the Soviets valuable intelligence capabilities—that while all those things made highly undesirable our having such a hostile government so close by, we simply could not expect the American people now to support any kind of military action against Cuba, let alone a full-scale war that they would first hear about the morning after Al's proposed invasion. The others seemed to agree and the meeting then did end; but Al Haig clearly was not going to accept his loss in this skirmish as a final defeat.

It is important to appreciate the flavor and atmosphere of this first of the many meetings and discussions on security problems we would have over the next seven years. While I think we were all conscious of dealing with issues that quite literally could mean war or peace, life or death, there was nothing forced, uneasy, or pretentious in the approaches or points made by the participants. I think that may well have been because some may have felt they were still discussing more of an academic problem than the series of issues that we would have to decide, and that the consequences of these decisions either way could have massive implications for the lives and security of the millions of people in our country and elsewhere.

While many among us had dealt with such issues in the past, some were getting their first taste of the reality of security problems. Still, the atmosphere remained largely calm and pleasant; I think *interesting* is really the best word to describe the discussion. I attribute that to the President and his influence.

Ronald Reagan is a genuinely decent, extremely nice man, who has both an enormous and a sophisticated sense of humor and a strong and civilized desire to have people around him feel as comfortable and happy as he does. He has extraordinarily well-honed skills in creating and securing this kind of atmosphere in meetings of all descriptions and with all different kinds of agendas and people.

I have found it quite literally impossible to feel or reflect depression, despair, or panic in a meeting over which the President presides. There is more to it than that, of course, because the President's skill at putting people at ease brings out the best in everyone present.

The President used this great skill on almost every occasion, not because he is consciously "being nice" or "funny," but simply because that is his way. It is one of the factors that has given him such high standing and deserved popularity among his counterparts in so many other countries. I have seen this "magic" at work many times.

While it is frequently derided, by those who have not been exposed to it, as simply the penchant of a President unfamiliar with the issues who likes to tell endless jokes, the fact is that the President's magic not only puts otherwise quite stiff and difficult heads of state, or heads of government, or congressmen, or senators and others, very much at their ease, but it also creates an atmosphere in which those present would like to make the President, or the American side, as pleased with the meeting as they are becoming. This can and does produce some vital agreements that neither logic, nor table pounding, nor cajoling could bring about.

That magic works very quickly, of course, with people who are initially basically receptive to the President. I saw this at work a few years later in one delightful luncheon that the President gave for Prime Minister Brian Mulroney of Canada. Each of these two heads of government had elaborate briefing books, with detailed discussions of major issues, including the points that the other was expected to raise and means of countering those arguments, and much useful background material.

However, we were some thirty minutes into one of the excellent White House luncheons, in the small "family dining room" off the large State dining room, before a single weighty issue was introduced. The President and the Prime Minister had been exchanging Irish stories at a fast and furious pace; for once the President had encountered a memory bank for jokes almost as extensive as his own. When we did reach item one on the agenda, the discussion sailed along far more smoothly and quickly than anyone had expected.

But the same magic also works with those less receptive initially to the President. We used to say that in the most difficult cases it would sometimes take President Reagan fifteen minutes to secure another firm friend and warm admirer of the United States.

That first meeting at Blair House had pointed the new Administration in the direction we were to follow for all the years of the President's two terms. We would make it unmistakably clear that actions adverse to freedom, actions that could harm our friends or potential friends, would be met by our firm and vigorous response. We would not embark upon impulsive adventures of high risk without full preparation, not only of our military forces, but with due regard for the vital need to have a supportive country.

I think most of us were (and certainly the President was) fully convinced that public support was an absolutely vital part of any successful policy of a free democratic country; its absence had been such a marked feature of our war in Vietnam. Public support for any military action would require the clearest possible and completely credible explanations and presentations, so that the public would be aware that the future security of the United States depended upon the successful outcome of the actions we might have to propose.

One other point, as I have said, was not discussed so much at that first meeting, but must have been implicit in the minds of many. It was a point that I mentioned briefly and privately with the President as we were leaving the meeting. I said that he should know, as I was sure he now did, that our military capabilities were sadly very low and that the chances of our being able to impress the Soviets with our military strength and dissuade them from taking any action they wanted to take in Poland at that time were virtually nonexistent.

The President-elect said yes, he was indeed aware of that; and he told me that his top priority was to reverse the situation, to give us the military capabilities to back up such decisions as we had just taken. The President said that in his view there was nothing worse than an empty threat or an idle boast or bluff. "If you get called and cannot respond, your chances of being believed a second time are exceedingly low," he said. Still, we agreed that it was important to send very strong signals to the Soviets on Poland, "But," said the President, "we must never again be in a position where no one will believe us if we send signals like that."

Two things were very clear to me from that first meeting and from my more private discussion at Blair House with the President-elect. Certainly he was deadly serious about carrying out his oft-repeated pledge of the 1980 campaign to restore the military strength of the United States as quickly as possible, even though keeping that vow might dictate that we would not get the balanced budget we had hoped for. And second, it was vital to do this not just to fulfill a campaign pledge; but actually to regain our strength as quickly as we could. Only that strength would persuade the Soviets that they could not take actions such as those they had taken in the 1970s in Angola and Afghanistan, and earlier in Cuba, Nicaragua, Ethiopia and elsewhere, with no hindrances and at no peril to themselves. I was quite sure that Poland would not be our only test, and that it was vital that we regain an effective and credible deterrent strength quickly.

These were extremely important conclusions. They came during a week in which I was receiving increasingly discouraging briefings about the Soviet gains in offensive military strength during the 1970s—and about the losses we had suffered by cutting our defense investment during the same decade by more than twenty percent—losses in readiness, in new equipment, in spare parts, in research and development and, particularly, in the morale of our troops and our youth. These losses were demonstrating almost every day that an all-volunteer system could not work unless it was better led and supported.

How did we communicate our important conclusions to the Soviet Union? I think a conversation I had on March 15 with then Soviet Ambassador Antoliy F. Dobrynin at the sixtieth birthday party dinner for the Chief Executive of Pepsico, Don Kendall (which dinner I attended as a retiring director of Pepsi Co.), sums up in a nutshell the *new* Administration's policy.[4]

At the predinner reception Dobrynin asked if he could have a word with me, and I replied noncommittally and continued talking with a number of other guests. Eventually, Kendall brought Dobrynin over to me and the following conversation ensued:

DOBRYNIN: In what direction do you see our two countries moving? Why is there so much rhetoric in the air now?

WEINBERGER: I think that part of it is because people in Washington feel it is important that the Soviets and the world know that the U.S. has changed, and that we have, and will acquire, much greater strength as well as greater firmness and resolve during this Administration, and that there is also great concern here about the Soviet actions in Afghanistan and around Poland.

DOBRYNIN: I assure you that my country knows very well how much the U.S. has changed. I tell them, I am a good reporter. But don't you think it is important that our two countries talk to each other and not just exchange statements?

WEINBERGER: Yes, if the atmosphere and circumstances are such that there is some prospect of effective talks, and some possibility of successful conclusion to such talks. If the Soviets went into Poland, it would be a clear signal that such talks would be useless.

4. At the Twentieth Party Congress of the Communist Party in mid-February, General Secretary Leonid I. Brezhnev had suggested that the Soviets *would* intervene in Poland if the Polish Party's control of the situation there deteriorated further.

DOBRYNIN: Poland! It is essential in Poland that we not have aggressive actions on our own border. You would not allow it [on your border].

WEINBERGER: But many of our allies do things we do not like, but we do not maneuver on their borders or threaten their independence.

DOBRYNIN: But the Warsaw Pact is different. We cannot have hostile governments on our borders. In any event, we should talk.

At that point, several other people drifted by and I did not encourage continuance of a further one-on-one discussion.

I think I made it clear that the times had indeed changed.[5]

---

5. Paraphrased from a classified memo I prepared for the President after that dinner. I believe that even with all the changes occurring so rapidly in Eastern Europe in the autumn of 1989, the Soviets would always insist that they "cannot have hostile governments on [their] borders"; and would take military action against any government they defined as "hostile."

II

President Reagan's First Defense Budgets

*A*n incoming President, who is inaugurated on January 20, inherits, along with the White House and an empty oval office, the budget left by his predecessor.

The question of adequate appropriations for America's defenses, not only for 1981 but for the four years of the Carter Administration, had been one of the principal issues in the presidential campaign. During the decade of 1970–1980, the amount we invested in our defense *declined* by more than twenty percent; and that was in real terms, *after* inflation. During the last year of the Carter Administration, however, and in response to the 1980 election and congressional pressure, the fiscal year 1982 defense budget request willed to the new Administration included a 5.5 percent increase in real growth over the 1981 budget. There were many who assumed, because of my budget cutting activities as Director of Finance in California and as Director of the Office of Management and Budget (OMB) in Washington, that I favored reducing budgets of all kinds and at all times.

Actually, what I tried to do in each post was to budget according to needs. In California, facing a big deficit and knowing that any degree of deficit was forbidden by the State Constitution, we obviously had to cut expenses. And in the early seventies, there was general agreement that we should deal with rapidly increasing Federal expenditures ("hemorrhaging" expenditures, as George Shultz put it). We did that, but nevertheless I have always recognized that not all government spending is of equal importance or necessity. Indeed, while I was at OMB, I took pains to underline the importance of national security: "The objectives of defense spending are . . . nothing less than our survival as a free nation in a world that cannot be considered completely friendly."[1] And I said in a 1972 conference of the American Enterprise Institute: "If our defense budget is inadequate, nothing else will be of much moment, and we will only know it when it is too late."[2]

However, I must admit that I was a little too optimistic at that AEI conference when I offered the following argument on behalf of the B-1 bomber: "It is necessary to develop the B-1 as a potential replacement for our aging bomber fleet. The B-52 will have been in use almost twenty years when the B-1 becomes operational in the late 1970s." I could hardly know at the time that I was nearly a decade too early in my forecast: President Carter canceled the whole B-1 program in 1977. It would take a new administration to restart the program and deliver the plane ten years later.

The new Administration was, of course, more than ordinarily interested in the appropriation requests left by the outgoing Pres-

1. *New York Times*, October 15, 1970.

2. "The Defense Budget," Town Hall Meeting, Washington, American Enterprise Institute, 1972.

ident. Portions of that budget were made available to the new Administration prior to inauguration. In the Defense Department, where I had been given temporary offices and the fullest possible cooperation by all of the outgoing policy officials, as well as by the permanent staff, we had looked over the Carter budget with very close attention.[3]

In some of my confirmation hearings, which were held before Inauguration Day, I was asked many times what addition, if any, we would request to the Carter budget for defense. The question was pressed most particularly by Senator John Tower, the Chairman of the Senate Armed Services Committee, which was the forum for my confirmation hearings. In the Department, both before and after Inauguration Day, we were engaged in a great many other issues, including interviews of potential appointees, rapid familiarization with the developing situation along the Soviet-Polish border and preparation for the confirmation hearings

3. A sidelight: A minor problem then arose, when it became apparent that the so-called "Defense Transition Team," one of a number of groups intended to help prepare for a smooth turnover from the outgoing Administration, had taken on a life of its own. In December, after receiving numerous complaints from military personnel that the Transition Team seemed more interested in finding out details of the existing highly classified military plans to deal with a possible attack on the United States than on helping to plan the transition, I asked the head of the Team, Dr. William Van Cleave, when he anticipated the Team would complete its work. "Oh, possibly by next June," he replied. Having seen a part of its product to date and not finding it helpful, and having in mind that Inauguration Day was January 20, I thanked him and told him the Team's services would no longer be needed.

I was told that Van Cleave then asked Will Taft, who was to be the new General Counsel of the Department, if "Weinberger really was sure he wanted to let the Transition Team go." Will correctly replied, "Mr. Weinberger was more sure of that decision than about any other of his decisions."

On February 18, Ed Meese wrote to me asking for my formal comments on the Defense Transition Team. In answer to the question, Was there any service "provided to you by the transition team which you considered useful?" I wrote in reply: "No. Because the transition team had an agenda of its own, it was not useful to me in developing the President's program; it was, in fact, the source of a number of problems."

It is somewhat ironic that in answer to Ed's question about "any problems with the outgoing Administration personnel," I wrote: "The outgoing Administration personnel were extremely helpful."

themselves, as well as many discussions and papers, requested by the President-elect, on the question of the Cabinet and executive office structure for the President. In the midst of all this, however, it was essential that we begin work on the changes to President Carter's last defense budget.

Incidentally, having to consider a multiplicity of issues simultaneously would prove to be a condition of my office as Secretary of Defense almost every day for seven years. There was never a day when we could discuss major issues separately, or one at a time. That is one of the reasons that, when congressmen and senators would ask with varying degrees of exasperation, "What is your highest priority?" I had to reply that I had several and that no one in my position at that time could have one "highest priority." So in the middle of everything else and almost as soon as we had copies of the Carter budget from OMB, we sent them to each of the armed services for their comments, recommendations and proposed additions or deletions.

In this budget area I worked closely with Frank Carlucci, whom I had recommended for the Deputy Secretary's position and who had been nominated for the post by the President, despite intense opposition from some of the new White House staff. The opposition was based on the rather irrelevant fact that he had held office in the outgoing Carter Administration. Carlucci had also held office with me in the Nixon and Ford Administrations, and I knew he was, and would be, both loyal and very competent. He fulfilled all those expectations: as Deputy Secretary; later, as National Security Advisor; and as my successor as Secretary.

We held a series of budget and strategy meetings with the Chiefs of Staff and others in the three services, even though at that point I had not yet decided whom to recommend to the President for appointment as the secretaries of each service.

In keeping with an organizational preference that I have long held and that I put into effect while I was Chairman of the Federal Trade Commission in 1970, I determined that the individual service secretaries should have greater authority in their areas for making recommendations, not only for the changes in the Carter budget, but for future budgets. My views were embodied in a memorandum to various Pentagon officials, which I wrote for the Deputy Secretary to sign. The basic idea is quite simple. It is that the people with the responsibility for a particular activity should have the authority to participate actively in the budget process, as well as in the allocation of any funds that may be appropriated for the activities for which they were responsible.

Over the years there was considerable public discussion and questioning of that method of mine, because it ran counter to the highly centralized procedures that had been imposed on the Defense Department by Secretary of Defense Robert S. McNamara almost exactly twenty years before. As a result of the McNamara belief that the Office of the Secretary of Defense should have all authority, the offices of secretaries of the Army, Navy and Air Force had been reduced virtually to ceremonial positions.

I also believed that the Joint Chiefs of Staff, the officers who had risen to the top of their very difficult professions, should have a larger role both in budgeting (including planning budgets) and in selecting the weapons and organizing the training necessary to carry out strategies and policies determined as a result of *joint* efforts by the Secretary of Defense, the Chiefs and others.

Basically, my purpose was to ensure *centralized* control of policy *formation direction*, but to move toward a more *decentralized execution* of the policies.

Many people familiar with the McNamara ideas and favorable to them, quite content to have the bulk of the power lodged in the office of the Secretary of Defense, complained strongly that, in the words of one detractor, we were "giving each service what they wanted and simply allowing each service a third of the total budget to do with as they pleased."

That was one of the myths that was to be repeated many times during my tenure, and it taught me how hard it is to expunge a basic error from media discussion. Many such errors result from a single inaccurate column, or from a comment on a hurried television report striving to compress a half-hour story into the ninety seconds that is usually the maximum allotted to everything except major disasters. Almost invariably the error occurred because the journalist relied entirely on a single source and never bothered to ask me, or others in the Department, if the source was correct. Once entered into the public's thinking, such errors are at least as hard to remove and correct as erroneous data in computers.

When our new team arrived at the Department, we found to our astonishment that the three service secretaries had been so downgraded that they were not even members of the Defense Resources Board, the top management group of the budget of the Department. So of course I *added* to that Board the Secretary of the Army, the Secretary of the Navy, and the Secretary of the Air Force.

Emphatically, the purpose was not to give each service a "third of the budget" to do with as it pleased. Rather, it was to ensure that those with the responsibility for the *development and execution of the programs* needed to carry out previously determined policies on the recruitment, training, equipment and readiness of each service—which functions are the assignment and duty of each service secretary—would have the authority to manage the resources allocated to those programs. There was never any suggestion that *policy* decisions should be delegated to the service secretaries (or to anyone else), nor that they should have any organizational or strategic responsibilities: It was quite clear that those decisions had to be made by the Secretary of Defense; and so they were. I have no doubt that the service secretaries and the service chiefs will be the best witnesses that they did not get all they wanted, either in budget totals or in the makeup of each budget.

Among other virtues I felt my plan would have was that it would enable the Secretary of Defense to concentrate on major policy decisions and goals and to secure the resources needed to achieve them.

In addition, of course, to considering the budget that the President inherited from the previous Administration for the fiscal year 1982, which was to begin October 1, 1981, we had to consider what, if any, changes would be desirable and necessary in the 1981 fiscal year budget, which had been given to the Congress the year before by President Carter but was not yet enacted.

It may not be amiss to describe the budget itself at this point. The budget of the U.S. Government is usually contained in two or three bound, printed volumes, each larger than the Manhattan telephone book. They include a budget message from the President and the Director of OMB and many pages listing, in great detail, the amounts requested for each department and agency. Also included are the amounts expended for each line of the Department's request for the prior fiscal year, the current year and the year of the request. The budget books, and voluminous subsidiary documents, also include "justifications" for each appropriation, for new reductions and new appropriations sought, and an explanation of economies and reductions proposed. Those requests are, of course, the President's proposals and requests to Congress for the funds to operate the Federal Government.

The President's budget, normally submitted at the end of January or, more often, in early February, is accompanied by some smaller volumes. One, the "Budget in Brief," about 200 pages long, attempts to give a broad overview of the budget's highlights.

The budget books are very complex documents, and it certainly helped me to have had several years' previous experience as Deputy Director and then Director of OMB in the 1970s.

The Congress considers the budget in two types of bills. The authorization bills are heard in the so-called substantive committees (for Defense there is an Armed Services Committee in both the Senate and the House). The authorization bills "authorize," or provide congressional permission for, various programs, and set outside limits on the amounts that can be expended. Some bills contain the authorization for several governmental departments. Also, there is one authorization bill for Defense, and a separate bill for military construction.

But before any money can be spent, a second bill, specifically *appropriating* the funds, must be passed. The appropriation bills the Congress considers are the compilations of the line item requests, in dollars, for the items in the President's budget. After passage of the *authorization* bill, the *appropriation* bills are then heard by the Appropriations Committee and its subcommittees for each department. Bitter fights between "authorizers" and the "appropriators" are common.

There are very real problems in working as far ahead as the budget process requires. The fiscal year begins October 1. (The period October 1, 1989, to September 30, 1990, for example, is called the 1990 fiscal year). As I have said, the budget for that year is submitted in final form by the President to Congress usually in early February. (In 1989, President Bush, who took office on January 20, made his changes to President Reagan's last budget about a month later.) Congress then has until October 1 to complete action on the budget. It hardly ever meets that deadline.

The major flaw of that system is that the departments begin work on their part of the budget for FY 1990, for example, usually in June of the prior year, 1988, that is about eighteen to twenty-four months before Congress will enact their requests.

Finally, some commentators and even some congressmen seem to believe there is a line item called "Fraud, Waste and Abuse" that can be cut each year. There is no such line, of course.

What we could do, and did do, was to eliminate much of the cost increases that had been more or less automatically accepted in the procurement of weapons and to make other savings based on such structural changes as multi-year procurement.

I devised the plan of regular meetings with the program managers of our major weapons systems to expose anything that was apt to cause an increase in costs, spending, overestimates, or delays in delivery of goods ordered or of programs scheduled. (I adapted this system from the pattern used at Bechtel Corporation where, for five years just before taking the Defense post, I had been the Corporation's General Counsel and Vice President.) At the end of three years, with the use of that management tool and others, the average annual *increase* of seventeen percent above the estimate for our eighty-nine major weapons systems, which had been a regular experience in the past, had been cut to *minus one percent*. In short, after three years the actual costs of our major weapons were coming in *below* estimates.

The upshot of our early 1981 discussions with the three services, and of my decision to reject many of their requests, was my final decision to recommend to the Congress that *increases* of approximately $32.6 billion in Defense appropriations requested by the Carter Administration be voted by the Congress for the two fiscal years 1981–1982.

That was about $6.8 billion more than President Carter requested the year before for FY 1981; and some $25.8 billion more for the FY 1982 budget we had just inherited.

Once I had determined the amounts required after those discussions with the services, and with the Joint Chiefs, and among ourselves at Defense, we asked the new Budget Director, a former congressman named David Stockman, to come over to the Pentagon to hear the conclusions. I knew, from my previous work as Director of OMB, that he would need to know about one of the largest overall budget changes that the President would be recommending and that it would be useful to have the Budget Director's support.

The meeting took place late in the day, perhaps about half past six in my office, at the round table that I used for most of the smaller meetings. Present were Frank Carlucci, Stockman and perhaps one or two others from OMB.

I had met Stockman during the campaign and saw a bit of him occasionally during the transition. He had impressed me as being very bright, basically quite knowledgeable about budgetary matters; a quick study with a rather glib and authoritative way of answering questions or making his points.

He had helped in the preparation for the President's debate with President Carter the previous fall. In the rehearsals he had taken the role of President Carter, projecting an accurate portrait of the man and the positions he was most likely to take. Stockman managed, at the same time, to present this in such an irritating fashion that the President-to-be once stopped in the middle of a session long enough to say, with a broad smile, "Stockman, if I didn't know you were helping to prepare me for this debate, I could begin to dislike you very quickly!"

Those exercises took place in an old barn, converted to look like an auditorium, in the Virginia hunt country home of Bill Clements, onetime Deputy Secretary of Defense, now Governor of Texas. They were a very important part of the campaign and its success.

Following the election, and during the transition period, I

worked from time to time with Stockman. We went over some of the expenditure reduction plans that, right after his election, the President-elect had asked me to put together for him in areas other than Defense. In the process, I became a little troubled by the quickness and positiveness with which he would take positions and make his points. Particularly troubling was that he was most positive when he did not yet quite have his facts straight.

But our meeting in the Pentagon that evening about the additions to the Carter Budget was amicable, consisting primarily of our presenting to Stockman the totals and the broad outlines of the additions and the changes we were recommending, for both the 1982 budget we had inherited and the 1981 budget that had not yet been enacted by the Congress. Stockman made a few notes, asked one or two questions that seemed to be based on his desire to be sure he understood the purposes of the increases, and said at the conclusion, after about an hour's meeting, that he agreed with our recommendations, that OMB would interpose no objections and that we should proceed.[4]

All of us at Defense were much encouraged by his statement, and hoped that it portended the beginning of a period in which all parts of the Administration would work together to help the President carry out his first priority.

Our additions covered a wide number of requirements, as recommended by the three services and the Joint Chiefs, all of which requirements had been reviewed very carefully by the Deputy Secretary and by me, as well as by many of the continuing permanent civilian officials who were acting in posts to which new appointments had not yet been made by the President. Of

4. The account of this meeting in Stockman's book, *The Triumph of Politics*, Harper & Row, is most politely described as fanciful.

course many of the requests of the three services and the Chiefs had to be rejected, or set aside for future years, because I was well aware of the President's desire that we should not spend more than was strictly necessary. The whole process had taken from mid-January to the beginning of March, and had required our heavily concentrated efforts while at the same time we had worked intensively also on many other issues then pending. Such a full-scale budget exercise normally takes at least eight months.

We did *not*, as some who were not there have claimed, simply select a large total budget figure and let the services spend up to that limit. Almost all of our detailed recommendations were approved by Congress in a comparatively short time.

They included funds for improving preparedness and for modernizing both the conventional and strategic forces. We faced the need to replace and modernize our triad of strategic forces, the neglect of all of which during the previous decade had seriously eroded our deterrent capability. It is vastly more expensive to replace all major elements of our strategic deterrent at once; but our nation's earlier, long-term failure to make regular consecutive replacements, and the great expansion and continued deployment of new and improved systems by the Soviets, gave us no choice. In particular our command and control capabilities, the "nerve center" of our strategic forces, needed both complete modernization and "hardening" so that a Soviet surprise attack on it could not totally cripple our capabilities to respond.

That need to strengthen our command and control capabilities led me to oppose, in Cabinet meetings and in testimony before the Senate Armed Services Committee, the Justice Department's suit, begun many years before, to break up the highly successful and effective telephone system run by AT&T. It seemed to me the suit was based only on the idea that it is bad to be big. I felt strongly too that the attempt to break up AT&T failed to consider the rights and benefits of consumers and that such a breakup, if effected, would endanger our ability to have the rapid and secure communications we had to have with our missile systems and our worldwide commands.[5]

Most of all, we had to restore fairness and equity to our treatment of military personnel. The all volunteer system was no longer working by the end of 1980. Enlisted men and women were not joining in sufficient numbers, and many of those in the service were not reenlisting. Only about sixty percent were high school graduates and many were scoring very low on the aptitude test. Also, many of our best noncommissioned officers and company and field grade officers, on whom we relied heavily for training, were leaving.

At my confirmation hearings, most questioners assumed we would have to return to the draft. For them it was not a question of *whether*, but *when*. The President and I both strongly opposed the draft, vastly preferring volunteer service. As usual the President phrased it better than any of us.

At a Pentagon ceremony on September 10, 1981, marking the dedication of a corridor to General Douglas MacArthur, under whom I had served in World War II, the President passed along the line of smartly saluting troops. At the end, he turned to me and said, "Cap, I would infinitely rather know that all of these men and women are here because they want to be, instead of being drafted and forced to be here."

So we urged in our budget amendments that we continue along the path on which Congress had embarked in the fall of 1980, to restore military pay and benefits—the most expensive and most important component of any defense budget.

More than that, we had to demonstrate to the troops that not

---

5. Our Justice Department felt it had to proceed with the action, but ultimately we were able to secure provisions in the court's order that helped protect our communication links with our missile systems.

only did the President and the Defense Department care about their welfare, but the American people as a whole also respected, honored and appreciated the importance of what our military forces were doing for the country.

The President took care of that most vital aspect of restoring morale. Almost single-handedly he led the country, by a number of symbolic acts, by his matchless speeches and by showing the genuine affection that he had always had for our fighting forces. He changed the nation's outlook; and the men and women of the military knew it, and responded.

One specific incident that was completely typical of the President stands out in my memory. The award of a Congressional Medal of Honor to Staff Sergeant Roy Benavidez had been approved several months before we took office, but the actual award ceremony still had not been held. Sergeant Benavidez had performed incredible feats of bravery in Vietnam, and the citation for the Medal, which of course is our highest award for valor in battle, was exceptionally moving.

The Benavidez file, together with a diffident note from the staff, inquiring whether I thought we should have an award ceremony, appeared in my in-basket early in February 1981. I did not understand the staff inquiry. Why in the world should there be any question about an award ceremony in this case? It turned out that the Carter Administration had not wanted to do anything that reminded the people of Vietnam, and the Pentagon, being the essence of the military, had taken their cue from that policy. I was really being asked if the Carter policy was to be changed.

I could think of no reason for not paying the highest tribute possible for the heroism Sergeant Benavidez had displayed, so I told the staff that not only would we have a ceremony, but I would ask the President to make the award himself. I approached the President, and he accepted eagerly. He was as moved as I had been when he read this citation:

The President of the United States of America,
authorized by Act of Congress, March 3, 1863,
has awarded in the name of the Congress
the Medal of Honor to

MASTER SERGEANT ROY P. BENAVIDEZ
UNITED STATES ARMY, RETIRED

for conspicuous gallantry and intrepidity in action
at the risk of his life above and beyond
the call of duty:

On May 2, 1968, Master Sergeant (then Staff Sergeant) Roy P. Benavidez distinguished himself by a series of daring and extremely valorous actions while assigned to Detachment B-56, 5th Special Forces Group (Airborne), 1st Special Forces, Republic of Vietnam. On the morning of May 2, 1968, a 12-man Special Forces Reconnaissance Team was inserted by helicopters in a dense jungle area west of Loc Ninth, Vietnam to gather intelligence information about confirmed large-scale enemy activity. This area was controlled and routinely patrolled by the North Vietnamese Army. After a short period of time on the ground, the team met heavy enemy resistance, and requested emergency extraction. Three helicopters attempted extraction, but were unable to land due to intense enemy small arms and anti-aircraft fire. Sergeant Benavidez was at the Forward Operating Base in Loc Ninth monitoring the operation by radio when these helicopters returned to off-load wounded crewmembers and to assess aircraft damage. Sergeant Benavidez voluntarily boarded a returning aircraft to assist in another extraction attempt. Realizing that all the team members were either dead or wounded and unable to move to the pickup zone, he directed the aircraft to a nearby clearing where he jumped from the hovering helicopter, and ran approximately 75 meters under withering small arms fire to the crippled team. Prior to reaching the team's position, he was wounded in his right leg, face, and head. Despite these painful injuries, he took charge, repositioning the team members and directing their fire to facilitate the landing of an extraction aircraft, and the loading of wounded and dead team members. He then threw smoke cannisters to direct the aircraft to the team's position. Despite his severe wounds and under the intense enemy fire, he carried and dragged half of the wounded team members to the awaiting aircraft. He then provided protective fire by running alongside the aircraft as it moved to pick up the remaining team members. As the enemy's fire intensified, he hurried to recover the body and the classified documents on the dead team leader. When he reached the team leader's body, Sergeant Benavidez was severely wounded by small arms fire in the abdomen and grenade fragments in his back. At nearly the same moment, the aircraft pilot was mortally wounded, and his helicopter crashed. Although in extremely critical condition due to his multiple wounds, Sergeant Benavidez secured the classified documents and made his way back to the wreckage, where he aided the wounded out of the overturned aircraft, and gathered the stunned survivors into a defensive perimeter. Under increasing enemy automatic weapons and grenade fire, he moved around the perimeter distributing water and ammunition to his weary men, reinstilling in them a will to live and fight. Facing a build-up of enemy opposition with a beleaguered team, Sergeant Benavidez mustered his strength, and began calling in tactical air strikes and directing the fire from supporting gunships to suppress the enemy's fire and so permit another extraction attempt. He was wounded again in his thigh by small arms fire while administering first aid to a wounded team member just before another extraction helicopter was able to land. His indomitable spirit kept him going as he began to ferry his comrades to the craft. On his second trip with the wounded, he was clubbed from behind by an enemy soldier. In the ensuing hand-to-hand combat, he sustained additional wounds to his head and arms before killing his adversary. He then continued under devastating fire to carry the wounded to the helicopter. Upon reaching the aircraft, he spotted and killed two enemy soldiers who were rushing the craft from an angle that prevented the aircraft door gunner from firing upon them. With little strength remaining he made one last trip to the perimeter to ensure that all classified material had been collected or destroyed, and to bring in the remaining wounded. Only then, in extremely serious condition from numerous wounds and loss of blood, did he allow himself to be pulled into the extraction aircraft. Sergeant Benavidez's gallant choice to join voluntarily his comrades who were in critical straits, to expose himself constantly to withering enemy fire, and his refusal to be stopped despite numerous severe wounds, saved the lives of at least eight men. His fearless personal leadership, tenacious devotion to duty, and extremely valorous actions in the face of overwhelming odds were in keeping with the highest traditions of the military service, and reflect the utmost credit on him and the United States Army.

The President then asked about the ceremony itself. I told him that we would have the citation read, and then the President would put the collar with the medal over the head of the Sergeant. I described the rest of the ceremony parade and events, but it appeared that the President was thinking of something else.

"Who reads the citation?" he inquired.

"Oh we have a soldier with a trained voice do that, offstage, so to speak," I said.

The President hesitated a moment, and then said, gently and diffidently, "I have a trained voice."

Finally, in my somewhat-less-than-quick way, I understood. "Mr. President," I said, "would you like to read the citation?"

"Yes," he said. "I would, very much, if it would not violate protocol."

I said I was quite sure I could arrange it.

Our protocol officers at the Pentagon were delighted by the prospect, the ceremony was amended and on February 24, with all flags flying and a huge crowd assembled in the Pentagon's inner court, the President of the United States, for the first time in the history of the award, read the citation himself and then placed the light blue collar with its myriad white stars, the Medal of Honor below, around the neck of Sergeant Benavidez. And if anyone had thought the citation moving just by seeing it in print, they should have heard the President's matchless voice and delivery bring it alive. It was one of those moments that remains fixed in the memory as one of the bright spots of the Presidency, just a month after the inauguration. Such moments should be savored. Just over a month later a would-be assassin's bullet hit the President and put in jeopardy all the changes, and all the goals and plans the new President embodied.

Within a few months of the inauguration, enlistments and retentions rose spectacularly, quality, measured by the percentage of high school graduates and IQ test results, increased similarly, and morale was restored, and then vastly increased. The compensation and support of our service men and women was my highest budgetary priority in 1981 and remained so all the time I was Secretary of Defense. But many other priorities were close behind.

The condition of the Navy we inherited clearly required substantial increases in both the number of ships and their capabilities. The appropriations we needed, of course, were the result of ten years of neglect, during which we had not kept pace with the rapidly growing Soviet Navy, nor even with the normal maintenance, overhaul and repairs of the ships we did have. We would, if our proposals were approved, be well embarked on the goal of achieving the 600 ship Navy that our commitments and our security required. All our studies indicated that there would be need for a *global* presence of the Navy, and that that would require 15 aircraft carrier task forces, compared with the 455 ships with 12 carrier forces that we inherited. Also, sadly, many of those 455 ships of the fleet in 1981 were in need of expensive overhaul, maintenance and modernization, all of which had long been deferred in the name of economy.

The Air Force had similar needs; and the readiness, the mobility and the fire power and indeed the general capability of both the Army and the Marine Corps also would have to be increased.

Not all the recommendations, however, were for increases. I urged that a little over $4 billion of the Carter proposals be eliminated. Much of that amount came from our rejection of the Carter proposals to base 200 of the new MX missiles in some 4,600 shelters with shuttle trucks running back and forth to try to deceive the Soviets. Since the Soviets would have the exact location by coordinates of all of the silos, it seemed to me that we ran the risk the Soviets would overcome our "deception" simply by increasing the size of their attack. We knew we had to have the new MX missile with its ten very accurate warheads and its ability to destroy Soviet hardened targets, to deter the Soviets from using their new SS-18s, but we hoped to have a more cost effective way of deploying them.

A number of additional savings could be achieved if Congress would allow us to use multi-year procurement, which simply meant buying arms on long-term orders, instead of the annual installments that had been used for too many years.

Use of long-term orders could save more than a billion a year starting in 1985. This simple and vastly superior method of purchasing had always been strongly opposed by Congress because they felt it prevented their reviewing each program each year. It also, of course, required small increases in the first years, but the savings were undeniable. We believed we could reduce spending by fifteen to twenty percent a unit with multi-year procurement, since military suppliers, knowing they had long-term contracts with the Government, could keep their skilled labor forces together and make more economical and efficient arrangements with their subcontractors and suppliers.

Predictably, the congressional staff comments on our proposal talked about the "loss of congressional flexibility," which simply meant that Congress would not be able to block previously approved programs, as they had so frequently done, or amend, or alter them from year to year. As it turned out, we finally persuaded Congress to allow some multi-year procurement, although not nearly as much as we had requested; thus we lost much of the savings we had hoped to achieve. Authorizing defense programs a year at a time is about the most inefficient way to buy anything.

Other provisions of the budget changes we proposed attracted great attention even though they required relatively small expenditures. One such item was the runway improvements that we sought for Diego Garcia, the mid-Indian Ocean island that would enable us to support any activity we might have to undertake in the Persian Gulf. The British government had always been extremely cooperative in allowing us to develop the island into a key military base. We determined that doing so was important enough to override objections from a number of the Third World nations.

As it has turned out over the years, the decision was a very necessary one: Our ability to support our forces in the Gulf was not only a crucial part of our operations later on, but was also critically important to the perception that we *could* maintain a presence in the Gulf and thus reduce the temptation for the Soviets, or anyone else, to try to take actions against our interests there.

Another provision of the budget amendments that attracted much attention was the plan to reactivate four of the mothballed battleships that had been out of service for many years. They were enormously powerful platforms from which to project American naval power, should it be required in those parts of the world where we did not have any land bases.

From 1981 onwards, that proposal was subjected to continuing criticisms, but by the end of the Reagan Administration all four of those mighty engines of deterrence were back in service. Even if they do not fire any more broadsides during their new lives, they will have added greatly to our deterrent capabilities and so to our ability to keep our peace and our freedom.

I have said that virtually all of our first recommendations were approved by Congress, and in a comparatively short time.

That does not, however, convey the full flavor of the nature of the process by which that approval was obtained, nor indeed does it convey any sort of picture of congressional hearings, which had already formed a considerable part of my prior experiences in Washington and were to occupy a very great deal of time during all the years I served as Secretary.

All those hearings followed a similar format, and it was one that I had become familiar with during my service in the Federal Trade Commission, the Office of Management and Budget and the Department of Health, Education, and Welfare.

One must never be late for a congressional hearing—a rule, however, to which very few of the members, or even sometimes the Chairman, adhere. Their lateness or absence is not always their fault, though. All members of the House and Senate are members of several committees, and nearly always there are conflicting schedules of hearings or committee meetings. In any event, you always try to arrive a few minutes ahead of time; and the press photographers then expend a great deal of film portraying you unpacking your briefcase, conferring briefly with members of the Department who have come to the hearings, or just waiting for the Committee to assemble. As soon as the Chairman appears, obligatory photographs are taken as you go from the witness table to the Chairman's lofty eminence above the floor of the Committee room. With those pictures out of the way, you return to your seat at the witness table and the hearing begins.

Customarily the Chairman makes an opening statement; another follows from the ranking minority member of the Committee. Those opening sallies are often couched in varying degrees of hostility. They are carefully prepared by the Committee staff and are usually read word-for-word by the Committee Chairman, or by a ranking member. Copies will of course have been distributed to the press well in advance of the hearing. Once those statements are completed, the witnesses make theirs. Most Committee members will have seen those statements, since the Committee rules require that they be submitted forty-eight hours before the hearing. You can, if you wish, read your statement word-for-word; or if you choose not to do so, to the Committee's evident relief, you can paraphrase and shorten it. I generally illustrated my statement with charts and graphics, which I hoped might interest either the Committee or, via the press covering the hearing, the public. I used my opening statements primarily to try to bring home to the public, as well as the Committee, the basis for our request, the need as we saw it, and our reasons, and indeed ammunition, for supporting our budgetary requests.

The questioning begins; and now the hearing takes on usually its most adversarial and confrontational aspect. Committee members each are generally given five minutes for questions. Normally the Chairman poses the first questions; then he calls upon a member of the Minority, then upon a member of the Majority, for their questions. Usually the "questions" consist primarily of lengthy statements of the member's position, the reasons for his unhappiness with some aspect of the Defense Department, and then perhaps an actual question, based often upon some (usually wildly erroneous) statement appearing in the morning newspaper. In my particular case, those questions quite often assumed that the item in the newspaper was gospel, and were sharply critical of me or the Department for some transgression alleged in the article. The questioners sometimes are quite irritated by having their questions answered, since that would consume part of their five minutes, which they would much rather use themselves. The witness's problem with their seizing all five minutes is that if statements made during that time go uncontravened, they will most likely be reported as uncontested statements of the simple truth.

In any event, the process goes on for several hours, because some of the committees, and particularly the Armed Services Committees, are very large, and members drift in and out, and then back in again in time to claim their five minutes. If by any chance all members present have used their five minutes, they will then frequently ask for, and receive, a second and a third increment of a few minutes. And as the hours wear on, the witness starts a mental calculation of how much longer the proceedings will last based on the number of members then present. That exercise is usually a serious mistake, because inevitably as the last member present is using the last increment of his five-minute period, three or four other members more will trickle in, and the process continues.

Throughout all of this, the witness must strive to remember

the cardinal rule: Any slight slip, any silly answer (and after three or four hours' intensive grilling I am quite capable of several silly answers), will form the basis of the media reporting and thus the public's views on the hearing. Its other four or five hours (or whatever span of time was consumed) will be completely forgotten. So it is essential that you stay on your guard at all times, a posture that adds to the tiring nature of the process.

The process for you as a witness resembles that experienced by an attorney conducting a trial in court: You cannot relax for a moment, for fear of missing the opportunity for either an objection you should make or an important question you should ask. And the possibility of your asking an unwise question or giving an injudicious statement is always before you.

The congressional hearing process is reasonably exhausting for the witness—and for the most part, I regret to say, quite futile; most of the questions do not turn on broad issues of national security policy, but are concerned with narrow, parochial interests that are of major importance to each congressman in his own district. That is understandable and an inherent part of our system: Members of Congress and the Senate must have an opportunity to question the executive branch, charged with the administration of the various departments, on even such very detailed and local matters.

Having made detailed preparations on every conceivable question of global strategy and all known military problems, I well recall one of the first questions fired at me by a House Committee member: Why, he demanded to know, had we contracted out to a private company the laundry and dry cleaning service at a Florida base? (Answer: to save money.)

There are several other important points about hearings. The first is that without exhaustive preparation, no one should go to a hearing as a witness (or even, really, as a member of the Committee, though the Committee would consider it quite presumptuous of a nonmember to point that out). I do not believe I ever went to a congressional hearing without having put in at least twice as many hours in the preparation as we anticipated the hearing itself would consume. The risk of erroneous or silly answers is too great; and the opportunities for the Secretary to present the case of the Administration and the Department are too important to leave to chance. Even with all that preparation, you may get a surprise question, like the one on the laundry in Florida. Since the questioner frequently does not expect an immediate answer, then you may "take the question," offering to provide the information later. A year's-worth of hearings may require hundreds of pages of such postsessional answers to questions. I have never ceased to be grateful to the enormously hardworking Defense staff who invested hundreds of hours each month in providing that followup information.

The sad truth, though, is that the hearings themselves rarely decide anything, most members already having made up their minds: generally, to make reductions in your request; to use the opportunity to voice their strong criticisms of the Department; to redress fancied wrongs borne by their constituents. Therefore, the hearing itself turns into an extended forum in which the Secretary is available for a number of political purposes that rarely seem to have a great deal to do with the major issues of the day.

But it is important to understand too that the congressional hearing process, tiring and irrelevant though much of it seems to participants and observers alike (and must seem to anyone unfamiliar with it), is a vital part of our American system of government. It is extremely important that the Executive make itself available to the Legislative Branch for the detailed and local-issue questioning that is inevitably the staple of congressional hearings.

Congress also considers it essential that Administration requests not be granted in full. Therefore many are questions based on the idea that since reduction of a budget request is inevitable, the Secretary must help congressmen by identifying what can be cut. Since I had already spent a very considerable amount of time preparing our budget submission, and already made a number of reductions in requests and eliminated various items asked for by the services, I did not come to the hearing with any eagerness to see further reductions or other changes made. Because I frankly said so, many times, and was not cooperative in helping congressmen find ways to make further reductions that I felt were unwise, and because I tried hard to stave off unwanted *additions* for many projects supported by a few representatives or senators for local purposes, I acquired a reputation of being stubborn, uncompromising, immoderate and unpragmatic. All those traits are considered rather serious shortcomings by many members, since the congressional process is made up almost completely of charge and countercharge, proposal, opposition, and inevitable compromise from which each side can claim a victory.

However, I felt strongly that most of those normal rules should be set aside on matters as vital as a rapid regaining of our military strength; and during the hearings on the President's first budget proposal and on the changes he made to the Carter budget of 1981, for the most part the Congress cooperated. The hearings were brisk, and there were controversial exchanges, but ultimately almost everything the President requested was approved. Congress perceived that the public wanted our military strengthened, and complied.

This sounds much easier than was actually the case, because there are always six, and usually eight, committees to which the same testimony has to be given, and many of the same questions have to be answered. These are the two Committees on the Armed Services, the Armed Services Subcommittees of the Appropriation Committees, the two Budget Committees, and usually the two Foreign Affairs Committees.

One of those stands out in my memory for the very positive way in which the Chairman managed affairs. It was the House Committee on Foreign Affairs, whose Chairman was the long-time Florida Democratic Congressman Dante Fascell; and whose ranking Republican member was Bill Broomfield, an able and experienced congressman from Michigan. Fascell has many of the attitudes common to Southern Democrats. He is a very practical, pleasant man, and he always conducts fair hearings. He may disagree with every thing the witness says, but you can hardly tell that from his treatment of witnesses. He regularly invited the Secretary of Defense to an informal breakfast with his Committee just before opening his hearings on the budget. After breakfast we would work around the room as we explored in some depth, with a total absence of rancor, a number of questions of concern to the Committee members. There were no press and no television cameras present, and the whole process was a model of how committee hearings should be conducted. After about two hours of informal discussion on such matters as the program for weapons systems, basing the MX missile, Soviet capabilities, base closing measures, relations with Israel, NATO, and Japan, we then went out to the public arena. Nevertheless, while much of the posturing and time wasting that accompany a standard hearing was absent, there were always a few congressmen who in public took positions somewhat different from those they had professed in private.

The hearings managed by Congressman Fascell produced far more civilized, useful and searching inquiries than most others and were far more likely to further the knowledge of the Committee. They also afforded witnesses a better opportunity to present the Administration's views.

That the Congress granted the President virtually everything he asked in 1981 should nevertheless not obscure that congressional consent came only after those eight long congressional hearings, many meetings, several conference committee discussions, and quite long debates, actions on amendments, and final votes that stretched on into the fall of 1981.

By that time, of course, we were well embarked on the work for the following year's budget, which had to be submitted to Congress at the end of January 1982. It too would require increases. In the preparation of *this* budget, several in the Administration, unwilling to face the hard fact that the nation's security costs a great deal, began to lose stomach for the rearmament of America—which remained the basic pledge and goal of the President.

The next budget decisions were not to be made in the Pentagon alone. Now the increasingly active White House staff took a hand, worried by their inability to persuade Congress to accept domestic spending cuts, after enactment of the President's tax cut.

Now voices were raised against the execution of the second year rearmament plan, and there were many attempts to make major reductions in it—as was borne in upon me when I was en route to Honolulu on September 2, 1981, to respond to an invitation to talk to the American Legion Convention there and to inspect our forces in the Pacific area.

On the plane going out, I heard that "the White House" had already announced that the second year appropriation request of the President for defense would be reduced by some $35 billion from the $222 billion that the President and we in the Department had previously agreed to request of Congress. When I landed in Honolulu, the press naturally opened their questioning on that subject. I replied that this was the first I had heard of such a reduction and to the best of my knowledge the President had not agreed to anything of the kind. I was able to make so flat a statement because I had spoken to the President from my plane immediately after hearing that "the White House" had agreed to that very deep slash in the second year request of the President. He told me that he had no idea where such a report came from, that he had not agreed to it. So my firm denial of it returned the matter to an issue to be debated further, rather than an issue already decided against the Pentagon.

The ultimate result of that debate, following many meetings with the President, with his Chief of Staff and others, as well as a private meeting between the President, OMB Director Stockman and me, was that over a three year period there would be a reduction in the original five year plan of some $13 billion in outlays, rather than $35 billion in budget authority in one year. Thus in Fiscal Year 1982, we would trim out $8 billion from our authority figures, to $213 billion, but only $2 billion in outlay cuts, with reductions of $5 or $6 billion for the next two years for a total of $13 billion reduction in outlays. (For 1983, the Congress approved $253.6 billion in budget authority, and $214 billion in outlays.) The reduction of $13 billion for three years could be accepted at that time, without undue harm to the military, because by then the monthly figures of the Labor Department's Bureau of Statistics had shown that we were getting a much firmer grip on inflation—much sooner than we had even hoped—and so would be able to buy more for each dollar than we had previously thought would be possible.

That debate, however, in the fall of 1981, hard on the heels of the passage of the President's spring 1981 request, was the forerunner of long and increasingly difficult disputes within the Administration, and of course later with the Congress, over the amount of defense spending. Congress, which had granted the President his tax cutting legislation, was increasingly reluctant to reduce the normal headlong increases in domestic spending, and increasingly anxious to find some area for cutting expenditures.

Defense is never a popular expenditure in democracies, and the Department was now subject to increasing criticism both from various factions within the Administration and from members of both parties in Congress. Congress did not want to agree to major domestic spending cuts, and the deficit persisted. The easiest candidate for cuts was Defense; but as long as it was perceived that the public supported our increases, the President's leadership prevented severe Defense cuts. It did so until the appropriation bill for Fiscal Year 1987 was passed late in 1986. Cabinet meetings became increasingly difficult year after year, since Defense was the only Department whose expansions were being authorized by the President; other department heads were under growing pressure for increases from special interest groups.

Changes in Budget Authority, 1980–1993

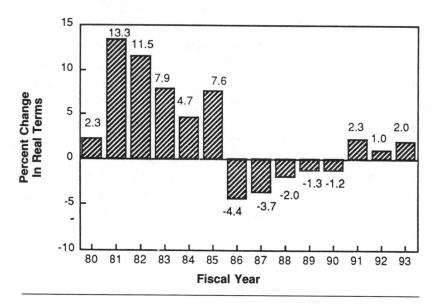

SOURCE: Office of the Assistant Secretary of Defense (Comptroller), *National Defense Budget Estimates for FY 1990/1991,* March 1989, p. 96; "Briefing Tables FY 1990/1991 Defense Budget," Secretary of Defense Richard Cheney (Washington, DC: Department of Defense). NOTE: Through 1989 is actual; the rest is "projected" or "estimated."

Nevertheless, the President remained firmly committed to the broad general outlines of our rearmament requirements; and the people *had* supported our increases for five and a half years. It is my belief that public support weakened thereafter primarily because the people generally felt we had accomplished our rearmament, that the job was finished.

The simple fact was that modernizing and renewing all three legs of the strategic Triad and the command and control system, improving personnel benefits to preserve the all-volunteer system, and repairing the deficiencies of the 1970s in operation and maintenance costs and in conventional forces, as well as regaining the lead we had to have in research and development, was bound to be a very expensive proposition for a number of years to come.

Congressmen and senators would regularly plead with me, both in open sessions of the Committees and in private meetings, to "be more reasonable," to "give some," to "compromise," to participate in the familiar rites of spring on Capitol Hill. They never had any specific cuts in mind. What they wanted was an overall percentage reduction that they could tell their constituents I had supported, so there would be no political pain to them. In 1987 I was told to bring in a Defense budget of a size that Congress would approve without confrontation. That, of course, would have required me to guess in advance what Congress would approve. None of those congressional pleas or demands was based on military needs; they were all designed simply to reduce defense spending for *political* reasons.

I could not bring myself to believe that I would be serving the President's interests, or the country's, by agreeing to such reductions, when we knew that the Soviet capabilities were increasing every day, and increasing from a level already far above ours. The Soviet Union had not had a twenty percent reduction in the 1970s, as we had had. I knew how much we had to do; I also knew that public opinion would not for long support major defense increases. I particularly could not bring myself to believe that additional cuts were safe when I had already made deep reductions in the requests of the various services before submitting anything to Congress.

Such strains and strictures made for a series of difficult confrontations at committee hearing after committee hearing in Congress, and within the Administration itself, until it not only seemed, but really was the case, that only the President and two or three of his principal officials, such as William P. Clark, who was Deputy Secretary of State and, later, National Security Advisor to the President, were on the side of adequate defense.

Certainly, one of the more annoying and damaging actions was the habit of David Stockman, the President's Budget Director, to meet privately with various congressmen and senators to tell them that, and where, he felt the President's defense budget should be cut. That activity was consistent with Stockman's continued support for tax increases, but quite inconsistent with any loyalty to the President.

Added to all those burdens was another: We were, in 1982, in the middle of a long-predicted economic recession, which exacerbated the problems of seeking domestic cuts. It also led to all kinds of demagogic outbursts from frustrated senators and congressmen who urgently wanted a return to far more traditional policies and to a far more traditional President, who would seek normal increases in domestic spending, not support defense increases, and would be willing to compromise on any issue on which Congress showed any resistance. I am now frequently asked if it would not have been better to seek much smaller defense increases each year "to preserve the public's consensus for Defense." Certainly not, I thought then, in 1982, and I still think. Public support for defense expenditures in a democracy in peacetime is always very shallow. Indeed, I do not believe America had *ever* previously supported a peacetime defense increase for more than about twenty months. I think it was evident to anyone, including Congress, who looked at comparative intelligence reports of our forces and those of the USSR, that we had to make up very quickly for our failures and neglect in the past. I knew that asking for an increase of one or two percent a year would not give us what we needed, and that the support for even that increase would soon erode, as indeed it did after 1988.

So I remain very grateful for the President's continuing support for what we had to do, unpopular politically though it was thought to be. I am also grateful for the congressional support we did have that enabled us to continue regaining our vitally needed military strength for over five years—until the Congress rebelled.

I was told by some that my "stubbornness" was hurting the President, so I was particularly grateful and pleased when in 1984 he was re-elected by one of the largest margins in our history. This is not to say, of course, that he was re-elected *because* of the defense buildup—but clearly he was not hurt by it. It was also a source of great gratification to me that he left office with a higher popular approval rating than any President since such assessments of public opinion have been taken.

That defense buildup he championed so valiantly produced something else he had always cherished: an arms-reduction treaty and better relations with the Soviets. But that is another chapter.

One of the most extreme examples of virulent demagoguery I remember was uttered by Senator Donald W. Riegle Jr. (Democrat of Michigan) at a budget hearing on February 3, 1983, at which he blamed the recession, the rising unemployment in his state and indeed most of the ills of mankind upon me personally. Our encounter was much noted at the time and is worth recalling again:

SENATOR RIEGLE. Thank you, Mr. Chairman. It has been very frustrating to sit and listen and not have an opportunity to engage in discussion along the way on some of the points that have been raised today, but that is the nature of the system that we have. Mr. Weinberger, I have served in the Congress now for 17 years under five Presidents, as both a Republican and a Democrat, and for the first time, I think we have a Secretary of Defense whose basic judgment is dangerous to our country. You give every appearance of being an inflexible idealogue who has lost any sense of rational proportion when it comes to assessing the defense needs of our country. By your really fanatical insistence on defense increases that are larger than needed, larger than we can afford, I believe that you are damaging our national security.

SECRETARY WEINBERGER. Well, Senator, I have to—

SENATOR RIEGLE. Now, I beg your pardon, sir. I did not interrupt you—

SECRETARY WEINBERGER. Yes; that is right, but you are—

SENATOR RIEGLE. I did not interrupt you, and when I finish —I have the floor—

SECRETARY WEINBERGER. Yes, but you are making an attack on me, personally, and I have to say—

SENATOR RIEGLE. I have the floor. I do not feel that I am, sir, and I have the floor—

SECRETARY WEINBERGER. Well, I would let anybody judge that—

SENATOR RIEGLE. Mr. Chairman, I would ask that the Secretary—

CHAIRMAN DOMENICI. Would you both refrain for a moment? All right, Senator, would you start over now?

SENATOR RIEGLE. I believe that these policies and this approach is damaging our national security and I want to repeat it for emphasis: I think you are making America weaker, not stronger, and I think this perverse reality is actually serving the interests of the Soviet Union, which is the most dangerous irony of all.

I think it is absurd to believe that the United States can plausibly project strength abroad when we lack economic strength at home. Today, one-third of our national plant and equipment is sitting idle. We have over 12 million Americans out of work, and we have bankruptcies and foreclosures in this country at the highest rate in 50 years, and despite these realities, you are insisting on obsolete, multibillion dollar weapons systems like the B-1 bomber; you are insisting upon the MX missile system, when even Joint Chiefs do not agree with your Dense Pack basing mode. By your refusal to accept a more reasonable, orderly strengthening of defense capabilities, I think you are creating a strengthening public opposition to defense increases.

I think that your overspending on defense is distorting the economy, bloating the deficits, adding to unemployment, keeping interest rates at excessively high levels. You are mortgaging our future with enormous permanent increases in the national debt, and you are allowing our allies to do less than their full share in bearing the free world defense burden.

As someone said earlier, you had the reputation before when you were at HEW as "Cap the Knife," and at the Defense Department, you certainly have become "Cap the Spendthrift," in every sense of the word.

These are not just my personal views. I have been out, throughout my State in the last year and a half, as those of us who were running for reelection, I can tell you that what I am saying here reflects the views of a substantial part of the 9.5 million people in the State of Michigan that I represent.

We need to make major cuts in the projected defense increases that you have brought before this committee. Your presentation is deceptive in terms of the point that Senator Chiles and others have made about changing the baseline numbers, creating the fiction of cuts when in fact, they are not real cuts, in terms of the actions that were taken here one year ago and which was understood by members of both parties to be the case. I am going to do everything that I possibly can to make these cuts.

Mr. Chairman, I have a number of questions that I am going to submit to the Secretary, that I would like him to answer for the record.

SECRETARY WEINBERGER. I would like to answer one now, if I might, Mr. Chairman. May I be recognized?

CHAIRMAN DOMENICI. You are granted as much time as you like, Mr. Secretary.

SECRETARY WEINBERGER. Senator, I think you have accomplished your principal purpose, which was to launch a demagogic attack on me in time for the afternoon and evening editions. I want to tell you that I think everything you have said is both insulting and wrong, and fully consistent with, basically, some of the things that have been evidenced in the past to me about you.

I wonder if your people in Michigan with whom you have talked know that if you are going to impose the kinds of cuts you are talking about, you will lose something in the neighborhood of 154,000 jobs in your State, and I wonder how that will improve unemployment and how that will help the economy. I wonder how it will help the Soviets [for us] to have the proper amounts that are necessary for defense, in the opinion of the person who has the responsibility to recommend them to Congress, how does that help them?

I wonder if you can tell me how I can spend one nickel of defense money that has not been appropriated by the Congress—by you and your colleagues—and I am sure you have taken full credit for any contracts that came home to Michigan.

SENATOR RIEGLE. There have been very few of those, Mr. Secretary.

SECRETARY WEINBERGER. I am sorry?

SENATOR RIEGLE. There have been very few of those, if you will remember.

SECRETARY WEINBERGER. There have been a lot of them, and—

SENATOR RIEGLE. We have 750,000 people unemployed in Michigan today.

SECRETARY WEINBERGER. Yes, and do you want to add 154,000 to their numbers? The other thing—

SENATOR RIEGLE. You have helped add 154,000 to their numbers.

CHAIRMAN DOMENICI. Senator, I think the Secretary deserves to answer.

You may proceed, Mr. Secretary.

SECRETARY WEINBERGER. Thank you.

You have offered no evidence whatever to support a lot of extraneous and demagogic-type statements, that I am sure you think will appeal to the headlines.

The simple fact of the matter is, I have certain responsibilities. I do not have the luxury of sitting up there and guessing at what might happen. I have the responsibility of looking at the threat as I see it and looking at how that threat has grown and looking at what is necessary, in my opinion, to advise the Congress and the President what we must do about it. The Congress thus far authorized the amounts that we are spending. To say that I am spending the country into bankruptcy is to say the Congress has authorized too much. I do not think they have. I think they have authorized what is enough, although I think last year, more should have been done on specific systems.

I have a totally different mission now than what [when] my mission was coming in here [while I was at OMB], which was to try to get a hold on a serious inflation problem and a budget that had been allowed to increase [domestically] because of decreases in defense spending.

We have examined everything in the Department of Defense just as carefully as we did at OMB, all of the requests have been scrubbed, and all of them have been reduced. As I told Senator Kassebaum, many of the requests are for over twice what is actually approved. To think that you can improve the situation, or lessen the peril that this country faces, by sitting up there and closing your eyes to it and making a lot of statements designed for headline treatment, and a lot of extremely unfair personal attacks, strikes me as fully consistent with what I had heard about you.

I think we would all serve our country a lot better if we examined dispassionately the threats and the needs and determine what we have to do to recover from them [and] to realize in doing that, we do not hurt our economy or add to unemployment, which is one of the principal problems in your State.

Mr. Chairman, I appreciate very much your allowing me to make this statement.

CHAIRMAN DOMENICI. Thank you.

The day-by-day struggles need not be recounted in detail here. Suffice it to say that each year's budget battle was a long *campaign*, with hearings, meetings, breakfast with various congressmen and senators at the Pentagon and elsewhere, individual calls on members of the Senate and the House. And in my efforts to secure public support not only for the broad outline of the President's military rearmament program but for many of its details, I made far more television and radio appearances than I wanted to make, held innumerable meetings with newspaper editorial boards, individual reporters and columnists, shared dinners with opinion leaders, and delivered far more speeches than I care to remember.

At the same time, the Department of Defense was also preparing, each year over a period of almost a year, the following year's budgets, and making major reductions in the requests of the three services and the individual agencies within the Department. Those were but some of the many matters we worked on during each year of which more will be said in later chapters. The budget fights with Congress and within the Administration, and the problems of presenting them in their true perspective to a public that often based its views on erroneous and partial presentations by the media, constituted a continuing and increasingly difficult problem for the Department each day of each year.

I understood perfectly that good news is not considered very newsworthy, and that the thing that could excite the public most would be bad news, weapons systems not working, outrageous prices attempted to be charged by various manufacturers, and basically any deviation from the conventional wisdom in the choice of weapons or in tactics.

Simple statements by us—that, for example, if the United States were ever forced into a war, nuclear or otherwise, it was vital that we win; or that if the Soviets believed they could fight a protracted nuclear war, we must be prepared to resist that too, so as to deter it—were enough to generate scores of articles stating that we were warlike hawks eager for a fight, hoping to drop the bomb, and at the very least, plainly militaristic. Those charges would be repeated, without independent examination, by other columnists and writers, at home and abroad, and would be taken as unquestioned facts by most readers or listeners. My contrary statements, *that we did not believe a nuclear war could be won by anyone, and thus must never be fought*, were usually ignored.

Also ignored were our statements that we never paid the outrageous prices attempted to be charged for hammers and coffeepots, and indeed that it was our own audits that had discovered the charges. The erroneous charge that we *paid* those prices was a much "better" story, and more likely to be selected for the front pages or the evening television news. Also rarely reported were the facts about all the refunds we obtained after those few occasions when initial payment of the absurd prices had been approved.

I took all of those attacks and stories very seriously, because I knew the damage they could do by undermining public support for the appropriations we urgently needed; I knew the ammunition they could give those who generally opposed defense spending in any amounts.

Nevertheless, for over five years Congress supported, after strenuous arguments, substantial increases in defense and approved well over ninety percent of the President's requests and proposals for regaining our military strength.

But as the public increasingly felt we had already secured vastly increased military strength and capability, the public's willingness to support military investment, on any scale, eroded, and the public resumed its normal posture of opposing military spending.

The support had been neither easily won nor gladly given—but I am convinced that if we had played the game by the usual rules, and given in at each sign of congressional resistance, we would never have secured the great military recovery we achieved—and most certainly I am convinced that we could not have achieved what we did within those five years.

That is why I disagree completely with those who say that we "lost the defense consensus," or that we should have proceeded "much more slowly," or that we had no strategy.

Our strategy was simple to state and very difficult to achieve; it was to regain, as quickly as possible, sufficient military strength to convince our friends to stay closely allied with us and to convince the Soviets they could not win any war they might start against us or our allies. We did that.

III

The Attempted Assassination of the President

On March 30, 1981, shortly before 2:15 in the afternoon, a would-be assassin named John Hinckley shot the President outside the Washington Hilton Hotel, where the President had delivered a luncheon talk.

For a time during the long and fateful hours of that afternoon and evening, there was always the terrible possibility that the President would not recover, and that all of the hopes that he and his friends had for the changes he planned to bring to America, and indeed to the world, would come crashing down in the aftermath of that single mad act.

There have been many accounts of that act and its aftermath, some written from the self-serving point of view of those who felt it necessary to try to correct the record of their activities; some by those who simply wanted to set down the events of the historic afternoon and evening; and some by those who had little firsthand knowledge of what had happened, but felt compelled to write about it anyway on the basis of one or two accounts they seem to have picked up from reports of others.

At the Cabinet meeting chaired by Vice President George Bush on March 31, the morning after the assassination attempt, one of the points discussed was a request by the White House staff that each of us who participated in the meetings in the Situation Room of the White House following the assassination attempt, set down our account of what happened. We were asked particularly to concentrate on the first stages of the events, and tell how we heard of the attempt and what we did before each of us arrived in the Situation Room.

The rationale for the request was that it was vital to put together as contemporaneous a record as possible, toward correcting any procedural problems and toward planning how best to handle any similar incident in the future.

My response to that request, a memorandum dated April 7, was actually dictated off and on during a two day period before that.

The following is a paraphrase of most of that memorandum, with some additions to help readers picture the scene more accurately. I chose to paraphrase the memorandum, rather than reproduce it here in its entirety, because I do not feel that a memorandum sent to the President's staff (and therefore for all practical purposes to the President himself) should be published without at least some minor modifications. I also made some editing changes to spell out for general readers the abbreviations and military shorthand used in the memorandum. Nevertheless, what follows is my account of the post-assassination attempt activities, written for the most part within a week of the attempt itself:

On Monday afternoon, March 30, about 2:30, my naval aide, Captain Bovey, appeared at the door of my office to advise me there was a radio report that there had just been a shooting outside the hotel where President Reagan had been speaking at lunch. I glanced over to the President's schedule on my desk and noted that he was scheduled to be through with his talk and depart the hotel at 2:35. I asked if the President had been near the shooting, and Bovey said the radio reports did not indicate so.

I continued work on the briefing papers for my next meeting, which was to be a talk with Admiral Bobby Inman, who was introducing his successor at the National Security Agency, General Lincoln Faurer.

As they came in, Captain Bovey again appeared and said that the radio had now reported that the shooting had taken place in the presence of the President, but that it appeared the President had not been hit and was in his car, apparently going to the hospital to see how some of the people who had been hit, and who had been taken there, were faring. I said, This sounds completely typical of the President, and then turned my own radio on. The radio was now reporting that the President was on his way to the hospital but had not been hit. Admiral Inman and General Faurer came in, but almost immediately my secretary told me that the White House had called, and I was wanted at the Situation Room immediately.

Admiral Inman excused himself, and we called for my driver [the imperturbable and very efficient Matt Turner, who served me so well for seven years, and who became a great friend of my wife's and mine]. They did not locate him immediately, so Admiral Inman offered to take me to the White House. I rode with him, arriving in the Situation Room in the White House a few minutes before 3:00, I believe.

On the car radio we heard more and more detailed accounts on the incident. They were now reporting that the President had indeed been hit, and was under treatment at the hospital; that Jim Brady had been seriously hurt and that two others, a Secret Service man and a policeman, had also been shot, but that the extent of their injuries was not known. There were accounts too that the suspect was in custody.

Almost immediately after hearing this, I began to think of other assassination attempts, and most of all I thought of the shooting of President Lincoln, and the fact that the Booth conspirators had also planned and started to carry out assassinations of others in the government. I also thought of the assassination of President Kennedy and the theories still held by some writers that that tragedy had been part of a larger conspiracy.

I wondered if the gunman had been acting only on his own disordered mind, or if there were some larger plan.

[The White House Situation Room is a small windowless conference room in the basement of the West Wing, next to the White House staff mess. Normally, when Security Council Planning Group sessions are held there, the President sits at the left end (as you enter the room) of the table, which fills most of the space in the room. There is room for a few chairs along the side walls, for staff. That afternoon many people were milling about and virtually no one sat at the table for more than a few minutes.]

In the Situation Room when I arrived were Dick Allen, Al Haig, Don Regan, Bill Casey, and several other people I did not know. Others kept moving in and out. I believe it was shortly thereafter that Bill French Smith, the Attorney General, came in. Various aides of those men were also present. There was a small tape recorder on the table, and occasionally Dick Allen changed tapes. The television set mounted near the ceiling of the room was giving repeated accounts of the incident and showing films of the actual shooting.

There was a copy of the book and coded materials carried in the "football" briefcase, which concern procedures in the event of an imminent nuclear attack on the United States and which always accompany the President, on the Situation Room table.

Very shortly after arriving at the Situation Room, I inquired about Ed Meese and Mike Deaver. I was told that Mike had been with the President but was apparently not hurt, and that Ed Meese was at the hospital.

The television films showed Mike Deaver either ducking or falling, and I was concerned he had been shot. Various calls were coming in and were being answered by anyone close to the phone. Al Haig had one of the secure phones in front of him near one end of the table, and another phone in the room was busy. I stepped out to call Ed Meese at the hospital, or Ed Meese called me, I cannot recall which, at approximately 3:15, or perhaps closer to 3:30. My conversation with Ed Meese was somewhat reassuring in that he told me that he did not think the President was seriously hurt, but that they were going to have exploratory surgery. He then said to me, "Under these circumstances, it is my understanding the National Command Authority devolves on you." I said that I believed the chain started with the Vice President. Ed Meese said the Vice President was on a plane in Texas that was being diverted back to Washington, and that it would take him approximately two hours to get here. I asked about the communication to the plane, and asked which plane it was, and Ed said that he did not know, but he did not think there was secure communication. He mentioned again the chain of leadership under the National Command Authority, and I confirmed that I was the next in line after the Vice President. [That had been clarified in one of the first directives that I had presented to the President-elect a few days before his inauguration. The directives were designed to insure that there was no gap in the chain of command between the ending of one Administration and the beginning of the next. I knew from past experience of the White House that an incoming President is almost literally buried under mountains of paper, reams of new regulations being added upon the usual massive flow of paperwork into the White House; and I thought it vital to get chain of command and other critical matters arranged ahead of the flood.]

We talked a bit more about the condition of the President, and I returned to the Situation Room to see if one of the secure phones was free. It was not, but there was considerable discussion going on about the television appearance of Larry Speakes, who was in the White House Press Room and whose statement was coming over the television set at that time. Speakes was responding to questions from the press about the location of the Vice President, the condition of the President, and about whether there had been any transfer of the authority from the President. He answered no or occasionally "I don't know" to those questions. Al Haig was visibly restless during this performance, and said Speakes should not be answering questions. I agreed, saying that in my opinion a short statement should be handed out and no questions taken, at least until we knew a great deal more. Haig in turn seemed to agree with that.

The phones were still busy, so I stepped outside the room to another secure telephone and called General David Jones, the holdover Chairman of the Joint Chiefs of Staff. He said that he had heard the news about the President. I passed on Ed Meese's statements about the President's having exploratory surgery but appearing to be in good condition and not badly hurt.

I then asked about the alert condition of our forces. General Jones said there had been no change in the alert and that the major part of the forces were in the condition called DEFCON 5 (Defense Condition 5),[1] except that, as was normal, some Strategic Air Command bomber crews and other forces were on the next higher degree of alert, called DEFCON 4.

---

1. Defense Condition 5 essentially means that our forces are in their normal peacetime condition: some in training, some on leave, etc. There are four Defense Conditions requiring higher degrees of readiness and alertness. In DEFCON 4, there are always some Air Force crews ready to take off in 12 to 15 minutes. DEFCON 1, the highest degree of readiness, would be declared if hostilities were imminent or actually under way.

I asked General Jones if he had information about any other activities that might indicate attempts by the Soviets, or anyone else, to take advantage of the news of the attempt on the President's life; or if he had any information from any source to indicate whether or not this was merely an isolated attempt on the President as opposed to being linked to some sort of co-ordinated activity. General Jones said he had no such information. I asked about the position of the Soviet forces, and he said they were more or less normal except that there were two Soviet submarines "outside the box." That expression reflects that there is a normal pattern of Soviet submarines operating off the East Coast of the United States. USSR submarines within that normal area are called "inside the box." The two that General Jones referred to that were "outside the box" were somewhat closer to the United States than was normal. The "box" represents an area measured in the minutes it would take Soviet nuclear missiles fired from their submarines to reach targets in the United States. Thus the boundaries of the "box" are not static. General Jones said that having two Soviet subs outside the box was not considered extremely unusual, and that it did occur from time to time, but that it was outside the normal pattern.

We discussed the general differences between DEFCON 5 and DEFCON 4. I still had in mind the possibility that more than the assassination of the President was intended, so I then told General Jones that we should increase the alert for the Strategic Air Command forces, not raising it to DEFCON 3, but that instead of having the alert bomber crews on regular alert and restricted to their *bases* (which is the normal condition under DEFCON 4 for the alert bomber crews), they should now be restricted to the *alert area* within the base, which would save anywhere from three to six or seven minutes in getting the bombers aloft if need be.

I also inquired about the condition of the NEACP, the National Emergency Airborne Command Post plane, and was told it was in the normal condition of alertness at Andrews Air Force Base. The crews were not aboard the airplane, but they were within a minute or two at the most of being able to board. I concluded that there was no immediate need for changing the condition of the alert status of the plane, since the Command Authority was at this point in Washington, a good ten minutes from Andrews.

I then asked General Jones to ask all of the Commanders in Chief of our designated and specified commands, as well as the Defense Intelligence Agency and others, to be on the alert specifically for any activity of any kind that might be interpreted as the Soviets or anyone else trying to take advantage of the situation, or proceeding in accordance with any sort of plan or actions that might involve hostile action of any sort against the United States. I told him we were not going to do all the formal changes involved in "raising the DEFCON," including a formal recommendation from the Secretary of Defense to the Joint Chiefs, formal adoption by the Joint Chiefs of the higher DEFCON transmissions, formal notice to all Commands, etc., but that I wanted every commander to be told immediately by informal message that it was the Secretary's direction that they be particularly vigilant and on the alert, until further notice.

General Jones reported that the NEACP had hardened Very High Frequency radio capability, which meant that its communications have some degree of protection against atomic blasts. He also reported that there were 249 B-52 bomber planes and crews on the alert at Strategic Air Command (SAC) bases, and 8 command and control planes and crews similarly on the alert. He reported that all of our North American Air Defense Command (NORAD) sensors were green (that is, no enemy activity).

I returned to the Situation Room and noticed everyone watching the television screen, upon which Al Haig had appeared and was responding to questions about presidential succession. I said (to no one in particular), "I wonder why they're running an old tape of Al Haig's." Someone responded that it was not a tape, that Al Haig was in the press room. I said, "But I thought he was right here."

When Haig stated on television that the line of succession was from President to Vice President to Secretary of State and that he was in charge at the White House, someone said "That's a mistake." Haig was now saying that no alert had been given to our forces, or contemplated, and that none was necessary.

Shortly thereafter, Haig returned to the Situation Room and said we should all act in accordance with the statements he had just made.

I said, "Al, one problem with that is that you should know I have already ordered an increase, although a very small one, in the alert conditions of the Strategic Air crews," and I then told him of my call to General Jones.

Haig said, "Did you do this simply because of the Soviet subs, or because of the incident?" I said that I did it because of the incident, and because I did not know whether it was simply an isolated incident or the opening episode of some coordinated plan, and that the location of the two Soviet subs mentioned above had indeed also been part of the reason.

He pressed again, stating in effect that the only reason I had changed the alert was because of the subs.

I said that, no, it was because I did not know enough about the whole matter, and that it seemed to me a prudent and necessary thing to do. He argued that the fact that I had taken that step might get out, and would tend to discredit his previous statement on television. He seemed unable or unwilling to accept that there could be an increase in the vigilance of our Commands, without going through all the technical and procedural changes involved in "raising the DEFCON."

I told him that it was only a small increase in the alert posture, that I had not raised the regular SAC alert condition to DEFCON 3, that there was no reason for anyone to know, or be alarmed, about the additional alert I had ordered, but that in any event it seemed more important to me to make that increase in the alert than to worry about whether any statements he had just made on television were contradicted or not. He pressed again on the matter, saying something to the effect that it wouldn't be a good thing for the fact that I had changed that alert to get out.

I responded that it was my understanding that I had to make decisions in that field, and that the decision I had made represented my best judgment. He said that I should read the Constitution. Haig seemed to be referring to the old statute, under the now superseded constitutional provisions, that established the Secretary of State as the next to take over in the event of the death or disability of the President and the Vice President. That statute has long since been changed by the Congress, by Acts of September 9, 1965, and October 15, 1966, under the Twenty-fifth Amendment to the Constitution, to provide that after the President and Vice President, the succession devolves, not upon the Secretary of State, but on the Speaker of the House and then the President Pro Tem of the Senate. I repressed an impulse to tell him that if he had read the current version of the Constitution he would find that some of his statements on television were not correct.

More reports were now coming in, by phone calls to Dick Allen and others, and the matter was dropped. Dick, or someone else, about this time reported that the President was now in surgery. Bill French Smith said he had more information about the gun and the assailant, whose name was Hinckley.

I called Ed Meese at the hospital and he confirmed that the

President was in surgery. Ed wanted to know the name of the assailant, and I relayed the information to him that Bill Smith had provided to the group in the Situation Room. I also advised Ed of the increased alertness that I had ordered, and of the information about the submarines, but advised him again that there was nothing very unusual about the presence of the two Soviet subs. I also reported to Ed Meese that Al Haig had felt this additional alertness I had ordered should not have been done, but that I continued to believe it was a small but necessary precaution taken until we had an opportunity to receive reports from various commands around the world, and from other sources.

Ed Meese concurred, and he advised again that the Vice President was expected to arrive now about 6:30, and that, very preliminarily, one of the doctors had advised Ed that the President appeared to be in good condition, and that the doctors were confident the wound would not be fatal, but that the surgery was considered necessary.

I then again called General Jones, who reported that all NORAD sensors continued green. We discussed the fact that a NORAD exercise with a simulated incoming missile attack had been planned for the next day. We both concluded immediately that this exercise should be canceled. I inquired whether any messages had been received from the Moscow link and was told that none had, and there were no reports of any unusual nature.

Bill French Smith, by this time, had a photocopy of the statute relating to presidential succession and was discussing the alternatives: that the President might transfer authority to the Vice President in the event of the President's disability; or in the event the President was not in condition to transmit authority, that the decision would then be made by the Vice President and the majority of the Cabinet. At this time, I noticed that Secretary Block and Secretary Edwards, and I think Secretary Baldrige, had come into the Situation Room.

The discussion flowed back and forth, with attention being divided between reports on the television screen and conversation about the arrival of the Vice President, and the points that should be made in briefing him. Admiral Murphy, the Vice President's Chief of Staff (who had been in the room from the beginning) was making a list of points to bring to the Vice President's attention when he arrived, including such matters as tomorrow's schedule, the constitutional provisions Bill Smith had just mentioned, the alert condition of the armed forces, a draft of a public statement to be made, and the status of any pending legislation requiring the President's action.

Secretary Regan had information about the Secret Service, and reported that he was tracing ownership of the gun through the Treasury tax people. He also reported that there were no unusual incidents around the country that had been reported to the Secret Service. At about this time, Dan Rather reported on television that Jim Brady had died from his wounds. That report was corrected in 10 to 15 minutes.

It was now perhaps 5:15 or 5:30.

I had previously called Deputy Secretary Carlucci and advised him of the situation and also of the provisions I had taken in increasing the alert. I then called the National Military Command Center to see if any further information had been received. There was none. General Jones called me to advise the same thing, and a number of other messages were coming in for other people. I talked again to Ed Meese, who reported that the surgery had been completed about 5:30 and that the preliminary indications were that the President had come through extremely well. The President was in the intensive care unit. George Bush was expected at Andrews at 6:30 and would first go to the vice presidential residence, then come to the Situation Room, being expected there about 7:00.

In the Situation Room, Dick Allen was going over a list of additional points to be presented to the Vice President, including tomorrow's schedule, and the desirability of having a Cabinet meeting in the morning, and the fact that the President had been scheduled to meet with the congressional leadership. I said I thought it would be very important for those meetings, both the Cabinet meeting and the meeting with the congressional leadership, to be held as scheduled. Al Haig said that Andreas van Agt, the Prime Minister of the Netherlands, was due for various meetings and that he felt there should be no attempt to postpone those meetings.

Jim Baker had come to the Situation Room now and reported that the President had actually lost almost 4 pints of blood; that he said when he saw Mrs. Reagan, "Honey, I forgot to duck"; and that on the way into the operating room he had winked when he saw Baker and Meese standing by and put his thumbs up, indicating that everything would be all right. Even though because of the oxygen mask and the anesthesia apparatus he was not able to talk, he did smile on his way into the surgery.

I checked again with the Military Command Center and General Jones on the secure phone and was advised that the position of the Russian subs remained virtually unchanged; that there had been no incidents of any kind reported from anywhere around the world and that the NORAD sensors were still all green.

I told General Jones to advise the Commanders in Chief of the specified and designated commands that the shooting was apparently an isolated incident, and that no information to the contrary had been received, but that they should continue to remain vigilant.

I reported that discussion to the group in the Situation Room. Jim Baker advised that there had been a FEMA (Federal Emergency Management Administration) exercise scheduled for the next day on presidential succession, with the general title "Nine Lives." By an immediate consensus, it was agreed that exercise should also be canceled.

At almost exactly 7:00, the Vice President came to the Situation Room and very calmly assumed the chair at the head of the table. The first question presented to him was that of the Dairy Price Support Bill, the first one passed by this Congress and hence the first one required to be acted on by President Reagan. That bill was awaiting signature and Tuesday was the last day on which it could be signed. Bill French Smith advised that the Vice President could sign it, but the Vice President said that he wanted to wait until he saw how the President felt tomorrow, and that the President might perfectly well be able to sign it. I was struck by the incongruity of our worrying about such legislation at such a time. I said I was sure that in any event Congress would reenact such a measure in a matter of one day so as to start a new time period running if necessary.

The Vice President asked for my report on the status of the forces, and I gave it to him. Then he (or it may have been Jim Baker) mentioned that a plane was needed for Jim Brady's family to get them from Chicago, where they were having trouble getting space on a commercial airline. I responded that we could take care of that, of course. Someone else said that "No, it has been arranged by now for one of the White House planes to be used." Ed Meese had also arrived with the Vice President and reported on the President's condition, and also on the condition of Jim Brady and the others.

The Vice President then asked "What's next?" and we discussed tomorrow's schedule. The Vice President agreed that he would have the National Security Council briefing normally given to the President in the morning, and agreed also with the recommendation that the Cabinet meeting should be held and the congressional leadership briefed. It was concluded with very little discussion that instead of the Republican leadership meeting normally scheduled for the next day, the leadership briefing should be a bipartisan briefing. The Vice President also agreed that he would meet with van Agt, the Netherlands Prime Minister, and then said, "Let's try to keep everything as normal as possible, including the scheduling."

Don Regan said we should have some reassuring bulletin out before the markets opened, and there was general agreement to that effect. Bill French Smith then reported that all FBI reports concurred with the information I had received; that the shooting was a completely isolated incident and that the assassin, John Hinckley, with a previous record in Nashville, seemed to be a "Bremmer" type, a reference to the attempted assassin of George Wallace.

There was one suggestion by Jim Baker that perhaps the Cabinet not be called because it called attention to the absence of the President, but the Vice President said, "Let's do it and make it a very short meeting so that everyone can get both information and guidance for answering the press."

It was agreed that all statements concerning all of the activities of the afternoon should be made by the White House Press Office and by no one else. The Vice President also cautioned the group in general, "Please be sure that we level with the American people and give them full and accurate information."

At that point, approximately 7:50, I telephoned General Jones and told him since none of us had any information to indicate this was anything except an isolated incident by some individual madman, we should now return to the normal DEFCON 4 alert conditions for the Strategic Air Command crews (that is, they would be allowed out of the more confined alert area and would again be restricted only to the bases). I asked him to advise the Commanders in Chief to be particularly alert for any unusual incidents during the course of the next few days. He reported that the location of the Russian subs remained virtually the same.

CONCLUSION

The above is a generalized running account as I remember the events of the afternoon and early evening, aided by some rough notes I made at the time. Although there were a number of people doing a number of things more or less simultaneously, there was not any real confusion. The difficult problem was that while there were massive numbers of reports coming in from the wire services, newspapers and television screens, there was no way of knowing which of them were accurate. For example, when it was announced about 4:30 that Jim Brady had died and that a "White House spokesman" had confirmed it, some time was spent trying to locate who that "spokesman" might have been.

Al Haig reported that he was notifying the embassies to deliver reassuring messages to the foreign governments around the world; and he said that some wires from foreign leaders, such as Mrs. Thatcher, and later Mr. Brezhnev, were being received. I was making the calls reported above with respect to the status of the Armed Forces, and Bill French Smith was reporting on the legal matters involving presidential succession, and FBI information about the suspect. Don Regan was reporting about the Secret Service, and tracing out information about the gun.

Someone, I'm not quite sure who, had already said there had been phone calls to the former Presidents (it was reported that one complained he had not been notified soon enough), and others, I believe Max Friedersdorf, head White House legislative liaison, had notified the Speaker of the House and the President Pro Tem of the Senate.

For the future, I would recommend that access to the Situation Room be restricted. (Dick Allen tried manfully to do that from time to time throughout the afternoon, but there continued to be a constant movement in and out of the Situation Room by various people with messages, requests for phone calls, delivering additional information, etc.)

At no time was there any "violent quarrel" or any major disagreement between Al Haig and me as reported by a few columnists and reporters, none of whom bothered to call me. The conversations as described above were low key and represented simply different views as to the necessity and desirability of increasing the alert condition of the Strategic Air crews. I never felt I had, or was supposed to have, "command of the Situation Room," nor did I object to Al Haig's actions.

At no time was any classified information improperly disclosed and at no time was there any discussion of anything connected with the National Command Authority except a recital of the matters contained in the published Department of Defense Directive on the subject. The "conversations" and direct quotes alleged in the press to have occurred in the Situation Room between Al Haig and me, simply did not take place. At no time did we argue about who had the authority or anything of the kind, other than as recorded above.

I remained in the White House until about 10:30 that night, when the President was reported to have retired for the night in good condition.

That completes my near contemporaneous account, as requested by the White House, of the activities as I saw them from the Situation Room.

But of course no such account could convey the mixture of horror, anger and worry I felt about what had befallen the President. From time to time I wondered, If he indeed recovers, will he be as I have always known him? I knew that he was putting on a bold front for his wife, his doctors and nurses all about him, but I hoped he would be allowed full rest during his postoperative recovery period. I also remembered how quickly and drastically one's condition might change after apparently successful surgery.

97

The next morning, and indeed several times that night, I called the hospital, and all the reports were reassuring. In the Cabinet room the next morning, just before the meeting started, I saw Dr. Daniel Ruge, the President's personal physician. I asked if the President had had a restful night. "No," said Dr. Ruge, "I have to tell you, he did not. He apparently felt it was necessary for him to entertain his doctors and nurses, and so although we did not let him talk, we could not stop him from writing jokes out for his nurses during the night. He is much better this morning, but he will have to rest for several days."

The Cabinet meeting proceeded under the Vice President's calm direction, and reassuring and accurate statements were put out for the press.

On April 3 I went to see the President at the George Washington University Hospital, because I had to leave for a NATO meeting that night. The security was extraordinarily heavy, even for a President. I had to pass through at least five checkpoints to be identified and checked before I came to the President's darkened room.

I hope that my expression did not betray my utter shock at his appearance. For the first time in all the years I had known him, he looked exhausted and very ill. His face seemed almost collapsed. Nancy was there, and indeed rarely left his bedside. We talked very briefly. I gave him a book of amusing military cartoons, and had planned to brief him a bit about the NATO meeting, but I decided I should let him get as much rest as possible, and so moved to take my leave after a short visit. He wished me well at the NATO meeting and said he would like a full report when I returned.

A few weeks later he presided at his first Cabinet meeting since the shooting and looked vastly improved, with the smile and the humor substantially restored. He visited his ranch in California, and in a short time he was out cutting brush and riding about as usual.

Six weeks after the shooting the President appeared fully recovered, and thereafter I never saw any aftereffects or ill effects in him. His powers of recovery were immense, as he demonstrated again after two subsequent operations. The relief I felt was as strong. It would have been a bitter blow for the country if this happy, secure and shining President had been cut down just as he began the long and difficult task of restoring America's hopes, her greatness and strength.

IV

Grenada

*T*he history of the Grenada action began many months before the island was saved by American exertions and skill and one thousand American students and other United States citizens were rescued from the anarchy and chaos into which Grenada had plunged.

First some background.

Grenada is a small island nation in the Caribbean with a population of about one hundred thousand. Formerly a British colony, it became independent on February 7, 1974. In the elections of 1976, however, a coalition of the New Jewel Movement (NJM) and other opposition parties received forty-eight percent of the vote. The New Jewel Movement took advantage of Prime Minister Sir Eric Gairy's visit to New York in March 1979 to carry out a coup d'état. (Gairy was no exemplar of rationality. In fact his agenda in New York included a talk to the United Nations on Unidentified Flying Objects.)

There was little resistance to the coup, and Maurice Bishop

was named Prime Minister on March 13, 1979. Promises of early elections and respect for human rights were never honored by the Bishop regime. Instead, it suspended the Constitution, ridiculed English-style democracy as "Westminster hypocrisy" and proceeded to implement a Cuban model of totalitarian dictatorship with Cuban aid.

The government broke up and dispersed political protest meetings in July 1979. In November 1979 they forcibly closed the *Torchlight*, a newspaper critical of both Gairy and his successor. In June 1981 the government arrested the editor of a new paper, *The Grenadian View*; and in June 1982 "People's Law Number 18" banned all opposition newspapers.

Bishop also established close ties with the Soviet Union. Grenada and Cuba in January 1980 voted against a United Nations resolution condemning the USSR for the Soviet "invasion of Afghanistan." By 1980, Cuban military advisors and several hundred Cuban construction workers were in Grenada, ostensibly engaged in building a new airport for tourism. On October 27, 1980, Grenada's Minister of Defense signed a major military aid agreement with the USSR in Havana. Another such agreement was signed on July 27, 1982. Later Grenada signed trade agreements with the USSR, Bulgaria, East Germany and Czechoslovakia. In 1982, ninety-two percent of Grenada's votes were cast with the Soviet bloc in the UN General Assembly.

By 1983, Grenadians were thoroughly unhappy with the regime. Grenada's state farming experiments had failed, and her cash crops were in low demand in the world markets. A Cuban fisheries program collapsed. The government raised electric power rates, but frequent outages occurred.

A power struggle developed between Prime Minister Bishop and Deputy Prime Minister Bernard Coard. Although Coard lacked popular support, he was the leader of the radical faction of the NJM. He was viewed as a hardline Marxist ideologue who engineered a reduction in Bishop's power inside the NJM's Central Committee. Bishop was accused of not moving fast enough to "socialize" the economy and not consolidating the revolution. He was also accused of using dictatorial methods.

This debate continued in the NJM's Central Committee throughout the summer of 1983, as revealed in documents we later captured, including minutes of the Central Committee meetings. On September 27 Bishop departed Grenada for a visit to Moscow, Eastern Europe and Cuba. He returned to Grenada on October 8 and again tried to regain the leadership of the NJM. But on October 12 the Central Committee voted to place Bishop under house arrest, and on October 14 he was expelled from the Party. After being freed from "house arrest" by a group of his followers, Bishop and four members of his cabinet were murdered on October 19 by the so-called People's Revolutionary Army Troops, loyal to the Central Committee.

A spirited account of this incident appears in "Operation Urgent Fury: The United States Army in Joint Operation," by Major Bruce R. Pirnie of the U.S. Army Center of Military History in Washington:

> Events moved to the end like a political passion play. On the morning of 19 October, a crowd of several thousand people gathered in St. George's [capital and largest city in Grenada]. A large group ascended the hill to the Prime Minister's residence chanting "We want Maurice!" and "No Bishop, no revo!" Soldiers guarding the residence fired a few shots, but seemed irresolute. The crowd pushed past an armored vehicle and approached the residence from the rear. The people found Bishop and his mistress Jacqueline Creft tied to beds. Bishop seemed weakened by the confinement and disoriented. The jubilant people bore Bishop and Creft away in a miniature motorcade. Rather than going to the Market Square, where a crowd was waiting for Bishop to appear, the motorcade turned

towards Fort Rupert overlooking the harbor. After a brief scuffle, the small garrison of the fort dispersed. Bishop entered the operations room on the first floor.

Some time after noon, three Revolutionary Government BTR-60 armored personnel carriers emerged from Fort Frederick east of St. George's. As these vehicles approached Fort Rupert, the crews opened fire with heavy machine guns and RPG-7 rockets. The union leader Vincent Noel died in front of the fort. According to the reports issued by the People's Revolutionary Armed Forces, at least four soldiers were killed in a brief fire fight with Bishop's supporters. A large number of people were hit by fire or injured as they fled. Bishop reportedly exclaimed: "Oh God, oh God, they turned their guns against the masses." The soldiers ceased fire and ordered Bishop and his followers to leave the fort. As they emerged, the soldiers ordered certain ones into the courtyard: Keith Hailing, Evelyn Bullen, Evelyn Maitland, Unison Whiteman, Fitzroy Bain, Narris Bain, Jacqueline Creft, and Maurice Bishop. The soldiers apparently murdered all of them with automatic fire in the courtyard of the fort.

The Coard faction had murdered Bishop under the press of events because his popularity threatened their power. On the following day, the Main Political Department of the armed forces announced a great victory over "counterrevolutionaries," "betrayers of the masses," and "opportunist elements" opposed to socialism. The bombastic, Soviet-style jargon sounded hollow and absurd when applied to Grenada. V. S. Naipaul later wrote:

> The revolution was a revolution of words. The words had appeared as an illumination, a shortcut to dignity, to newly educated men who had nothing in the com-

munity to measure themselves against and who, finally, valued little in their own community. But the words were mimicry. They were too big; they didn't fit; they remained words. The revolution blew away; and what was left in Grenada was a murder story.

I had begun receiving regular intelligence briefings on Grenada early in the new Administration; they confirmed the development and construction, largely by Cuban labor, of a very large new airport on that small island in the eastern Caribbean. The airport was far larger than anything that might be required by even the most expanded tourist trade, and it was clear from that size, as well as from the nature of the runways and the supporting facilities, that a great deal more than commercial use was intended. When the President saw the evidence, he felt it necessary to tell the American people about it—and also to make known the seriousness of our objections to having that particular type of construction so close to our own continent. He did that on March 23, 1983, in the same nationally televised speech in which he unveiled his Strategic Defense Initiative. Here is what he said:

> On the small island of Grenada, at the southern end of the Caribbean chain, the Cubans, with Soviet financing and backing, are in the process of building an airfield with a ten-thousand-foot runway. Grenada doesn't even have an air force. Who is it intended for? The Caribbean is a very important passageway for our international commerce and military lines of communication. More than half of all American oil imports now pass through the Caribbean. The rapid buildup of Grenada's military potential is unrelated to any conceivable threat to this island country of under one hundred ten thousand people and totally at odds with the pattern of other eastern Caribbean States, most of which are unarmed.

The Soviet-Cuban militarization of Grenada, in short, can only be seen as power projection into the region.

We had provided the President with pictures showing the progress of construction, and he used them in his address to the nation. (Two weeks before, on March 10, 1983, the President had also referred, warningly, to Grenada's apparent preparations to be a military base.)

Bishop visited the United States, and on June 7, 1983, he met with National Security Advisor William Clark. Clark and the other representatives at the meeting encouraged Bishop to follow a more moderate course, and expressed unhappiness over his having jailed his political opponents and recklessly denounced the United States. His response led us to conclude that we should review United States policy toward Grenada and also to start thinking what we should do if the Americans in Grenada were threatened or taken hostage.

We continued to monitor the construction of the airfield; but even more worrisome was the course of other events occurring in Grenada. It became increasingly apparent that this small island was being used as a laboratory for the imposition of a far leftist regime, with what appeared to be growing and active Cuban and probably Soviet support.

The drama continued to play out as the factions grew more violent. At 9:00 in the evening on October 19, and after Prime Minister Bishop was murdered that same day, General Hudson Austin, Commander of the Grenadian Armed Forces, issued a twenty-four-hour curfew with a warning that anyone seen in public would be shot.

We could not dismiss that violence and that threat of more to come as a mere aberration of a small irrational group of people on an unimportant island.

For one thing, Grenada is part of the eastern Caribbean chain, a group of islands that hangs like a long, detached earring in the eastern Caribbean. Grenada is a member of the Organization of Eastern Caribbean States (OECS), whose other members have always been very friendly toward us and supportive of our policies. For another, there was a medical school in Grenada, the St. George's University School of Medicine, owned by some American investors, with headquarters in Brooklyn, New York. Some eight hundred American medical students were enrolled there.

Once the announcement of the twenty-four-hour curfew, with its open license to kill, was made by the most fanatical and irresponsible of the leftist elements in Grenada, who had already murdered Bishop and his colleagues, we naturally had to think about how we could either extricate the Americans there or prevent their being seized as hostages in a reprise of the Iranian seizure of our citizens and capture of our Embassy in Teheran, in 1979.

Matters came to a head in Grenada after the Bishop Government was so violently overthrown. There was no effective government on the island thereafter.[1]

---

1. Two returning members of the bipartisan fourteen-member congressional fact-finding mission to Grenada gave a very detailed description of the great risk to Americans at the time and the extensive diplomatic effort beforehand to secure their release.

Representative Dick Cheney stated in a November 14 opinion editorial in *The Washington Post* that:

> One such meeting [with the congressional fact-finding delegation] was a session with five State Department personnel assigned to the eastern Caribbean and working out of our embassy in Barbados. All five had spent the days prior to the U.S. rescue operation trying by every means possible to arrange for the safe evacuation of the hundreds of American citizens who wanted to leave Grenada after the bloody events of Oct. 19.

> One of these State Department employees gave an especially eloquent description of the plight of Americans on the island. Cut off from the outside world, dependent on the People's Revolutionary Army for food and water, and confined to their quarters on pain of death, they were, the State Department employees believed, already hostages. All five officials stated they felt the only way to guarantee the security of the Americans on Grenada was through a military rescue operation.

Representative William S. Broomfield, the ranking minority member of the House For-

Eugenia Charles, head of the OECS and Prime Minister of
Dominica, one of Grenada's neighboring eastern Caribbean islands, had informed the President of the "great risks for us all"
in the rapidly deteriorating situation in Grenada.

Before any presidential decisions were made, I had asked the
Chairman of the Joint Chiefs to proceed with some preliminary
planning, to see what courses might be available to us on a very
quick basis, and to review existing plans to consider what could
be done to safeguard both students and democracy if the President should so decide.

Meanwhile, the Brooklyn-based office of the American medical
school in Grenada, in a series of extremely unhelpful and incorrect
statements, kept announcing that its students were in no peril,
and that any suggestion of American intervention would be most
unwelcome. The Chancellor of the school, Charles Modica, secure in Brooklyn, seemed far more concerned with whether his
school was going to be able to continue to collect tuition fees
than he was with the actual conditions on the island itself—or
with the very real risk that his students faced, particularly in view
of the twenty-four-hour curfew that had been imposed. In fact,
even as late as October 21, Modica stated publicly that the school
expected to continue to have good relations with the "Government" of Grenada, overlooking the fact that by then there was
no government except a group of murderers.

The planning effort I had asked for was now underway in the
Joint Staff, and I was being given reports of the availability of

---

eign Affairs Committee, provided an even more detailed description in a companion
piece. He wrote:

> I am absolutely convinced that had the United States not intervened, inaction
> would have been comparable to playing Russian roulette with the lives of more
> than 1,000 Americans on the island. As Rep. Tom Foley, chairman of the dele-
> gation has said, the President did not have the luxury of waiting a week to see
> how things developed before making a decision. "Waiting a week was a decision,"
> he said. There is no doubt in my mind that the President would have been irre-
> sponsible had he risked so many American lives by delay.

Marine and other units that were bound for normal replacement duties in the Mediterranean off Lebanon, as well as Army and Navy units that were relatively nearby and available.

On October 20, the day after Bishop was murdered, I approved General Vessey's recommendation that we turn southward two units—the carrier *Independence* and its Battle Group, and the Marine replacement group that was then under way for normal rotation with units in the Lebanon area—in case they would be needed near Grenada.

We also, of course, had our alert battalions and alert airborne division at Fort Bragg, North Carolina, and Fort Campbell, South Carolina, which were ready at all times for anything the President might call upon them to do.

The planning was greatly complicated by the continuing crisis in Lebanon. Our Marine battalion was stationed in Beirut Airport as part of the multinational force that many months before had been sent in to act as a buffer between the forces of Syria and Israel, which were supposed to withdraw from their very hostile positions opposite each other. But withdrawal was not agreed upon, and as a result, I was increasingly worried about our role in the international force—and especially about the extremely vulnerable position our Marines were in, sitting as they were at the airport at Beirut, with only the inadequate arms permitted by the terms governing the international peacekeeping force, and without authority even to move out of the airport and secure any of the surrounding high ground necessary to protect their position should they be attacked.

That situation was a subject of a whole separate set of meetings, and we will come to it in the chapters of this book about the Middle East. The important thing to bear in mind now is that the Grenada activities and the preliminary planning effort that I had started were all taking place as a kind of sideshow, or at least as a very important, but separate and simultaneous, activity added to those other problems that then required our daily and active attention. Lebanon and the future of our forces there required virtually continuous meetings at this time with the President, the State Department and the National Security Council (NSC). At the same time, of course, rumors had begun to spread in the press that we were thinking about some kind of intervention in Grenada.

Meanwhile, the Joint Chiefs had, as I had asked, refined and developed plans for the insertion of our forces into Grenada. The broad objectives of the plan called for us to move as quickly as possible to Point Salines to seal off the new airfield, which was not yet fully operational,[2] as well as the older and operational airport at Pearls, on the eastern side of the island; to secure the two campuses of the medical school in the southwestern portion of the island, so that our students could be freed and brought home; and to rescue the Governor General and other political prisoners from imprisonment.

At 4:45 on Thursday, October 20, there was a meeting of the Special Situation Group (SSG), a small group of the NSC. Vice President Bush presided, the President having gone to Augusta, Georgia. The SSG decided to advance the planning and to alert our Commanders again.

General Vessey immediately notified the Commander in Chief of the Atlantic Forces to prepare options as to how to evacuate American citizens from Grenada in a hostile environment.

The plan involved the landing of Marines in the northeastern part of the island near the Pearls commercial airport, and parachuting Army Rangers into the new airport in southeastern Grenada, with its ten-thousand-foot runway. The linkup between Marines and Rangers was to be made as quickly as possible, and they were then to turn north and west for the rescue of the medical students, and to work with our Special Operations

2. The Grenada government had planned, according to documents we captured, to dedicate and open this new airport on March 13, 1984.

Forces, to secure the release of the Governor General, capture the radio station, and free other political prisoners in buildings at Fort Ruppert and Richmond Hill.

The practical requirements and logistics of such an action are very large, and the planning time required is normally far longer than the few days we had, particularly when we had spent the first two days looking at the matter in a more or less academic way to determine what we could do to evacuate American citizens. Normally, of course, we would have liked massive pre-landing reconnaissance and much more knowledge than we had of the size and composition of Cuban forces at the airport and on other parts of the island, as well as Cuban capabilities for reinforcement. Ideally, we also would have had much greater knowledge of local facilities that we could take over and use. Finally, we had to consider the delay caused by the simple fact that our available forces were several hours away. These forces included the Marines, who were at that time loaded on naval ships, and while always "prepared" for war, were intended, at this time, for normal rotation with the *lightly armed* multinational force in the Middle East. Obviously the Marines had not rehearsed for operations in Grenada. But all these considerations and the plan itself were ready to be presented to the President, together with the risks involved.[3]

General Vessey and I did that, in a secure call to the President

---

3. Some (John Lehman, then Secretary of the Navy, for one) have said that it was a mistake to use Army Rangers, because the Marines could have done it "all by themselves." Perhaps. But my invariable practice was to double, at least, any Joint Chief recommendations as to the size of a force required, since I always had in mind that one of the major problems with our attempt to rescue our hostages in Iran in 1979 was that we sent too few helicopters.

In any event, the service Secretaries are not operational officers, and do not participate in the planning or conduct of operations. That is done by and under the direction of the Chiefs of Staff of each service. The service Secretaries' task is to have their services trained and equipped for whatever the President decides the Secretary of Defense is to undertake.

in Augusta, Georgia at 2:00 Saturday morning, October 22. We discussed our plans, the fact of the other Caribbean States' request that we intervene,[4] and the shortness of time to gather intelligence. The President was aware of the difficulties, but generally seemed to me to be willing to accept the risks. He urged us to continue developing the detailed plans, and I sensed he had just about decided we should go in.

At 9:00 that Saturday morning, the National Security Council Planning Group (NSPG) met in the Situation Room. The Vice President presided, and we kept in communication with the President by secure phone. He did not return from Augusta at once, so as not to attract unneeded attention.

This Saturday morning meeting approved my recommendation to use SEALs to get what prelanding intelligence we could, and to continue our detailed Grenada planning. The SEALs (so called from the acronym for Sea, Air, Land) are the Navy's special forces who conduct pre-landing and other reconnaissance missions and carry out various special and difficult operations. They are highly trained for a number of risky but vital tasks. The President at this time also approved an expanded mission for us that included restoring a democratic government to Grenada.

Following the NSC planning group meeting, I went back to the Pentagon to meet with the Joint Chiefs in the Tank to review the progress of the planning. Again, I told them to double whatever forces the field Commander said he would need.

The President returned to Washington at 8:40 Sunday morning and, owing to the attack on the Marines in Beirut, imme-

---

4. On Friday, October 21, the OECS met in Bridgetown, Barbados. Its membership included Antigua, Grenada, Montserrat, St. Kitts-Nevis, St. Lucia, St. Vincent and the Grenadines and Dominica. That evening Eugenia Charles communicated the unanimous resolution requesting intervention to the U.S. Deputy Assistant Secretary for Inter-American Affairs, Tony Gillespie, who was in the area at the time. Mrs. Charles stressed that there was no hesitation in issuing the request. As a legal justification for the intervention, Article Eight of the OECS treaty was adduced.

diately convened a meeting of the NSPG. The President said to me as he came into the Situation Room, "Remind me never to go away again. Look what happens," referring both to the heightening of the Grenada crisis and to the bombing of our Marine barracks in Lebanon, details of which were just coming in. At this meeting, he also reaffirmed his determination to intervene in Grenada.

At 4:00 that Sunday afternoon the NSPG met again in the Situation Room. Both the Grenada planning and the Beirut bombing were gone into at length. Following that meeting, the President signed the order approving "Operation Urgent Fury," as it was called, and the Joint Chiefs sent the Rules of Engagement to Admiral Wesley McDonald, Commander in Chief, Atlantic Forces (CINCLANT), and later the formal operations order was sent to him.

At noon, on Monday, I met again with General Vessey. He has since reminded me that my final word to him as we left to meet with the President was, "Be sure we have enough strength." I also authorized him to use the 82d Airborne Division as a backup if we encountered more opposition than expected.

We then rode together across the river and met with the President and the JCS in the Cabinet Room. The President polled each Chief of Staff and each told him the plan would work; but each said he was concerned about the lack of time to get intelligence, and to rehearse and practice several of the more difficult aspects of the operation. By now it was clear to me from his comments and questions that the President had decided to move into Grenada unless Grenada took some measure to free the American students from danger.

Later that afternoon, the President formally advised me that his decision was to proceed with the action and the attempt to rescue our students, and Grenada. Fortunately we had actual orders all prepared as part of the planning, including the orders to divert from their previous assignments the forces to be used.

For example, as I have said we had delayed the scheduled rotation of the Marine units in Lebanon by diverting the relief forces on their way to Lebanon to Grenada also. The task of assembling all the logistical support had begun.

The President concluded that he should notify the congressional leadership as well as some of our allies, and it was important that this be done very shortly, before the actual landing of our troops.

The utmost secrecy needed to be observed, because we knew that our principal ally would have to be surprise. Also because of the need to conduct the rescue of the students as soon as possible, we were not able to do the prelanding reconnaissance as much in advance as we would have liked, nor could we risk alerting the Cubans, Soviets and others by any kind of leaks, or indications, that we were diverting Marine forces bound for the Middle East. For the same reason we could not place our alert forces on planes for the operation. Despite our best efforts, there were television reports that the Marine contingents bound for the Middle East had been diverted south, and whenever our alert forces in the United States began any preparations to move, rumors always begin to spread.

My original instructions to the Joint Chiefs had been that we should plan to begin the operation at the soonest possible time consistent with the maximum safety to our forces, and consistent with the actual time needed to assemble both the forces and supplies for a successful action. The JCS Chairman, General Vessey, advised me on Friday that if the President ordered, we could go in shortly after first light on Tuesday, October 25, with a good degree of certainty that we would be able to free the American students very quickly thereafter—although there were clearly elements of risk in the shortness of time for planning and in the lack of full scale reconnaissance.

We had received a strong request from the task force Commander, Vice Admiral Joseph Metcalf, reinforced by Admiral McDonald, CINCLANT, his immediate superior, that no press or additional personnel of any kind be permitted to go into Grenada with the landings—and in any event, most certainly not until a secure beachhead had been obtained. The need for secrecy was urgent; and the limited transport available required that we would have to have some of our forces, with critical and few communication facilities, based in Barbados.

In fact, the operation would be staged not only from the naval ships and from the planes carrying the troops, but (to whatever extent we could manage) from neighboring Barbados. Our transport, limited as it was, would have to be used entirely for necessary follow-up supplies, additional ammunition, communications support facilities and all of the implements required for invasions.

In matters of this kind, and although aware of the unhappiness the decision would cause, I felt the Commander should be supported; so I accepted and agreed to the task force Commander's request, with the understanding we would make every effort to get the press in at the end of the first day. He was the man we had entrusted with the responsibility for the success of the operation. It would have been a very bad start, it seemed to me, if we overruled his first recommendation, a recommendation that indeed seemed to me to have considerable justification and reason behind it. In the event, Admiral Metcalf did not get the press in by the end of the first day, and the Joint Chiefs and I had to direct him to get them in on the second.

Again I must mention that we could not and cannot isolate particular crises or events in the constantly shifting history of security issues. Early on Sunday morning we received word of the bombing of the Marine barracks at Beirut Airport, with the awful loss of life that was entailed, and with the frustrating and horrifying knowledge, as far as I was concerned, that I had not been persuasive enough, throughout a long series of prior meetings, to secure approval for the withdrawal of our Marines from the international force. Besides stressing the especial danger they faced, I had argued and reargued many times a point that had seemed clear to me: The international force as constituted was totally incapable of carrying out the mission of interposing itself as peacekeepers between withdrawing Israeli and Syrian troops. The mission itself was frustrated, because the Israeli and Syrian troops were *not* withdrawing.

To add to the complexity and problems of the day, I had agreed some weeks before to be a guest on a new CBS Sunday public affairs program. There was ample reason to cancel, in view of the news we were getting on that Sunday morning and Sunday noon, October 23, 1983, about the Beirut disaster, and the simultaneous urgency of our still very secret planning on Grenada. But I felt that I should keep my word, and that the American public was entitled immediately to know as much as possible about our grievous losses to terrorism in Lebanon. The only condition I made was that I could not leave the vicinity of the Situation Room.

CBS sent its camera crew over to the Roosevelt Room at the White House, and I emerged from the National Security Council meeting in the Situation Room, downstairs in the White House, and went upstairs to be queried about all matters (particularly about what retaliation we planned, and whether we planned to leave the Marines in), by the new hostess of the program, Leslie Stahl.

I felt such programs were not to be treated lightly. I was very well aware that today, one inadvertence or one awkward answer on my part could cause a very great deal of damage. I was greatly relieved when the end of the half hour was signaled, and I could dash back downstairs again to continue discussions of what we should do after we were able to bring as much treatment as possible to the injured Marines, and to evacuate the injured and the dead as quickly as we could. But that program had been particularly difficult for me. Because my argument for withdrawing our Marines had not yet become our official policy, I could not discuss my own viewpoint on the matter; nor could I discuss the by then very advanced planning for the Grenada rescue operations.

The President decided to notify the congressional leadership about our Grenada operation on Monday night. He asked that they be brought to the upstairs family sitting room by a variety of means, so as to minimize rumors that would fly at the unusual hour for assembling congressional and military leadership. So we gathered in the upstairs sitting room at the White House. It is a beautifully decorated room, with gold the predominant color. We sat on two of the large sofas that faced the fireplace across the room from the balcony[5] that looked out on the Washington Monument and the Mall. It was a cool October Washington evening, and the fire in the fireplace was most welcome. The President and members of the Security Council, the Secretary of State, the National Security Advisor, and the Chairman of the Joint Chiefs and I were there before the congressional leadership came in. I outlined again the details of the invasion plan, scheduled for the next morning, mentioning some of the risks as well as our hopes. The President was firmly and resolutely determined to proceed.

I reported to the President that we had launched again some of our special action naval forces to do as much of a pre-landing reconnaissance as possible along the selected beaches, with full instructions to minimize any possibility of their being discovered,

---

5. This is the famous (or infamous, at the time of its construction) Truman Balcony, which many feared would impair the architectural integrity of the White House. In fact it did not; it was an addition much prized by many of Truman's successors.

or their purpose divined. Their effort was actually under way now, although we did not get the reports of their actions until several hours later.[6] The President was most interested in their work, particularly in the extraordinarily risky nature of it and the great bravery that would be asked of the men in these special, so-called "Seal Teams."

After a short time the congressional leaders came in, with at least a clear inkling that some major event was under way; evening gatherings in the family sitting room at the White House are by no means the rule. The President opened with a brief but thorough summary of the situation, emphasizing the risks to the American students, the evidence we had of growing Cuban involvement, the increasing madness of the regime presently in power in Grenada, as exemplified in the twenty-four-hour shoot-on-sight curfew, the risk of extensive and violent civil war there, and the knowledge we had had for a long time of both Soviet and Cuban involvement in the island itself, beyond the building of the new airfield. And, of course, he emphasized the plight of our students and our fears they might all be held as hostages, or worse. The President reported on the urgent plea that had come to us from the neighboring eastern Caribbean islands, and concluded, "I feel we have absolutely no alternative but to comply with this request. I think the risks of not moving are far greater than the risks of taking the action we have planned."

He then asked me to outline the military plan, which I did. And I presented General Vessey, who described the plan in detail, crisply and effectively. The President advised the congressional leadership of the hour of landing on the next day, and, naturally, urged that they maintain the security of the operation.

There was very little comment from the leadership. Speaker O'Neill seemed lost in thought for a time, and then said, "I can

6. The previous evening, four SEALs had drowned in heavy seas and the mission was aborted.

only say, Mr. President, God be with you, and good luck to us all." Senator Byrd, the Senate Democratic leader, had a few questions about the invasion plans—How many troops would be involved? How many Grenadians and Cubans did we think we would encounter? Were there any Soviets there?—which we were able to answer. Others said very little, but there did seem to be an understanding of the risks and an acceptance that we really had no alternative. The President was at his best in this meeting: cordial, frank, friendly, and very clearly making the congressional leaders aware of, and part of, the whole decision, and the whole action.

After they left, the President said that even as late as it was in London, he felt he should now confer with Prime Minister Thatcher, who had sent a cable to the President expressing her "gravest concerns" about the impending operation. This cable had arrived as the meeting with the congressmen was ending. (The President had cabled Prime Minister Thatcher twice that day, once to inform her that the United States had received a formal OECS request to intervene, and the second time to inform her we had accepted it.)

He stepped into the next room. The door was open, and we could hear one side of what was obviously a very vigorous discussion; the unhappiness being expressed from London by the Prime Minister came through very clearly. The President carefully went over the details of both the plan and the provocations, mentioned the absence of any effective government in Grenada, referred to the fact that the Queen's representative, Sir Paul Scoon, was himself a prisoner (and had himself requested assistance);[7] and he asserted the lack of any real alternative in view

7. On October 23, the Governor-General of Grenada, Sir Paul Scoon, orally requested outside assistance from an OECS peacekeeping force. On October 27, the Barbados Government released the text of the formal request, which was in the form of a letter to Barbados's Prime Minister, John Adams. They did not release it until the Governor

of the pleas from the neighboring nations and the uncertain fate of our own citizens. At the conclusion of that conversation, the President returned with a rather rueful look on his face, which made it clear that even his persuasive powers had limits, and he had not convinced the Prime Minister.

As we arose to leave, the President said to Jack Vessey, "What are you fellows going to do now?"

Jack said, "I'm going home and go to bed. You have approved our plan, and it is now in the hands of competent commanders and troops. There is nothing more we can do now."

The President said, "Good. I'll do the same." General Vessey is a man who inspires and justifies enormous confidence, and the President and I shared the greatest admiration for him.

We left shortly thereafter, and I returned to the Pentagon with the Joint Chiefs to issue the "execute" order, to go over the final details once more, and to receive any reports from the assembling forces. Bad news was not long in coming—we knew at least one of the SEALs' rubber boats had foundered in very high seas after hitting a patrol boat, and we greatly feared at least two more of the SEALs were lost; and we had no real pre-landing intelligence.

General was rescued. The letter reads:

Government House, St. George's, Grenada, October 24, 1983

Dear Prime Minister,

You are aware that there is a vacuum of authority in Grenada following the killing of the prime minister and the subsequent serious violations of human rights and bloodshed. I am, therefore, seriously concerned over the lack of internal security in Grenada. Consequently I am requesting your help to assist me in stabilising this grave and dangerous situation. It is my desire that a peace-keeping force should be established in Grenada to facilitate a rapid return to peace and tranquillity and also a return to democratic rule. In this connection I am also seeking assistance from the United States, from Jamaica, and from the Organisation of Eastern Caribbean States through its current chairman, the Hon. Eugenia Charles, in the spirit of the treaty establishing that organisation to which my country is a signatory.

I have the honour to be
[Signed]
Sir Paul Scoon, Governor-General.

At 8:00 on that Monday night, the Organization of Eastern Caribbean States was notified that we had accepted their plea to intervene. At 8:36 the first planes carrying in the Rangers were airborne.

Early Tuesday morning, October 25, Eugenia Charles flew to Washington to meet with the President and the National Security Council in the Cabinet Room. Mrs. Charles is a large, strong lady, and the very picture of calm, secure confidence. She is extraordinarily eloquent and persuasive.

She described in detail to the Security Council, as she had to the President, the horrors being imposed on the people of Grenada by the increasingly leftist regime, and the bloodily brutal internal battles between the factions. She also discussed with us privately, the amount of Soviet and Cuban involvement in that troubled island, and expressed the feeling of all of her neighbors among the eastern Caribbean nations that there was only one thing that could save the situation, and that was our military intervention. She pronounced herself greatly relieved that we had agreed to the urgent request of all the members of the Organization of Eastern Caribbean States, plus Jamaica and Barbados, for us to go into Grenada to prevent further violent bloodshed. The President and others of us questioned her closely, particularly about whether there would be any dissension among the people of the OECS nations along the lines that America, with its military might, had intervened in the affairs of a small neighboring Caribbean republic, carrying with it the baggage of "Yankee Big Brotherism."

She very firmly rejected that kind of argument. She said that she and her neighboring heads of government took full responsibility for having invited us to come to Grenada, and that she knew that if we did not intervene now, to save Grenada as well as our own American students, it would not only be infinitely more difficult militarily later for us to do so, but our inaction would contribute in the meantime to the impression that America had not the resolve, and perhaps not even the strength, to take decisive action when it was required.

Her eloquence made a great impression on the entire Council, as indeed it had earlier on the President.

Following this meeting I went to a press conference with the President and Prime Minister Charles, and then at 11:00 over to Capitol Hill for a previously scheduled hearing on the situation in Lebanon before the Senate Armed Services Committee. Needless to say, the members were interested also in what was happening in Grenada, so I gave them a summary of our ongoing operation, stressing the urgency of the request from the OECS and the need to evacuate American citizens, and also describing what I knew about the current status of our forces there. I also remarked, in answer to a question from Senator Gary Hart about how long the American forces would be on the island, that "the sooner we can get them out, the happier we will all be."

I then had a brief lunch in my office and received more of the reports coming into the Pentagon.

In the early afternoon, I reported on both Grenada and Lebanon to the House and Senate Committees, and attended an NSC meeting in the White House Situation Room to bring the latest reports of our progress to the President.

The Congress was truly, and quite understandably, clamoring for information now, so I returned to the Hill, first to a group of senators, and then to a separate meeting with House members. The House sessions reversed the format of my usual experience, since I was seated on the Committee bench, and the room was filled with congressmen, who listened and questioned intensely.

There were, of course, other things happening in the Department. The next day, Wednesday, October 26, I was scheduled to go to Canada for a regular NATO Nuclear Planning Group two day meeting. And later still on this Tuesday evening, October 25, I was to go to a long-scheduled dinner at the Italian Embassy for their Minister of Defense, my good friend and the former Prime Minister, Giovanni Spadolini.

Although a bit tired, and despite the constant flow of messages about both Grenada and Lebanon, I felt it was both proper and necessary to go to the dinner for Minister Spadolini Tuesday night. During all my years at the Pentagon, Italy was one of the staunchest friends of the United States, and Minister Spadolini was paying us an official visit. But, I must confess, it was not my sense of duty alone that impelled my decision.

Dinners and indeed all invitations for the Italian Embassy, the beautiful Villa Fierenza, are highly prized. Ambassador Rinaldo Petrignani is a highly skilled and effective diplomat with a great command of languages and issues, and his wife, Anne Merete, is by unanimous agreement one of the finest and most delightful hostesses in Washington. Indeed, we used to say that if you were invited to dinner at the Italian embassy, and World War III broke out in the afternoon, everyone still would come to the Italian Embassy that night.

That Tuesday evening there was the usual splendid dinner; but I left rather early, having found I was spending too much of my time at the Villa responding to phone calls from the Pentagon.

The first reports of the landing of the Airborne forces, the other Army and Marine forces and those allied forces from nearby Caribbean islands, had been very encouraging; and, as we now know, they moved from objective to objective with commendable speed and appeared at the gates of the beleaguered American medical school, brushing aside the resistance that was there before the Cubans could bring their newly arrived forces into position. As a result, by the second day we freed all of the nearly one thousand American students and other United States citizens, without injury and without the loss of life of a single American civilian.

I emphasize that the force that had landed on Grenada in the morning of October 25, 1983, also included contingents from Jamaica, Barbados, and four OECS member states (Antigua, Dominica, St. Lucia and St. Vincent). The contingents were small, but it should be recognized that those elements *were* part of the force.

There were about seven hundred Cubans on the island. The Cuban Government referred to them as "construction workers"—but we found their organizational and duty rosters, which disclosed that they were organized in military fashion into "Company A and B, Mortar Company, and Machine Gun Company." As I told the House Appropriations Committee at its hearing on November 8, 1983, this was not the way other construction companies organized their workers. Also, the Cubans, unlike other construction workers, were equipped with Soviet AK-47 automatic assault rifles and heavy weapons.

Reports of our own casualties were light, but even so, and particularly in view of the heavy loss of life two days before in Beirut, each reported casualty felt to me like a personal wound. The final toll was 18 killed, 93 wounded and 16 missing. Cuban and Soviet reaction was, as expected, intense and infuriated, because it was quite clear they had been caught totally by surprise. They had no idea that the Americans would or could attempt so audacious an operation as the Grenada landings.

The Grenadian casualties were: 45 killed; 337 wounded. Of Grenadian dead, 24 were civilians, including 21 killed in the accidental bombing of a mental hospital located right next to an antiaircraft installation that we had to silence as part of normal landing procedures. The Cubans lost 24 killed in action, and 59 wounded. In addition, some 600 of the Cuban "construction workers" were taken prisoner. By November 9, all Cubans (except for 2 Cuban diplomats), 17 Libyans, 15 North Koreans, 49 Soviets, 10 East Germans and 3 Bulgarians had been returned to their countries.

There is no need to to recall in detail here the further, familiar story of the precision and skill with which our objectives were taken and the island cleared, the airport captured, and Cuban and other resistance reduced and eliminated in a matter of a few days and hours. General Jack Vessey, Chairman of the Joint Chiefs, and I were able to announce to the press on Wednesday, October 26, 1983, that we had 3,000 troops on the ground, that both campuses of the medical school had been taken and all students were safe and being evacuated. We also reported on the capture of the 600 Cubans.

Earlier that day we had held a Full Honors ceremony and parade for Italian Defense Minister Spadolini; and at 7:00 that night, I flew to Ottawa from Andrews for the NATO meeting in Montebello, Canada.

Several popular misperceptions about the Grenada action need discussion. Some of them stemmed from the anger of the press over their not being allowed to land with the troops and their consequent and apparent eagerness to find fault with everything that we had done in their absence.

There was the allegation that we did not assemble our forces based on military necessity, but rather to give both the Army and the Marine Corps, as well as the Navy, important parts to play.

To anyone who was connected with the operation from its very inception, as I was, these charges seemed almost too ludicrous to comment on. We had to take the forces that were available and close enough to land quickly, and forces that were specially trained and that we could equip quickly to carry out a very difficult and potentially very dangerous mission of rescuing our students, without time for either the planning or the pre-landing reconnaissance that any military commander would want to have.

Much was made also in the press of a few comparatively small items that did go wrong, largely because of the speed with which we had to plan and execute the operation, and which were easy to report as major disasters. As invariably happens in combat, a bomb from one of our planes fell on a hospital, although the hospital was, contrary to all rules of war, being used by enemy troops for non-hospital purposes. The available maps were not as detailed as we would have liked, and some of our troop commanders had not been fully briefed on all our very precise tactical objectives. Also, there was some lack of communication capability between some of the Marine and Army units, although it was never impossible for those units to keep in touch with each other. Some had to do so by more indirect means than we would have liked; but at that very time the Department was moving toward the much fuller integration of communication equipment, between all our services, that is now in place for use worldwide.

Also, some of the criticisms stemmed from the fact that most of the people writing of the alleged mishaps and errors were sufficiently unfamiliar with combat to know that combat—and indeed security crises of all kinds—are not tidy nor disciplined events, in which things occur exactly as they are either planned or hoped for. Instead, all manner of things can and do go wrong, both in practice training maneuvers and in actual combat. The important thing is to have the preparation, and the capability and the equipment to respond quickly and flexibly to fix things that do go wrong, so that the basic objectives can be achieved.

In Grenada the basic objectives were all achieved in a very few days, with very small casualties on our part. A difficult and dangerous situation for about a thousand American students and other American citizens was reversed; and the basically mad and anarchical Grenadian factions were all removed. Further, the way was paved for free elections that were held less than two months later, on December 19, 1983, followed by the full withdrawal of all American forces.

In many ways, it was the complete model for future such activities, should our armed forces be called upon to undertake them at such short notice as we were in Grenada. If the measure of success is attaining our political objectives at minimum cost, in the shortest possible time, then the Grenada operation has to be judged to have been a complete success.[8]

A number of articles appeared reporting our "failures" in Grenada. The authors did not seem to realize the potential risks and dangers facing our American students, the speed with which we had to move once the decision to go in was taken, nor the longer range risks to America's own defense and security, had there been another Cuban-Soviet base established on the island of Grenada, with all of the attendant problems and risks involved in our then trying to claw out a very undesirable established force. One Cuba, we felt, quite emphatically was enough.

The press was regularly briefed in the Pentagon in the aftermath of the invasion by General Vessey and by me, but that did not appease them, and they continued to rankle over the fact that they had not been allowed to go in the first day, even though by the exercise of Herculean efforts, we did manage to get various groups of the press in beginning on day two, and more every day thereafter. Later we developed rules, generally approved and accepted by the press, for pools of press representatives to be selected by the press, to enable us to get the press in as soon as possible in the future, should we have to have another such operation with such limited transport from only one staging base.

There were still occasional voices heard making the point that there had not been any real danger to the American students. One such voice belonged to NBC-TV "Today" host Bryant Gumbel. Here is an excerpt from an October 26 interview:

BRYANT GUMBEL. For the second time this week American servicemen have been killed—they have been wounded in a foreign country. Many Americans this morning are asking why some of those casualties came on a tiny Caribbean island

---

8. As was our operation in Panama in January 1990, which also encountered some unwarranted criticism.

called Grenada. One of those answering that question is Defense Secretary Caspar Weinberger, who joins us this morning from the Pentagon. . . .

SECRETARY WEINBERGER. Good morning.

Q: Mr. Secretary, the President says we had to invade Grenada to protect Americans on that island. Can you give us any hard evidence those Americans were in any real danger?

A: Well, when you're in a twenty-four-hour curfew and you're told that if you're found on the street you will be shot without any questions asked, I would classify that as at least a pretty uncomfortable condition. Also in those circumstances you always have to be worried about hostages being taken and we have had a pretty recent experience when hostages were taken and it took four hundred and some days to get them back. So it seems to me it was entirely proper to consider those one thousand American citizens in danger.

Q: Before choosing to participate in the invasion force then why did we not exercise all diplomatic efforts available?

A: Well, you have the diplomatic efforts that were exercised by the neighbors of this small island that have no armed forces, who regard themselves as practically part of the entire island chain and who urgently and almost desperately appealed to us to come in and be of some assistance to them in trying to restore democratic government to Grenada.

Q: Mr. Secretary, as we heard Andrea Mitchell's report moments ago we heard the word "warmonger" brought up for the first time in quite a while. It's a word we are going to be hearing an awful lot I believe in the coming months. As we sit here we have peacekeepers in Beirut, we have advisors in Central America, we have invaders in Grenada, and a lot of Americans are asking this morning where do we draw the line? To these Americans, what do you say?

A: Well, I say that if you are one of the students or one of the families of students in an area that is threatened by lawless anarchy—that's not a bad idea to have American soldiers, sailors, marines, airmen, able to relieve some of your worries and protect American citizens wherever they may be. I don't think that's "warmongering," particularly not when you're not just invited, but—urgently—pleaded for to come in and take care of the situation on that island and get a democratic government back. We don't plan to stay a minute more than we have to to get a government that is chosen by the people back into authority.

Anyone who has ever had anything to do with security matters knows that no one in their right minds would court or permit any use of our military in that way, and that it was only with the greatest reluctance, and full appreciation of the risks involved, that we concluded we had to take this action.

Any suggestion that the students did not fear they had been in danger was set at rest finally, completely, and in very dramatic form, by the pictures of the American students' arrival at Charleston Air Force Base after they were successfully evacuated from Grenada. The first of the students, in a completely spontaneous gesture, stepped off the plane and bent down to kiss the Charleston soil. That scene, reported in newspapers and shown on national television, epitomized more than any press conference or speech both the necessity of the operation and the fullness of its success.

Later, on November 7, nearly five hundred of the students came to Washington, at their own expense, to visit the President and thank him for their rescue. They, at least, had no doubt they had been in peril. One of the student leaders said that before the events occurred he had been what he called a "typical student with little affection for anything military." But, he told the President, "It only takes one rescue by our forces to make us all true believers."

Whatever their Chancellor in Brooklyn, New York, or the other owners of the school, may have thought, the students themselves felt they were in very real danger, and that the American military forces had rescued them; and so indeed they had. Over the next few months increasing stability was added to the various civilian groups in Grenada. There was never any question about the desire of the people of Grenada to have stable and sensible government. They did not wish to become a left-wing laboratory, or a subsidiary of Cuba or the Soviet Union. Within less than a year, violence had been ended and basic living conditions had been not only restored but vastly improved. Free political parties were able to choose their own candidates; and a free election was held on December 19, 1983. Four days before the election, to the considerable amazement of many of our critics in Grenada and the United States and elsewhere, the American forces simply left. By December 15, 1983, less than two months after they went in, United States combat forces had all been withdrawn from Grenada. We left behind only training, police, medical and support elements.

The next time a high American official visited Grenada was on the first anniversary of the landing, when the President was invited to come down. During that visit, on which I accompanied him, he received one of the most tumultuous welcomes of his long career. Nearly half the island population of nearly one hundred thousand turned out, too, to cheer his speech at the end of the day. It was quite apparent that the people of Grenada were delighted, and welcomed the opportunity to say a heartfelt thank you for their rescue. Given such circumstances, I could not describe the Grenada operation as anything other than a necessary activity and a complete success.

I took personal satisfaction again from the high degree of readiness our forces had clearly displayed, the skill with which they conducted the operation; the rapidity and effectiveness of our foreshortened planning period—all those things were once again a source of great gratification to me. They were further evidence that the military was now performing as it was supposed to—that is, as an instrument to carry out and help realize the objectives of the President's foreign policy. That was precisely what we were unable to do in 1980, and what we were now manifestly able to do, and do very well, less than three years later.

However one may view the invasion of Grenada of October 1983, the historical significance of the event is undeniable, if only because of the resulting disclosure of the so-called "Grenada Documents" uncovered during our operation. They offer a rare view into the workings of a Third World Marxist-Leninist state and should be a clear signal of the situation developing in Nicaragua and Central America and what happens in countries vulnerable to Soviet and Cuban influence.

In its 1973 Manifesto, the New Jewel Movement called for the transformation of Grenada into a "new society" for the "new Grenadian man" free of outmoded values. The New Jewel Movement through front organizations was also calling for the violent overthrow of the existing government.

Grenada represents the first instance in which a society subdued by a communist-dominated, Soviet-supported government has been liberated from without, shattering the Brezhnev Doctrine's claim of "irreversibility."

When the New Jewel Movement took power in 1979, Grenada had a British-style constabulary and a small and lightly armed defense force. By October 25, 1983, Grenada had a regular army approaching 1,500, supplemented by a militia estimated at 2,000.

Although its forces already dwarfed those of its OECS neighbors, Grenada's leftist rulers were planning to field three more active battalions and nine more battalions in reserve. All that was established in the documents we captured.

A July 2, 1982, request by the People's Revolutionary Armed Forces of Grenada to the Armed Forces of the Soviet Union revealed a plan for development of the Grenada Armed Forces during the three year period 1983–1985. The proposed 18-battalion force would put between 7,200 and 10,000 men and women under arms, depending on battalion size, excluding personnel on the general staff and other support functions. In proportion to population, that plan would have given Grenada one of the largest military forces of any country in the world.

Documents found on the island indicated that in the previous three years Grenada signed at least five secret military assistance agreements: three with the Soviet Union, one with Cuba and one with North Korea. Other documents also pointed to the existence of similar agreements with Czechoslovakia and Bulgaria.[9]

9. Taken together, the agreements provided for delivery by 1986 of the following:

about 10,000 assault and other rifles, including Soviet AK-47s, Czech M-52/57s, sniper rifles and carbines;

more than 4,500 submachine and machine guns;

more than 11.5 million rounds of 7-62mm ammunition;

295 portable rocket launchers with more than 16,000 rockets;

84 82mm mortars with more than 4,800 mortar shells;

60 crew-served antiaircraft guns of various sizes, with almost 600,000 rounds of ammunition;

15,000 hand grenades;

7,000 land mines;

30 76mm 21S-3 field guns with almost 11,000 rounds of ammunition;

50 GRAD-P howitzers with 1,800 122mm projectiles;

60 armored personnel carriers and patrol vehicles;

86 other vehicles and earth movers;

Cuba began to provide arms as soon as the NJM seized power. Cuba and the Soviet Union provided military and intelligence training and assigned "specialists" to the General Staff and units in the field. Economic "cover" was used to ship arms and ammunition to Grenada: The United States–Caribbean security forces found Soviet weaponry in crates marked "Oficina Economica Cubana."

We discovered large numbers of weapons, many still in crates, on Grenada. The single largest concentration was at Frequente. There were six warehouses full of weapons at that site.

Much of the media initially treated our Grenada operation as an unprovoked aggression against a peaceful Caribbean island of no strategic importance. The impression given was that the ordinary people of Grenada resented and resisted the intervention. In reality, an astonishing 97 percent of Grenadians polled later believed that they had truly been rescued by "Papa Reagan."

Grenada was a particularly well-performed military operation, and one that served very well the interests of America and our allies.

4 coastal patrol boats;

156 radio sets or transmission equipment;

more than 20,000 sets of uniforms; and

tents capable of sheltering more than 5,000 persons.

This listing would outfit a force of 10,000, with half that number in the field.

(These figures were first published in "Grenada, a Preliminary Report," December 16, 1983, by the Department of State and the Department of Defense.)

Lebanon

*T*he story of our association with Lebanon is mainly an unhappy one, extending back for many years. One reason for that unfortunate fact is that in many ways Lebanon is not really a country. It is more like the creation of a committee that operated from a map rather than from any sense of a history that produces nationalities and countries. Even the boundaries are artificial, and virtually all of the elements of instability are contained in that small, narrow, and unhappy land. Indeed, by January 1981 Lebanon was in its sixth year of what can charitably be described as chaos.

Mr. Elias Sarkis, the President of the Connecticut-size republic in 1981, was a decent, kind and soft-spoken man who faced one essential problem: The governmental authority he had embodied since 1976 now covered the Presidential Palace, the Ministry of Defense and precious little else. The balance of Lebanon, and most particularly the capital city, Beirut, was run by a disparate collection of foreign armies and indigenous militias.

Lebanon had become a killing ground where the conflicting interests of Syria, Israel and the Palestine Liberation Organization (PLO) combined with local Lebanese antagonisms to produce a nightmare of epic proportions.

Civil war prevailed in 1981. The PLO was entrenched in Beirut, and running operations in southern Lebanon as well that threatened Israel—particularly the firing of mortars and rockets. The Christian militia (Lebanese forces), fighting against the PLO, was gaining momentum under the direction of Bashir Gemayel.

In 1981 none of us in the incoming Administration was sanguine about the ability of the United States unilaterally to piece Lebanon back together. Had Lebanon been a remote island republic, quite possibly its peculiar system of allocating political power among religious sects may have persisted for quite some time. For nearly thirty years, Lebanon *had* maintained the facade of parliamentary democracy while Beirut became one of the main commercial centers of the Middle East. The wealth of Beirut imparted a certain discipline into the situation: No one wanted to lose the financial benefits it brought to Lebanon. Yet as early as the 1950s, it had become clear that the combination of sectarian differences, a weak central government and Lebanon's vulnerability to inter-Arab disputes and Arab-Israeli conflicts had made the country a very precarious republic.

President Eisenhower felt obliged in 1958 to send in United States forces to preempt what was widely perceived to be a Nasserist attempt to overthrow the government. He sent about seventeen thousand Marines and Army troops into Lebanon at the request of Lebanese President Camille Chamoun. Order was restored, and American forces were withdrawn after the election of General Fuad Shehab as President. The deployment lasted about four months.

That 1958 intervention in Lebanon turned out well. The Government was not overthrown, and stability, undergirded by the general knowledge that America's strength had supported the Lebanese Government, was restored for several years. Also, our intervening troops left; and that is always, to my mind, the sign of a successful intervention. By the 1980s, however, the situation had become much more complicated.

Lebanon's weak central government, which had quite accurately reflected the absence of national consensus among Lebanon's sectarian-based local power brokers, proved unable to regulate the activities of Palestinian commandos; in the early 1970s, they began to use Lebanese territory to mount operations against Israel. As the PLO-Israeli conflict heated up, all of the internal Lebanese antagonisms broke into the open. Maronite Christian political leaders, who dominated Lebanon's government and economy, blamed the Palestinians for bringing ruin to Lebanon. Lebanon's Muslims, aggrieved by what they saw as disproportionate Maronite power and wealth, made common cause with the PLO. The result was civil war fueled by Syria and Israel, both of which had considerable stakes in the contest for power within Lebanon. Yet another complicating factor, dimly seen in early 1981, lurked just beneath the surface: the growing aspirations and frustrations of Lebanon's largest and most impoverished sectarian community, the Shiite Muslims.

The Shiites are also the most fanatical and the most basically anti-Western Muslim sect. They do not place any great value on the preservation of human life. Their real goal is to enter into their spiritual paradise, which they feel they can accomplish by fierce and unswerving devotion to their concept of Muhammad's teaching.

Shiism is an offshoot of Islam based upon worship of Ali, the cousin and son-in-law of the prophet Muhammad. In Lebanon, the Shiite community had long been the least well-off economically, as well as the least powerful politically. The Shiites believe that they are entitled to a more significant political role in Lebanon. Their claim is resisted by both the Christians and the Sunni Muslims of Lebanon, who hold the Presidency and the Prime Ministership, respectively.

So while no one in the new Administration had any real idea of how best to reconstitute Lebanon, one fact was transparently clear: Lebanon was a powder keg, a place where yet another Arab-Israeli conflict could ignite, placing in jeopardy Western interests throughout the region. A succession of very capable American ambassadors in Beirut held to one central theme: that the United States supported Lebanon's territorial integrity and would continue to recognize Lebanon's constitutional government, such as it was. Beyond this declaratory policy, accompanied by repeated appeals for Syrian and Israeli restraint, there was little of a practical nature we could do to restore unity to this very troubled land.

For many years the divisions between the various Christian and Muslim elements in Lebanon were kept balanced and accommodated essentially by a recognition that to do otherwise would be to commit national suicide, and to cause immense problems beyond the loss of nationality for both Muslims and Christians. Also, as I have said, the success of Beirut was paramount; the center held.

Thus, there were constitutional and other provisions for sharing of the high offices of government, and recognition that certain Christian and Muslim sanctuaries were to be respected and preserved.

From time to time those arrangements were strained or upset, and bloodshed and destruction resulted; but generally, a reasonable stability was achieved for many years. Beirut prospered further, and was thought to be not only a beautiful but basically a safe city for many business, educational and social activities; many thought of it as the financial and intellectual capital of the Middle East.

One of the difficult problems with which leaders in Lebanon

had to contend was that neither the Christian nor the Muslim communities were in any way unified among themselves, nor were all Christians or all Muslims situated in easily definable geographical areas. There were regional pockets for each community, but they were not completely separate. More than one group contested for some areas, such as Beirut and the Shuf, the mountainous region overlooking the city. There were a number of competing small factions, and family feuds within each of those communities.

The stability that was achieved was secured because all factions recognized that stability was far better than civil warfare. That recognition was aided by reasonably enlightened leadership. The institutions of the government managed to function and maintain legitimacy, albeit tenuously at times. But when those wise and restrained viewpoints were neglected or rejected, then civil war broke out with varying degrees of intensity and ferocity.

In the early 1970s the Palestinian military groups, which had developed a virtual "state within a state" in Lebanon after fleeing from the West Bank and Gaza in the 1967 war, began to mount attacks on Israel and others. Factions in Lebanon such as the Maronite Christians blamed the PLO for mounting tensions, and Lebanon's Muslims, glad to have a basis for attacking the Christians, did so. Syria helped the PLO—except that, to add to the confusion, Syria intervened in 1976 *against* the PLO to help the Christians, carrying out Hafez al Assad's strategy to ensure that no one group became too powerful in Lebanon.

Israel helped the Maronites. And the Shiite Moslems eyed everyone with deep suspicion bordering on hate. They believed that an accurate census would show their numbers to be at least a plurality in Lebanon, entitling them to far more of a voice in the country's affairs.

Both Syria and Israel regarded Lebanon as either a potential threat or as a potential base for attacks against the other. The Israelis were concerned about raids and various hostile acts mounted from points along their border with Lebanon. And the Syrians, beginning in 1976, consistently maintained tens of thousands of their troops there to help achieve the virtual hegemony they felt they needed over Lebanon. Lebanon, of course, was never strong enough to resist either of its powerful neighbors, or indeed any of the other potential threats to its existence— threats that were present in virtually every community and every area of the country.

Our fears with respect to an Arab-Israeli war breaking out in Lebanon began to assume a very ominous shape in April 1981, when Syrian-Lebanese Christian fighting around the town of Zahlah led to an Israeli shootdown of a Syrian helicopter, followed immediately by Syrian deployment of SA-6 antiaircraft missiles in Lebanon's Bekaa Valley. The situation became even more ominous in June and July of 1981, when Israeli air strikes on PLO positions in Lebanon led to Palestinian artillery and rocket attacks against northern Israel. Ambassador Philip Habib succeeded in negotiating a cease-fire, but I knew of no one in the Administration who believed that his very adept diplomacy had ended the threat to Middle East peace.

In fact, the Israelis had a very fundamental objective in Lebanon, which was nothing less than the eradication of the PLO army. Having rooted itself in Lebanon, the PLO army inadvertently gave Israel a golden opportunity to destroy it, and along with it the nationalistic aspirations of Palestinians living on the West Bank and in the Gaza Strip; or so the Israelis reasoned. In short, by Israel's killing off the PLO army in Lebanon, Israel theorized, the PLO itself would be made impotent to oppose the Israelis effectively in the territories occupied by Israel since June 1967.

Tension continued to mount throughout the balance of 1981 and on into the spring of 1982. Israel adopted a very liberal interpretation of the Habib cease-fire, arguing that Palestinian attacks against Jews anywhere in the world constituted violations.[1] This position was, according to Phil Habib, wholly untenable; the terms of the cease-fire applied only to actions in Lebanon. That the PLO complied with the cease-fire greatly vexed Israeli Defense Minister Ariel Sharon, who needed a pretext to deliver a knockout blow. Sharon also sought to obtain from the Reagan Administration a tacit approval of his plans by arguing repeatedly that the prospective destruction of the PLO would amount to a defeat for the Soviet Union and international terrorism. Although I can add nothing to the controversy about whether or not Al Haig gave Sharon a "green light" to invade Lebanon, I do know that Sharon's line of argument had a certain amount of appeal to Al and to others who tended to view the Palestinian-Israeli problem as a subset of the Cold War.

In any event, Sharon received his pretext in early June 1982, when a Palestinian assailant severely wounded Israel's Ambassador in London. That the perpetrator belonged to the anti-Arafat Abu Nidal organization, therefore raising the possibility of a deliberate third-party provocation, did not deter Israel in the least. Having just completed its treaty-mandated withdrawal from the Sinai at the end of April, thereby placing its relationship with Egypt on a firm footing, Israel was now ready to devote its full attention to the PLO in Lebanon. The Israeli attack was launched on June 6, 1982.

Israeli forces moved swiftly up the coast and through the heart of southern Lebanon, brushing aside UN observer forces and engaging Syrian units. Syria, which for its own reasons would shed no tears over the PLO's destruction, nevertheless managed to burnish its image in Arab circles as a "confrontation state" by offering resistance, however ineffective, to the Israeli invaders.

---

1. One of the other and more creative interpretations of the term "cease-fire" was Begin's claim, after the Israeli Defence Forces invaded Lebanon in June 1982, that he did not believe a cease-fire was a "cease-fire in place." And so the Israelis felt they could advance as long as they did not fire, and if the other side fired to halt the Israeli advance it was a violation of the cease-fire.

But most of the Syrian ground units were located in the Bekaa Valley, and Israel's real objective was to finish off the PLO army once and for all in Beirut. So the Israelis halted well south of the Beirut-Damascus highway, and concentrated their full attention on the real prize: Yasir Arafat's PLO army trapped in West Beirut.

In the aftermath of the Israelis' 1982 invasion, we spent considerable time and resources trying to strengthen the Lebanese government, train and equip its army, and generally secure for Lebanon the blessings of a sovereign and safe nation. We were by that time already part of a United Nations observer force that was supposed to help keep the peace after Israel's 1978 invasion of southern Lebanon—but in June 1982 that force was brushed aside like an annoying fly by the Israelis, when they concluded that their interest required them to invade and occupy southern Lebanon.

Though our intelligence sources supported the belief that the Israeli Ambassador to London had been shot by an Abu Nidal unit in an anti-Arafat gesture, Prime Minister Menachem Begin and Defense Minister Ariel Sharon, as we have seen, blamed the PLO for the assassination. The Israeli invasion was "supposed" to go forty kilometers into Lebanon to clear out PLO snipers. Begin said that Israel did not covet "one inch" of Lebanese territory; but Ariel Sharon did, and soon Beirut was under siege. Nor were the Syrians prepared to stand aside, notwithstanding Israel's technological superiority, particularly in the air. In only a few hours, the Israeli Air Force had shot down and destroyed over seventy Syrian planes with virtually no Israeli losses.

The six year term of Elias Sarkis as President expired in September 1982. Lebanon's chronic weakness was magnified by a return to the earlier disputes about how to maintain the legitimacy of the presidency and the government, and thus the government of Lebanon became an easy prey to its powerful neighbors.

The Israelis were determined to eliminate the presence of the

PLO army in Lebanon, thereby removing a political-military threat to their northern areas, and weakening Palestinian nationalism. They claimed the PLO had been firing into northern Israel since late 1981 despite the July 1981 cease-fire. As I said, the Israelis' invasion not only occupied the southern border areas of Lebanon, but continued on north, in what they described as their "self-defense" role—until they ran into the Syrians, who were moving to engage them from various vantage points in and beyond the Bekaa Valley. In Beirut, the PLO was fighting for its survival, and incidentally thereby supporting Syrian interests as well as its own. That factor added to Israel's military problems, because the PLO's central base of operations was in various strongholds in Beirut itself.

The Israelis were more than eager to destroy the PLO army, but in Washington we were all, I think, very worried about the effect of the house-to-house fighting in Beirut that we were sure would come about if something were not done to try to halt the conflict.

The Israelis, preparing for their attack on the city, had sealed it off, cutting water and electricity supplies. Minor epidemics in West Beirut had broken out and the Beirut hospitals had appealed to international organizations for relief and supplies. As a result of those worries, and after many meetings, conferences, debates and pleas, we agreed to the formation of the Multinational Force (MNF),[2] not under United Nations control,[3] but simply the

---

2. In the middle of all this, Alexander Haig resigned as Secretary of State, on June 25, 1982. This was not the first Haig "resignation," but it was the first one the President accepted. Haig was a one hundred percent supporter of Israel on all issues, and many felt he left because our policy in the Middle East was becoming more evenhanded.

Two weeks before his last resignation, Haig had successfully opposed the White House staff, who thought that the United States should join the other members of the Security Council of the UN in a resolution demanding Israel's withdrawal from Beirut in order to let the trapped PLO army withdraw from that city. Haig ordered our UN representatives to veto (thus block) this resolution the day after his final resignation, although earlier we had voted for UN Resolution 508, calling for Israeli withdrawal.

product of cooperation of the participating countries. General Vessey and I argued that we should not be one of the participants; but this argument we lost, and ultimately this first MNF was composed of troops from the United States, Italy and France. The force, with representatives from each of the three countries, was assembled, equipped, transported and landed with the full consent and agreement of the Lebanese Government. It deployed to agreed-upon positions in July 1982. The MNF then, in accordance with an agreement arranged by our Special Envoy, Ambassador Philip Habib, supervised the departure of the PLO from Beirut and dispersed its members by sea to various other countries, including Algeria, North Yemen, and Tunisia, where the PLO headquarters was based.

During that period the President was increasingly worried and unhappy about the fate of the people living in Beirut, including many American citizens. He was very critical of the Israelis' use of force and particularly their use of the CBU or "cluster" bomb units, which we had given to Israel to use in their own defense; they had used them in urban areas, inflicting heavy casualties on civilians. As a result, the President was a strong supporter of the plan to send in the first MNF.

I judged the MNF action to be a complete success because with virtually no losses, we had not only taken out the PLO army, one of the principal magnets for an Israeli house-to-house

---

Actually, most of Haig's final threat to resign was caused by his unhappiness over his treatment by the White House staff on the President's European trip in 1982. The staff differed with Haig about which planes and helicopters he should ride in as part of the presidential entourage. Haig always referred to such differences on protocol as part of the "guerrilla warfare" being waged against him by the White House staff.

3. I understand that United States diplomats initially pressed for a UN force to supervise the withdrawal of the Israeli forces from Beirut and the departure of PLO fighers from Lebanon, but Israel said no. It did not trust UN forces, did not want them on its flanks, and insisted that the United States contingent of the MNF be stationed in the southern part of Beirut contiguous to Israeli lines.

attack through Beirut, but we had removed a principal cause of instability in Lebanon itself. With this first MNF, we also had greatly eased conditions for all the people living in Beirut. The MNF's entry was not only timely, but lifesaving.

Finally, the PLO army never again regained anything resembling effectiveness or unity.

I knew that the President was planning to offer a new peace plan after the PLO army left Beirut. I was particularly pleased that his plan recognized that one of the root causes of disorder and instability in the Middle East was the plight of the Palestinians on the West Bank and in various refugee camps in Beirut, the Gaza Strip and elsewhere.

The President's peace plan, revealed in a speech on September 1, 1982, had been prepared by career experts in the State Department, in coordination with the NSC staff. It reflected the President's desire to build upon the momentum of the Egypt-Israeli peace achieved at Camp David. The Administration had held off from putting forward its plan until Israel carried out its withdrawal from the Sinai on April 25, 1982. Perhaps the President would have given his speech soon afterward, but Israel prevented any such peace momentum with its invasion of Lebanon on June 6, 1982.

The President's plan, which I discussed with the new Secretary of State, George Shultz, seemed to me to be the most creative and imaginative plan yet put forth. It offered a measure of self-rule to the Palestinians by placing the West Bank in a loose form of federation with Jordan, whose King is one of the wisest and most courageous leaders in the Middle East. King Hussein had a full understanding of the security needs of Israel and was, along with Presidents Sadat and Mubarak of Egypt and King Hassan II of Morocco, one of the few heads of state in the area willing to talk to the Israelis and to try to help them. The plan seemed to me to offer the Palestinian people the first real hope they had had; and even though it did not provide for an independent

Palestinian state (an anathema to the Israelis), it did provide for Palestinians to have a large amount of self rule and participation in other governmental units under overall Jordanian governance. The plan was deliberately vague as to details, to permit considerable negotiating flexibility; but it recognized the Palestinians' needs and rights to more self-rule without giving them the status of a new country. I was pleased also that the plan seemed consistent with the great concern George Shultz had expressed during his confirmation hearings for the plight of the Palestinian people. I had supported George strongly in this worry.

I had planned to visit the MNF before it left Lebanon, to congratulate our forces on their fine performance and to meet with leaders in Israel and Egypt. With the announcement of the President's plan approaching, I planned to arrive in Beirut on September 1.

The State Department fed stories to its favorite columnists that the Department disapproved of my trip, but I had called Phil Habib, after meeting with the Joint Chiefs, from the secure telephone in a small conference room off the Tank (as the conference room of the Joint Chiefs was called), and asked him whether he thought I should come or not. He was most enthusiastic about the idea.

I arrived in Beirut on September 1, where the very anticipation of the President's speech had stirred great excitement.

While I was there, I met with Bashir Gemayel, President-elect of Lebanon, a vigorous, enthusiastic young leader who seemed to me to offer a hope of unifying and strengthening Lebanon. He made a strange proposal to me: The United States should consider and use Lebanon as its strategic outpost in the Middle East. Lebanon was not quite to be our fifty-first state, but its relationship with us might not have been altogether dissimilar from that condition if Bashir Gemayel's plan had been approved. From his point of view, of course, it made good strategic sense: It would have assured him of a permanent large American troop presence and would have been a major factor in denying both Syria and Israel their presumed right to wander across Lebanon's borders at will. From Israel's point of view Lebanon could not be used as a staging ground for attacks on Israel's northern border. From my point of view, however, it would have committed us far too permanently to a presence (and a responsibility) in that powder keg.

To me, Gemayel's plan was little more than a wild idea. Here was a small country torn by civil war, without strategically important resources, whose main claim to American attention was its ability to serve as a breeding ground for trouble in a very volatile region of the world. Lacking any real leverage, Bashir Gemayel put forth the political equivalent of a "blank check"— saying, in effect, "Do anything you want with Lebanon—just save us."

I, of course, reported Gemayel's idea fully to the President and to State, and discussed it with my Defense staff. No one reached a conclusion different from mine.

Next on that trip, I had the always happy and congenial task of visiting with our troops. The Marine elements of the MNF were in the process of packing to leave. It gave me a sense of some continuity to see, amid all the high-tech new weaponry, the familiar canvas lister bags for water, which the Marines were carefully packing. This was one of the few items that continued to look familiar to me from my service in New Guinea in World War II.

The Marines' assignment had been carried out quickly and efficiently. My visit with the French and Italian elements of the MNF was equally pleasant and congenial, and they all seemed glad to be recognized for their highly valuable services. Of course they also all seemed to be glad to be going home.

In Israel my reception was somewhat mixed. There Prime Minister Begin harangued me for nearly four hours about the inequities of the President's peace plan. Mr. Begin is not a man who likes to be interrupted or argued with, and as a result it was virtually a four-hour monologue. I did point out some of the major advantages to Israel in the plan, but the Prime Minister simply went on to his next prepared paragraph and continued. His major point—indeed his only point—seemed to be that Israel owned the West Bank, needed it for its own security, and would not give it up.

His long monologue made me very late for the dinner that our Ambassador, Sam Lewis, had planned for me. At that dinner, however, Shimon Peres, then out of office, warmly endorsed the President's plan in a conversation with me and agreed that it offered the only real hope of peace in the area. That approval was consistent with his basically broad and politically courageous approach to the problems of securing Israel's safety. He knew that Israel could not live in peace with fiercely antagonistic neighbors on the West Bank, or elsewhere, and he was sure the President's plan would give the Palestinians many of their rightful demands without hurting Israel. Peres has always taken a more flexible view of the issue of determining the final status of the lands contested by Israel and its neighboring peoples.

These were tiring days, because Ariel Sharon took me on a day-long helicopter trip to innumerable Israeli West Bank settlements. In some cases, the helicopter would land, we would conduct a quick examination and return to the helicopter, and many times we simply observed the settlements from the air. The United States had opposed those settlements as a violation of the 1949 Geneva Convention, and I believe Sharon's choice of sights for me to see was designed to try to display some indirect American approval of the settlements. In the Golan Heights, we also were given a demonstration of the capability of the Israeli forces.

At the end of the day, I asked the then Defense Minister if it was all a "coincidence" that every Israeli West Bank settlement

I had seen occupied higher ground then any of the Arab settlements nearby.

"Of course not," said Sharon. "We have placed our settlements for the maximum military advantage."

I was also shown the Israeli camera-carrying drone, a remotely piloted vehicle that had made video tape recordings of me the day before, on my visit to our troops in Beirut.

It was a most impressive technical achievement. The drone was in effect a model airplane, but one equipped with sophisticated photographic and recording capabilities. Its small size and low cost were also welcome features, particularly for short range battlefield reconnaissance. Especially appealing was the fact that the drone did not put lives at risk, and was hard to detect, given its small size. Later, I directed the Joint Chiefs to give us that same capability again: That Israeli drone had actually been developed by us, but the Congress had refused to fund its deployment. It was then sold to the Israelis.

The Egyptians also treated me most hospitably; but far better and far more important was their immediate and enthusiastic acceptance of the President's peace plan.

Sadly, despite the high hopes the plan had brought and the depth of support for it in Egypt and within important elements in Israel, our own support for it seemed to wane as Begin's opposition to it mounted. There developed a feeling that perhaps it would be better to "get things quieted down in Lebanon" before we began active work to secure the benefits of the President's peace plan. Unhappily, things never "quieted down in Lebanon," and we never pushed for adoption of the plan. That was a source of great sorrow to me, because I thought then, and still think, that properly developed, and with carefully nurtured and gathered support from various elements in the Middle East, it could have succeeded in realizing the President's vision of a stable peace there, with Israel and her neighbors living side by side and accepting each other's sovereignty. And thus, ultimately, might be removed one of the major, centuries-old reasons for the constant turmoil that has been the principal characteristic of the Middle East.

The actual departure of the Multinational Force took place on September 14, a few days after I had left the area. Frequently in the case of such special forces, there is not a sufficiently clear-cut objective, so no one can tell when the objective has been secured (whether or not we had "won"); and thus when it is time to leave. In this case we had not only secured our objective, but agreed with our associates that after ten quiet days following the departure of the PLO forces, it was time to leave, and we left. Some wanted to leave the MNF in longer and assign it other missions, but it had been sized and equipped for the single mission it had accomplished. Moreover, I felt, as President Eisenhower had felt twenty-five years earlier, that we should not have a permanent presence in Lebanon.

So far so good. The Israelis, however, having paused at the edge of Beirut, remained there instead of continuing to pull back southward. Nearly a year later they did move the main body of their forces south to the Awali River, but at this time they remained on the outskirts of Beirut. I felt that if the Israelis *had* pulled back then, the Lebanese Armed Forces could have deployed to the areas they vacated. The Syrians had withdrawn their so-called Arab Deterrent Force (ADF) from Beirut while the PLO was taken out. But with the Israelis in position on the outskirts of Beirut, the Syrians, well inside Lebanon, stayed in the Bekaa Valley with very substantial numbers, generally estimated to be about fifty thousand.

On September 14, shortly after I returned to the U.S., Bashir Gemayel, the young strongman of the Maronite Christian militia and the President-elect of Lebanon, was assassinated along with many of his political lieutenants. Within days the Israeli army moved back into Beirut itself, and there was a massacre of some seven hundred unarmed Palestinian refugees in the Sabra and Shatila refugee camps, in Beirut, where the homeless Palestinians had lived for years. The Phalangist militia, formerly led by Bashir Gemayel, was the force that committed the indefensible and terrible massacres. At that time it was under the leadership of Elie Hobeika. Israeli forces, under the command of Brigadier General Amos Yaron, remained on the periphery.[4]

The spiraling panic in Beirut was intensified. Ambassador Phil Habib had promised the departing PLO fighters that Israeli forces would not reenter the city and threaten their women and children—a promise that the Israeli reentry into Beirut after Gemayel's assassination made impossible to keep. Gemayel had promised that the Palestinians in the Beirut camps would be safe.

Against this background, many people urged the President to send in another multinational force consisting of troops from the same nations. Actually, the NSC staff, including Bud McFarlane, at that time a Deputy to the NSC Adviser Bill Clark, in keeping with their passionate desire to use our military, wanted to send in a major force, of several American divisions and some French divisions, to "force withdrawal" of both Syrians and Israelis. A force of that size would, of course, almost certainly become embroiled in major combat while "peacekeeping" between Syrians and Israelis. I opposed the whole idea, as did the Joint Chiefs, and this time we prevailed.

Thereupon, MacFarlane's demands for another MNF, supported by the State Department, became more petulant. I still objected, of course, very strongly, because this MNF would not have any mission that could be defined. Its objectives were stated in the fuzziest possible terms; and then later, when that objective

---

4. Yaron was relieved of field command for at least three years by Israel's Kahan Commission, which investigated the massacres. He subsequently served as Israel's Defense Attaché in Washington, after the Canadian government refused to accept him because of what they felt to be his involvement in the atrocity.

---

was "clarified," the newly defined objective was demonstrably unobtainable. The Joint Chiefs were also strongly opposed to the reentry of a multinational force, because without a clearly defined objective, determining the proper size and armament and rules of engagement for such a force is difficult at best.

But on September 29 the MNF returned, following the President's conclusion that he felt it was necessary to have the force back in Lebanon even though this time it had no mission other than to "establish a presence." It now appeared that Israel and Syria would continue to face each other in a wider struggle.

Later, the "mission" was defined to be the interposition of the multinational force between the withdrawing armies of Israel and Syria, until the Lebanese armed forces were sufficiently trained and equipped to take over that role. It is quite reasonable to have such a buffer in the event an agreement for withdrawal *is* secured. When forces are in direct contact with each other and are asked to withdraw, each is understandably deeply suspicious of the other, and the withdrawing forces are extremely vulnerable to any violation by their adversaries of the withdrawal agreement. So it would not have been in any way unreasonable to constitute an independent, neutral force to come between the Syrians and the Israelis, who were in direct combat with each other, and thus to permit an agreed-upon withdrawal to take place in an orderly fashion.

The problem, of course, was that there was *not* an agreed-upon withdrawal. There was, however, a great eagerness by the State Department and the NSC staff, and by Israel, to have an American troop presence in Lebanon even without any defined objective. When the second Multinational Force landed, there was still not an agreement for withdrawal. Indeed, a tentative, wholly unworkable agreement was reached only eight long months later, during which period the Syrians, whose air force had been largely destroyed and its army weakened by the Israelis, were rearmed by the Soviets. Meanwhile, and as a result, the tasks assigned to the elements of the MNF were very limited and circumscribed.

Our part of the force was assigned to the Beirut Airport, with the idea of trying to keep the airport open—something that the Government of Lebanon was not able to do. Other forces—French, Italians and, beginning in January 1983, a small contingent of British observers—were scattered about to the north and east of the airport with other individual assignments. There were virtually no contiguous deployments, although their patrols frequently crossed paths; and the forces of the four nations that formed the group had to maintain direct liaison by going to, from and around the always volatile and dangerous streets of Beirut and surrounding countryside, where the armed tribes of anarchy roamed at will. There was a coordinating committee in Beirut that tried its best to deal both with military liaison and with some political issues, but there was no overall *command* of the force, and the coordination was best described as "loose."

The government in Beirut had legally approved the entry of the first Multinational Force, which had secured the elimination of the PLO army from Lebanon, and that position had been concurred in by the various Christian and Moslem factions in Lebanon. But this time those factions were at war with each other in a series of anarchical and tribal conflicts, which the government of Lebanon was totally unable or unwilling even to try to stop. Those factions waited until it was clear the Israelis and Syrians would not withdraw; then they began to attack the MNF and each other and anyone else in sight. Sadly, but understandably, the training and equipment that we poured in in lavish amounts to help the Lebanese Army was not sufficient to enable it to deal with fifty thousand Syrians and at least a similar number of Israelis at each other's throats; nor could it deal even even with factional Lebanese militias.

Also the Syrians began to receive the SA-5s (very accurate,

long range surface-to-air missiles) from the USSR, and now felt increasingly confident they could prevent another shattering defeat of their air force by the Israelis. The result was that the scattered elements of the second MNF basically came to be viewed by many of the warring factions as simply a prop for an unpopular Lebanese government whose writ was too weak to run except in the areas where the MNF was billeted, and certainly not elsewhere in Lebanon.

By the same token, the MNF was lightly armed, since its only mission was to interpose itself between forces that might theoretically agree to a withdrawal. It was not only lightly armed, but was quite insufficient in numbers or configuration to deal militarily with either the Israelis or the Syrians, and certainly not with all of the factional militias of Christians and Moslems who fought each other with great ferocity and had been doing so for many years. Indeed the second MNF was not designed or intended to deal militarily with *any* other forces. The militias saw that, and began their season of rising threats with the April 1983 bombing of our Embassy.

Those were some of the reasons that I so strongly opposed our participation in this second MNF. Nevertheless, I supported the President's decision fully after he sent in the second MNF, and we both made major efforts to spur the strengthening of the Lebanese Armed Forces.

On April 18, our Embassy in West Beirut was bombed, and seventeen Americans, among them Robert Ames, were killed. A small truck packed with explosives penetrated the checkpoint on the street and drove under the front of the Embassy, collapsing several floors and killing the Americans and many others, mostly Lebanese. Ambassador Robert Dillon, dressed for jogging, was in his eighth floor office and survived the blast, although he was hurled into the rubble.

Successful terrorist activities always produce a reaction in which fury and frustration are combined, succeeded by an unswerving desire for vengeance. That cycle is what makes it so very difficult to pursue a reasonable focus on the terrorists themselves, and not to yield to the temptation to launch an indiscriminate bombing in revenge. When and if we have the proof, as we did in the case of Libya's responsibility for the Berlin discotheque bombing, then an appropriate response against the terrorists connected with the terrorism is essential.

On May 17, 1983, eight months after the second MNF went in, an agreement was finally signed by Lebanon and Israel, but not by Syria.

It was a curious agreement. Israel, after requiring that significant economic benefits accrue to it as a consequence of its withdrawal, said it would withdraw from its advanced position if Syria would also withdraw. But in a secret side letter, accepted by Secretary Shultz but apparently unknown to Amin Gemayel, who had been elected President of Lebanon after his brother's assassination, Israel said it would not withdraw if Syria did not withdraw simultaneously.[5] The side letter also required that Israel receive information about all previous Israeli MIAs, and the return of all POWs and remains of dead Israeli soldiers—all of this *prior to* Israel's withdrawal from Lebanon. Why such an agreement was reported to us in such glowing terms by George Shultz

---

5. On two or three occasions in late 1982, Syria had made known its willingness to withdraw its troops from Lebanon. However, Syria believed that its own forces had entered and remained in Lebanon legally and legitimately, at the request of the government of Lebanon. Syria's Arab Deterrent Force (ADF) received its initial mandate from the Arab League on October 26, 1976.

The mandate was renewed nine times, until July 1982, when the Arab League called for the withdrawal of all non-Lebanese armed forces from Lebanese territory, and the Lebanese government declined to ask for a renewal of the ADF mandate.

In light of this background, Syria was loath to equate its own armed presence in Lebanon with that of Israel, the legitimacy of whose armed presence in Lebanon had been called into question by UN Security Council Resolutions 425 in 1978 and 508 in 1982. Thus, our Middle East experts well understood that Syria's willingness to withdraw, if indeed it was genuine, would be undermined by any agreement or resolution that suggested legal and "moral" equivalence with the Israeli presence and withdrawal.

has always remained a mystery to me. This agreement with its secret side letter gave President Assad of Syria veto power over any withdrawal and thus over Israel's ability to establish better relations with a key Arab neighbor, Lebanon. In retrospect, it was also a veto over America's entire Middle East policy. Assad promptly exercised this by not withdrawing.

I pointed all this out, many times, to Secretary Shultz, first at a meeting even before the agreement was formally signed. We met in his hotel on his way home from his Middle East trip on May 11, 1983. I was in Paris to meet with the Saudi Defense Minister, Prince Sultan.

On the way into George's suite, I noticed in the living room an enormous, fifteen- to twenty-pound box of chocolates the French government had presented to George. As a confirmed and unabashed chocoholic, I felt a brief pang of envy, which I manfully suppressed.

George was extremely proud and protective of his agreement, and none of my arguments that it was not worthwhile, nor in our interest, made the slightest visible impression on him. On the way out, I picked up Rich Armitage, who had been meeting with Nicholas Veliotes, Assistant Secretary of State for Near Eastern and South Asian Affairs, and one of the best of the State Department's experts on the Middle East. Both raised their eyebrows inquisitively. I shook my head, and there was no need for any further briefing.

Our whole policy, including the MNF presence and the build-up of the Lebanese Armed Forces, was premised on achieving a *diplomatic* success—an agreement that would *require* both Israelis and Syrians to withdraw. Absent this, there was no *military* action that could succeed, unless we declared war and tried to force the occupying troops out of Lebanon.

Our Marines at the airport, now with no mission since there was no withdrawal agreement, were shelled from time to time. At the end of August, we did authorize responsive fire to take out the artillery doing the shelling, but we did not and could not, under the basic terms of the MNF agreement, equip or authorize our Marines to take the kind of normal responsive actions Marines are trained to do to protect themselves in combat. That would include seizing and holding the high ground around their basic position and patrolling aggressively to insure that the airport was not only occupied but was fully secured.

In August 1983, the Marines were shelled repeatedly from the mountains, and often sniper fire came from the southern Beirut slum areas. As a result of this intermittent, harassing shelling and sniper fire of the Marines at the airport, a decision was made, in the field, to billet the Marines in the only reinforced concrete building in the area to protect them from sniper fire, shrapnel and the inevitable injuries and deaths that result from indiscriminate shelling. (Toward the end of 1983, we also built bunkers for the MNF, showing how radically their "presence mission" had changed.)

I had urged many times, in various meetings, that we recognize that the objectives of the MNF could not be achieved in the absence of any agreement by the Syrians and the Israelis to withdraw; that the May 17 "agreement" was not only absurd, but was nullified from the start, by giving President Assad of Syria a veto power over withdrawal; and that our position was becoming increasingly dangerous, and was in fact useless. The MNF could no longer contribute either to stability or peace by our Marines remaining in what I described as the "bull's-eye" of a large target at Beirut Airport, with artillery, small arms and other harassing agents continually sniping at them.

The arguments I had in the National Security Council and in the National Security Planning Group, with Secretary of State Shultz, and before the President, were vigorous and intense and exposed differing philosophies. I felt—and certainly my feeling was colored by the fact that I had, and felt keenly, the responsibility for the safety of our troops—that we could not either guarantee their safety, nor give them the means to provide for their own security, under the arrangements and conditions then prevailing in Lebanon. Because we could not achieve the objectives for which we had entered, I urged repeatedly that we should dissolve the MNF and leave. The Joint Chiefs of Staff shared that view. I did not regard it as either a defeat or a shameful act; it was simply a recognition that the goal and mission of the forces as it was finally developed, namely to act as a buffer force between withdrawing Syrians and Israelis, could hardly be secured in the absence of any withdrawal. But State stubbornly clung to its "agreement" as if it were a major diplomatic triumph. Because the Israelis had insisted on Syria's parallel withdrawal, subject to major new preconditions, the stillborn agreement meant nothing.

For military reasons the Israelis moved south to the Awali River in the late summer of 1983. The Syrians stayed in the Bekaa, and the situation around Beirut unraveled daily. The Syrians had been receiving the Soviet SA-5 missiles from the USSR since early 1983, restoring Syrian confidence (and obstinacy) after their shattering defeat by Israel's air force. Yet our State Department still thought the Syrians would withdraw.

We also had unsettling reports, from sources of varying reliability, that prior to departing the Shuf region, which overlooked both the city of Beirut and our Marines at the airport, the Israelis were operating in close coordination with both the Christian and Druze militias and warning each against the other.

We also had credible reports that the Israeli forces had repeatedly prevented the American-trained Lebanese Armed Forces from sending exploratory patrols up into the mountainous area to prepare for a possible deployment after the Israeli withdrawal under the May 17 agreement. When the Israeli Defense Forces withdrew from the Shuf, the Christian militias moved in and "reclaimed" areas that had most recently been held by the Druze, while the Druze militia took equally aggressive retaliatory action against the Christians. Many civilians reportedly were killed in the factional fighting on the mountain.

The result was that the security in and around Beirut deteriorated and the United States-backed Lebanese government and army were seen to be impotent. Now the Marines were in far greater danger than before.

The State Department and Secretary of State Shultz particularly, and the National Security staff as it was then constituted, had long had the feeling that many situations in the world required the "intermixture of diplomacy and the military." Roughly translated, that meant that we should not hesitate to put a battalion or so of American forces in various places in the world where we desired to achieve particular objectives of stability, or changes of government, or support of governments or whatever else. Their feeling seemed to be that an American troop presence would add a desirable bit of pressure and leverage to diplomatic efforts, and that we should be willing to do that freely and virtually without hesitation. The NSC staff were even more militant, with a number of its members seeming to me, and to the Joint Chiefs, to spend most of their time thinking up ever more wild adventures for our troops, later going so far as to suggest that we should persuade the Egyptians that we, and they, should invade Libya in a rerun of General Montgomery's Desert War. The NSC staff's eagerness to get us into a fight somewhere—anywhere—coupled with their apparent lack of concern for the safety of our troops, and with no responsibility therefor, reminded me of the old joke "Let's you and him fight this out."

My own feeling was that we should not commit American troops to any situation unless the objectives were so important to American interests that we had to fight, and that if those conditions were met, and all diplomatic efforts failed, then we had to commit, as a last resort, not just token forces to provide an American presence, but enough forces to win and win over-whelmingly.[6]

The arguments raged back and forth, with the President always being concerned about how it would look to the rest of the world if the MNF were removed. The State Department and the NSC staff played to that worry of the President's by telling him that it would always appear that we had "cut and run," that we had been "driven out," and similar phrases designed to encourage the belief that only if we stayed in Lebanon could we demonstrate our manhood or secure any of the objectives we wanted.

I always made the point that we were totally unable to accomplish anything with this second Multinational Force, because it had been correctly sized to act only as an interposition force, as a buffer between the withdrawing armies. It was not sized or structured to perform other actions; and, since the warring armies were not withdrawing, the mission of the Multinational Force was already frustrated. Finally, I urged that our Marines were in a position of increasing vulnerability as they sat, in effect, in the middle of a target, unable to do what was required to protect any occupied position.[7]

Toward the end of these discussions and debates we were also heavily involved in the actions of Grenada. It was quickly apparent that the principal forces we would have to draw upon for Grenada were Marines headed for the relief of the Marine Amphibious Ready Group now in Lebanon, and that was a complicating factor.

---

6. I set forth this view in detail in a talk, entitled "The Uses of Military Power," which I gave to the National Press Club on November 28, 1984. The full text is set out in the Appendix of this book.

7. During some of the last days of those arguments, I even proposed that we take our Marines out of Lebanon, but keep them on our Navy ships 400 to 500 yards offshore. Then they would be far safer, yet available quickly should the situation change. Bill Clark supported that proposal, as well as my earlier plea to get our forces out now that their mission had become impossible; all to no avail. The State Department's continued claims that it would appear we had "cut and run" always carried the day, until after the October 23 bombing of our Marine barracks.

Ultimately, as we all know now, a tragedy occurred on October 23, 1983, when the suicide terrorists of some faction, to this day still unknown, blew up the building in which the Marines were housed, and another building where French Multinational Forces were located, with a fearful loss of life.

I was infuriated by various specious charges made later that I had refused Israeli offers of medical help after this tragedy. The offers were first brought to my attention in a telephone conversation with Mr. Moshe Arens, then the Israeli Defense Minister, eleven hours after the tragic bombing, and long after the evacuation of many of our Marines to American military hospitals was well under way. The offers also were made to other United States headquarters, all of whom on their own and, of course, without directions from me, decided that our own medical contingency plans, resources and facilities did not require Israel augmentation. We did request medical body bags from Israel and were grateful to receive them. A few days later, on November 4, Israel's forces were subjected to a bombing. I offered medical help to Mr. Arens. He declined with thanks, saying they did not need the assistance. There were no angry letters to the editor about his refusal of my offer.

While I am dealing with myths and canards, let me try to set at rest another:

The NSC staff people, always eager for combat at all time, circulated a report that I had been "ordered" to participate with the French in a joint attack on Syria's position in the Bekaa Valley, but I had refused at the last minute to carry out that order. This is, of course, absurd; because, on the face of it, if I had been ordered by the President to do anything and refused, I would not have been around for several more years.

The facts are that I received a telephone call from Charles Hernu, the French Minister of Defense, in the morning of November 16, telling me French planes were going to attack Syrian positions in about two to three hours. I had received no orders or notifications from the President or anyone prior to that phone call from Paris.

I thanked my friend Charles Hernu, wished him and his pilots good luck, and said, "Unfortunately it is a bit too late for us to join you in this one." Of such a chimerical collection of threads are woven lies of whole cloth. This is another instance when McFarlane's "recollections," well known to be "flexible," differed sharply from those of other other participants.[8]

A final myth, that I prevented closer liaison between the Israeli occupying forces and the United States MNF contingent, received wide currency in the United States. This was also absurd, since the mission of the MNF required—and there was—ample liaison between the MNF and the Israelis, including redundant communication nets and established mechanisms for working out operational problems as they arose. Occasionally, as frequently happens when troops of different countries operate in the same area, provocative actions required extreme patience on the part of our Marines, as detailed to me in a long angry letter from General Robert Barrow, Commandant of the Marine Corps. He set out eight instances between January 5 and March 12, 1983, in which the Israeli Defense Forces harassed our forces and those of the UN Truce Supervising Organization. Our Marines exhibited that patience.

Given the magnitude of the Beirut barracks disaster, with 241 American servicemen killed and United States policy in Lebanon reeling from the effects of a bomb-laden truck driven by a suicidal driver against U.S. forces that I did not think should have been there in the first place, I believed that an independent inquiry into what had happened was absolutely necessary. I secured the services of the best man for the job: retired Admiral Robert L. J. Long, who until recently had been serving as our

8. See David Martin and John Walcott, *Best Laid Plans* (New York: Harper & Row, 1988), pp. 138–139.

Commander in Chief, Pacific, and whom I knew well from his work there.

The "DOD Commission on Beirut International Airport Terrorist Act, October 23, 1983" was established by me on November 7, 1983. The Commission quickly became known as the "Long Commission" after its Chairman. He was very ably assisted by four distinguished commissioners—former Navy Undersecretary Robert J. Murray of Harvard, Army Lieutenant General Joseph T. Palastra Jr., retired Marine Lieutenant General Lawrence F. Snowden, and retired Air Force Lieutenant General Eugene F. Tighe Jr.

I told Admiral Long at the outset that although his inquiry would of necessity focus on the tragic events of October 23, 1983, he should not consider himself fettered by tight terms of reference or a restrictive charter. The events themselves dictated that the Long Commission focus on matters such as rules of engagement and the adequacy of security measures, both before and after the attack. Yet I wanted to make certain that the Commission was able to place its specific findings in a context understandable to me, the President, Congress and the American people. For this reason I told Admiral Long that I would neither influence his findings nor limit the scope of his investigation. I also directed that, once the report was finished, the commission produce an unclassified version of its findings for public release, a decision I made without having read the report or even knowing of its conclusions generally.

The publication of the unclassified Long Commission report on December 20, 1983, was itself a bombshell. The Commission's findings placed before the public many of the arguments I had been making privately for well over a year, such as the abysmal inadequacy of using a word such as "presence" as a substitute for a valid and properly equipped military mission, and the nonsensical emphasis on quite inadequate military options as a tool of influence when, in fact, the Lebanese political landscape was cracking beneath our feet.

Naturally, George Shultz and others who had pressed that course of action on the President reacted with anger to the publication of the Commission's findings, claiming that Long had exceeded his brief. Some viewed the Long Commission report as a veiled outlet for my policy disagreements with others, including George Shultz. Since I had created the Commission and given Admiral Long a brief with the widest possible latitude, I was uniquely qualified to reject all such arguments.

The Commission demonstrated its independence by concluding that inadequate rules of engagement had contributed to a sense of laxity within the USMNF; that the USMNF's operational chain of command had failed to correct or amend the USMNF's defensive posture prior to the bombing; that intelligence support to the MNF commander had been inadequate; that the Marine commanders on the ground had failed to take adequate security measures; that post-attack security measures for the USMNF had been inadequate; and that the USMNF had not been trained, organized, staffed or supported to deal effectively with the terrorist threat in Lebanon. Although those criticisms were directed primarily at the operational chain-of-command, they hardly constituted the sort of news that brightens the day of the Secretary of Defense. Had I been inclined to dictate the results of Bob Long's inquiry, I might have begun by taking out all those findings.

As it happened, the proper and useful thing for me to do was to take prompt action on the Commission's recommendations. Within six weeks or so I was able to report progress on a number of fronts. Within the NSC, I was pursuing aggressively the arguments that we must get our men out of the impossible situation that had contributed so much to the tragedy. Within our Department, a single set of Rules of Engagement was implemented for all Marines in Lebanon; the chain of command was shortened and strengthened; the U.S. European Command took an active and creative role in security enhancement measures for the USMNF; Bill Casey and I had begun discussions that would lead to greatly improved intelligence with respect to terrorist threats to United States forces; and steps were taken to improve significantly the antiterrorism capability within all the services. Most of those actions were unclassified, but they were based on our increased knowledge of terrorist tactics and weapons and the development of those weapons and training for our forces.

The work done by Admiral Long and his colleagues has withstood the test of time both in terms of its intellectual honesty and its usefulness as a guide for future action.

There was, of course, one footnote to the Long Commission episode that caused some controversy at the time. The Commission recommended that "the Secretary of Defense take whatever administrative or disciplinary action he deems appropriate, citing the failure of the BLT (Battalion Landing Team) and MAU (Marine Amphibious Units) commanders to take the security measures necessary to preclude the catastropic loss of life in the attack of 23 October 1983." However the President, in his statement of December 27, 1983, took the view that the local commanders, "men who have already suffered quite enough," ought not be punished for not comprehending fully the nature of terrorism. The President, quite manfully, accepted the blame for what had happened.

My own view is that the President was not to blame for whatever people on the ground in Beirut did or failed to do. Our military, very properly, places great emphasis on individual accountability, a view Bob Long took great pains to articulate. By the same token, however, the Long Commission itself went to great lengths to detail the impossible position in which our Marines had been placed by people who had urged the USMNF "presence" mission on the President. This made it difficult for me to use a word like "negligence" to apply only to two Marine colonels. Eventually Secretary Lehman issued nonpunitive letters of instruction[9] to the two commanding officers, a step I regarded as sufficient.

After the October 23 bombing and amid intelligence reports that the Syrians might become "more belligerent," we seemed to be agreed that any Syrian forces that fired on our own should be met with a "vigorous and prompt response." The President was firm in his conviction, however, that our retaliatory measures should be directed only against the forces that actually fired at Americans.

I was in Paris on Friday, December 2, for discussions with the French, when President Reagan, Vice President Bush, Secretary Shultz, General Vessey, Bud McFarlane, and my Deputy at the time, Paul Thayer, met to go over *how* the United States would respond to future attacks. It was correctly decided that General Vessey would draw up specific contingency plans.

Those plans were tested more quickly than expected. The next day the Syrians fired surface-to-air missiles at two of our reconnaissance planes, missing both. President Reagan was at Camp David at the time and shortly thereafter asked me to plan and execute a response. I gave the order to execute at about 9:40 P.M., Paris time.[10]

At dawn on Sunday, Beirut time, 28 bombers from the carriers *Kennedy* and *Independence* struck three Syrian missile launching sites. Two of our planes were shot down. One airman was killed and another, Lieutenant Robert Goodman, was captured.[11] At a

9. A nonpunitive letter of instruction is a letter, placed in an officer's file, that attempts to tell him how to perform his duties better in the future, based on lessons learned from his past.

10. American forces can be sent into action only by the specific order of the Secretary of Defense.

11. On January 4, 1984, Lieutenant Goodman was released by Syrian President Assad to Democratic presidential candidate Jesse Jackson, and shortly thereafter President Reagan invited the flier and Rev. Jackson to a ceremony at the White House.

short press conference that afternoon, President Reagan said that in the future, "if our forces are attacked, we will respond."

On December 14, for the first time since arriving off the coast of Lebanon, the battleship *New Jersey* fired its huge, 16-inch guns at Syrian targets—five minutes after Syrian antiaircraft positions had fired, once again, on our reconnaissance planes.

But those actions were all exercises in futility, because the measures did not have anything to do with "winning," nor, for that matter, was it possible to win our mission there in the first place. That is, the problem with "presence" missions, or missions to separate withdrawing forces, are the forces that *do not* withdraw.

The October 23 bombing of our Marine barracks drove that message home with a terrible vengeance, and it became apparent in the shocked discussions that followed that the President agreed that the mission of the Multinational Force could not be achieved, because of factors totally outside our control. The subsequent four months, however, until the actual departure of the Marines from Beirut, were a period of considerable turmoil: within Lebanon itself, and within our own Government, as arguments continued about withdrawal of the MNF. One school of thought in the United States Government, particularly at the NSC, wanted the United States to step up the military pressure against Syria. My view was that tensions of that sort served no meaningful purpose, since they were not part of any policy initiative.

In December 1983 I had Rich Armitage and his staff begin work on a quiet reassessment of our policy objectives and levers of influence in Lebanon. Not surprisingly, given the situation, the paper was aptly titled, "Strategy for Disengagement in Lebanon." Soon afterward, subcabinet officials from my staff, State, NSC and JCS met "off the record" to admit frankly what some had for so long refused to recognize; namely that we were engaging fruitless tactics in pursuit of unreachable goals. A "non-paper" prepared for President Reagan in late December told him that the May 17 agreement was standing in the way of withdrawal of foreign forces; that the May 17 agreement was virtually useless; and that the solution to the Lebanese crisis was not to be found through a continued or increased employment of American military force.

Finally, at the President's request, I asked the Joint Chiefs, on very short notice, to prepare a plan for withdrawal of our forces. There was, of course, already an emergency evacuation plan, but it obviously needed to be refined before execution.

For whatever reason, the staff of the Joint Chiefs put together a plan that did not provide a timetable for full withdrawal, and some of the other essentials that I felt necessary to protect our people while they were being taken off. The President had made a firm decision that we would withdraw, and told me I was to present the plan to him the next day.

The Chiefs' plan was delayed. I kept asking for it, but I first saw a copy of it in the car going over to the White House. General Ed Tixier, who was the ranking Middle East policy official on Rich Armitage's staff in International Security Affairs, was with me; he too had just received the plan. As I read the paper on the way over to the White House, its lack of specific withdrawal requirements and times became more and more apparent. At the NSPG meeting, at which the Vice President was presiding in the absence of the President, he asked me about the status of the plan and I told the Vice President that I would have it the next morning at 7:30. The Secretary of State, who was still strongly opposed to any withdrawal, also wanted to see the plan, and I advised all of them that I would give it to the Vice President in the morning. On the way back to the Pentagon, General Tixier, who shared my dismay, said that he would get the Joint Staff to rework it. I told him no; that I wanted him to do it, because he understood all of the requirements that I had in mind for a quick and safe withdrawal. He had to work all night to revise the plan, and had typists come in to finish his version at 4:30 in the morning. By 7:00 his version of the plan was finished, and he brought it to me in the office. This one was satisfactorily specific as to full withdrawal and the times needed to accomplish it. All action was to start after the President's final decision. I made a few minor changes and asked the General to send it directly to the Vice President. I also told him that he could leave a copy for the Secretary of State and the Joint Staff, who had heard that I was doing a plan on my own. That was causing great consternation.

Ultimately, the plan that we submitted was approved; and after as much consultation as possible with Italy, France and the UK—all three of which had joined the MNF at our urgent behest—the withdrawal took place, on the predetermined timetable that was part of the approved plan. The fact that the Lebanese Army collapsed at, or about the same time, in its confrontation with Muslim militias was an unfortunate coincidence that had long been anticipated. It was not caused by the departure of the MNF. The last Marines left the beach near their ill-fated airport positions on February 26.

Meanwhile, I had long been committed to a debate at the Oxford Union Society of Oxford University. The subject was "Resolved, there is no moral difference between the foreign policies of the US and the USSR," and my opponent was to be Professor E. P. Thompson, a prominent Marxist (his own designation) Oxford professor.

Our Embassy in London and several others warned me that this was a foolish risk, that such a debate could not be won, and that the loss would be a big story, at least in Europe. However, I felt fully committed by my agreement with the students and went ahead with it, although I had been on my feet in the Union only five minutes when I decided the Embassy was absolutely right.

In any event, we left Andrews late on the evening of February

27, and arrived in London early on the morning of the twenty-eighth, where I immediately launched into a busy day meeting with Ministry Defense officials and those of other agencies.

Although I carried a background book with me on which to base my arguments for the debate, and had been briefed in the Pentagon, I actually had had very little time to prepare because of the Lebanon situation. As our plane was taking off from Andrews, my Assistant, Kay Leisz, was already ensconced in the seat across from me, and I was dictating to her in an effort to get a few arguments and points on cards. The loudness of the engines (this not being our normal plane) particularly on takeoff, was quite deafening, and we both found the process a bit difficult.

In the late afternoon of the twenty-eighth I went to Oxford, and that evening participated in the debate in the historic Oxford Union building, surrounded by portraits of all the prime ministers whose political skills had been honed in the Union. I was also surrounded by a huge crowd of students, well behaved but intensely interested in the proceedings. I tried to sum up all the ways in which our system was superior to the Soviets' by saying at the end of the debate that I hoped the members would vote against the resolution "so that they could come again" to debates like this. After I finished, I was driven back to my hotel in London, without knowing the results; the students could vote until 1:00 or 2:00 in the morning.

I went to sleep immediately. The next morning I had a phone call and a very familiar female voice said: "You know you won, don't you?"

I had not known. But I have always remembered Prime Minister Thatcher's generous thoughtfulness, and her delight that we had won. It was a telephone call I greatly treasured.

Later that day, I flew on to Cyprus, landing at Larnaca. Six of us then took a helicopter to the USS *Guam* to talk to our Marines, who had finally been withdrawn to their ships offshore. With me were my Military Assistant, Major General Colin Powell; Assistant Secretary of Defense for Public Affairs, Mike Burch; Assistant for Security Joe Zaice; Lebanon Country Director Linc Bloomfield; and Commander Sixth Fleet, Vice Admiral Ed Martin.

On the *Guam*, I spoke to Marines in the area below decks and met with the press. I then toured the ship, right down to the boiler room and working up, talking and visiting with the crew members individually.

After the *Guam*, I flew to the USS *Trenton*. Again I toured the ship, talking with many sailors, and then addressed the Marines on deck, with the city of Beirut two or three miles away as a backdrop. Standing along the rail with the Marines were eight rather peaked-looking Army troops from Fort Sill, Oklahoma, who had been operating counter-mortar radars, which our forces had used to defend against shelling from the mountainous area east of the airport.

On both ships, I told our Marines, sailors and soldiers, of my pride in their performance as they had carried out their hopeless task—and of my deep sorrow at our losses. It was a very difficult moment.

My last stop was in Beirut itself. Because President Amin Gemayel was in Damascus that day, I did not make any calls on Lebanese officials. Instead, I walked down the grim streets of the Corniche area in West Beirut, talking with Marine Embassy guards as they stood watch over our "sandbag city." They were very nervous about my peering over the sandbags to get a better look at the area nearby. Then I walked over to meet with the officials at our Embassy. Having been bombed out of our Embassy a year earlier, our diplomats operated out of the British Embassy. There I met with our Ambassador Reginald Bartholomew; the Joint Task Force Commander, Brigadier General Joy; U.S. Defense Attaché, Colonel Fadlo Massabni; and OMC Chief, Colonel Al Baker. Everyone wore flak vests and helmets, since the city had been subjected to random mortar and artillery shelling in recent days. It was a very wise precaution judging from the sound of gunshots, mortars and other fire, which at times were none too distant.

Upon returning to Cyprus, I spoke to the press over the din of the roaring helicopters. We then rejoined the remainder of our traveling party, who had spent a relaxing, and I am told, an enjoyable day in sunny Larnaca.

On the plane ride back to Washington, I found it hard to erase the stark and compelling images of just a few hours before: Marines lifting weights to keep in condition in sandbagged entryways to their dugouts along the Beirut Corniche; the hollow, hunted look in the eyes of our military representatives in the Embassy, going about their business as shells landed at random in their midst; and the silent echo of my own voice addressing a few hundred brave men on the *Trenton*'s deck, bobbing gently up and down in the gathering twilight over Beirut, behind them.

I returned to Andrews that same night or day—arriving at the usual 7:00 in the morning; I went immediately to a long scheduled breakfast with the House Appropriations Committee, and briefed them on my trip; then I testified for four hours to the Committee in support of our budget and about the Lebanon situation.

While the State Department kept alive its unhappiness at our having pulled our forces out, the rest of the world did not attach the negative view that State had worried about, and I felt we had averted another tragedy. The rest of the world appeared to understand the pointlessness of our remaining. The French, Italian and British MNF contingents quietly pulled out shortly thereafter, and conditions in Lebanon remained unchanged—that is, anarchical groups roamed in terrorist fashion all over the country; the Shiites were mainly in control in West and South Beirut; the Israelis remained in control of southern Lebanon, and the Syrians in control of eastern and some of northern Lebanon; and the government's writ shrank until it ran only in a small Christian enclave north of Beirut.

If ever there was an illustration of the Hobbesian view that "life is nasty, brutish and short," Lebanon, sadly, is it.

Yet somehow, the people there continued some form of existence, with the wreckage of smashed buildings all about them and occasional bombs still going off. People struggled through their daily lives, engaged in some rudimentary businesses, and continued to exist. When it came time to change the government, the remnant that was still slightly responsive to the central government was unable to fulfill any of the Lebanese constitutional requirements as to election of a president, and the country was quite literally without an effective head. Unfortunately, by that time positions had deteriorated to the extent that most Lebanese did not even knew whether there was a head of government or not, nor did it make any particular difference to the lives of the individuals there.

There were and are many other issues involving the Middle East, the most promising of which, of course, is the possibility that Iran, having sued for peace as a result of its inability to close the Gulf and block peaceful commerce by intimidation or attack in that area, will eventually reach a settlement in its long and bloody war with the Iraqis.[12]

But Lebanon will, in my mind, always stand as a major reproach to me because I was not more persuasive, in all the meetings we held, to prevent the worst loss of military lives to occur during the time I was at the Pentagon.

I perhaps felt this most keenly and immediately at the rain-soaked memorial service for the dead Marines at Camp LeJeune, South Carolina on December 7, 1983.

12. The topic is discussed more fully in Chapter 13 on the Persian Gulf.

The President and Nancy attended, and after the outdoor service on a grassy knoll at the Camp, visited with and personally comforted each of the families, many of whom were weeping uncontrollably. That too was a time I will never forget.

This was particularly difficult for the President, but it was clear to me, as I witnessed the responses and the changed expressions, that he had brought some very real comfort and consolation to almost all of the families.

In the end, our forces had responded to a country and a people in real need; we had helped them while giving diplomacy a real chance to untangle a political conflict; and our forces had exhibited courage, loyalty and complete professionalism for the many long months it took their superiors in Washington to face the unhappy truth that the second MNF was a sad and grievous error.

VI

Libya

*I*n 1981 Libya had been under the command and complete domination for twelve years of Muammar al-Qaddafi, one of the strangest heads of state in the world.

Qaddafi is a theatrically posturing, fake mystic, with a considerable dollop of madness thrown in. Rumors have long circulated in intelligence circles that he suffers from an incurable venereal disease, and that the disease accounts for occasional bouts of madness exhibiting hysteria, braggadocio and extreme theatricalism. However, those stories have never been authenticated. And from time to time, intelligence sources at home and abroad have reported that his military, or at least the top echelons of his military, were basically against him, but could do little in view of his complete domination of all other aspects of Libyan government. The closed societies that are a feature of small military dictatorships obviously resist analysis. One finds it difficult to be completely sure of what is happening; but I recall many reports, during the Reagan Administration, of the execution or self-exile of several high-ranking Libyan officers.

Libya has substantial oil and gas revenues; but it is a very poor country, because its revenues are devoted largely to Qaddafi's various extravagances, and to very large—but largely ineffective—expenditures on its military. In short, Libya was one of the newly rich oil countries in which the average citizen not only did not benefit from the oil revenues, but very greatly suffered during their influx. At the food stores, lines were long and supplies short; housing, education and health services for the average citizen were such that most westerners would not tolerate them. Libya is no longer so newly oil rich; but its so-called "quality of life" remains exceedingly low.

Qaddafi had long maintained claims, insupportable under international law, that he controlled the entire Gulf of Sidra, the great body of Mediterranean water that lies between Tripoli and Benghazi north of Libya, and that everything within that Gulf should be considered Libyan territory. He also claimed that Libyan territorial jurisdiction extended northward an indefinite number of miles beyond what even Libya defined as the Gulf of Sidra.

Our Mediterranean fleet for many years had maneuvered and exercised in all those international waters now claimed by Qaddafi. I felt it was vital that we continue to do so; that we not give any credence to the Libyan claim of jurisdiction over the Gulf. Such a claim, if honored, would have serious precedent for other bodies of international water around the world. Our forbearing to go into territories Qaddafi baselessly claimed as his own would signal that his absurd claims were being taken seriously.

Thus, when Qaddafi issued a specific warning that he would destroy any American naval units or planes inside—that is, south of—the 32°–30 minutes line in the Gulf of Sidra (roughly the northern line of the Gulf of Sidra), I concluded that we would have to ignore those claims, and continue our planned exercises for that region. Qaddafi now had to decide whether to take active measures to try to deny us our right to exercise and move freely in the international maritime areas he claimed as his own, or be recognized internationally for what he actually was—an empty braggart easily able to make threats, but able to do little more than indulge in an overflow of rhetoric, or use his oil revenues to employ terrorists to try to carry out his threats.

Our naval maneuvers in 1981 called for various firing and other exercises above the 32–30 line, but our plans also required that carrier borne naval aircraft fly over the Gulf of Sidra area as part of their normal patrolling and protection of the carriers. I made it clear to the Joint Chiefs in our regular weekly meetings, and in individual discussions with the Chairman, that I did not wish our plans modified, either in response to Qaddafi's threats or indeed for any purpose.

Thus it came about that on the night of August 18, 1981, we had two navy F-14s in the air south of the 32°–30 minutes line when they were challenged by two Libyan fighter planes—Soviet made SU-22s. Our pilots responded to Libyan warnings by telling them we were in international waters. Then one of the Libyan planes fired on our planes and the other was locking its radar onto our F-14s. Our pilots responded immediately, each firing an AIM 9-L, a heat seeking missile, with a high degree of skill. The result was that both Libyan planes were shot down into the Mediterranean. Their pilots were rescued, but in one short and decisive action lasting probably between 30 and 40 seconds, we had told the Libyans, and the world, that we rejected any claim or threat that the Gulf of Sidra was within the territorial waters of Libya, and that we were going to treat those waters and the air above them as we always had—as being open.

We had demonstrated not only a greatly increased American resolve, but also a greatly increased American capability for dealing with the enemy quickly and decisively. That alone did more to reassure our allies than any budget amounts we were committed to spend, or any amount of rhetoric, no matter how well delivered.

The reaction was immediate and for the most part extraordinarily favorable, with only a few voices being raised to express their dismay that there actually had been shots fired. Those first shots, of course, came from the Libyans; and our two planes, legally and properly in international airspace, could have been destroyed had we not responded as quickly and effectively as we had.

All of this action took place the night of a day, August 18, on which I had returned from Los Angeles; there, in the Century Plaza Hotel, I had made long presentations to the President toward saving our Defense budget, then under attack by the Office of Management and Budget (OMB) and the White House staff. After those discussions and lunch with the President, I had flown back to Andrews, arriving about 11:00. I was buoyed by the President's continued support for Defense budget increases and by his birthday call to my plane, and by a fine birthday cake prepared by Air Force personnel assigned to the plane.

I turned in about 1:00, after packing for a long-planned trip to London, on which I was to depart the following evening. (I knew there would be little time to pack during the day, with a trip to Philadelphia and many other meetings scheduled for both the morning and the afternoon of August 19.) But almost immediately after I went to bed, reports of an action in the Mediterranean started coming in to me by secure telephone calls from General Phil Gast, at that time Director of Operations for the Joint Staff of our three services. We had had earlier routine reports from the fleet of our planes taking off, and reports of other aspects of the naval maneuver. Those and later reports were received in the Pentagon, and I was notified immediately by a secure phone to my home many times during that night.

I kept in touch directly with Ed Meese, the President's co-

Chief of Staff, who had remained in California with the President, and with Bill Clark, acting Secretary of State. After the decisive action, I suggested to Ed that he notify the President.

Just a day or two before, in response to a question from me based on the possibility that the Libyans might indeed shoot at our planes or ships, the President specifically authorized us to "shoot 'em down if they fire first."

Ed now said that he felt there was no need to notify the President, since that would have involved awakening him at about midnight (Pacific time), and since anyhow it appeared that the action was over. He asked me to let him know if any further developments occurred.

I told Ed that there might be further events, since some of the Navy people had suggested canceling the rest of the air-naval exercise and pulling our ships back well north of any of the lines claimed by Qaddafi. I told him I had vetoed the idea at once, on the ground that if we did that, the Libyans—despite what had occurred in the area—would be able to claim that they had driven us off and forced us to stop our planned exercise. Ed did not demur, and I continued to monitor the action during what was left of the night. Nothing further occurred except that our planes made frequent trips into Qaddafi's claimed waters without any reaction whatever from Libyan aircraft. We were able to observe that the Libyan pilots had been picked up by their rescue squads. We penetrated the airspace frequently with other reconnaissance flights during the night, but again with no reaction from the Libyans. After 4:00 in the morning, the reports from the area showed no activity at all taking place there. That phase of our maneuvers had been completed.

I continued to keep in close touch with White House staff and with Ed Meese in California.

I went to the office early and received a full debriefing of the night's activities, talked with Ed Meese again so that he would have full data before the morning staff meetings at the "western

White House." Our press office also had been in touch with the White House press office in order to coordinate their briefings.

Then at 7:45 I had a press conference in the Pentagon briefing room, to give the press all the data we had, including later reports from our pilots and reconnaissance planes. I remember the first question from the press: "Was our being there in any way a provocation to them?"

A: "No . . . these are international waters."

And later, **Q:** "You said that they [United States pilots] carried out their mission extremely well. It seemed as though [sic] you are almost proud of the way—"

A: "I don't think it's necessary to do any amateur psycho-analysis at this time. . . . The mission of the planes was to fly patrol, and if attacked, if fired upon, to respond. That's exactly what they did, and I would say again, without leaving myself open to any other interpretations, that I think they carried out their mission extremely well."

I then had breakfast with Bill Clark, who was as delighted as I with the performance of our military.

For a long time, I had had scheduled a talk that morning (August 19) to the annual convention of the Veterans of Foreign Wars in Philadelphia. So after the breakfast, I went to the Pentagon helipad and took a helicopter to Andrews, and from there a small Air Force plane to Philadelphia. Although the press and television had been carrying reports of the action since my early morning press conference, many at the convention had not heard about it, so I gave the delegates a report of all that had happened.

The hall exploded with the most enthusiastic applause I had heard in a long time; it was clear that our decisive and continuing action, and our refusal to be intimidated by threats from Qaddafi, was an extremely popular course with the VFW. I believed too that the country as a whole felt our actions were necessary, and welcomed them.

Early in my talk, I mentioned two lessons I hoped we had

learned from Vietnam: "If a war is not serious enough for us to have to win it, it is not serious enough to enter it"; and "I hope and believe that we will never again become involved in another war unless we mean to win it. We inflicted a heavy blow on our youth when we asked them to fight in a war that we did not intend to win."

This was also very well received.

I then flew back to Washington, to preside at a Defense Resources Board meeting and to report to it on my budget discussion in California. The Defense Resources Board was, as always, faced with more requests from the services than it could fund. So it was vital that its members know as soon as possible how our budget request would fare. So far all seemed to be well, but there were more budget meetings scheduled for the following week in Santa Barbara; and at those there would be more arguments and pleas from OMB for me to agree to cuts in the President's original budget proposals. Ed Meese, almost alone of the White House staff, supported my opposition to those arguments.

On the night of August 19, after quite a long day in Washington and Philadelphia, I flew overnight to London for long-scheduled meetings with the Defense Ministry and other officials, all of whom seemed impressed and pleased with the Gulf of Sidra demonstration of our military capabilities and with our resolve.

On August 26, after I returned from Europe, I reported on all this to the President at his hilltop ranch above Santa Barbara. It was evident how much he loved that property, with its superb views and its rugged trails and brush covered country, and its simple early California cabin. Seated at a rustic mission style table, with the jeans-clad President clearly very happy, we discussed the Defense budget of the United States. It was evident that the President had not wavered from his recognition of the need to rebuild our defenses as quickly as possible. And the results our pilots had obtained over the Gulf of Sidra had strengthened his resolve.

I mentioned to the President the suggestion that had been made to me about our Libyan encounter: that after the aerial combat we should have terminated the exercise. I told him I had directed otherwise. The President strongly approved what had been done, and felt that our action that night was a turning point, that now both our friends and enemies realized that they had a very much different America to deal with, an America that was stronger, better and a more reliable ally, and a country that would not be intimidated or diverted by threats from people like Qaddafi.

We would learn of more such threats in years to come from intelligence sources. Still others would be made publicly: His March 28, 1986, threat calling on "all Arab people to attack anything American" was issued as a formal statement from Libya.

Also in March 1986, Qaddafi repeated his 1981 attempts to close off the international waters of the Gulf of Sidra. In fact, Qaddafi renamed the area in and above the Gulf of Sidra "the Zone of Death," and again vowed to destroy any American ships or planes that penetrated it. He had also deployed Soviet-made SA-5s—long-range antiaircraft missiles—and SA-2s, all capable of hitting our aircraft flying in international waters below the 32°–30 minutes line.

Since 1981, we had continued our regularly planned naval exercises designed to keep the Navy fit and experienced with various kinds of activities in which they might have to engage. Some of those plans called for our ships and planes to be within that "Zone of Death" from time to time.

This time there was very little discussion within the National Security Council whether we should or should not carry out our exercise plans. There were some who felt that if we did so in the face of Qaddafi's threats, our acts would be "provocative" and might disturb some of our allies; but those views were not pressed with any vigor. At the March 14, 1986, National Security Planning Group (NSPG) meeting, the President decided that our exercises should proceed as planned, including south of the 32 −30 line.

So we issued the usual notices of our naval air exercise, defining the areas in the international waters where we would be operating. They are the regular "Notice to Airmen and Mariners" that we use as formal statements of the Government. This particular "NOTAM" (Notice to Airmen and Mariners) was issued on March 21, 1986, and set forth our long-planned exercise. This was the nineteenth naval exercise we had done in the area since 1981, and it was the eighth in which we operated below, inside, Qaddafi's "line of death."

The redefined Rules of Engagement—which are, in effect, the "charter" for our ship and plane captains when they operate in foreign waters—were issued to Admiral Frank B. Kelso II, then Commander of our Sixth Fleet in the Mediterranean. Especially given that Libyan or Soviet missiles can cover so many miles in just a few seconds, our commanders in the field must have full authority, within broad basic guidelines, to take any action they think necessary to protect themselves and to enable them to complete their assignment, without asking Washington or other headquarters for permission to take responsive actions.

These rules of engagement had been approved by the President earlier. They provided that if there were some indications of hostile intent by Libyan ships or planes in the areas where we had told the Libyans and others our naval exercises were to be held, then *all* Libyans present would be presumed to be hostile, and our ships and planes were to open fire. That decision seemed quite reasonable in view of the many statements by Qaddafi of Libyan intent to destroy any ship they wished south of the 32–30 line.

I was quite sure that this time the Libyans would try to carry out some of their threats, and I knew that various interpretations could be put on Rules of Engagement, no matter how carefully drawn. So I decided to discuss the matter with Admiral Kelso.

We met in my hotel in London when I was on my way back from a NATO meeting. I began by saying "Admiral, I know that no matter how carefully and precisely we may try to draft orders and Rules of Engagement, there always can be different interpretations, and even different means that can be given to the Rules. So I wanted you to know exactly what I had in mind with these Rules, and wanted to give us an opportunity to discuss them so that in the end there should be no differences in our views."

"That's unusual, but I appreciate it," said Admiral Kelso.

"First of all," I went on, "we must have the freedom to go wherever we wish on open, international seas. But as you know, the Libyans have openly threatened to block us from doing that, and in fact Qaddafi has said he will destroy us.

"Now, I signed these new Rules because I want you to have the maximum freedom to do whatever you have to do to enable us to move freely on the open waters."

Admiral Kelso nodded, thought a moment, and then he said, "I believe that if any of our aircraft cross Qaddafi's so-called 'line of death' as part of our maneuvers, the Libyans will fire their SA-5s at us. I take it that would show 'hostile intent,' " he said with a slow smile.

"Indeed it would," I said. "That would be a clear and unmistakable sign of intent; that is about as hostile as you get.

"As a result," I continued, "under those circumstances you would be free to fire on any and all Libyan forces in international waters. That is what is new about these Rules, and Admiral, I want you to know—and that is why I wanted to meet with you here—that I will back and support you to the full in any action *you* feel you have to take."

I added, "I understand there may be losses on our side, and I know you will do all you can to minimize these. But most of all, I want you to know that it is extremely important that Qaddafi not be allowed either to intimidate us or to carry out any of his threats."

I concluded, "I know you are going to be sailing into a difficult and dangerous situation, and my intent and the intent of the Rules of Engagement are that you should do what you feel is necessary to complete all our planned exercises: No one is to be allowed to prevent that, and I will support you fully on any judgment you may make as to when hostile intent is shown. You have full authority to act as you see fit after you make such a finding. And now tell me if there is anything else you need."

"No," he said, "I think I have all I need, and your instructions are very clear and most helpful. It was a good idea to meet like this."

Admiral Kelso is not a man who wastes words, and he said little else then. He is a man who inspires great confidence. I felt very comfortable and grateful that he was in command during the encounters with Libya; and that is why I would be most delighted later to have the President's and our NATO allies' approval of my recommendation that he be named Commander-in-Chief of the Atlantic Command.

And too, that is why I would especially appreciate Admiral Kelso's coming up to me on July 4, 1986, on board the USS *Iowa* at the big Fourth of July Celebration in New York, to say, "I want you to know how much that talk we had in London encouraged and—yes—inspired me."

I told him again what superb leadership he had given to the fleet in the engagements it would indeed experience with the Libyans.

My revisions of the Rules of Engagement, and my meeting with Admiral Kelso, turned out to be fortunate precautions, because this time the Libyan reaction was rather extensive—but far more devastating to them than their previous attempts to keep us out of international waters.

In short, the Libyans confirmed Admiral Kelso's predictions. They fired their USSR-provided SA-5s first, at 7:52 A.M. Eastern time on March 24, 1986, when the first two of their new SA-5 missiles were fired from the site at Sirte at our aircraft, which were flying in the Gulf of Sidra as part of normal patrols with the ships, but below the 32°–30 minutes line. Those missiles missed.

Late in the morning, but before we started firing back, two Libyan MiG-25s (Soviet-made fighter planes) approached our patrol aircraft; but they were intercepted by our pilots and turned back. No other Libyan planes left the airspace over Libyan land during the rest of our exercise. The only Libyan aircraft that were airborne were operating well south of the Mediterranean, over the desert in the central and southern portions of Libya, where there were no other aircraft. Some of those Libyan Air Force planes often misrepresented their positions to their own air traffic controllers in an attempt to show they were still engaging our pilots!

Two more SA-5 missiles were fired at our forces during the morning, and an additional SA-2 missile; but again they scored no hits.

At about 2:30 that afternoon, March 24, one of our carrier-based A6 planes destroyed a Libyan fast-missile patrol boat that was approaching some of our naval units in the area.

Later that afternoon other carrier-based American planes put the Libyan radars at the SA-5 site out of action.

At 4:15 that same afternoon we attacked another Soviet-made Libyan missile boat approaching our naval forces and sent it back to its port heavily damaged. And then at 7:00, when one of the SA-5 missile sites was found to be emitting radar waves and trying to lock onto our planes, two more of our carrier planes attacked the SA-5 site.

After that, the Libyans ceased all threatening actions and removed their ships—their planes were, of course, long since gone—and our exercise was not further disturbed.

We gave very exhaustive press briefings during this response (and our earlier responses) to Libyan attacks on our planes. While the questions from the reporters were often hostile (seeming to indicate a strong desire to find the United States somehow at fault), I was determined to let the American people know of the attacks on our properly conducted naval exercise in open international waters.

Frequently, the penalty for holding press conferences very close to the actual event was that we did not yet have full information; but we knew the interest of the press in being informed of results immediately. We tried to caution that some of the reports we had might have to be changed as later information from the pilots and the fleets came in. Nonetheless, there was frequent criticism whenever we came up with information at a subsequent briefing that was slightly different from that furnished immediately after the event. Sometimes our first reports showed that a ship had been destroyed; later we saw it limping toward a Libyan port. Sometimes it worked the other way: A ship that we believed had been damaged would turn out to have been hit so severely that it sank shortly thereafter.

Qaddafi now turned to the use of terrorism to try to secure some advantage and escape from the continued humiliation he suffered as the world perceived how idle were his threats, and unequal his courage, for taking any military action to match his words.

On March 28, 1986, three days after his heavy losses caused by his threats to our naval forces, Qaddafi put out his formal statement encouraging "all Arab people" to attack anything American, "be it an interest, goods, ship, plane or a person." On April 5 a Libyan bomb, placed by Libyan-employed terrorists, exploded in a West Berlin establishment, the La Belle Discotheque, killing an American serviceman and a Turkish woman and injuring 230 people, among them some fifty American military personnel.

We had had many internal discussions within the NSPG and with the President as to the course we would follow if we could ever identify a terrorist or a group of terrorists who had carried out an attack on us or on one of our allies. A number of people, particularly in the State Department, supported what is called an "unfocused" response; that is, an immediate retaliatory action, such as bombing a Syrian or Iranian city if we believed the terrorist act originated there. I always argued against that simple "revenge" approach, as did the President. He very much opposed anything that could hurt or kill innocent people. So we, the President and I, had agreed that we would make a "focused" response whenever we identified and located a terrorist; that is, a response appropriate to the terrorist action, and a response that had as its aim the discouragement of any country or any person using terrorism from ever doing it again. On December 28, 1985, following early indications that Libya was behind the terrorist attacks at the Rome and Vienna airports, we also had begun contingency planning against possible targets in Libya.

When I first received the reports of the Berlin bombing, I was on my plane on a trip to one of our regular consultative meetings with our Korean ally and visits to some of our other Pacific friends. I took the message, as it was handed to me from the communications officer on the plane, straight to Rich Armitage, who was working on briefing papers for the rest of our Pacific trip. I asked him, "Is this finally our smoking gun?"

He read it carefully, and sent off signals to Washington asking for additional details and intelligence assessments. A short time later he told me, "I believe this *is* indeed a smoking gun. We know Qaddafi has done this."

In short, this time we had our proof. And so we decided to give the focused response to terrorism that we had always planned to deliver when our proof was clear. Essentially, it consisted (after the Joint Chiefs, working with Will Taft, the Deputy Secretary, went over and recommended staff-prepared detailed plans) of an attack on various Libyan targets associated with the terrorism. Those included terrorist training grounds, the headquarters where their command and control was located (which happened to be part of Qaddafi's personal compound), airfields and aircraft on the ground that had been, or could be, used for additional terrorist acts. The purpose of our plan was to teach Qaddafi and others the lesson that the practice of terrorism would not be free of cost to themselves; that indeed they would pay a terrible price for practicing it.

All that involved very careful and coordinated joint planning. The main attack would be delivered by Air Force F-111 fighter-bombers based in Britain, and by many carrier-based attack planes from our carriers in the Mediterranean.[1] We would also need aircraft for reconnaissance, and search and rescue missions (which would come by Navy carriers in the fleet); and Libyan radars would have to be disabled before the bombers went in, also by planes from our Mediterranean fleet; and additionally the fleet would provide aerial damage assessments following the raid. The coordination and logistics required for such an attack are formidable. We would have more than one hundred planes involved, and many would have to come from great distances. Their activities would have to be coordinated to the split second to get the bombers from Britain and the Navy pilots over their targets with as much tactical surprise as possible immediately following the destruction of the Libyan radars.

Many reports and rumors were published saying that we were planning activities of some kind to respond to the Libyan bomb-

---

1. The F-111s were used because they could drop two-thousand-pound laser-guided bombs at night, thus giving us both the accuracy to avoid collateral damage *and* the destructive power to inflict maximum damage on the Libyan targets. The Navy planes alone could not deal with all five primary targets.

ing of the Berlin restaurant, but it still would be possible and highly desirable to achieve tactical surprise; and that we were able to do. I reviewed the plans several times, in Asia and on the way home, by means of a secure voice telephone call to Will Taft, who had been meeting with the Joint Chiefs and the President in the Oval Office. Will reported that the President was anxious to do the attack as soon as all was ready, but that he was always most insistent that each target be clearly associated with the Libyan-employed, Libyan-trained terrorists, and that we take all possible precautions to avoid any casualties or danger to civilians. The President particularly applauded the Joint Chiefs' plan that required any pilot who might have any malfunction, or who was not sure of hitting his assigned target, to abort his mission, and not to drop his bombs at random. I repeatedly urged that we have more than enough resources to assure full damage to all terrorist targets.

This was another of the many times that events and crises refused to stay in separate boxes, or to confine themselves to single countries.

I had been in Korea, Japan, Thailand, the Philippines and Australia from April 1 to April 13. During a very large part of that time, on the plane and otherwise when we were not engaged in the always hectic and tightly packed ground schedules for such trips, I was working with Rich Armitage and talking with Will Taft, refining the plans to respond to the Libyan acts of terrorism in Berlin.

I recall that while in Australia we had to delay a meeting with the Australian Foreign Minister (Bill Haydon, now Governor-General) and our own Ambassador, Bill Lane, my good friend from California, while I went over the plans by secure phone calls, and discussed with the Joint Chiefs how best to carry out, with minimum risk to our forces, the focused response the President had ordered. I was also very concerned with the efforts that were being made to secure British approval for the use of our facilities there, and French permission to fly over French air space.

I also had in mind the President's long-standing worries about any attacks we might have to make that could cause "collateral damage"; that is, damage to civilian or nonmilitary targets. We wanted the attack to hit only Libyan sites that were associated with or part of their terrorist activities.

Full discussion of all such matters required lengthy secure phone calls to Will Taft in Washington, many of which were made, in this case, from Ambassador Lane's private study in the beautiful Georgian-style American Embassy residence in Canberra.

During these calls Rich Armitage stationed himself at the door and blocked all attempts to enter, including even those attempts of the Ambassador to remind me of my next engagement, while I went over all the details of the plan.

It was not until much later that we were able to reveal the substance of all those secure calls while the Australians and our Ambassador were awaiting our meetings.

I arrived back at Andrews from that trip on Sunday morning, April 13 at 7:00, having spent most of the last long leg from Sydney going over attack plans against Libya, and all the things that could go wrong, and what we might do in each such instance, and indeed whether we had covered all possible contingencies. At 3:00 that afternoon I convened a meeting with Will Taft and our military commanders in the Pentagon to go over the military aspects of the plan once more, and returned home at about 8:00 for one of my wife's special dinners. She is rightly regarded as one of Washington's premier chefs, and she outdid herself that night.

There had been frequent reports to the President of the sufficiency of the plans, the adequacy of our forces, and the risks that were inevitably involved, including the precautions we were taking to avoid civilian damage and to concentrate on targets that we knew from our intelligence were directly associated with Libyan terrorist activities. By this time we knew that, thanks to the President's personal calls to the Prime Minister, the British had agreed that our F-111s based in Britain could be used in the attack. We also knew that the French had refused us permission for the F-111s to fly over French air space. In what seemed a typical, but still infuriating action, President François Mitterrand gave us some gratuitous advice as to how to conduct the raid—"Don't inflict a mere pinprick," he said, advising that we inflict heavy damage—but not to use French air space. By the time we received that guidance, our plans were long since complete. It would not be a pinprick.

The President was most actively engaged in the whole process, and made the final decisions about which targets we would hit. As always, we had secondary priority targets planned in case weather or other factors prevented us from attacking primary targets.

Of the five targets, the President chose four that had direct terrorist connections, and added a fifth to protect our forces.

1. The facilities at Murrat Sidi Bilal were known to be a swimmers/commando training school.
2. The Azziziyah barracks were the command, control and communications center for Libya's terrorist related activities.
3. The Tripoli International Airfield had Libya's IL-76/CANDID large transport planes and also was identified as a terrorist logistics "node."
4. The Benghazi barracks housed many of Qaddafi's elite guards, and others involved in terrorist activities.
5. The Benina Airfield was not directly tied to terrorist activity, but was targeted to ensure that the Libyan air defense forces did not intercept our strike forces.

The President's goal was to preempt, or disrupt, and discourage further Libyan operations abroad and to teach Qaddafi a lesson that the practice of state-sponsored terrorism carried a high cost.

We proceeded throughout this operation greatly supported and buoyed by the knowledge that we were carrying out the President's policies—the primary, and really the only, mission of the Pentagon.

Our action had been planned so that the bombs would hit the targets in Libya at 2:00 A.M., Libyan time. On Monday afternoon, April 14, we began the delicate but vital process of notifying the congressional leadership. They gathered in the new Situation Room, ordered by the NSC staff, in the Old Executive Building. The congressional reaction was somewhat muted. There was some grumbling, and there were many questions about the operational details of the attack. In the interest of telling the full story, we even advised our audience of the time the attack would go in. The possible lack of wisdom in our being so candid was demonstrated when a senior member of Congress emerged from the briefing to tell reporters that he could not say anything, but they should turn on their television sets about 6 P.M.

The long flight of the F-111s, from Britain, made many hours longer by Mitterrand's refusal to let us use French air space, required four refuelings, all at night, with radio silence. The refuelings occurred near the French coast, then Spain, then at a point just north of Algeria, and one final time, before the attack, north of Tunisia. Refueling an aircraft always seems a spectacularly risky affair to this former foot soldier, although the Air Force constantly dismisses it as a simple matter. But to do it at night, with no radio contact permitted, is indeed a tricky business for anyone. We were enormously proud: of the skills of our bomber crews for the very long fourteen hour trip down from England, detouring around France, and back again; of the carrier-based planes, each with only a few moments over the target, for the skill with which they all carried out their assignments. Special words of praise need also to be added for the refueling tankers, the AWACS crews, which included Air Force women, and indeed everyone who took part.

We started getting reports shortly after the planes took off from Britain; but eager though we were to know all the details, I gave orders that we should not harass unduly the people conducting the operation, with requests for more and more information. As a result, there were long and agonizing periods when we heard nothing, primarily because there was nothing to report.

About an hour before midnight in Libya, which was 5 P.M. in Washington, I went directly from the briefings for the congressional leadership, in the Old Executive Office Building, to the Situation Room in the Pentagon—there to receive the reports directly, as they were coming in from our various headquarters and from the carriers. Admiral William Crowe, the Chairman of the Joint Chiefs, Rich Armitage and I went to a small room off the Pentagon's Situation Room, where General Richard Burpee, the Air Force officer who was then Director of Operations for the Joint Staff, was receiving reports. But so well had our security held that the regular watch officers, seated just outside, were quite astonished to see the Chairman and the Secretary walk through the watch room into the small crisis room.

The first reports were uniformly good, and we were able to follow the action quite carefully. Shortly after the first bombs went in at 2:00 A.M., Libyan time, radio and television reports began to issue from reporters located in Libya. Thus we had another source from which we could track the progress of our raids.

"Feet wet" is the terminology pilots used to indicate that the planes had completed their assignment over the target and were on their way back. Those came in in encouraging numbers; except that about an hour after the attack, there was still one of our fighter bombers not reporting "feet wet." We kept up hope for that plane all night, hoping that perhaps there had been a radio or other communication problem preventing the word's getting through. Finally, at the end of the next day, we had to acknowledge that the plane had probably gone down in the water.

At 9:15 the night of the attack, I held a joint briefing for the White House Press Corps with George Shultz. Using a lecturer's pointer and a map perched on an easel, I showed the route of the bombers from England, and the long detour required by President Mitterrand's refusal to let us fly over France. I declined the offer, by way of several press questions, to criticize Mitterrand. But of course, everyone connected with the attack was furious with both his casual refusal (based, in my judgment, on his fears of domestic political problems), combined with his "advice" that we hit the Libyans very hard. But at the press conference, and so as not to add any fuel to our unhappiness with the French reaction, I simply let the map tell the story of the greatly added risk to our pilots that Mitterrand's refusal had caused us. The contrast to Mrs. Thatcher's agreement to let the bombers go from England could not have been more marked.

The last reports were in, and, except for the one missing F-111, all planes were back or on their way before 9 P.M. Washington time.

Later the Libyans frequently claimed that they had recovered the one plane that went down, and its crew, but they never proved that. They did return the body of one pilot, Fernando Ribas, to the United States, in January 1989. That long delay, and the Libyans' continued silence as to the other pilot, typifies the way that government acts.

The results of the raid were extremely impressive, but guided alone by newspaper accounts, the innocent reader would be pardoned in thinking that the only thing that had happened was that one of our planes released one bomb early and hit an apartment house near the French Embassy, and near an intelligence connected building.[2] That did indeed happen, but one accidental miscue in an operation of that complexity seemed to me to be fully excusable. Another story widely reported was that some allegedly adopted child or children of Qaddafi's had been killed or injured during the attack. That claim was, and is to this day, completely unverified, and was based only on highly suspect Libyan reports;[3] yet virtually every story about our raid accepted without question Qaddafi's statements that that event had happened.

We took enormous precautions in our planning to avoid any so-called collateral damage—meaning, of course, damage to those not responsible for the terrorist act. As I have said, the concern about collateral damage and injuries to civilians weighed heavily with the President whenever we talked about any retaliatory measures. I believe it is a proper ground for worry, and through holding to that belief I was frequently called "too cautious." Without that concern, however, we could have been criticized correctly as "brutal" or "reckless." Fear of criticism cannot be the basis for making decisions. Our Libyan plans were very carefully drawn to do everything we could to prevent any collateral damage. We knew, however, that almost inevitably a bomb or two would go astray. A raid flown by young pilots at an altitude of 200 feet at night, over a city in an environment with intense antiaircraft and surface-to-air missile defenses, in which only one bomb went astray, is a remarkable feat. It was a bit like picking out a specific building in Washington, D.C., with strict orders not to hit any other. We had no target practice areas available like that, and in the nature of things, could not have.

Naturally Libya, and those opposed to our attack, made the most of our one miscue. Also, there seemed to be far more

2. Ironically, the intelligence building had been proposed as a target, but had been rejected by the President because it was too close to the civilian apartment building.

3. One reporter told me that the only source he had heard was Qaddafi's doctor.

emphasis in many reports on alleged injuries to those various alleged adopted "children of Qaddafi" than to the real aspects and results of the attack. These were our efforts to respond to the proven use of terrorism by Libya, and to try to let them know what a terrible price they had to pay for using terrorism, and would have to pay if they used it again. These were some of the circumstances that led me in the press briefing on the night of the raid and after the attack, when all of our planes but one were on their way back to England or to their carriers, to state that the action was a complete success, and that all objectives had been achieved. The real point of the raid, as Admiral Kelso said later, was that we had "the will to act against terrorism, and the noise and blast of the bombs sent the message clearly."

All actions of that kind are not only immensely complex, but are subject to all manner of events that cannot be predicted, no matter how carefully, or for how long, the action is planned. Since bad news appears to be the most newsworthy aspect of any event, it is, I suppose, understandable that the press will concentrate most heavily on reporting any adverse aspects to an activity. But that emphasis makes it more difficult for the public to understand what really happened. This was to happen in Grenada; and it happened in connection with the Libyan raid. The fact of an attack of that magnitude on a country that had practiced terrorism without hindrance in the past, was of course a major news event, but the one plane that was lost, and the one bomb that fell short in the hundred plane raid, drew far more attention than the positive and skillful results achieved.

In any event, the surest way to measure the success of an enterprise is to ask whether it achieved its objectives. Our objective here was to end Qaddafi's belief that he could use terrorism without cost. That was accomplished, thanks to some very able and brave people who undertook the action for us all.

Qaddafi, in common with a number of braggarts, appears to be more than a bit of a coward personally. He slept in a different place almost every night; and when we attacked his command and control headquarters, a quite legitimate and very necessary military target, we had no idea whether or not he was in residence that particular night at the adjacent tent. Amazingly enough, that we destroyed part of his tent in the attack on the command and control units seems to many commentators to be another basis for attacking our raid.

The fact is even with my rigid instructions to avoid "collateral damage" as much as possible, and my consequent requirement that all aircraft be "fully operational" before dropping any bombs, which caused some of our aircraft to turn away just before reaching their targets (even though they would have dropped their bombs nearby in the absence of my instructions), because of relatively minor technical malfunctions, and despite the extreme difficulty of the mission, the raid did indeed accomplish its assigned mission.

Here are the *real* results of the attack: The Sidi Bilal military complex was severely damaged. The Azziziyah barracks received substantial damage. The Tripoli International Airport was hit hard, and the five IL-76/CANDID heavy transport aircraft on the apron were destroyed. The Benghazi barracks were hit and a warehouse in the complex, involved in MIG assembly, was destroyed. At the Benina Airfield many planes were damaged or destroyed, including at least four MIGs; but most important, the Libyans were unable to launch planes from the airport during, or immediately after, the attack.

Perhaps the most dramatic evidence of our success came from the actual in-flight films provided us by the Air Force lead pilot for the Tripoli Military Airfield target. The film showed the rapidly moving terrain and gave a very real sense of the extreme difficulty in maneuvering at 200 feet above the ground and 500 miles per hour in the dark. As the pilot found the target—a large apron upon which sat the large Soviet-built military transports

—the camera zoomed in. You could clearly see the laser-guided bombs release and home in on the target, and then the entire apron disappear in a huge cloud of smoke as the bombs obliterated the Soviet transports. I took that tape to the White House and showed it to the President, and later released it to the press.

Several days after the action, we had the flight leaders from both the Air Force and the Navy flown in to the Pentagon for debriefing. The Air Force Flight Leader—an outstanding young Lieutenant Colonel—told us that because of the requirement to maintain radio silence for the entire mission out of England (fourteen hours en route the Mediterranean), he had no way of telling if the mission would succeed. He made his final turn to begin his attack route into Libya, when suddenly off to his left he saw a Navy carrier-based aircraft fire a Harm missile to suppress the Libyan radar and missile sites. He then for the first time felt very confident in the success of the mission. The split second timing of these two superb forces, staged from thousands of miles apart, was absolutely essential to the overall success of the action.

The allied reaction was predictable. People in opposition parties in England, Germany, the Netherlands, and some in Italy, protested most violently, sensing some political gain from their attacks on our raid. But after a short time, it appeared that a very great number of people, including many governments, were delighted that someone was able to teach Qaddafi a lesson; and his resulting silence and indeed, virtual disappearance, indicated very clearly that the lesson had been taught and learned.

For nothing was heard from Qaddafi for many months after the attack. He canceled many scheduled public appearances, and pretty well vanished into the desert for an extended period. Thus, our goals were realized, and one source of the export of terrorism was stopped at least temporarily. The President gained a great deal of credibility and strength at home as well as abroad. For my part, I was particularly delighted with the performance of our forces. It was all the vindication that anyone should need of our correctness in rebuilding our military strength and in deciding when to use it.

It is tempting for many to exploit our renewed military strength. My feeling always has been that military strength should be used only when we have, and can achieve, a proper objective; and then we must use it in the amounts necessary to achieve that objective as quickly as possible. But military actions should never be used except as a last resort, and when all else has failed. Military forces should certainly not be used on any occasion unless a matter of major national importance is involved.

All of those tests of mine seemed to me to be fulfilled by the President's decision to use our military in Libya. Once that decision was made, it then became essential, from my point of view, that we assemble sufficient forces, and act decisively and effectively, to achieve all the President's objectives. It is important to remember that one of the President's objectives, aside from teaching Qaddafi that he should never use terrorism again, was to minimize so-called collateral damage and to pick targets where the chances of that collateral damage were not great, recognizing that it would not be possible ever to guarantee that there would not be any collateral damage done.

So, at least twice[4] Qaddafi had tried by overt attacks, intimidation, threats and bluster, to assert control over international waters. He failed each time. When he saw that he could not accomplish his aim overtly, he then tried the covert use of terrorism. Here our response to him was so immediate and so devastating that for over a year he took no action of any kind.

---

4. In January 1989, Libya again tried to frighten away our carrier pilots from the USS *John F. Kennedy*, flying regular air patrol in the vicinity of our carrier over a hundred miles from Libya. Two Libyan MiG-24s repeatedly put themselves in position to attack our F-14s. As the Libyans closed, their aggressive intent seemed clear. Our pilots correctly fired missiles at them, shooting both down in an action markedly similar to that of August 1981.

Coupled with that failure was his unsuccessful attempts to defeat much smaller forces in Chad, to his south, so that by the end of 1986 his credibility was virtually nonexistent. That was a vastly better result than some of the particularly silly suggestions that had been made earlier by various members of the National Security Council staff, and by Robert C. McFarlane when he was the National Security Advisor, that we should encourage, promote and support, with many American infantry divisions, a full-scale attack by Egypt upon Libya as a way of dealing with Qaddafi. President Hosni Mubarak of Egypt correctly diagnosed and disposed of that absurdity by his hearty laughter.

And so, as the natural result of the President's refusal to be intimidated by threats or by actual attacks, and thanks to his strong resolution and determination to use America's newly regained military power to insure that we and other nations had the right to use and exercise our Navy in international waters, we gained additional strength and respect in the world. Our use of our greatly increased military strength had amply demonstrated that no Qaddafi or other dictator could, by any means, drive us out of the places we had a right to be.

So our allies and our potential foes now had a far more accurate realization that neither threats nor terrorism could succeed against a newly strengthened America. Our people and our allies took comfort from that proof, and another step had been taken to demonstrate why military strength is vital for peace—and why it is sometimes necessary to fight for peace.

VII

The Falklands

O n April 2, 1982, the armed forces of Argentina invaded the Falkland Islands claiming that they owned these British islands. The next day they invaded the South Georgia Islands, a Falklands dependency. They thus seized territories over which Britain had exercised full sovereignty for nearly one hundred fifty years. The Argentine military dictatorship, under General Leopoldo Galtieri, apparently felt that the time was ripe for it not just to assert its claim to the Islands, but to settle the matter once and for all by force. The primary motive for the endeavor, I am sure, was to distract the disgruntled Argentine people's attention from the faltering economy and from the leadership's lack of political legitimacy. The military junta said that no matter what course later discussions might take, it would not give up the newly acquired territories; but it made a major miscalculation in assuming that Britain neither would nor could resist the junta in any effective way.

Certainly there were no British defense forces on the Islands that could offer any such resistance. But it was quite clear that the residents of the Islands were British citizens and wanted to remain that way. In fact, ninety-seven percent of the Falklands population is of British origin.

Argentina's military dictators overlooked the possibility that Britain would mount an *active* resistance to the invasion from some eight thousand miles away. That resistance ultimately led to the total defeat of the Argentinian forces, the ousting and disgrace of their military dictators, and a clear statement by Britain to the world that aggression would not be allowed to succeed, no matter how improbable were the odds that it could be resisted.

On the face of it, resistance seemed absurd even to contemplate. Not only was the logistical line from Britain to the Falklands impossibly long, but there were no preparations in England for mounting an invasion over a logistical line of any considerable length. There had been no real belief in England that the Argentinians would invade; and although the opposition of Argentina to British sovereignty in the Falklands had been known for years, there had been no recent indications that the Argentinians planned any sort of attack. The task of raising and equipping task forces that would have to travel those eight thousand miles, land, and drive out invaders who were already in possession of the Islands—which were only four hundred miles from the Argentine mainland—seemed, to most, not just a very formidable task, but an impossible one. The immense preparations required to put together the forces, the ships, the planes and all the impedimenta required by any military action would normally, under the best of circumstances, require many months. Procurement of many items not ordinarily stocked would have to be achieved in a very short time. The training of British forces is generally at a high level, and they are normally in a high state of readiness; but in 1982 their principal training certainly did not include successfully executing an opposed landing on islands so many thousands of miles from home.

So the Argentine dictators dismissed the possibility of Britain's mounting any kind of military opposition to their invasion. They also refused to discuss giving up their possession of the Islands.

Fortunately, quite the opposite view was taken by Prime Minister Margaret Thatcher. Despite advice by some of her senior military leaders that a military operation could not succeed, she nevertheless ordered all preparations to be made for a full-scale counterinvasion to retake the Falklands. She added a very memorable phrase which served as the keynote for the entire British campaign. Mrs. Thatcher said, "The possibility of defeat simply does not exist."

The American reaction to the news of the Argentinian invasion of the Falklands was mixed. Some of us (and I was one) felt that if the British were going to mount a counterattack and try to retake the Islands, we should, without any question, help them to the utmost of our ability. We should do so, I felt, not only because they were our principal ally, but because I felt that naked aggression, as practiced by the Argentinian military dictatorship, should neither be encouraged nor indirectly supported by our indifference or our neutrality (which two terms I took to be synonymous in this case).

I therefore passed the word to the Department that all existing requests from the United Kingdom for military equipment were to be honored at once; and that if the British made any new requests for any other equipment or other types of support, short of our actual participation in their military action, those requests should also be granted, and honored immediately. I knew how vital speed would be for the extraordinarily difficult operation they were about to undertake.

Others, notably our State Department under Secretary of State Alexander Haig, tried to institute negotiations to see if the matter could be settled. But Haig had delivered himself, on April 14, of one of his more convoluted sentences: "The United States," he said, "had not acceded to requests that would go beyond the scope of customary patterns of cooperation based on bilateral agreements." That verbal mess was correctly translated by the British to mean that Secretary Haig was trying to keep the United States neutral in a war between an aggressor and America's closest friend, whose territory had just been invaded. In furtherance of his aim, Secretary Haig went to England, and from there attempted to operate "shuttle diplomacy" between the United Kingdom and Argentina, following a technique practiced with a high degree of success by former Secretary of State Henry Kissinger, who some years earlier had moved quickly back and forth between Israel, Syria and other Middle East capitals.

One problem with shuttle diplomacy between England and Argentina was, of course, the immense distance involved. Further, the Argentines, having invaded the Falklands, would have to be persuaded to give up and return home: No other conditions would, or could have satisfied the British, acting for their citizens who had been invaded and who wanted British rule restored to their islands.

The difficulties of negotiation under those circumstances proved to be too great. After several flights by the Secretary of State between the United Kingdom, Argentina and the United States, occasionally slowed by arguments over which planes were available for the Secretary's use,[1] the negotiations were given up. But British preparations for retaking the islands continued, as they had throughout those negotiation attempts.

Within our government were also raised other voices objecting to our encouragement or support of the British. We should at least remain neutral, according to those voices, in any controversy involving a South American or a Central American state; they feared we would worsen "relationships" with Argentina, and

---

1. Air Force transport planes with windows are much prized by Washington staffs, even though the windowless versions are faster and require fewer refuelings. Secretary Haig's staff sometimes preferred to delay his flights until a plane with windows was available.

---

indeed all of Latin America, if we supported any kind of military action against any Latin American nation. Adherents to that philosophy could be readily identified by their determined and quite self-conscious use of the label "Malvinas Islands" (the Argentine name for the Falklands).

In many National Security Council meetings and in forums elsewhere in April, I vigorously expressed my view that the rest of Latin America had no interest in helping an invasion perpetrated by the Argentine military dictators; that there would be no support by other South American countries for Argentina; that there would be no adverse reactions by any of those countries if we helped Britain. On the other hand, there would be fury in the British Isles, and serious loss of confidence in America as a friend among our NATO and our Pacific allies—and among Latin American nations too—if we supinely accepted aggression, and stood by wringing our hands as we talked "negotiations" and "settlements."

Ultimately that view prevailed. The President agreed that it would be unthinkable for the United States to remain neutral when our oldest friend had been attacked in such a fashion; and he also supported very vigorously the idea that we could not condone, by silence or inaction, naked aggression anywhere, and certainly not in our own hemisphere. He was willing to allow Secretary Haig's attempts at negotiations, but I never had any doubt that the President's heart was with Britain.

The arguments were sharp and vigorous, but the President's decision in favor of our helping Britain carried the day on April 30.

The President's decision was threefold. He formally blamed Argentina for the failure of Al Haig's mediation efforts; he announced sanctions against Argentina; and he pledged that we would give the British "material support."

I was of course very pleased with the President's clear-cut action. We could now openly and even more quickly supply

Britain's needs, as they approached the date of their counter-landings on the Falklands. In fact, the first ship convoys of UK forces sailed on April 5, 1982.

On Sunday, May 2, two days after the President's decision, Francis Pym, the newly appointed British Foreign Secretary, came to Washington for the second time in a week. I met with him and Sir Nicholas Henderson, the skilled and highly effective British Ambassador, at the British Embassy, a most beautiful setting on that spring Sunday. The gardens of the Embassy are magnificent all year, but never more so than in the spring, and we had a fine view of them as we sat on the terrace that leads out from the broad hall corridor.

Nicco Henderson is a tall, lanky man who had officially retired from the British Foreign Service, and then written a very penetrating article for *The Economist*. In it he pointed out the reasons for England's decline in the past years and stressed the need to make changes of the kind Mrs. Thatcher had in mind. She persuaded him to come out of retirement and take the Ambassadorship to the United States. Henderson was highly persuasive in his discussions with American officials about the Falklands. He has a superb and subtle sense of humor, and he took great delight in violating many of Savile Row's ideas of proper dress.

Those serene gardens were an incongruous site for our discussions of the supply of arms, ammunition and war supplies for the British seaborne counterattack convoys approaching the Falklands. We all knew of the enormous military odds against Britain, but at least our own position was now unequivocally settled in favor of the British and against Argentina, and I made it clear that we would supply them with everything they needed that we could spare, and that we were able to do it very quickly.

We did this. Former Secretary Haig said he spent some time at his negotiating sessions with the Argentines in telling them we had refused to fulfill British requests for arms. If he did tell them that, he was simply wrong.

Washington, January 6, 1981. Caspar Weinberger, President-elect Ronald
Reagan's choice for Secretary of Defense, prior to the start of his
confirmation hearings before the Senate Armed Services Committee.
(*Associated Press/Harrity*)

Secretary and Mrs. Caspar W. Weinberger during thier visit to India in October 1986. *(photo by Kay Leisz)*

Award Presentations to Immediate Staff upon Secretary's last day in office, November 23, 1987. *(private collection)*

The showdown with Budget director David Stockman over the Defense Budget before the President, on September 1, 1981. (*The White House*)

Laying the presidential wreath at the Tomb of the Unknown Soldier on November 11, 1986, at Arlington National Cemetery. (*private collection*)

In Beirut, Lebanon, on February 29, 1984, with Ambassador to Lebanon Robert S. Dillon and Major General Colin Powell (*far right*). (*private collection*)

Indian Ocean—observing flight operations during a visit to the USS *Constellation*, February 10, 1982. (*courtesy of the Pentagon*)

Meeting with Infantry troops at the National Training Center, Fort Irwin, CA, November 7, 1984. (*courtesy of the Pentagon*)

Secretary Weinberger briefing the National Security Council on the Defense
Budget, September 9, 1981. (*The White House*)

National Security Council meeting with President Reagan, Vice President George Bush and National Security Adviser Bill Clark (*center*) and Secretary of State George Schultz (*second from right*) in the Oval Office, May 8, 1983. (*The White House*)

Secretary Weinberger observing an Army exercise at Fort Ord in California, on November 8, 1985. (*private collection*)

Presentation of Defense Budget to President Reagan, September 9, 1981.
(*The White House*)

Briefing reporters at a Pentagon press conference on October 28, 1982.
(*courtesy of the Pentagon*)

In a highlight of Secretary Weinberger's career, President Reagan read the tribute to Medal of Honor Recipient Master Sergeant Roy P. Benavidez. By awarding this honor for service in Vietnam, the Reagan Administration made a historic stride in healing America's wounds inflicted by that war, and in restoring respect for the members of the armed forces. February 24, 1981. (*courtesy of the Pentagon*)

Secretary Weinberger hosted a Joint Services Full Honor Arrival Ceremony for Prime Minister Margaret Thatcher of the United Kingdom, July 26, 1985, in the Pentagon courtyard. Prime Minister Thatcher and Secretary Weinberger, escorted by Colonel William R. Williamson, Commander, 3rd United States Infantry, are shown Trooping the Line. (*Department of Defense/Sfc. Jimmy Wood*)

The Strategic Defense Initiative Organization and Air Force Systems Command, Space Systems Division, successfully conducted a long-duration, laboratory flight test to demonstrate technologies for a Space-Based Interceptor (SBI) on April 24, 1989, at Edwards Air Force Base, CA. (*Department of Defense*)

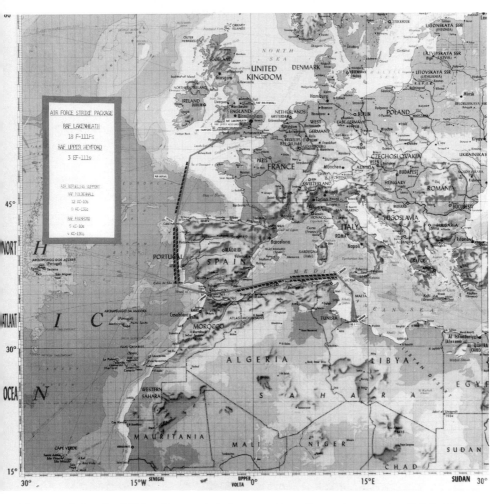

Map used for the White House briefing on the Libyan Action, April 15, 1986.
(*Department of Defense*)

A news briefing to discuss changes in the Defense Budget, March 4, 1981, in the Pentagon. (*Department of Defense*)

Meeting with Israeli Minister of Defense Yitzhak Rabin on November 14, 1985, in the Pentagon. (*Department of Defense/Helene Stikkel*)

April 6, 1986: In Tokyo breaking open a container of sake with Japanese Minister of Defense Kato as a sign of enthusiastic good will. *(photo by Kay Leisz)*

White House ceremony for Grenada students who came to thank President Reagan for their rescue by American forces, November 7, 1983. (*The White House*)

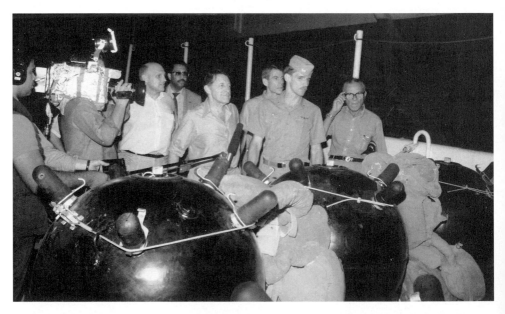

During a September 25, 1987, visit to U.S. forces in the Persian Gulf. Confiscated Iranian mines with Captain H. Rottenour, Commanding Officer, USS *LaSalle* (AGF 3). The mines, which Iran denied they had, were transferred to the *LaSalle* from captured Iran Air vessel. (*private collection*)

A reception for Minister and Mrs. Yoon of Korea during the Korean-U.S. Security Consultation Meeting in Washington on May 6, 1985. (*private collection*)

April 15, 1985. In the Cabinet Room the Secretary of State, George Shultz, sits at the right of the President and the Secretary of Defense sits on the President's left. (*The White House*)

President Reagan with the Secretary proceeding to meeting with Vice President Bush and the Deputy Secretary Will Taft IV, now U.S. Ambassador to NATO, and the Chairman and Joint Chiefs of Staff in the Pentagon, June 22, 1984. (*private collection*)

The President awards Secretary Weinberger the Presidential Medal of Freedom at the Secretary's retirement ceremony on November 18, 1987. (*Associated Press/Barry Thumma*)

Pym had succeeded Lord Peter Carrington as Foreign Minister when Carrington, quite unnecessarily, we thought, had resigned, assuming blame for the Argentine invasion. (Fortunately for us all, Lord Carrington was later elected Secretary-General of NATO and served with extraordinary skill and effectiveness there.)

Pym is a pleasant and basically cheerful man, who some years later fell out of favor with the Prime Minister—largely, it is thought, because he suggested, just before the next general election, that it was not a good thing politically for any party to have too large a majority. Mrs. Thatcher felt no such alarm at the prospect of a large majority, which of course the voters gave her. Shortly thereafter Geoffrey Howe became Foreign Minister.

Pym quite neatly summed up our support by saying, after he met that same day with Secretary of State Haig, "Last week I came here to see Mr. Haig in his role as a mediator. Today I have come back to consult with him as an ally." Haig was still not quite so sure. He told reporters afterward that despite the breakdown in the mediation attempts, "the United States remained committed to seeking a diplomatic solution before the fighting worsened." That was not quite what the President had had in mind, nor what I envisioned. I had told Mr. Pym that our arms supply effort would intensify, and that we would work as effectively as we could to support the British counterattack.

The next day a British submarine torpedoed and sank Argentina's only cruiser, the *General Belgrano*. Argentina's military dictatorship promptly called the British report a "lie" and "psychological warfare," but that claim was a bit hard to sustain when it became known that the *Belgrano* actually had been sunk.

That political opponents will go to great lengths to discredit a government policy was manifest in the claim by some Labour politicians that the sinking of the *Belgrano* was a "provocative act" and essentially a "dirty trick," and that war might have been averted if only the British had not sunk the *Belgrano*. A better way to avoid the war would have been for Argentina's military dictatorship to have decided not to invade the Falklands.

The day after the sinking of the *Belgrano*, I left for Brussels and the regular gathering of the NATO defense ministers. There I had several meetings with John Nott, then British Defense Minister. My previous meetings with him had always involved my expressing my worries that in keeping with his government's desire to reduce all spending, the British were mothballing too many of their Royal Navy ships. Nott always took the position that they could bring them back on line quickly; but on the basis of our own experiences, I was not so sure.

At those May meetings, after the Falklands war was under way, John Nott obviously no longer raised the question of putting more British ships in reserve status. We discussed arms and military supplies Britain might need, but the Defense Minister was anxious to have it appear publicly that the British could do the Falkland operations by themselves. That was, I am sure, why he told his press that "no assistance was needed at this time." Shortly thereafter all of their other regular requests were augmented by a formal memo asking for the loan of one of our long-range transport planes. We were happy to comply.

Communiqués were issued after each meeting of the NATO Defense Ministers; and I felt it important that this one express the support of the Atlantic alliance for England, in keeping with the NATO charter provision that an attack on one NATO member would be considered an attack on all. The communiqué we issued after some internal skirmishes was, I felt, quite satisfactory.

NATO communiqués are never easy to draft or agree upon. This one was easier than most; but the process always reminded me of the task of the official starter of a horse race. When all of the horses but one have been cajoled into their stalls in the gate, that last horse is always the most difficult. Then, when he is persuaded to enter the gate, one or two of the others back out.

At this NATO meeting, questions about the Falklands resolution were raised informally by Greece, Norway and the Netherlands. But eventually they were satisfied that Argentina should be condemned.

The communiqué, issued on May 6, openly sided with Britain and condemned Argentina's "armed invasion of the Falkland Islands and dependencies and her failure to comply with United Nations Security Resolution 502." (That resolution called for an immediate Argentine withdrawal and a negotiated settlement.) The communiqué also emphasized the importance of upholding the principle "that aggression or occupation of territory by force should not be allowed to succeed."

At that May meeting I also resumed my plea with NATO on "out of area actions." I had long urged NATO to recognize that events outside its borders could affect its mission and its ability to defend Europe. The British requirements in the Falklands made it necessary for England to detach part of the forces it had committed to NATO, and I made the point that while this was only a "temporary displacement," and not a loss, the detachment did underline NATO's need to concern itself with events outside its borders, including events in the Middle East that could disrupt vital oil supplies. I proposed that NATO do some contingency planning for such events.

The Royal Navy, next to ours, was the biggest and most effective in NATO. It carried out nearly seventy percent of the Atlantic alliance's antisubmarine patrols in areas through which Soviet subs would most likely move in the event of any Soviet action against the United States.

But the Falklands required nearly half of the British fleet of 62 major surface warships; and four Royal Navy ships were sunk in the Falklands action. Most British detached naval forces were soon returned to NATO activities, but the Falklands war emphasized, as nothing had before, that NATO at the very least needed contingency plans to backfill any national forces that might have to be diverted to national requirements. I told NATO ministers that the United States too might have to use our NATO committed forces elsewhere temporarily. The NATO contingency planning that I had been urging for out-of-area activities began shortly thereafter.

There were still, of course, voices at home loudly worrying about the "damage" to United States–Latin American relations that would occur as a result of the President's decision. But that talk would fade out after the British victory and when Raúl Alfonsín, with his new civilian government, took over the reins in Argentina after the military junta was deposed—that is to say, when its miserable performance could no longer be hidden.

Meanwhile the British plan for their military action and the movement of their forces continued, greatly buoyed by the President's April 30 decision.

It is also undoubtedly true that the President's close personal relationship with Mrs. Thatcher and the virtual identity of their views on so many matters, were part of the reason for the President's immediate and strong support of the United Kingdom. Now that the President's decision had been formally made and he had telephoned it to Mrs. Thatcher, we were able to be more useful to England.

We had previously and quietly advised Mrs. Thatcher's government that we would honor, as rapidly and as completely as we possibly could, all of their requests for military and other assistance, despite the opinion of most of our military leaders that the British decision to retake the Falklands was a futile and impossible effort.

On paper it would have seemed that the military advice was correct. Britain's 8,000-mile distance from the islands it would have to recapture was an extraordinarily formidable obstacle—particularly when the only stopping point on the whole long, lonely trail was Ascension Island, a small point on maps of the Atlantic, about 3,800 miles south of England and about 1,700 miles west of Africa. There we held lease rights from the British, and had established military facilities—our "Wideawake" base. I told the British they would have full availability of our facilities there. This was consistent with our basic offer: to help with everything short of actual participation in the military action itself.

Our military leaders advised that lack of shipping, among other factors, made Mrs. Thatcher's position and plans impossible to carry out. They also noted that Britain's lack of air transport, and the length of time the Argentines would have to prepare defenses against the English attempt to retake the Falkland Islands, and all of the normal difficulties inherent in making an opposed landing, not to mention the peculiar difficulties of doing that after a 8,000-mile trip with no real intermediate bases—all those factors led our military leaders to conclude the British action could not succeed.

Meanwhile, many of Mrs. Thatcher's own military advisers had reached virtually the same conclusion; but they fully respected her decision and that of her government, that the military operation would be undertaken. They proceeded with exceptional skill to make plans, many of them improvised very quickly, to assemble the necessary shipping from private sources, and to commit their limited helicopter carriers, and short takeoff and landing carriers, and all of their available, but limited, naval strength to the action.

Very shortly after our unequivocal decision to help, British requests for materials and supplies of all kind began coming into the Pentagon.

In the normal course, those requests would have been handled in a routine fashion, which consisted of careful examination, often by several different offices, of the request itself, and particularly including our own estimate as to whether the British actually needed the things requested. There would normally be some consideration of British stocks of particular supplies; and there would of course be consideration whether we were able to fulfill the request—and if so, whether there would be any effect on our own readiness. That process would normally involve a vast number of Defense Department civilian and military offices in the Pentagon and elsewhere. Each office, of course, has many in-baskets through which each of those requests would have to flow. Also in the normal course, those matters would have been considered along with many other questions and requests from other countries for military assistance and sales.

It was apparent to me from the beginning that "the normal course" could not be followed if we were now to be of any real assistance. Therefore I directed that all of the British requests have immediate and first priority—and particularly that our staff examination be drastically shortened, so that we would examine only the effect that fulfilling the request would have on our own supplies and readiness. I also directed that each of those requests come straight to my desk, something that would otherwise not have happened. Finally, I directed that I be told, within twenty-four hours of our receipt of a British request, whether it had been granted; and if not, why not, and when would it be granted?

The Pentagon "bureaucracy," so often derided in the press and so frequently a target for criticism by those who do not like any manner of military action or defense spending, responded magnificently.

My instructions were carried out precisely. Dov Zakheim, one of our new appointees, was particularly efficient in insuring that my orders were understood and followed. Some fifteen in-baskets of the normal chain were eliminated. The outward flow of materials of all kinds began immediately, and continued at a rapid pace to the various destinations requested by the British, including the British Isles themselves, Ascension Island, and—later—the task force standing off, and eventually on, the Falklands, as the British military operations proceeded in an exemplary fashion to recapture their Islands.[2]

The first requests were for missiles, particularly our Sidewinders, the AIM 9-L air-to-air missiles, with which the British wreaked such havoc on the Argentines, and aircraft fuel. But initially we had to, and did, add enormously to the facilities at Ascension to receive and deliver the fuel and other supplies to the British task forces' ships and planes. (We also sold them twelve of our F-4 fighter planes at a "bargain basement" price after the war, in order to allow the British to keep a Phantom squadron on the Falklands.)

A small British task force first took the South Georgia Islands on April 25; and less than a month later, on May 21, 1982, the British main body of forces landed on the Falklands themselves. Just over three weeks later, on June 14, Argentina surrendered at Port Stanley. Mrs. Thatcher's pronouncement turned out to be correct: The possibility of defeat *did not* exist, because the British forces would not permit it to exist.

Some said later that the British could not have succeeded if we had not helped.[3] This is not so—I think the decisive factor was Mrs. Thatcher's firm and immediate decision to retake the Islands, despite the impressive military and other advice to the effect that such an action could not succeed.

Her decisions and her subsequent resoluteness in carrying them out were the essence of leadership, and demonstrated once again that such leadership can overcome very heavy odds.

We certainly helped substantially, and quickly. Our help consisted primarily in the rapid supply of things England might otherwise have had supplied from elsewhere, but much more slowly.

---

2. An excellent account of the entire operation is *The Battle for the Falklands*, by Max Hastings and Simon Jenkins (London: Pan Books Ltd., 1983).

3. *The Economist*, March 3, 1984, p. 23 (American edition, p. 29).

Nearly seven years later, at a dinner in 10 Downing Street, I described my role as being that of an assistant supply sergeant, or an assistant quartermaster. I am told that not even during World War II had we been able to respond so quickly to requests for military assistance; and speed was what the British most needed. Most of their requests to me were approved and sent on their way in twenty-four hours. One of their requests, for radio receivers to talk to intelligence-gathering sources, took only six hours from their original request until they began receiving the radios.

We were also able to assist in producing and sharing intelligence. Normally our surveillance and general intelligence gathering did not include keeping an eye on the Falklands. However we have, because we vitally need, a high degree of flexibility in those arrangements; and shortly we were able to let the British see what we could see in that area. That capability, added to our joint efforts to gather intelligence, gave the British valuable advance knowledge of Argentine movements and intentions. We were also able to provide some real help with our worldwide communications lines. The combined results—of British resolve and military skill and our substantial logistical assistance—were uniformly excellent.

The Falklands were completely retaken in a very short time. The corrupt Argentine military dictatorship was ousted, and Raúl Alfonsín's civilian government, quite friendly to the United States, was installed. None of the dire consequences predicted for our relationships with Latin America occurred. Our allies, who were also Britain's allies, were uniformly admiring, and reassured that America was a far more reliable and helpful friend than they had thought.[4]

---

4. Argentina's first civilian government in many years, although a vast improvement over military dictatorships, did not prove able to deal successfully with the many economic problems inherited. Alfonsín was succeeded by Carlos Saúl Menem. He was considered

As happened after other successful American actions, my colleagues in the defense ministries of our friends told me many times how much they admired and approved what we had done, and how helpful it was for them to have such evidence of our new capabilities and resolve. In some cases they could not say those things publicly; but the experience gave them valuable ammunition to use in discussions and debates in their own governments when questions arose about the reliability and constancy of America as an ally.

Most important of all, the British success in the Falkland Islands told the world that aggression would not be allowed to succeed; that freedom and the rule of law had strong and effective defenders.

---

a Perónist, but his initial moves have given some hope that he may have cast off the Perón mantle. In August of 1989, he agreed to open talks with Britain on restoring diplomatic relations without discussing the issue of sovereignty of the Falklands. Argentina's desperate economic situation dictated that all efforts be made to get assistance from anyone it could.

VIII

United States–Japan Defense Relations

*J*apan lies in one of the most strategically important geographic locations in the world and in the most vulnerable position vis-à-vis Soviet military power in the Pacific.

The Soviets necessarily have given first priority to their European border. Their second priority was clearly the long territorial border with China, which pins down up to fifty Soviet divisions—the great majority of its Asian ground forces. The rest of the Pacific, the importance of which Mr. Gorbachev appreciates far more than his predecessors, remained a third priority in Soviet military thinking, until recently. Those are very important considerations for Japan's self-preservation, and for our own Pacific strategy.

A line drawn west from the northernmost tip of Hokkaido Island intersects the east coast of the Soviet Union at a point three hundred miles north of the key Soviet naval port of Vladivostok, the only ice-free port of the eastern USSR. A similar line drawn west from the southernmost point of Okinawa Prefecture, near the Tropic of Cancer, touches Taiwan. If Japan is protected from nuclear blackmail by the umbrella of our retaliatory nuclear weapons, and if Japan gains effective air and submarine detection and destruction capability of its own in the seas and skies surrounding its territory, all Soviet ships and aircraft exiting Vladivostok would face surveillance for three hundred miles to the frigid north and could not avoid Japanese shadowing for over one thousand miles to the south. That combined Japanese-American capability significantly complicates the Soviets' increasingly aggressive Pacific planning.

The crux of our Pacific strategy is that by complicating that Soviet offensive planning we vastly increase our ability to deter any Soviet attack.

It is the essence of our policy that Japan, which is barely the size of the state of Montana—and for the most part only two hundred to five hundred miles from Soviet territory across the Sea of Japan—survive as an independent free nation; and that the United States and Japan continue to have uninterrupted access to the Pacific Basin—the new economic center of the world; and, finally, that Japan and the United States remain close friends and allies. If the United States and Japan can jointly deter the Soviets from attack or from gaining a dominant influence in the Pacific, the United States will have far more flexibility in using our forces to deter war in the Middle East, Europe and elsewhere.

It is important, however, to look back to the Second World War to understand how Japan's unique view of its military evolved.

Japan, of course, had virtually collapsed on August 15, 1945. The psychological as well as physical side of defeat was reflected in Japan's acceptance of an American-authored article in the postwar "MacArthur" Constitution, which went into effect on May 1, 1948, outlawing war "as a means of settling international disputes." The original MacArthur draft was reworded so that the possibility of having and using armed forces for purposes *other* than "settling international disputes"—or, by interpretation, for self-defense—was left open.

Nonetheless, the new Constitution was explained to the Japanese public in 1948 as outlawing military force for any purpose. Thus when the Allied Occupation of Japan ended, in 1952, and Japan agreed to take extremely modest measures for self-defense, less than half the population believed the measures were legal. The opposition parties branded as illegal the Safety Forces, which in 1954 were renamed the Self-Defense Forces. Fortunately, that extreme position was not accepted by a majority; however, many Japanese people were simply unsure through most of the 1960s whether the national defense forces were legitimate—a unique historical phenomenon for a democratic country.

Japan's first postwar defense budget was almost two percent of GNP, a fact unknown to many Americans, who mistakenly believe that Japan's Constitution has a quantitative limit. Also, the Japanese military budget has increased every year in nominal and real terms; however, the percentage of GNP devoted to defense started falling, particularly through the 1960s, when Japan's economy galloped ahead annually in double digits.

Japan's rapid economic growth, coupled with the necessity of our bolstering all our defense capabilities and commitments to meet the challenge of greatly increased Soviet military power, brought about increasing charges in the 1970s from the Congress that Japan was "free riding" on the United States for Japan's defense. It was certainly true in 1980 that Japan had not spent enough to give itself forces capable of defending itself independently. In fact, owing to extreme vulnerabilities in all three of its Self-Defense Forces, Japan was contributing very little to its own defense, much less to overall Pacific security.

That low estate was the natural result of some thirty-five consecutive years of low Japanese military budgets. Indeed, Japan's policy of not spending more than one percent of its gross national product on defense had become virtually enshrined into law.

Despite the major economic recovery miracle that transformed the utter devastation that was Japan in 1945 into the strongest and most vibrant economy in the Pacific in 1980, spending less than one percent of its GNP on defense did not give Japan the self-defense capability it required.

When the Reagan Administration took office, in January 1981, one of my principal goals was to chart a better relationship with all our allies, particularly with Japan. It had become a cliché that Japan needed to do more in the defense area; but we had never really discussed with the Japanese what we *wanted* them to do. There were those angry claims in the Congress that to its great detriment the United States was almost totally funding Japanese defense; and American officials held press conferences attacking the Japanese effort and demanding that they "do more." I always felt that stridency was the worst way to secure what we needed: a greater Japanese investment to improve their own self-defense capabilities. Of course many of Japan's neighbors feared any revival of the militarism that gripped Japan in the 1930s and 1940s, and so they were not in favor of any expansion of the Japanese military for any purpose.

Thus the Japanese were, in effect, being told both to do more and to do less militarily.

Japan's self-defense role has positive, vital and direct local and regional effects, and, indirectly of course, global results as well.

I shared the President's view that we needed to give far more attention to the Pacific Basin, without weakening in any way our NATO ties, and that Japan now was the major and critical power economically in the Pacific. China, of course, was also vital to our interests; but that is the next chapter. So, in 1981, I favored an early approach to the Japanese in defense matters. I thought we should explain to them frankly, but privately, what we would like to see them do as part of a mutual defense effort in cooperation with the United States.

That "privately" was important. Few people, and even fewer

Japanese, respond well to public criticism, particularly criticism on defense from the United States, after we had cut our own defense investment by more than twenty percent in the decade of the 1970s.

Our State Department offered some opposition to meetings of the type I proposed. It was never really comfortable with the idea of the Defense Department's meeting with officials of other countries. State also felt that defense was a sensitive area in which Japan had to set its own pace without help from us. The President, however, had wisely reappointed Mike Mansfield as our ambassador; and in late January Ambassador Mansfield wrote the President, urging him to let the Japanese know privately, and soon, what we wanted Japan to do in defense and trade. The President looked favorably upon the Ambassador's suggestion, and the approach that I favored became United States national policy the next week.

The State Department grumblings came largely from careerists who did not oppose the substance of the approach I favored; their opposition was of the "not invented here" variety. They simply did not want another department involved in United States–Japan relations even in the military areas. But the letter from Ambassador Mansfield to President Reagan required a substantive response for which the Defense Department was well prepared.

On March 4, 1981, I told the Senate Armed Services Committee that a rational division of labor among the United States, its NATO allies and Japan would be a central thrust of our Administration's defense policy.

Later the same month, I laid out the rationale for such a division of labor when I met in Washington with Masayoshi Ito, Japan's Foreign Minister. I told him that the United States understood that Japan could not become a military superpower owing to its constitutional provisions limiting its military to a strict self-defense role; and that the feelings of its own people and those of its Asian neighbors would, in all likelihood, always forbid a return to any type of military adventurism in Japan.

I mentioned to the Foreign Minister, as tactfully but as forcefully as possible, that I was well aware of the feelings of Japan's neighbors, since my own war service had been in Australia, New Guinea and the Philippines. I said that the United States would continue to provide Japan with both a nuclear umbrella and such American forces as might be necessary to protect Japan from invasion. I did not have to tell the Minister that the defense of Japan was vitally important to our own security. Part of our support for Japan was indeed altruistic, but we both knew that any successful invasion of Japan would make the defense of the United States infinitely more difficult. I also pledged that we would remain in the Korean peninsula, clearly differentiating the new Department of Defense from a Carter Administration defense official's "private" suggestion that Japan consider taking over the American role in the Republic of Korea—an idea equally unacceptable to the Japanese and the Koreans.

Few people understand how much turmoil is created, particularly in the Orient, by casual suggestions of drastic changes in policies. In my discussions with Minister Ito at the Pentagon, I said that in the Southwest Pacific and Indian oceans, areas as critical to Japanese security as those surrounding Japan itself (given Japan's need to import virtually all of its oil from abroad, and most of that from the Middle East), the United States would provide both a nuclear umbrella and the forces necessary to protect those areas too, and that we would provide sea-lane protection forces on Japan's behalf. I said that I left it to Japan's discretion to choose its own roles if it agreed to participate; but I offered a suggestion that Japan consider assuming responsibility for the defense of its own territory, the airspace around Japan and the sea-lanes of the Northwest Pacific, north of the Philippines and west of Guam.

Foreign Minister Ito said that Japan would respond later about its willingness to join us in such a division of responsibilities. He was quite dubious, however, that Japan could accept responsibility for defense of the sea-lanes in the Northwest Pacific, as that would be seen as a *regional* defense role, and thus a role that, constitutionally, Japan could not play.

The President and Prime Minister Zenko Suzuki met in May 1981, and Japanese defense efforts were a major issue in the President's briefing book for their talks. The meetings preparatory to the Prime Minister's visit established a pattern that was to become familiar. The State Department prepared a very thick briefing book; I had the Japan desk of our International Security Affairs unit prepare a smaller book. After studying both volumes, the heads of the various departments involved met with the President in the Cabinet room. Mike Mansfield, our great and long-time ambassador to Japan, was there too, ever vigilant to protest against ideas that would weaken United States relations with Japan.

The communiqué to be issued after a meeting between the President and a prime minister is one of the items most carefully considered in those preparatory sessions. In effect we work backward, starting weeks ahead with a draft communiqué that summarizes the meetings as we would like them to have happened; and in our preparatory meetings we present the arguments and reasons why the meetings should go as the draft communiqué proposes to say they did go.

Most of the President's meetings with the Prime Minister took place in the Oval Office, interpreters being the only other people present. When those meetings were concluded, the President and the Prime Minister came to the Cabinet room, where we had been meeting informally with our Japanese counterparts, and a larger and more formal meeting began. The defense issues were discussed without any firm resolution.

The President and I sought to divide defense responsibilities between the two countries fairly. Japan had always been reluctant to state clearly what its responsibilities were, given its earlier mentioned political sensitivities at home and the fears of Japan in other Asian countries. The Prime Minister seemed to understand the President's logic but was still cautious about what could be said publicly.

Later, I had a very cordial meeting with Prime Minister Suzuki at Blair House, and explained to him how tightly stretched United States forces were, particularly across the Pacific and Indian oceans. The Prime Minister was very understanding, but still enigmatic—I had no real idea whether he agreed with my suggestions, which were similar to those the President had made to him earlier, and which I had made to the Foreign Minister three months before. So I was delighted when Japan did agree to the joint communiqué, which was nearly identical to the draft we had originally prepared—a draft that set forth our hopes for this meeting. The final communiqué was issued shortly after my meeting with the Prime Minister.

In that communiqué, and for the *first time* in the postwar era, the United States and Japan agreed that a division of defense responsibilities in the Pacific was appropriate.

The Prime Minister pledged that Japan would increase its defense efforts as well as its support for United States forces in Japan. While the specifics of Japan's defense role were not spelled out in the communiqué, and although neither the American nor the Japanese press recognized it then, a precedent for much more meaningful United States–Japan defense cooperation had been established.

Rather than saying only what had always been said previously—that Japan would repel an invasion on its shores should one ever come—this communiqué established the rationale for a more forward, logical, and increased Japanese self-defense role as a cooperative effort with the United States; and it clarified that that role would not necessarily be limited to repelling an invasion. This was the key paragraph of the May 8, 1981, Communiqué:

> 8. The Prime Minister and the President reaffirmed their belief that the Japan-U.S. Treaty of Mutual Cooperation and Security is the foundation of peace and stability in the Far East and the defense of Japan. In insuring peace and stability in the region and the defense of Japan, they acknowledged the desirability of an appropriate division of roles between Japan and the United States. The Prime Minister stated that Japan, on its own initiative and in accordance with its Constitution and basic defense policy, will seek to make even greater efforts for improving its defense capabilities in Japanese territories and in this surrounding sea and air space, and for further alleviating the financial burden of U.S. forces in Japan. The President expressed his understanding of the statement by the Prime Minister. They recognized their common interests in contributing to the defense of Japan, and expressed the hope for even more fruitful dialogue between the two countries on security matters.
>
> —from "Joint Communiqué Between
> Prime Minister Zenko Suzuki and
> President Ronald Reagan"

The following day the Prime Minister addressed the National Press Club, a large gathering of newspaper and television correspondents and others. It is one of the best forums in Washington, because its events are particularly well covered by print, television, and radio reporters. It is a standard part of the agenda for all major foreign visitors. The obligatory question-and-answer period following the speech turns the event into a large press conference. There the Prime Minister was asked what now was the limit of the Japanese defense capability under its Constitution, given the joint communiqué's language on future defense co-operation. Prime Minister Suzuki responded that Japan could, within the limits of its Constitution, defend its own territory, the surrounding seas and skies, and its sea-lanes out to 1,000 miles. (Left unsaid was that "sea-lanes out to 1,000 miles" happened to include most of the Northwest Pacific.) He also said that that defensive perimeter was Japan's national policy.

Due primarily to a domestic political flap upon Suzuki's return to Tokyo about the Prime Minister's use of the word *alliance* in speaking of United States–Japan relations, the Japanese Foreign Office emphasized that the Prime Minister had not made any new commitments during his visit to Washington.

The Japanese word for ally—"domei koku"—had been used to describe Japan's wartime relationship with Germany. In the postwar period Japan's connection with the United States had usually been described as a treaty—"joyaku"—relationship. Although former Prime Minister Masayoshi Ohira had used the word *ally* once previously in 1979, it had never been used in anything as official as a communiqué. When the Japanese press raised the issue with Prime Minister Suzuki, on the way back from Washington, he denied that his use of the word *alliance* fundamentally expanded Japan's military responsibilities.

I did not dispute that assertion in public. But I told my Japanese counterpart, Japanese Defense Agency chief Joji Omura, who visited the United States as my guest on June 29, 1981, that the U.S. Government fully supported the Prime Minister's statement of Japanese defense policy made the previous month. The only question was Japan's capability to meet those defense goals. I urged Mr. Omura to achieve that capability as quickly as possible—and during the 1980s.

But a credible commitment to achieve the Suzuki defense plan was to come only later, when Yasuhiro Nakasone became Prime Minister. Even so, I was surprised and pleased by the speed with which the Japanese agreed to share defense responsibilities with us, and add to their own defense capabilities. That agreement vindicated my feeling that we could make progress with the Japanese, if we approached them with the respect and dignity they deserve as a world power, and that defense was an issue that we could discuss frankly with them as befits a true partnership. That attitude was quite a departure in 1981. It became fairly routine in the next few years, but now too many congressional voices are raising old and unwelcome criticisms.

Japanese prime ministers usually change their cabinets almost annually, and thus there were seven reshufflings and five different Japanese heads of Defense during my tenure as Secretary of Defense.[1] There would have been seven had not Mr. Nakasone wisely chosen to reappoint two extremely capable ministers to second terms, Mr. Koichi Kato and Mr. Yuko Kurihara.

Joji Omura, the first Japanese Defense Minister I met, had been in poor health early in his term of office, suffering from stomach ulcers. When he called on me, we received him with the usual honors at the Pentagon: a large and most impressive parade (on the Pentagon parade ground) by the "Old Guard," expert marching units from all four services; a 19 gun salute; inspection of the troops by the foreign visitor; and the playing of the national anthems of both countries by one of the service bands.

Even after all that had happened during the years since 1941, it was still a strange feeling for me to see the flags of our two nations flying together; and ironic memories, reaching back to New Guinea, made it difficult for me to maintain the rigid demeanor required during the playing of the anthems and the inspection of our troops with a Japanese Defense Minister.

---

1. As part of the postwar downgrading of military affairs in Japan, Defense is not a Ministry, but an agency, whose head is Minister of State without Portfolio and the Director General of the Defense Agency. He was in the past usually called "Director General." Recently, he is most frequently addressed as "Minister," and is popularly referred to as "Minister of State for Defense" or, simply, "Defense Minister."

The honors ceremony then required that we proceed through lines of saluting troops to the Pentagon and up the stairs to my office on the third floor, where the first of our talks was held.

In addition to talking with him frankly but positively about the strategic importance of achieving as quickly as possible the defense goals promulgated by Prime Minister Suzuki, I asked Minister Omura if Japan could find a legal way to allow its industries to share defense technology with the United States, as the United States had done with Japan, and as the United States and its NATO allies were doing reciprocally. We knew that Japan had done some sophisticated and advanced work in electronics and avionics, and we believed that much of their achievements in those and similar areas would be of great military value to us. Minister Omura soberly advised me of the still lingering sensitivities in Japan about increasing defense strength and the difficulties of relaxing Japan's self-imposed restriction on the export of defense technology, but he thanked me for clearly stating American desires and pledged that he would communicate my views in Tokyo.

He seemed particularly pleased with my approach, and with the honors appropriately accorded him. At the dinner I had at the Pentagon in his honor that night, he drank wine for the first time since his stomach operation. When the time came for his toast, the Minister said he preferred to sing rather than speak, and he lustily rendered a Japanese folk song, showing great sincerity and emotion. I promised to have John Lehman respond with "Anchors Aweigh" when I visited Tokyo; but since the Secretary of the Navy did not accompany me when I made that trip, I had to use Deputy Assistant Secretary for East Asia, Rich Armitage, and Assistant for Japan, Jim Auer—two of the best Japan experts in Washington—for the musical toasts when the Minister recalled the pledge I had made during our first meeting. I could not fail to match Minister Omura's new defense reciprocity.

Far from incidentally, tribute here must be paid to Richard

Armitage, who served the Department and me with extraordinary fidelity and skill and unparalleled knowledge and good humor during all the time I was in office. A former Navy officer and a man with a physique that would have served well a professional football lineman, Rich was the resident expert on both the Near and the Far East. He was to a considerable extent responsible for our increasingly good relationships with Japan, China, Taiwan, the Philippines, Korea, Thailand, the Southwest Pacific, and all of the countries of the Middle East. Not only was he personally a walking encyclopedia of knowledge about those countries, their leaders and potential leaders; he had amassed an extraordinarily able staff, who worked untiringly for and with Rich, handling the complex problems and relationships of their assigned countries. They were, in my opinion, the best "state department" in Washington. Jim Auer was the head of our Japanese Desk under Rich; he is a brilliant and dedicated civil servant who, as one of the leading experts on Japan, is now directing the Center for U.S.–Japan Studies and Cooperation at Vanderbilt University. He too deserves a large part of the credit for the improved relationship between the two countries.

The importance of Japan's pledge at that May meeting with Prime Minister Suzuki about its share in defense responsibilities, and the crucial nature of what we proposed the next month in technology sharing are still not understood by nearly enough Americans. They are also, I think, not yet fully recognized by many Japanese.

In a March 26, 1982, speech in Tokyo on America's Asian policy, I said that if Japan increased its self-defense efforts to the levels necessary to meet the defense goals set out by Prime Minister Suzuki in Washington in 1981, its effort "would contribute to Japan's own security and to the stability of the entire free world."

On the technology side, Japanese assistance to us is no less significant a matter. Thus far the Soviet military has not made the cuts pledged by Mikhail Gorbachev in his 1988 speech at the United Nations. In both Europe and in the Far Eastern military districts, the Soviets continue to add to their strength without any real "pro-Western" changes visible, although their former satellites are moving toward western-style democracy in a most gratifying fashion. The Soviets currently have in the Pacific more than 55 divisions of ground forces, more than 800 ships in the Pacific Fleet alone, and at least 3,000 fixed-wing aircraft and helicopters, far more than the United States and Japan forces combined have in each of those three categories. To deter the Soviets despite those unfavorable numbers against us, we have to use not only the geographical advantage I have mentioned, but also our superior morale—which democracies enjoy because they reward innovation and have technology superior to that of the Soviets.

The Japanese arms industries were shut down by General MacArthur's headquarters in August 1945, but some were re-opened in 1950 to manufacture ammunition and equipment for United Nations forces during the Korean conflict. Those companies were still in business when Japan regained independence in 1952, and Japan exported small quantities of arms abroad until 1967. In that year Japan adopted, as Japanese Cabinet policy, a prohibition of arms export to Communist countries, countries under United Nations sanction, and countries at war. In 1976 this policy was widened to prohibit the export of defense items and defense technology to *all* foreign countries—a self-inflicted wound taken in the spirit of demonstrating Japan's continued aversion to becoming a major military power.

Even though Japan did not, and still does not, have much military technology per se, given the almost exclusively commercial orientation of Japanese business, so pervasive was the taboo, particularly as Japanese industries boomed throughout the 1960s and 1970s, that even export of commercial technology *not* prohibited by either the 1967 or the 1976 policy statements was avoided by Japanese industry, lest it be accused by the opposition Communist or Socialist parties, or by the media, of engaging in illegal, almost "immoral," activity.

I reasoned that in the thermonuclear age, we could hardly make weapons more destructive than those we already had; thus we did not need innovative Japanese military technology for our strategic forces. But we did need, and could make, weapons smaller, quieter and more accurate; so Japanese commercial technology was highly relevant to United States defense interests.

For example, sophisticated Japanese semiconductors could help make our missile systems more accurate than presently existing United States or Soviet weapons. In the future, Japanese electronics could lead to breakthroughs in pinpoint-accurate conventional weapons, the development of which could lessen the need for nuclear systems.

I believed that if transfers to us of Japanese defense technologies at which they are the most skilled, such as electronics and avionics, were legitimized, certainly commercial technology— which was likely to be what we most needed from Japan—would also become that much more available. I said in an interview with a Japanese newspaper in 1986, "There is no better way to maximize our leverage vis-à-vis the Soviets in Asia than by U.S.–Japan technological cooperation."

Despite the best efforts of Defense Minister Omura and his successor, Soichiro Ito, Prime Minister Suzuki did not act on my request that he try to find a way for Japanese technology to come to the United States. That would have been too bold a step forward for the long-established Japanese "consensus" against the export or exchange of anything that might be useful militarily to any other nation. Suzuki knew that a decision to transfer such technology to the United States would be politically unpopular; and, unlike his successor, Nakasone, he did not have the will to step up to it. He did, however, agree that Japan would continue to increase its already impressive support for American forces in

Japan, and to pay almost $300 million, or over eighty percent, of the support costs for the basing of two new squadrons of F-16 fighter planes at Misawa Air Base in northern Japan. Had we put those aircraft in the United States or in any other country, American taxpayers would have had to pay the attendant costs.

When Prime Minister Nakasone took office, in late November 1982, major changes in Japanese policy took place almost at once. Yasuhiro Nakasone was an original: He was strong and decisive enough to disregard prior Japanese consensus and favor bolder new policies, unhampered by the conventional wisdom and arguments of the past. In that respect, he resembled President Reagan, whom he greatly admired.

The President's personal magnetism had again helped secure our objectives. Nakasone immediately pledged his support for achieving the defense goals of the Reagan-Suzuki communiqué of 1981. Nakasone, as a defense expert and formerly Director General of the Japan Defense Agency, unlike his predecessors, clearly understood the communiqué's implications.

In preparation for a January 1983 trip to the United States, Mr. Nakasone's Cabinet took the courageous, but politically unpopular, step of exempting the United States alone from the prohibition of the export of defense technology. Japanese public opinion polls taken at the time showed that over eighty percent of the people opposed the transfer of technology, even though a greater percentage supported the United States–Japan Treaty.

With that decision, we had secured, in less than two years, commitments from the Japanese government to do everything we asked for in a division of defense responsibilities. We pushed our case hard at all meetings, but I was anxious that we not criticize Japan publicly; and I believe that that care on our part, together with Prime Minister Nakasone's strong political courage, enabled us to gain all our objectives.

Implementation was another matter. Japan had been running government deficits relatively larger than our own since the time of the worldwide rise in oil prices in the 1970s. Over one-third of its budget was financed by bonds. The powerful Japanese Ministry of Finance recommended reduction in all levels of Japanese spending, including defense. But the Nakasone cabinets approved budgets for 1983 through 1986, which treated defense as an exception while they generally kept government ministries and agencies—including politically popular ministries such as education, construction (public works) and welfare (social security)—at reduced levels. Defense actually grew five percent annually in real terms during those years.

I found that increase in defense spending extraordinarily supportive and forthcoming toward the United States, as did much of the Japanese press and public. (One newspaper cartoon showed me plying Nakasone's first Defense Minister, Kazuo Tanikawa, with a "Weinberger cocktail," a drink served in a glass the base of which rested on missile fins.)

But in June 1985, the United States Senate, which cut our 1986 defense budget, also passed a resolution in 40 minutes by a vote of 88-8 that Japan's 1976 National Defense Program Outline should specifically be revised to incorporate *formally* Prime Minister Suzuki's 1981 statement about defending Japan's sea-lanes to 1,000 miles. The 1976 document did not mention specific targets for sea-lane defense, and the Senate action was motivated to register displeasure over that omission during the visit of Koichi Kato, Mr. Nakasone's first two-term defense minister, to Washington.

I wondered privately how many of those who voted for the very specifically worded "Sense of the Senate" resolution would feel if the Japanese Diet had passed a resolution telling the United States what *we* should defend. I also wondered if many senators knew the contents of either Japanese statement. At least one Democratic senator, Christopher Dodd, of Connecticut, justified my doubts by voting *for* the resolution that repeatedly called for *sea-lane defense enhancement,* and the same week published a trip report of his recent Asian travels—in the Japanese section of which report he wrote that the *U.S. should stop urging Japan to defend its sea-lanes* and should instead encourage Japan to increase its *territorial* defense. We were in fact urging Japan to increase its territorial, air, *and* sea-lane defense; and Japan was doing so. The American press was not reporting it, and few American congressmen read Japanese newspapers.

In 1985, the Japan Defense Agency (JDA) completed planning its Mid-Term Defense Estimate for the period 1986–1990. The estimate was prepared under the leadership of Yuko Kurihara, a close associate of Prime Minister Nakasone. Kurihara was later named by the Prime Minister to serve an unusual second term as defense minister.

Kurihara had been very highly regarded by the late Prime Minister Ohira, who was a leading Liberal Democratic Party faction leader; and Kurihara probably would have become foreign minister had Ohira not died in office. He still maintains long-standing close ties, outside his faction, with Nakasone.

Kurihara became a close personal friend of mine, as did Koichi Kato, and we always made special efforts to make their visits successful and pleasant.

They in turn entertained me royally in Japan, not only when I was in office—even arranging for a great Japanese pianist to play a special concert for me, knowing how much I would enjoy that—but Kurihara also invited me to his home, a signal honor, when I went to Japan to receive a Japanese decoration some months after my resignation.

Kurihara proposed significant improvements for the three branches of the Japan Self-Defense Forces. There had been two previous plans, for the years 1980–1984 and for 1983–1987, but neither required expenditures greater than one percent of the gross national product.

In addition, the annual budgets, which had to be approved by the Diet, and, more important, by the powerful Ministry of Finance, achieved an average of only sixty percent of the defense items called for by the Defense Plans or estimates. Those estimates had been, in effect, the JDA's "wish lists," which were not recognized as anything more than that outside the JDA.

But the 1986–1990 estimate actually was designed to achieve the minimum peacetime force goals of the 1976 National Defense Program Outline. It included weapons that extended Japanese defense capability farther offshore to meet Mr. Nakasone's goal of achieving the minimum level of defense capability required. The estimate also called for considerable increases in spending for radars, and for support items like missiles, torpedoes and other kinds of ammunition, all of which had been a critical weakness of the Japan Self-Defense Forces.

However, there was still no guarantee of full *funding* for the 1986–90 estimate. The JDA had estimated that it would require an average annual defense expenditure in excess of one percent of GNP, and that excess would violate a policy adopted by the Japanese Cabinet in 1976. In September 1985, Prime Minister Nakasone tried and failed to gain the support of his ruling Liberal Democratic Party (LDP) and his Cabinet to change that one percent rule.

Nakasone failed then because his rivals argued that since the first year of the new plan could be carried out without going over the one percent barrier, there was no need to decide the issue at that time. But I was told that the major reason for the refusal of his request to do away with the one percent limit was the desire of other faction leaders to keep the highly capable Prime Minister from putting another feather in his cap.

Nonetheless, the Cabinet approved changing the status of the estimate from an internal JDA development paper, to an official 1986–1990 defense plan approved and endorsed by the Cabinet. (The annual budget request still required the approval of the Diet, but that approval was assured, given the LDP's absolute majority in both houses). As a result of that significant change in the status of the defense plan, in December 1985 the Nakasone Cabinet approved a defense budget fully funding the first year of the 1986–1990 program.

Earlier in 1985, I had invited Japan, along with our NATO allies and many other countries, to participate in SDI research. The media had speculated that the Prime Minister and certain Japanese companies favored participation. The companies felt SDI might drive future technological advances and did not want to be left out. But Japanese public reaction was not altogether positive, and the liberal press was opposed. The opposition in Japan argued that SDI research would involve Japan further in the "U.S. global strategy" that is sometimes portrayed as endangering rather than protecting Japan. I told my Japanese counterparts and other Japanese the rationale behind the President's decision on SDI; that its purpose was wholly defensive—to make the use of nuclear weapons much less likely—and that it was very much in keeping with both American and Japanese strategic objectives. I also told them frankly how effective I thought Japan's potential contribution could be, a contribution as valuable as that of any of our other allies.

Buoyed by an overwhelming LDP electoral victory that continued its traditional control of both houses of the Diet, in July 1986 Mr. Nakasone was awarded a one year extension in office beyond the mandatory limit of his LDP presidency. We again quietly urged that Japan cooperate with us on SDI, and that it abandon its self-imposed policy of limiting defense spending to one percent of GNP. A September 1986 Japanese Cabinet statement, while carefully worded, was still the most positive political endorsement of SDI made by any foreign government.

The same month, Defense Minister Kurihara visited Washington. He and I had by now developed a close working relationship as well as a personal friendship. Some felt that the rapid appreciation of the yen since September 1985 could help the

U.S. trade deficit in the long term; but immediately it had a negative effect, increasing the costs of maintaining United States forces in Japan, particularly the costs of paying the talented Japanese work force employed in our bases for ship and aircraft repair and other tasks. Since JDA buys more than one billion dollars per year of American equipment, the more the yen increases in value, the more Japan could save in its purchases. I told Minister Kurihara that fully funding the second year of the 1986–1990 defense program was our most important goal. But I said that if Japan would use money saved from yen appreciation toward increasing its voluntary share of the costs of United States forces based in Japan, such a gesture would be extremely effective in dealing with our congressional calls for reductions in United States overseas costs.

My suggestion complicated the JDA's budget request for the second year of the 1986–1990 defense plan. By early December of 1986, it was clear that Japan's fully funding the 1987 part of the five-year program, as well as increasing Japanese support for American labor costs by $100 million—a commitment that Minister Kurihara and Prime Minister Nakasone forced on an extremely reluctant Japanese bureaucracy—would require a defense budget slightly more than one percent of the expected GNP. A protracted discussion within the LDP and the Cabinet followed; but on December 30, a budget was adopted that provided full funding for the second year and increased labor costsharing by $100 million, all of which meant a defense budget that equaled 1.004 percent of GNP.

The following month the Cabinet formally discarded the one percent policy statement of 1976, and replaced it with a nonquantitative barrier based on several factors including the threat Japan faced in the international environment and the needs of the United States–Japan security arrangements. That policy was, in essence, what I always urged on our own Congress: that we should base our defense budget on our military needs, measured by the size of the threat against us, and not on some abstract fiscal formula.

However, Japan's opposition Komeito Party leader Junya Yano, who visited me at the Pentagon in February 1987, quoted Henry Kissinger as saying that the Administration had unwisely encouraged Japan to exceed one percent of GNP, and it was now inevitable that Japan someday would become a regional military power, contrary to United States interests. I told him I was not familiar with any such quotation from Kissinger, and that I did not think Japan was any more "dangerous" at 1.004 percent of GNP.

A budget at 1.004 percent of GNP is not fundamentally different from one of 0.996 percent (the 1986 figure). The important thing is that, given Japan's huge GNP, even one percent of it is not an insignificant amount: Japan's one percent budget is greater than the Republic of Korea's or the United Kingdom's five percent. Even more important is that Japan's budget is now funding a high technology defense network that greatly enhances deterrence when combined with our force. Japan could not continue to meet its defensive goals fully without going over one percent, but that figure had become a sacred cow thanks to the attention Japan's media and opposition parties successfully attached to it.

I told Yano that the important thing was that Japan was acting responsibly to meet legitimate and reasonable self-defense goals, which threatened no one.

The Soviets *were* complaining; that I understood. Their plans were being complicated by American and Japanese efforts as we strengthened our joint deterrence. The fact is that the President had changed and vastly improved our Asian policy, and Japanese relations with the United States were stronger than ever; Soviet complaints were quite irrelevant to that central fact.

When Japan abandoned that barrier of one percent of GNP,

full funding of the entire 1986–1990 defense program was a virtual certainty.

And indeed the next Japanese budget, for 1988, which kept the program on the route to full funding, and exceeded the one percent barrier by an even greater margin, was approved with almost no opposition within the Cabinet. Now the only part of the 1981 division of defense responsibilities that had not been implemented was Japan's earlier policy decision to permit its defense technology to flow to the United States as an exception to its normal rule that it could not sell weapons systems to anyone.

It had taken more than two years after the 1983 Nakasone Cabinet agreed in principle to such sales to arrange procedures for actual transfers of technology. I had indeed signed a memorandum of understanding with the government of Japan for Japanese SDI participation in mid-1987, but the negotiations were unnecessarily long and I had to become personally involved to ensure that bureaucratic objections on both sides were overridden.

There were always complicating factors: A Japanese company saw its stock plunge when it was sensationally revealed that a totally nonlethal component it manufactured was used in the nuclear-capable Tomahawk missile system. An American opponent of a legitimate offer from the Fujitsu Corporation to buy Fairchild—an American based, but foreign owned, subsidiary maker of computer chips—falsely named me as opposing the sale. Tokyo headlines stated my opposition, and Fujitsu withdrew before I had made any decision.

Finally, there was the damaging and illegal sale by a subsidiary of the Toshiba Corporation of milling machines that could make propellers of the Soviet submarines far quieter. The sale had been negotiated in 1981 and deliveries were made in 1983 and 1985; but the facts were not fully known until 1987, following the revelations of a former employee of a Japanese trading company and an investigation by the Japanese government. The incident inflamed many on the Hill, who immediately called for sanctions of dubious legality against any Toshiba sales in the United States. That response convinced some Japanese that the United States was using a national security rationale unfairly.

There was no doubt that those sales of submarine-quieting equipment, by both the Japanese and the Norwegian government-owned firm of Kongsberg, hurt us. But the sale also hurt the Japanese and the Norwegians, neither of whom had any interest in facing far quieter, and therefore far more dangerous, Soviet submarines.

That loss of submarine technology offered another opportunity for us to try our "quiet, reasonable, private" approach to our differences.

I met with Prime Minister Nakasone on June 28, 1987, and we went over in detail the severity of the loss and the added capability it gave the Soviets. I mentioned how undesirable I felt it could be if Congress passed some stridently anti-Japanese legislation.

I suggested that rather than trying to punish the offending Toshiba unit, we should make as certain as we could that those responsible would be dismissed and new procedures put into effect designed to prevent any recurrence.

Then I said that we preferred affirmative rather than negative actions, and that the main thing now was to regain our lead in submarine construction technology. I proposed that Japan and the United States, with Japanese funding, begin an intensive research and development program to secure better detection and quieter submarines than the Soviets'.

The Prime Minister eagerly agreed. He did not talk about referring it to the Cabinet, or having anyone study it. He said, "We will do this."

Also, he agreed to have Japan furnish a valuable and much needed navigational system to assist our minesweepers in the Persian Gulf, where they were helping to keep that international waterway open for oil shipments—many of which went to Japan and our other allies.

Meanwhile, there was still little progress in securing large imports of Japanese technology to the United States. The trade balance remained heavily in Japan's favor two years after the basic decision to let us have Japanese technology. Now in June 1987, Japan approached an already delayed decision to select its new air-to-ground support fighter for the 1990s, the FSX.

Some in Japanese industry argued that there was sufficient capability to build the aircraft entirely in Japan. They said that all existing American aircraft had at least some features that were not as advanced as state-of-the-art Japanese technology. American industry had tried and failed to get Commerce Secretary Mac Baldrige, George Shultz and me in 1985 to threaten the Japanese, and tell them that they must use an American plane for their FSX, a suggestion I strongly opposed. I insisted that trade and defense issues be kept separate.

Since 1985, I had been telling Ministers Kato and Kurihara, the capable and knowledgeable Nakasone two-term defense ministers, that FSX was their decision. I did not apply pressure as such, but gave them general performance information about American aircraft, and public data concerning maintenance costs and the suitability of our various planes for their defense needs. I left them in no doubt that they should buy a United States plane. I shared with them our experience, and reminded them of the problems and very great expense that some of our allies had encountered in trying to build their own planes; specifically, I mentioned Israel's enormously expensive Lavi fighter plane, which the Israeli government later canceled at our urging.

I argued that while Japan no doubt had technological developments superior to those of the United States in some areas, those excellent technologies could be added to an existing United States aircraft; there was no need to design a totally new one. I knew the fury that would be aroused on the Hill if Japan chose to build its own aircraft at the same time that Japan still had a huge trade surplus with the United States, and had been portrayed as selling out our security with Toshiba's sale of the quiet submarine propeller. But I also knew this was 1987, not 1947, when American governments simply ordered Tokyo to do what we wanted.

Our discussions occurred in many places; but the final phase, on June 28, 1987, in a top floor suite of the Okura Hotel in Tokyo, with all of the Japanese Defense and Foreign Ministry experts ringed around Minister Kurihara, seemed anything but propitious. They appeared clearly ready to proceed with building their own new plane. But I kept reciting all the arguments in favor of an American plane, and the problems we would both have if Japan decided to build its own plane—somewhat to the surprise of the Japanese, who had been told I was lukewarm on the subject. I had to rely on the hope that the good judgment of Minister Kurihara and Prime Minister Nakasone would prevail. It did.

For in September 1987, Minister Kurihara, in his third visit to Washington, the last of eight visits I received from Japanese defense chiefs, announced that Japan would select an American aircraft as its new fighter, to be called the FSX, and would use in it state-of-the-art Japanese technologies, exactly as we had suggested and wanted.

Subsequent negotiations resulted in Japan's agreement to spend over one billion dollars modifying the General Dynamics F-16 Falcon, with over one-third of the Japanese funded development work going to American firms, over and above the F-16 license production procurement program. Also, the United States would receive free flowback of any Japanese technology derived from American data, and would receive information on—and be permitted to buy—any state-of-the-art technology of Japanese origin incorporated into the FSX.

Amazingly, some in the United States have gone so far as to

criticize even those Japanese commitments as a Japanese "victory." Some have argued in virtually the same breath that the FSX will be a United States aircraft in name only, and that the JDA chose the F-16 as a "scheme," only to obtain F-16 technology cheaply. Now, both accusations cannot be true; and, in fact, neither is true. The FSX will incorporate U.S. *and* Japanese technologies. For the first time since I formally asked for it in June of 1981, we will now have access to Japanese technologies we never had before. Nevertheless, a number of the standard critics of everything Japanese continue, up to the date of this writing, to oppose the agreement and urge the United States to repudiate it.[2] The basic wrongheadedness of their position emerges when we list the losses we would accrue in overturning the agreement. We would lose the benefits of a highly effective Japanese fighter deployed against the Soviet threat, which is in U.S. as well as Japanese interest; would lose compensation for sunk American costs and significant numbers of American jobs; would lose the opportunity to benefit from Japan's technology; would demonstrate to the world that agreements with the American Government are virtually worthless.

The same opponents also argue that in sharing our technology with Japanese, we will enable them to build a civilian aircraft industry; apparently they forget that the Japanese have coproduced our F-15 for years, an even more sophisticated plane in many ways than the F-16, and that we had been sharing the technology on the plane for many years. Most important, for those who really fear an independent Japan, the FSX project joins the United States and Japan together in an informal partnership that makes an autonomous Japanese aviation industry less likely in the future than if we did not have the FSX agreement.

---

2. Our Congress in May 1989 narrowly defeated a resolution designed to kill the FSX agreement. It did add restrictions and attempted to change the agreement, but President Bush wisely vetoed that bill in August 1989.

So, looking back over the years since 1981, I take great pride in the Reagan Administration's defense relationship with Japan. I believe that the President's decision to give more attention to Asia in general and to Japan in particular was one of the wisest and most successful policies of his Administration. It gave birth to his close relationship with Prime Minister Nakasone, which carried over to that with Prime Minister Noboru Takeshita, until his resignation in April 1989, and to my close relationship and friendship with five Japanese Defense Ministers. Japan's defense spending pulled virtually abreast that of the United Kingdom, France and the Federal Republic of Germany in 1988. It has more than tripled in absolute *and* in per capita GNP dollar terms since 1981, and will clearly grow faster than the defense spending of any of those three countries in 1989 and 1990. Thus Japan will have the third largest military investment in the world, without any sign of an ominous return of Japanese militarism, because all of its investment simply adds to Japan's defense capability. All of this lessens our defense burden in the Pacific, and *increases* the security of both our countries.

Indeed, our Pacific security and deterrence have been significantly strengthened because of Japanese defense efforts. Japan's financial support for our forces in Japan exceeded $2.5 billion in 1988, more than $45,000 per American service-person assigned in Japan—the most generous host-nation support arrangement the United States has enjoyed anywhere in the world. Finally, the potential flow of Japanese technology to the United States through the FSX program and other technology-sharing projects in the 1990s bodes well for the future.

I believe Japan can and should do more—for its own self-defense, in support of American forces in Japan, and in technology-sharing in the future; just as I believe we can and should do more for *our* self-defense. But I continue to believe that the way to achieve those goals is to work with the Japanese privately and with respect, as the President and I did, rather than to confront them and attack them with politically popular statements released to the press.

The Japanese people and their Government have been most appreciative of the attitude we have taken, and I think it has already helped greatly to secure results we both need. I recall the time Mrs. Takako Doi, then the vice-chairwoman, later chief, of the Japan Socialist Party, visited the Pentagon several years ago together with the chairman of that party, a precedent-breaking event I welcomed. She told the press that before she met me she imagined that I was a "monster," but was surprised to see how "kind and gentle" I was. She was responding not so much to me personally as to my approach, a quiet behind-the-scenes appeal for a greater Japanese defense effort.

In May 1988 I was honored to receive the Grand Cordon of the Rising Sun, an award I am told has rarely, if ever, been bestowed on a foreigner, from the Foreign Minister Sosuke Uno[3] of Japan on behalf of the Emperor. Former Defense Ministers Kurihara and Kato attended the ceremony, and Minister Kurihara and Prime Minister Nakasone entertained our party with great hospitality. Overall, I am very comfortable with United States–Japan defense relations. I think they have been a true

3. Foreign Minister Uno succeeded Prime Minister Takeshita, who resigned in May 1989 in the wake of the Recruit stock scandal. Mr. Uno seemed to me to be a wise choice, but shortly he too was plagued with personal problems and embarrassments, and resigned in July 1989. It is far too soon to make any judgment about the new LDP Japanese Prime Minister, Toshiki Kaifu, elected by the Diet, after the Upper House voted for Mrs. Doi in an unprecedented action. What is most important in my view is that whoever ultimately becomes a long tenured prime minister have the opportunity and the will to pursue the policies of his predecessors—policies that, I believe, serve very well the interests of both the United States and Japan. The real risk for the future is that the current unhappiness with personal charges against some members of the Liberal Democratic Party could lead to a change of policy that might weaken Japan's ties with the United States.

This would be most unfortunate, since there is no indication of any lessening of public support for the LDP's defense policy. The victory of the LDP's candidate in an October 1989 by-election for the Upper House has solidified LDP support for Prime Minister Kaifu, and bodes well for the success of the Party in the 1990 elections.

success story of the 1980s, a major factor in our greatly improved deterrent strength in the Pacific and therefore in the world.

As for the long-term future, I think the recent predictions of Edwin Reischauer are both highly relevant and probable to occur.

Reischauer, in his book *The Japanese Today*,[4] said:

"Barring the occurrence of a worldwide catastrophe, it is certain that the Japanese will continue to be a major and increasingly unselfconscious part of the world. The contradictory pulls between uniqueness and internationalism that so grip the Japanese today will be resolved in favor of internationalism. And with the economic power and technical skills of the Japanese clearly lending themselves to that trend, Japan and the rest of the world will come appreciably closer to viable world order."

Let us hope he is right, and that there is no "worldwide catastrophe." If the United States and Japan stand together as allies, then I believe there is far less chance of such a catastrophe.

---

4. Edwin Reischauer, *The Japanese Today* (Cambridge: Harvard University Press, 1988), p. 412.

IX

China

America's relationship with the People's Republic of China during the years of the Reagan Administration was immensely more complex and difficult than were our relationships with the other major Pacific powers. A considerable identity of viewpoint and objectives has prevailed between the United States and Japan, Korea, Australia and even Indonesia ever since the end of World War II. In the case of Australia, of course, that identity extended back many years before the war.

But in the case of China, deep suspicions existed on both sides. In the 1950s and 1960s we were very unhappy with the close relationship between China and the Soviet Union, and with the aggressive philosophical attachment to Communism that characterized the People's Republic. Of course, we still held a considerable legacy of resentment over the Chinese Communists' defeat in 1949 of the Chinese Nationalists under Chiang Kai-shek, whom we had supported over many years before and during World War II. The PRC's support of North Korea, when we were supporting South Korea, was remembered too by our Government and by the thousands of Americans who had fought in Korea from 1950 well into 1953. We also remembered, of course, the PRC's early support of North Vietnam.

Following his defeat on the mainland, Chiang Kai-shek had taken his government, which had adopted as its name the Republic of China, to Taiwan. In a short time, the Republic of China achieved an economic miracle. Our relations with Chiang remained cordial and close. The People's Republic considered that closeness to be an intolerable affront to it; and throughout the 1960s and the 1970s, regular confrontations ensued, in the United Nations and elsewhere, over whether there existed one or two Chinas. We strongly and successfully opposed the admission of the People's Republic to the United Nations, until 1971, when the UN finally voted to admit the PRC.

As relations between China and the Soviet Union chilled, and then hardened into implacable hatred on the part of the Chinese, President Richard Nixon saw an opportunity and, with Henry Kissinger, developed and expanded it. They worked out arrangements by which we were able to keep our relationships with Taiwan, and at the same time begin a long, slow process of convincing the People's Republic that a reasonable working relationship with the United States was quite possible, and indeed held many advantages for both.

By 1979, the Chinese relationship seemed important enough to us that the Carter Administration was willing to accept most of the People's Republic's demands that we sharply reduce, and eventually reverse, our relationships with Taiwan. The Carter Administration agreed to a one year moratorium on arms sales to Taiwan; and many felt that had President Jimmy Carter been re-elected, his Administration would have continued the moratorium from year to year. The Taiwan Relations Act, adopted by the Congress and then signed by President Carter, did provide a framework for an unofficial relationship with Taiwan following our derecognition of the Republic of China. At the core of that Act was the requirement that the United States provide Taiwan with such defense articles and service as necessary for Taiwan to maintain a sufficient defense capability.

There were still considerable suspicions in the United States of the motives of the People's Republic, particularly among conservative Republicans; and indeed the new President from California, who had been very friendly with the Chinese in San Francisco and in other California communities, remained fervently loyal to the Chiang Kai-shek regime and its successors on Taiwan.

By 1981, when President Reagan took office, relations between China and the Soviet Union appeared to be colder and more intractable than ever. The factors that impelled President Nixon to go to China in the early 1970s still pertained, and argued strongly for establishing military-to-military relationships of our two countries. But that effort had never progressed, and was the least promising then of all the aspects of our relations with China.

In fact the Carter Administration, through Secretary of State Cyrus Vance (until after the Soviet invasion of Afghanistan), actually discouraged closer military relations with China, on the ground that movement in that direction would make more difficult the plans for a closer relationship with the Soviet Union.

That approach emphasized a very important difference between our strategy with the PRC and that of our predecessors. We saw the relationship between the United States and China as vital in and of itself, and not just as a function of a strategic triangle. (That is one reason I have urged recently that we not try to devise additional punishments for the Chinese as a result of the recent turmoil there, but constructively help them change.[1])

1. See Caspar W. Weinberger, "Commentary," *Forbes*, August 7, 1989, p. 31.

In January 1980, however, the then Secretary of Defense, Harold Brown, had visited China. His was the first of the high level U.S. military meetings with Chinese mainland leaders. Although the two sides agreed on a limited program of training and logistics exchanges, no arms sales agreements were reached.

In the fall, the 1980 Presidential election, with its very decisive results, showed that the American people were determined to regain our own military strength. Because neither China nor the United States was really ready in 1980 to accept a close military-to-military relationship, with all of the contacts that would entail, virtually no progress was made toward that relationship until several years later.

Mainly, China was still unsure about the extent to which it wanted to have foreign participation in its military modernization program. Its leaders knew they had to modernize their fighting forces, but they were not agreed on how they wanted to accomplish that.

In any event, the Chinese government seemed far more interested in economic modernization, and its major internal policy battles were being carried out with great secrecy, almost entirely beyond the comprehension of the West. As we know now, the question really was whether the People's Republic was willing and ready to recognize that if it wished to improve its economy and the quality of life for its people, it would have to modify the essentials of its long-term commitment to socialism and to Communist economic theory.

Deng Xiaoping, a leader of extraordinary capacity, courage, and staying power, had been one of the participants in the political struggle, not only against Chiang Kai-shek but later against various internal factions in the Chinese government. Those internal fights were particularly vicious during the Cultural Revolution. Now Deng had emerged as the undoubted leader of the People's Republic, and he was more than willing to try wholly new approaches, recognizing as he did that Communist and socialist economics had failed badly and could not produce what he knew China urgently needed now.

But it was clear to Deng and to the other members of the Chinese leadership, notably Zhao Ziyang, who later was to become Premier and the General Secretary of the Chinese Communist Party,[2] that economic "modernization" (which really was an increasing willingness to accept the economic principles of a freer market, with sharply increased private participation and sharply decreased state control), must precede any military modernization. That in turn meant that military modernization and the resulting changes in military relationships with the United States would have to wait several years, until Deng could find the funds.

But the Chinese leadership was not entirely sure it could modernize its military forces according to its own timetable. They were all too well aware of the Soviet divisions on their borders, and the immense and increasing military power of the USSR. So they were not unreceptive to a much closer military-to-military relationship with the United States; but they could not and would not appear to be eager for it.

On the American side, President Carter's Administration, beset by many problems and shortly to be voted out of office, had shown no willingness to reduce many of the fundamental tech-

---

2. And then to lose all of his power and position in the June 1989 crisis. It is not clear whether the military force used against the demonstrators in Tiananmen Square has ended cries for democracy in China. It is clear, however, that that military action has made it far more difficult for the United States to continue building on the greatly improved military-to-military relationship I helped establish in the 1980s. But nothing has changed the vital necessity for both the United States and the People's Republic of China to reestablish the relationship we developed in the 1980s.

That renewal will happen only when China shows more clemency toward the demonstrators and accepts that a nation cannot have economic freedom without political freedom; nor can China expect improved relations with the West without visibly changing the policies that resulted from the Tiananmen Square turmoil. Equally, it is important for us to urge change, quietly, in our communications with the Chinese, and not drive them into isolation or pro-Soviet policies by our criticisms or "punishments."

nology barriers that would ultimately have to be diminished if there were to be any improvement in the military relationship with the People's Republic.

In 1981, after President Reagan took over, our own military strengthening had to have first priority. We went about that as vigorously as we could. And with all the other issues confronting us—in NATO, the Middle East, Japan, elsewhere in the world and at home—the question of improving our military relationships with the People's Republic of China could not be addressed immediately with the urgency we knew it deserved.

Our legal requirement, under the Taiwan Relations Act, to continue arms sales to Taiwan, became a major problem with Deng Xiaoping. His adversaries at home, of whom there were still a great many, were, in the nature of political adversaries all over the world, anxious to secure political advantage by attacking him. It was easy enough for them to raise the cry that he was helping—or at least not fighting vigorously enough against—the Chinese on Taiwan, with their claim of being the "true" China, so long as he accepted continued arms sales by the United States to Taiwan and the Taiwan Relations Act.

Matters came to a climax in the long debate in the United States over Taiwan's 1980 request for a modern high performance fighter aircraft. Additional months of intense negotiations with the People's Republic by the new President, his Security Adviser and the State Department finally produced the August 17, 1982, communiqué that the People's Republic signed. Essentially, it sanctioned our continuing to provide weapons to Taiwan, but on a limited and diminishing scale; the key idea was that while we would help to maintain Taiwan's defensive capabilities, we would not give it anything, or do anything, that could upgrade, qualitatively or quantitatively, the levels and types of arms sales to Taiwan from the benchmark period 1979 to 1982. As a result, Taiwan later decided to embark on a program to build its own fighter plane, and felt we should help in its development as much as we could consistent with our agreements with the PRC. The prototype was completed by Taiwan in 1988, and gives promise of being an excellent addition to Taiwan's defensive strength.

A year after the communiqué, Secretary of Commerce Malcolm Baldrige visited China, in 1983. As a result of his visit we agreed to liberalize our guidelines on exports to China, particularly exports of seven so-called "dual use" items.[3] The phrase denotes that although those items did have some military use and capability, the exports were being approved so that China could have the benefits of their commercial, nonmilitary uses.

Most of the seven were things we did not export to the Soviet Union or its Communist allies. That distinction too demonstrated to China that we were placing it in a category apart from Communist nations generally and the Soviet Union and Warsaw Pact in particular. That in turn led the Chinese to be far more receptive to military visits and military discussions.

Thus it was that in the summer of 1983, I concluded that while we should continue to do all we could to nurture our relationship with Taiwan, it was time for me to accept the invitation from China's Minister of Defense. I would go to China as the best way to advance the cause of improved military relationships between our countries and to discuss with the Chinese the nature and extent of the Soviet threat against them. I felt I should take personal charge of our effort to secure a better military relationship with China, believing then, as now, that such a relationship could be of great help to both our countries and would show the Chinese clearly that they did not need to resume or strengthen their military ties to the Soviet Union.

That was not an easy decision for a Californian brought up in San Francisco with a great many Chinese friends and political

---

3. The specific identity of those "dual use" items is still classified information.

supporters all of whom were still strongly supportive of Taiwan, and very suspicious, to the point of hostility, toward Communist China.

Nevertheless, I reflected on a number of other arrangements, alliances and friendships we had with countries with whom we had strong differences about their internal policies. Also, I was particularly interested in China's relationship with the Soviet Union and the military threat that the Soviet Union clearly posed to the People's Republic. The Soviets regularly kept over fifty divisions stationed on their border with China, along with vast fleets of fighter and bomber planes; and the Soviet navy cruised at will and with rapidly increasing strength in and around Chinese waters.

I also was most interested in China's internal convulsions as its leaders moved to repair the shattering devastation of the Cultural Revolution. I thought they should be encouraged to move down the "capitalist road," although I knew they would never call it that, nor should we. But their increasing interest in and reliance on free market principles was evident, and very encouraging. This was, it seemed to me, the time to explore the possibility of a closer military relationship. Much excellent staff thought and work had gone into that effort; but I did not see any way that we could secure what we wanted without letting the Chinese know that the American Secretary of Defense, and indeed the President, were both *personally* interested in China, and in our future military relationships with China. And the best way to convey that message was by a personal visit.

I knew that anything we did would be viewed with great concern by Taiwan and by supporters of Taiwan, for many of whom I had long-standing affection and among whom I had many friendships. I also knew that China would view with the deepest suspicion any continued close relationships that we had with Taiwan. Thus it was quite apparent that I would have to walk a very narrow tightrope during my visit if I was to accomplish what we wanted. Our objectives were to open the door to future, and continued, close military relationships with China; and, at the same time, to maintain our friendship with and support for Taiwan.

My other objectives were to arrange a visit to the United States by Zhao Ziyang—a necessary preliminary to a visit by President Reagan to China—and also to convince the Chinese that we wanted to reclaim their friendship for its own sake and not just as a maneuver in our continuing struggle with the Soviets. Finally, we needed to convince the Chinese both of our general good will and of our desire to transfer military technologies to them that they would find useful but that would not harm us if they escaped to other countries.

There was, in fact, substantial distrust on both sides and, we felt, a considerable lack of understanding on the part of the Chinese as to how technology transfer worked in the United States. Also, we knew that they did not fully appreciate the fact that we had two governments in Washington: a congressional government as well as an executive government, and that even the executive government was not always in full agreement on a given issue.

I made sure that Richard Armitage, our Assistant Secretary with direct responsibility for our relationships in the Pacific, and my longtime friend and associate Will Taft, General Counsel of the Department, accompanied us. Also on the trip was James Wade, my Deputy Undersecretary most familiar with technology transfer procedures, and most knowledgeable about which technology could be safely transferred and which could not. General William Richardson represented the Joint Chiefs. He commanded the Army's Training and Doctrine Command, and knew which things the Chinese most needed in their quest for military modernization. General Richardson had the advantage of being born in China, the son of missionaries. We also had General Colin Powell, my Senior Military Assistant and one of the finest military officers and persons I had worked with over the years (he is now Chairman of the Joint Chiefs of Staff); and our Undersecretary for Policy, Fred Ikle, who was familiar with the Chinese and Pacific matters through long years of study; and Michael Burch, our Public Affairs Assistant Secretary. His relationships with the press were both good and necessary.

We also took representatives from the Department of State, including Paul Wolfowitz, who was the Assistant Secretary for East Asian and Pacific Affairs,[4] and one of our recognized China experts, Gaston Sigur, the Special Assistant to the President for Asian Affairs and one of our nation's foremost authorities on Asian matters. After we arrived, of course, our Ambassador, Arthur Hummel, was invariably helpful, understanding and effective.

I was insistent that our wives accompany us, not only for their and our sakes, but also because I thought it would send a unique signal to the Chinese that we regarded this occasion as a most important one. Ours certainly was a larger group than I normally took on trips. It demonstrated the enormous importance that we attached to the success of this mission, as well as the difficulties that we saw ahead of us.

September 1983 had been a particularly busy month in a long series of busy months. At the beginning of the month, I had made a three day trip to Central America to visit our forces there who were helping to train Honduran and Salvadoran troops. Our forces also were conducting extensive maneuvers then in Honduras. That had been a very quick and important trip, my first one to that area. I met with the American trainers in Salvador, and spoke to the Salvadoran forces being trained in Honduras, and visited the very large exercise we were conducting in Honduras. As usual, I met with the presidents, defense ministers, and

4. He is now the Undersecretary of Defense for Policy.

foreign ministers of Honduras and El Salvador, as well as their counterparts in Panama.

I was particularly impressed with the medical facilities that we set up in Honduras as part of our maneuvers there. There was a station hospital, housed completely in tents, which had been flown down from the United States and assembled in about a day and one-half. It was then ready to perform all forms of medical treatment, up to and including open heart surgery.

I returned from that trip on September 8 to Andrews Air Force Base, and the press there advised me that during my three days in Central America, I had had fourteen helicopter rides, two formal arrival ceremonies, a Panamian state dinner, many meetings with our three ambassadors, and dozens of other events visiting troops, including a life raft demonstration in the jungle training facility at Panama, and a visit to one of our "new" old battleships, the *New Jersey*, to observe a firing exercise—among other things. A battleship firing nine 16-inch guns hurling projectiles the size and weight of a Volkswagen 23 miles is the most cataclysmic sound I have ever heard.

On September 1, shortly before I had left for the Central American trip, the Soviets shot down the Korean airliner, and there were many calls back and forth to Washington during the trip as further details on that naked aggression were received and secure conference calls were held to consider appropriate responses. It seemed to me that that act should emphasize to the Chinese, and to the world, the nature and character of the Soviet threat; and that the Soviet claims that they thought the 747 Korean airliner was really an American 707 "spy plane" were too ludicrous to be of any value to the Soviets as by their denials they characteristically struggled to avoid worldwide stigma.

Also, in Lebanon, the Marines were coming under increasingly heavy attacks in their positions at Beirut Airport. It was becoming clear that there was no real possibility of our succeeding with the original mission of the multinational force, to interpose neutral troops between withdrawing Israelis and Syrians. It was now clear that neither the Syrians nor the Israelis were withdrawing; and it was also disturbingly clear that there were many warring factions and tribes milling about in Lebanon, and that the authority of the central government was being diminished every day.

All of those matters occupied a substantial amount of time, as did the preparation I was trying to do for the China trip, attending many briefings and reading large volumes of background material, prepared in most expert fashion by our staff.

One of the most helpful briefings I had was with my Harvard College classmate, the late Theodore H. White. Teddy White was one of the great China experts. He was trusted by the leadership of the PRC, and his advice and suggestions were enormously helpful to me. (At the time, however, he was held somewhat in disfavor in China due to a recent *Time* "cover story" in which he had written quite critically of some aspects of the Chinese regime, and concluded that they were a long way from a Western democracy.)

Teddy White told me of the great progress the Chinese economy was making as it shifted away from the Socialist Communist economic system. But he also warned me against my making any comment to the Chinese that they had in fact given up "Communist economics." He said that even if they were bitter enemies now of the Soviets, that did not reflect any lessening of their attachment to Communism as an idea and a dogma.

"But," said Teddy White, "the Chinese are very realistic, and they know the Soviets pose a real military threat to them and that we do not. So if you are patient and persuasive enough, you can eventually get a good military-to-military relationship established.

"But in addition to being practical and realistic, the Chinese are very proud and genuinely regard other countries, particularly our young one, as upstarts. It will probably take quite a time before they actually ask for anything."

I had many other helpful briefings by China experts from several administrations, including talks with my predecessor, Harold Brown.

Meanwhile, of course, the need to continue to mobilize public support for our efforts in Central America continued. I discussed my Central American trip on two networks the morning after I got back from that trip, and talked to the Air Force Association convention on the twelfth of September in Washington. On the fourteenth I was in Dayton, Ohio, for long-scheduled speeches there. Thereafter, I spoke at ceremonies in the White House Rose Garden honoring the Hispanic contribution to the United States. Meanwhile, of course, the regular routine continued, with morning staff meetings, and many National Security Council meetings, particularly in connection with the shooting down by the Soviets of the Korean airliner. State Department and arms control advocates were very anxious that we not take such strong steps as demanding Soviet apologies and reparations to the Koreans as a condition of our continuing any talks with the Soviets. I felt we should signal our extreme displeasure with what seemed to be the typically uncivilized behavior of the Soviet government. The arguments went on inconclusively for some time. The President decided that while we should indeed tell the world of our horror at the Soviet action, we should not link the incident to arms negotiations then going on with the Soviet Union. During that same time, we were working on new ways to improve contractual relationships between the military and major defense contractors to eliminate a number of the problems that had led to attempts to charge us outrageous prices for small procurement items.

In the middle of all this, the Chinese Ambassador to Washington, Zhang Wenjin, gave a very fine dinner at his embassy residence a few blocks from my home, for my wife and me and for our Pentagon party headed for China. At that party I learned about the enormous importance that the Chinese attached to toasts at a formal dinner. I had been in the habit of making generally spontaneous remarks as part of my toast; but Rich Armitage told me with considerable earnestness that that would not do in China, where every word and every punctuation mark in a toast was held up to microscopic examination by the Chinese later to see the number of meanings that could be extracted from the words. Toasts in China must be most carefully drafted and must be read word for word. That style was uncomfortable for me, but at the Chinese Ambassador's dinner we tried to comply; still, I could not resist a few general remarks, especially at the end, expressing my deep appreciation for all that had been done.

On Thursday morning, September 22, we all went to Andrews Air Force Base, and I met briefly with the reporters waiting in the small enclosed area at the foot of the steps leading up to the plane, to tell them something of our hopes for the visit. I was pleasantly surprised that the Ambassador from the People's Republic had taken the trouble to come to Andrews to bid me a formal farewell, a mark of particular politeness and again a demonstration of the importance that both sides attached to this trip.

We stopped in Honolulu for meetings and for dinner with Admiral Crowe at the official residence of the Commander in Chief of the Pacific. The house has guest quarters and is very comfortable; and it is in Pearl Harbor, directly across from Battleship Row. The next day we stopped for refueling at Midway, reviving memories of World War II and of our first naval success nearby.

At Midway, we were again treated to the splendid hospitality our forces all over the world always extended to me. The refueling stop was also a very good opportunity for us to meet with some of our forces there, and to make some of the additional necessary calls to Washington for any late information.

We arrived in Tokyo on the twenty-fourth after crossing the date line. The flight had been routine, but "routine" to Air Force pilots means an extremely comfortable plane with ample room for meetings as well as for resting and preparation of all kinds. The plane we had was one that I always hoped we could use on long trips. It had been Lyndon Johnson's Air Force One. It was old, but kept in perfect condition and equipped with full communication equipment, enabling me to talk securely to any point in the world and to receive written or oral messages from anywhere.

These flights were always "working flights" in every sense of the word. There were the enormous and extraordinarily comprehensive and detailed briefing books covering everything from histories of China to biographies of everyone we were to meet, and background on what we might see. Every event was set forth in great detail; and every issue we wanted to raise, and everything the Chinese might want to raise, was set out. Our objective as spelled out in the briefing books was to lay the foundation for each of the pillars of a military-to-military relationship with the Chinese—high level visits, functional exchanges, and military technology cooperation.

I held many briefing sessions with our staff Chinese experts, and I marveled then, as always, at the scope of their knowledge about even the smallest details of the trip, including full background on the new sights we had added to the schedule. This latter was better than any travel literature I had read.

We also had typewriters, copying machines, facsimile machines, and word processors aboard, which were most useful for speech drafts, toasts, and arrival and departure statements. All of those documents, current news summaries, facsimiles of newspaper articles, classified intelligence reports, and much more flowed from these machines in a steady stream. Inevitably, there was also a pile of paperwork that had accumulated at the office in the hours before our departure that had to be disposed of and returned to Washington. My longtime Executive Assistant, Kay Leisz, and my secretary, Thelma Stubbs, performed yeoman and deeply appreciated work on this and the many other trips I took, doing all of the things they did in their Pentagon offices with no letup or change, even while we flew all night, sometimes in quite turbulent weather.

Reporters were aboard the plane, and there were many informal meetings with them, as well as one or two formal press conferences in the conference room on the plane. They were conducted under much more informal and cheerful circumstances than most of the more formal press conferences; reporters gathered in a tight circle so that all could fit into the plane's small conference room. There were microphones and tape recorders everywhere, including, of course, those of our own public affairs staff. Before each of the formal press conferences, we met with the China experts on the trip, to go over questions that the press might be expected to ask.

At the Tokyo stopover, I said that we hoped to respond to the needs of the Chinese, as we perceived them, as well as to their requests, and pointed out that as two great powers we shared a number of strategic and economic interests. We also warned against expecting any dramatic agreements on arms sales or military cooperation. The press wrote that I had expressed an "almost unrestrained enthusiasm for helping China build its defenses." I did suggest that the recent Soviet murder of the South Koreans, and others in the Korean plane they shot down, underlined the common interest of the United States, Japan, China and Pakistan to be strong both economically and militarily. I said that I felt our whole ability to deter war and maintain peace "will be greatly increased if we can strengthen China in the ways they want to be strengthened."

I was also, of course, aware of alarms that might be set off in Japan and among our other allies in Southeast Asia if we were viewed as trying to arm China for any sort of offensive operations.

On landing in Japan, I had an opportunity to express again the appreciation we felt for the self-chosen role of Japan in defending both its own territories and the sea-lanes out to a thousand miles. I was also able to talk with Defense Minister Kazuo Tanikawa about the problems and needs of our forces based in Japan, and with him and Foreign Minister Shintaro Abe about the desirability of Japan's spending more on its own defense so that it could realize its chosen self-defense goals. Foreign Minister Abe was sympathetic but noncommittal. Ambassador Mike Mansfield helpfully arranged briefings on both Japan and China.

We flew on to China, arriving on Sunday, September 25. The Chinese airport ceremonies would be accurately described, I think, as "correct." Foreign Ministry and Defense Ministry officials met our party and advised us that more formal ceremonies would be held later. We were then loaded into Soviet-built cars and taken to the formal honors ceremony, held in front of a military museum in downtown Beijing.

Soldiers of the People's Liberation Army paraded, and I had the opportunity to inspect them. The expertly conducted ceremony included Chinese soldiers, sailors and airmen in special ceremonial units of the People's Liberation Army (all of whom seemed to have new uniforms, but all of them still devoid of any badges of rank, something that was not to change until 1988). A band played "The Star-Spangled Banner," very credibly, and the Chinese national anthem. The Chinese Defense Minister, Zhang Aiping, a former infantry division commander of one of the divisions of the People's Liberation Army that fought against the Japanese, and a veteran of the Long March, seemed a bit stiff in his formality. He was apparently uncertain how far to go in being cordial. I had learned that an American plane, shot down in Vietnam, was prominently on display in front of the museum, and looked about for it. It had been removed, and I took that to be a good sign. Cynics in our party suggested that it had merely been taken away to be repainted.

However, from that point on the visit was marked by increasing enthusiasm by our hosts, and, finally, even by expressions of great friendship. Zhang and I became and remained, ever after, close personal friends. His cordiality and thoughtfulness toward me on this visit and the one that followed were not exceeded anywhere else in the world that I visited.

Zhang is a frail looking man; we were told by one or two of our staff that he was not in good health, and that the schedules would probably have to be curtailed for that reason.

But Zhang completely belied his appearance. He turned out to be vigorous and strong in every way; and the more cordial our personal relationships became, the stronger he seemed to grow.

After some fascinating sightseeing during the rest of that day, which included a lengthy and most welcome tour of the Forbidden City, we were billeted in The Diaoyutai[5] national guest house. The Diaoyutai is a compound that had belonged to the Emperor before the Revolution; several houses have been built within it. The most lavish, a beautiful Chinese pagoda-style home set in the middle of a lake, was prepared for the visit of Queen Elizabeth to China in 1986. We were assigned very comfortable quarters, with rooms for all the principal members of our staff, in two or three of the cottages. There were wide hallways, and very large porches where the breeze was most welcome. Beijing in September was heavily tropical that year.

The opening banquet was given by the Chinese on that first evening, in the Great Hall of the People. I had gone over my formal toast, making several changes, just as if it were a communiqué, to respect its great importance to the Chinese.

The Great Hall is really a series of halls. Some of them are very large indeed, and some are smaller meeting rooms. All are im-

5. Literally: fishing platform. The guest houses themselves were constructed after 1949.

pressive in size, with wide corridors and high ceilings. We were first taken to one of the smaller halls, where the chairs were arranged in the usual long rectangle. Zhang Aiping and I sat next to each other; and then, strictly by rank, all of the other guests, with our wives, were arrayed down the remaining sides of the rectangle. We talked through interpreters in comparatively desultory fashion until it was time to go in to the banquet.

In such meetings of state the world over, it is always high protocol that no real business be conducted in the pre-dining sessions. Traditionally, light and unsubstantive matters only are to be gone into; and that tradition is strictly observed. Still, I had to convey to the Chinese Defense Minister my great appreciation for the hospitality that had already been extended, for the enjoyment we all had taken from the tour of the Forbidden City and the other sights we had seen, and for the great comfort of the guest rooms assigned to us. He seemed pleased with that. And we took pleasure in noting the presence of his wife, another mark of Chinese politeness and the importance they attached to our meetings. And as I learned later, they too especially appreciated that our wives had accompanied us. Their presence enabled both sides to treat the visit on a far friendlier basis than a formal protocol-ridden visit would have allowed.

We shortly adjourned to a much larger hall, where a splendid Chinese banquet took place. There were at least eighteen courses; and since I am a considerable fan of Chinese food, having been raised and trained in San Francisco, where there are many fine Chinese restaurants, I greatly enjoyed the meal.

I had been warned about the customarily constant consumption of mao-tai (140 proof), far beyond my normal intake of about two sips of such liquids. Nevertheless, I circulated around the room, accompanied by several of the Chinese officials and the Defense Minister, toasting all and sundry, but staying within my basic total allowance of two sips.

When the time came for the main toasts, I was not too surprised, but not especially encouraged, that Zhang Aiping indicated very little interest in any type of relationship, military or otherwise, with us. In his toast, apparently memorized, he said, "We will not attach ourselves to any big power or group of powers," and he recalled that China had been subjected to a number of most unwelcome foreign aggressions in the past—an unmistakable reference to European, Japanese and, as well, American forces in China. The Defense Minister concluded, "That is why we treasure our independence, sovereignty and military integrity." He added that he believed that "with our own initiative and our own hands we will be able to achieve the modernization of our country."

He was beginning to make my trip sound a bit unnecessary. And although he did conclude that China would be willing to cooperate to "speed up the modernization of the armed forces," small encouragement could be drawn from that.

In my own toast, I spoke of how the United States and China shared many important strategic concerns based on our common desire to live in peace and freedom—goals that could be threatened by the immense size of the Soviet forces, both strategic and conventional. And I expressed the hope that we would have "an enduring relationship," saying that close United States–China relations and cooperation in strategic areas would serve the interests of both our nations. I spoke of our Administration's "new policy on technology transfers," and conveyed that it gave us the opportunity in a responsible way to contribute to China's defense and modernization. I also asked for "candid exchanges of views" to enable us to "avoid the kinds of unjust perception in past U.S. policies which come from incomplete or inaccurate understanding of those policies." And I said that we anticipated continuing our meetings and discussions at a higher level. That statement, of course, was designed to encourage Chinese agreement to an exchange of visits by Premier Zhao Ziyang and President Reagan.

The next morning, on September 26, we met again in the

Great Hall. The Chinese officials were lined up in the normal configuration on one side of a long table covered in green baize, and our "visiting team" was lined up on the other side. Zhang Aiping did not appear ready to talk substantively at this point. He advised me, however, in a brief opening, that the Chinese felt that anyone who had come so far must be bearing great gifts for them; he then went on to say that in China a guest always speaks first, and so would I please open the meeting.

I would. I delivered a lengthy statement about our views on both global and regional issues, including our concerns about the growth of Soviet naval and air power in the Pacific and about their willingness to use it, as they had when they shot down the Korean airliner. I pointed out that that act of aggression clearly differentiated the Soviet Union from the United States. I told them of our rearmament plans and of the necessity for rearmament, and assured them that we had no aggressive or offensive motives or agendas toward any nation. With the translations, but no interruptions or questions from the Chinese, the whole presentation took well over an hour. It was designed to be as inclusive as possible.

With no discernible trace of irony, the Chinese Defense Minister thanked me for my "concise briefing," contenting himself with saying that he appreciated the opportunity to get to know us better, and that they would make a careful study of all of the many points I had raised.

I knew they were more interested in exchanges in military technology than in our views on the threats from the north, but I also thought it important for them to know what motivated our meeting; why we felt it necessary to continue the defense buildup in which we were then engaged. The Chinese Defense Minister did say that he was basically in agreement with much that I had said. His statement had a Delphic ring to it, sufficient to mean almost anything, or nothing.

He did want to have a future military technology cooperation agreement with us, he said, and to get that signed as soon as possible. By that he meant a basic agreement that we would give them essentially what they wanted without their being required first to list or define any specific things that might be approved for transfer.

Again our differences were evident. It seemed quite clear that the Chinese were unwilling to ask for the technologies or items unless they were sure they would not be turned down. So they did not wish to ask for specific items of military technology, but preferred to work out broad framework agreements. The Chinese are experts at sending indirect signals; at letting you know precisely what they want without their coming out directly and asking for it, risking a loss of face should they be turned down.

Nevertheless, despite those differences I sensed a growing cordiality on the part of Zhang Aiping. I had great respect for him personally because of his splendid war record and because he had been strong enough to survive the excesses of the Cultural Revolution. He had had a very bad time during that period, as had Deng Xiaoping. In addition to all his military capability, including expertise in the technical side of various military technologies, Zhang Aiping was a scholar and a noted calligrapher.

Some have since asked me, quite naively, how I could become friends with a Communist! Zhang Aiping was unquestionably a Communist, but he was an anti-Soviet Communist. We were basically agreed that China, regardless of its internal government, was quite capable of having, and needed to have, a good military relationship with us, and that such a relationship would serve the interests of both our countries.

He seemed to respect me, and our exchanges became more and more informal and friendly as time went on. He had been carefully briefed about my history in government. I think my having served in the Nixon Administration in four capacities was particularly helpful, because the Chinese have enormous respect for that former President. Perhaps Zhang may also have found it congenial that I too had served in the infantry in the Pacific during the war.

After our first long formal session, the Chinese did agree to have our two staffs meet to see what kind of military technology cooperation agreement could be worked out. Essentially, we wanted the kind of agreement we had with other countries: one saying that each item requested by the Chinese would be considered on a case-by-case basis. But, as we have seen, the Chinese wanted an agreement that spelled out the level of technology releasable to them, an agreement they could then use to authorize many of their actual requests without their having to apply for approval of those specific items.

Essentially the Chinese wanted an agreement that would allow them to go directly to American companies and negotiate on specific systems on their own terms. We, on the other hand, wanted to identify specific systems or programs that we could and would release to them, and then cooperate with them on a government-to-government basis.

While the staffs were meeting, I met in the late afternoon with Premier Zhao Ziyang to discuss the whole Chinese-American relationship, with emphasis on the possible exchange of visits between Zhao and President Reagan.

At that meeting I heard the first mention of Taiwan during our stay in China. I attempted to state our position and move on to another subject. Our position was that we would be bound by the August 17 communiqué, and would continue to make arms sales to Taiwan, but that we would do nothing that violated that communiqué or upgraded the Taiwan military capability.

Zhao, however, was apparently charged with the task of raising the difficult Taiwan question, to demonstrate that the Chinese took that issue very seriously and to impress upon us that Tawain was still an obstacle to better future relationships. He repeated the same points four or five times. At one point, my staff tells me, I gave the appearance of being asleep. I was no doubt meditating on Zhao's words. But in any event, I do recall that Zhao finally agreed to change the subject, and we got on to other matters.

The next day, September 27, featured a six-hour meeting, including staff from both sides, at our guest house at Diaoyutai. We discussed in detail their "1981 list,"[6] which had been brought to Washington earlier; but the long discussions produced nothing other than a reiteration of our desire to take up Chinese requests on a case-by-case basis, and the Chinese desire to have a broad framework so that everything they defined as fitting within that framework would automatically be given to them.

I was also taken to a garrison post near Beijing to be shown a firing exercise of a Chinese division. It demonstrated considerable achievement in accuracy, but also underlined the need of the Chinese Army to modernize itself in all respects.

Tuesday evening I gave our return dinner in the Great Hall of the People for our Chinese hosts; it was virtually a mirror image of theirs the night before.

Just before Monday's dinner, the Chinese told us the staffs could meet again, to try to break the deadlock. That session took place at Diaoyutai and lasted until about ten-thirty that night, with the result that some of our staff missed all eighteen courses of the dinner. As soon as the meeting was over, I asked that the Chinese be told that we wished to meet with them again in the morning. We still had no agreement, but we wanted to do something to convince the Chinese that we were serious about helping them modernize. The staffs met again the next day, from eleven-thirty until one-thirty; but again no progress was reported to me when I returned from the obligatory visit to the Great Wall.

Being an inveterate sightseer, I had been looking forward to the Great Wall for a long time. We began our drive northward

---

6. That list is still classified.

from Beijing, accompanied by the military officers assigned to me; they were uniformly extremely cordial and helpful. The countryside was quite spectacular, with beautiful mist-shrouded mountains looking like all the sketches by Chinese artists, and quite different from American or European mountains. The Great Wall is as wonderful as all the descriptions of it. I had been warned not to try to go all the way to the top of the rather innocent looking hill up which this section of the Great Wall climbed, and that was good advice. It was far steeper than it appeared. We were all deeply impressed with the extraordinary feats of military engineering required to build the wall. The Chinese were delighted with our delight at being there.

When we returned to Beijing in the afternoon, I met with our staff on the porch of our guest house to see if there was any way we could possibly reach agreement with the Chinese without giving up our own requirement that we should approach each weapons request on a case-by-case basis, which in fact meant that there had to be a formal Chinese request for any weapons system or specific technology.

We had been assured in Washington that anything we said in private in China would be listened to. As a result, we had brought along informal voice "protectors." They were like ether masks used in old hospitals to administer anesthetics. We spoke into our "ether" masks and were able to hear the responses; but anyone listening outside heard nothing but the most awful gibberish, because the CIA had also furnished us with a noise machine. It fitted conveniently under the table and set up a clatter that would frustrate the most determined listeners anywhere. That of course was the idea. For over an hour, we talked back and forth through the masks while the noise machine clacked away under the table. Eventually we concluded that much though we wanted to be helpful, we could not sign an agreement under which the Chinese would be able to claim various pieces of our technology without individual review: We had restraints on many items; and we had no track record of the way the Chinese would protect the technologies we were able to send to them. At one point in our discussions, a Chinese housekeeper came onto the porch, bound for cleaning operations in our rooms. When she heard the unearthly clatter of our discussions, she left hastily, firmly convinced, I fear, that all Westerners were indeed devils, as she had probably felt for years.

Finally, at another joint session after our dinner, we agreed that we could sign, if not an agreement, at least "minutes" of that meeting; its points would clarify the understanding on each side of what had taken place, and show what we still had to do.

By now it was Wednesday morning, and I had a meeting scheduled in just a few hours with Deng Xiaoping in the Great Hall. It was conducted in the same configuration as the meetings before each of the banquets, with large armchairs placed side by side, and the famous cuspidor that appears prominently in the middle of every picture of Deng meeting with anyone.

I got off to a good start with Deng Xiaoping. He asked me to sit on his left rather than the right, which would have been called for by protocol, because he had a hearing problem; I told him that I heard less well in the left ear anyway, so it would be an admirable arrangement as far as I was concerned. He seemed to enjoy that small joke very much, and we progressed quite smoothly from there.

It is critically important that the atmosphere of all diplomatic meetings, which is frequently set with the first few sentences, be cordial and friendly; and that tone is usually achieved by whatever small jokes or phrases can be put into your opening sentences. President Reagan is particularly gifted in that respect, and I tried to follow his very effective practices. He can put foreign and other visitors at their ease within a matter of a few minutes, whatever country they may come from.

Deng Xiaoping is very small, and still, at the age of nearly eighty, he appeared quite a lot younger than he was. I saw few signs of the indignities and privations he suffered during the Cultural Revolution; but he did at one point tell me that for several months during that lamentable period in Chinese history, he had been forced to scrub stone hospital floors. I mentioned that with some awe to Yang Dezhi, the Chief of the General Staff and vice chairman of the Military Committee under Deng, when Yang called on me in Washington a year or so later. Yang chuckled and said, "Deng had it easy." I never did find out what precisely were the indignities that Yang Dezhi suffered during the Cultural Revolution.

As part of my substantive discussions with Deng Xiaoping, I covered much of the world situation, technology transfers and American-Chinese relations. Then I touched briefly on Taiwan. I also expressed some concern about the continued Chinese support of North Korea, and the worries that support caused our ally South Korea. Deng advised me that he knew the North Koreans would never invade South Korea, for two reasons. One was that the North Koreans were militarily inferior to South Korea (I was greatly surprised to hear that, because we knew, to the contrary, of the very large superiority of weapons and numbers of active divisions the North Koreans had); and second, said Deng, "We know they would not invade, because we would not support them."

That was quite an astonishing admission of dominance over the North Koreans by the Chinese. It may have been that attitude, perhaps expressed more freely than the North Koreans wanted to hear, that caused them in the next few years to turn increasingly to the Soviets rather than to the Chinese for their military support. Deng also urged that I tell the South Koreans that they could or should reunite with the North Koreans and that the North would be willing to grant favorable terms for such a reunification.

Deng told me frankly that he would like to improve Chinese relations with the Soviet Union, but that the PRC's "Three Conditions" must be met first. Those were the thinning out of Soviet forces on China's border, the withdrawal of Soviet troops and help from Afghanistan, and the withdrawal of Soviet support for the Vietnamese-backed regime in Cambodia.[7]

The press was waiting for a scheduled press conference with me after the meeting with Deng Xiaoping, and I was very glad the Chinese had agreed that I could say that a final agreement had been reached on the visit of Zhao Ziyang, their Premier, to Washington to meet with President Reagan. During the flight to China, the White House had given me authority to announce that the President would come to Beijing if the Chinese visit was agreed to, and so that morning I was also able to tell the press that meetings in China of the President and the Chinese Prime Minister had been agreed to and arranged. And I announced that I had invited the Defense Minister, Zhang Aiping, and his wife to the United States, and that they had accepted. All those visits took place as scheduled; and the President's trip particularly, in June 1984, was a great success.

Our staff returned for the press conference and advised me that we and the Chinese had concluded that we could not resolve our differences over technologies transfers, but that we would sign minutes of the meeting now; and perhaps the agreement that had eluded us could be signed at a later time, perhaps in Washington in connection with the visits that I had just announced.

I was relieved that I had finally been able to meet with the press, both those accompanying me and the reporters stationed in Beijing permanently. We had tried our best in that press conference and other press meetings to discourage any rumors of victory for our side, knowing how much the Chinese would

---

7. Some progress on all three of those conditions led to a public thawing of the chill between the PRC and the USSR during General Secretary Gorbachev's visit to Beijing in May 1989.

object to such overblown claims, or to any other posture that indicated a foreigner's success at their expense. For that reason, I did not have a daily press conference to advise the press what was happening, which I would have preferred, but simply had Mike Burch, our press secretary, describe each day's events in very low-key fashion. I also made the announcements and other statements at my press conference in a very low-key manner. I recalled that in the recent past, after a very optimistic set of press conference statements by Al Haig when he was Secretary of State, the Chinese had advised the press that Mr. Haig was wrong, and that nothing of what he had described so glowingly had happened. I was particularly glad I had taken the advice of Rich Armitage and Paul Wolfowitz, and downplayed our press conference. We were told by our press later that the Chinese were most enthusiastic about the accomplishments of our trip after the Beijing press conference, and claimed more from my visit there than I did. (Our portrayal of my visit—unusually low-key, as the Chinese saw it—put them in the unfamiliar position of having to play up the success of the visit in their press briefings.)

On Wednesday, after our press conference, we flew from Beijing down to the Xian area, because I had expressed strong interest in having an opportunity to visit the Qin Emperor archaeological digs, where hundreds of terra-cotta Chinese soldier-statues were buried with the remains of the emperor. The Chinese had made it a condition that we use their aircraft, and so we were flown southward in a very comfortable Chinese government plane to Xian, and thence were driven to the excavations. The sight was breathtaking: row upon row of the terra-cotta statues of soldiers in full uniform, each with a quite individually carved head and face—hundreds and hundreds of them, all drawn up in military fashion. In all ways, it is one of the most fantastic archaeological finds of the last half century.

The Chinese, as a special honor for me, unveiled an ancient life-size bronze and gold chariot that had been uncovered at the excavation, and apparently was to be used by the departed emperor to travel to Paradise.

We were billeted in a large but seldom used guest house nearby. Its principal features were very, very large rooms, particularly large bathrooms and dressing rooms, and heavy red, quite old, velvet draping everywhere.

Another major dinner was scheduled for that evening, and I had been awaiting the draft of the written toast that I was to use for that banquet. The toast that evening was considered particularly important, because the press were watching everything very closely, as indeed were the Soviets, to see if there was to be any evidence of closer ties between the United States and the People's Republic. By the same token, if there was any hesitancy or any miscue, that would be seen and reported extensively.

I wanted the toast to mention that we had just visited the tomb of the Qin Emperor who also had constructed portions of the Great Wall. I also wanted to make the point that the present People's Liberation Army now had to serve as a Great Wall to protect China against the very real threats that now, as then, came from the North.

The toast draft incorporating those points was late—almost the only time there was such a staff transgression—and it had not arrived when I came downstairs to have dinner.

I later found out that Bob Young, our China desk officer, had arrived at the banquet hall at the last minute via a commandeered Chinese Army jeep—the official delegation having already taken all the assigned cars when we had left the guest house. With the draft in hand, Bob plunged between the densely grouped Chinese, and handed it to Rich Armitage, who uttered a well known expletive, and then handed it immediately to me, just seconds before I was supposed to speak.

It was worth waiting for.

The Chinese liked the concept of the People's Liberation Army as a modern Great Wall blocking the "Threat from the North."

Thereafter, in private and occasionally in public, they assured me that they knew where the real threat came from, and that it was indeed from the North—meaning of course the Soviets—and not from the East—and that they knew the United States had no hostile intentions but desired only friendly relations with the People's Republic.

The banquet was as sumptuous as the dinner in Beijing, and the mao-tai flowed as freely. My abstinence began to be noticed, but the Chinese were far too polite to urge me to "drink up," as the Soviets had when I was there in 1973.

The next morning we were taken to visit a nearby aircraft engine plant, which was running at apparently less than half its capacity. We then returned to Beijing in the Chinese military aircraft, and from there departed for Shanghai, the last leg of this China visit.

In Shanghai, we had a short "windshield" tour of the city, the military term for a drive through with no stops. The impressions one can form from such a tour are necessarily limited, particularly when there is animated, translated conversation with military and other officials going on the whole time. But I did get the impression of a more modern, crowded and bustling city than Beijing. This was also a city that looked a bit more western, or at least more familiar to western eyes, than the others I had seen.

Our main purpose in Shanghai was to visit the Shanghai Naval Base, and I took the opportunity to inspect at first hand an old former Soviet submarine that was now a part of the Chinese navy. My hosts seemed quite pleased I was willing to walk all through the sub, and ask many questions about it. A splendid luncheon was given to me by the officers of the Shanghai Naval Base. There we found a very great increase in warmth and cordiality. Whether it was a result of instructions sent from Beijing, or simply the natural friendship between military people of two nations, I did not know, but the Shanghai reception was the most cordial and warmest of all on this visit. It was also here, at the luncheon in the Shanghai Naval Base, during one of the toasts by the naval officers, that the Chinese advised me in the most explicit terms that they knew the real threat to their existence came from the North, and they were preparing to deal with it if necessary.

As we boarded our familiar Air Force plane in Shanghai on September 29, I was very conscious that it had been a long trip. And yet it was less than half over. We still had to go to Sri Lanka, Pakistan, Egypt and Italy, before returning to the United States on October 4, 1983.

It had been a very successful visit to China. We did not have a large number of agreements to sign, but we had arranged the visits of China's Premier and its Defense Minister to the United States, and of America's President to China. Those visits took place at the times we had agreed on, and they were generally hailed as substantial successes and—even more important—we had, we believed, convinced the Chinese that we sincerely wanted to help them, and that it was necessary for them to take the kind of help we could give. At the same time, we believed that we had convinced them we would not be overreaching, and would not attempt to do anything more than give them the kind of assistance they wanted. They in turn had responded with the great hospitality and kindness for which they are known to all who have traveled there. At the end of the visit, and after the press conference in which we did not try to claim any better results than had actually been achieved, they seemed particularly pleased. I understood that such fundamental changes as we hoped to bring about in our military-to-military relationships would take time and patience, but I felt we had made real progress and laid a solid foundation for the future.

And I was buoyed by the Chinese reception; by the agreements we had entered into; by the prospects of future, far closer, relationships; by the knowledge that the Chinese recognized the Soviets as a major threat and showed few signs of reviving the very strong ties that had once marked relations between the Soviet Union and China.

With all of those trips, no matter how successful, no matter how gracious the hospitality, there is a great sense of relief when, after the formal and very cordial departure ceremonies, and after the presentation of the final gifts, and the photo albums commemorating and serving as a very welcome souvenir of the trip, you mount the stairs to your U.S. Air Force plane, and come again under the sheltering care of all on board. It is only then that you can move partially offstage and relax the vigilance and care you must always exercise when representing your country abroad.

Unfortunately, I could be "offstage" only briefly. We were back in Washington on October 4; on October 10, the President asked me to head the United States delegation to the funeral services in Korea for the Korean Cabinet ministers murdered in Burma by agents of North Korea. So on October 11 I flew out to Korea for the funeral and meetings, then flew homeward via Japan, pausing there for more conferences with Japanese officials and our Embassy personnel. I was back in Washington again on October 14. Preparations for the liberation of Grenada, dealing with the bombing of the Marine barracks in Lebanon, liberating Grenada, and taking part in a NATO defense ministers' meeting on October 26 and 27 at Montebello, Canada, where we secured agreement to a U.S. plan for reduction of nuclear battlefield weapons, completed the month.

The Chinese took some time to decide how they would formally respond to my visit. But by the spring of 1984, approximately nine months later, they announced that the Defense Minister Zhang Aiping would come to the United States, and that his visit would be preceded by further discussions on military technology at the working level.

Those meetings—including the son of the Defense Minister, Zhang Pin; and the son-in-law of Deng Xiaoping, He Ping; and the son of former People's Liberation Army Marshall He Long, He Pengfei—began in February. We also gave the Chinese team an opportunity to visit a number of American companies and military installations. We concluded our discussions on March 7 in Washington.

In late March there were four more weeks of meetings at the staff level in China, and we finally achieved agreement on Chinese letters of request for programs in artillery, antitank and air defense. We believed these were the areas best suited for close cooperation with the Chinese, because those were the fields we had identified as the ones most in need of modernization in the People's Liberation Army.

In June of 1984, the Defense Minister Zhang Aiping arrived for his return visit. We had arranged a number of meetings at the Pentagon. I also included meetings for him with the President, and with Secretary of State George Shultz and with General Jack Vessey, the then Chairman of the Joint Chiefs of Staff, and many others. We also arranged an opportunity for Zhang to travel around the United States visiting defense contractors and military facilities. I was delighted to be able to sign with him, before he left on that tour, a military technology cooperation minute that set forth the basic principles to be incorporated in our relationship in the future. He was extremely cordial and complimentary toward me about what we had accomplished in China the previous year. All the restraint and stiffness of our first meeting were gone, and we had become firm personal friends.

The three specific programs mentioned in the joint minutes that we signed were the production of an antitank guided missile to deal with the huge number of Soviet tanks on the Chinese-Soviet border, large caliber artillery ammunition manufacturing, and the development of an avionics kit for China's older F-8 intercepter plane. On June 12, the President announced that China was now eligible for Foreign Military Sales (FMS) cash purchases, and I was most pleased that we were now ready to help to carry out the agreed FMS programs with the Chinese.

One of the events Zhang Aiping enjoyed most was a reunion we arranged for him. During World War II, an American air crew had been shot down near positions held by General Zhang Aiping's division. He had rescued the American crew, sheltered them in his division positions and had them repatriated.

The Pentagon's matchless record system located the American air crew, and we brought them to Washington to enable them to meet with Zhang Aiping and thank him again, and to exchange pictures with him of the rescue. He was completely surprised by the reunion, and delighted with it.

I was told that throughout his tour of the United States and after his return to China, Zhang Aiping was most pleased and complimentary, and so I felt we had accomplished a great deal. We also found that our representatives Bob Young and Ed Ross had established very good relationships with Zhang's son and the political commissars assigned to the visit. As is usually the case, the initial exchange of visits and the opportunity for staffs to work together had combined to produce a very excellent working atmosphere, all of which boded well for the future.

Other visits were to come later, including a naval visit that arranged for a passing exercise to be conducted between ships of the two navies in January 1986. Shortly before that, General Vessey and Admiral Crowe, who was at that time Commander in Chief of the Pacific (and would succeed General Vessey the following year as Chairman of the Joint Chiefs of Staff), visited China as the guests of the Chief of Staff, Yang Dezhi. Later, General Charles Gabriel, Chief of Staff of our Air Force, was the guest of the People's Liberation Army Air Force Commander.

The reciprocal training and logistic exercise exchanges continued and increased as the years wore on. It was clear that a valued military relationship was maturing in a number of ways, including the conducting of a People's Liberation Army training seminar in the United States, the passing exercise by the Navy, and even a visit to the United States by the PLA Air Force song and dance troop in September of 1986.

All of that struck me as very good news, and I watched with considerable appreciation the continued development and growth of those relationships.

By 1986, three years after my first visit, it seemed to me time that another visit by me would be useful, since significant progress was under way now toward reaching an actual agreement on a major cooperative foreign military sales program. Also, Zhang Aiping had been most insistent that I make a return trip.

This time my trip was marked by extraordinary cordiality, in addition to the fine hospitality that we had encountered on the first visit.

We had wide-ranging discussions on regional and global issues with Zhang Aiping and Deng Xiaoping and other Chinese political and military leaders. There was none of the stiffness or hesitancy or caution that we encountered at the beginning of my first trip. My first meeting with Zhang Aiping on this trip, which was originally scheduled for two hours, ran almost to four. It was a true give-and-take session, with the genuine strategic dialogue that we had been trying to encourage three years before, but only now were able to achieve. We discussed quite openly the Chinese distrust and fear of the Soviets, and what they would need in antitank and anti-air equipment to deal with any Soviet incursion. We also discussed their worries about India and the North Vietnamese.

Other meetings with Deng Xiaoping and Premier Zhao Ziyang were marked by extraordinary cordiality and absence of any discussion of Taiwan, and with many glowing references to the work that we had accomplished over the past three years. I was completely surprised when Deng raised the possibility of United States loans to China, similar to loans for military and economic assistance we extended to other countries. Nothing in my briefing books or preliminary preparation sessions had prepared me for that request, and it seemed so much at variance with China's normal pattern of not wanting to ask us for anything. I took it as another sign of how far our friendship had progressed! Nothing came of it, at that time, but we felt the approach showed that the Chinese felt far closer to us than we had ever estimated.

Again Deng volunteered how much he hoped he could establish better relationships with the Soviet Union. He told us his "traveling days" were over; but still, he added, "If I felt a trip to the Soviet Union could bring about the fulfillment of our three conditions to better relations, I would go tomorrow."

The first night of the 1986 visit was marked by a special example of how far our relationship had come. Defense Minister Zhang Aiping welcomed me with a small private dinner as an "old friend," before the official meetings were to start the next day. That dinner was very informal, very cordial and extremely warm.

I was also asked to address the National War College of the People's Liberation Army. That was one of the first times an American had been so honored. The only other senior American official to have spoken there was General Vessey. When I arrived at the War College, about a two-hour drive from Beijing, I found that the Defense Minister had called several times to be sure that I would be well received, and that everything was done to make the visit a success. I had urged that there be a question and answer period after my talk. The Chinese were reluctant, but finally agreed. One of the first questions was put by an apparently senior Chinese Army officer: "Why do you say you are friends of ours when you still sell arms to Taiwan?" Considerable embarrassment was evidenced on the part of both the translator and my hosts. They laughed loudly and tried to treat it as a joke. I gave our standard response about the requirements of the Taiwan Relations Act, and added that we had been friends of Taiwan for many years, and that I felt no one would respect us if we casually abandoned old friends. That observation, it seemed, was quite well received, and we went on to other topics.

We now had signed letters of offer and acceptance for programs that totaled about $30 million and involved technical data covering assistance for large caliber artillery fuses, and plants for the manufacture of a number of things, such as avionics modernization, that the Chinese needed for their defense. The avionics program, in its entirety, will cost about half a billion dollars; and some fifty fighter planes will be modified by the Chinese for installation of those avionic kits in China.

Before I left for home, I was treated to a visit to another Chinese division. The most memorable fact of that visit was a demonstration of Chinese hardheadedness, or concentration, or self-hypnosis. Several large Chinese soldiers stood at attention, their heads uncovered, while their colleagues broke beer bottles by banging them on their bare heads.

I was also taken south to be shown the Chinese space launch facilities at Xichang and was urged to recommend that American commercial interests use those Chinese facilities. That has since been accomplished.

While a short distance from China's southern border, I was given an extensive and very frank briefing on its military positions, its occasional raids in the mountains along the border to preserve those positions, and its problems with India.

We and the Chinese were now close and trusted friends. We enjoyed each other's company. I felt we had brought our military-to-military relationships to a vastly improved level.

The Administration recommended in 1987 that the Chinese be given our so-called fire-finder artillery locating radar. The equipment will be a very considerable assistance to them in defending their long borders with the Soviet army, which is very heavy in artillery and tanks.

I had been particularly pleased when Richard Halloran, the correspondent for the *New York Times* who accompanied me on the 1983 trip, reported then that I "seemed genuinely to enjoy meeting people at different nations and negotiating." Mr. Halloran said of my efforts on that trip, "He seemed indefatigable, he endured long flights, working on great stacks of papers in his compartment, phoning the White House or the Pentagon, holding staff meetings in his flying office, taking time off only for an occasional nap.

"On the ground Mr. Weinberger's schedule was packed. The Chinese in particular carried him for long distances to see a skimpy infantry demonstration, an obsolete aircraft engine factory and a naval base. He managed however to find diplomatic things to say on each occasion.

"Moreover, Mr. Weinberger was a fervent sightseer. He tramped through the Forbidden City, climbed the Great Wall, and followed a guide through an archeological dig near the ancient capital of Xian."

I kept busy during the 1986 trip too. The activity was indeed on the tiring side, but my sense of the importance and fruitfulness of what we were doing overrode any feelings of personal weariness. I was most pleased that the improved military relationship with the People's Republic seemed to have been accomplished at the same time we maintained the relationships we have made with Taiwan. For me, that was one of the most welcome accomplishments of my long tenure in the Defense Department.

I hope that despite the recent student demonstrations and their tragic ending, and despite the Gorbachev visit in May 1989, that our military-to-military relationship with China will return to normal. I found it significant that not only were the various student demonstrations not anti-American; their most visible symbol was a very credible replica of the Statue of Liberty. And I do think it is *vital* that we try to work continuously with the

Chinese to urge them to try to wipe out the stains on their reputation caused by the Tiananmen Square events. The Chinese have made great progress with economic reform, but political and economic reform must go hand in hand.

The first thing anyone writing about China should do is acknowledge that no one, really, knows what has been happening within the government. That is why so many can write so authoritatively about what caused the tragedy in Tiananmen Square. Nevertheless some comment on those matters, based on several trips I have made to China and my friendship with many of the Chinese leaders, may be useful to set them in proper perspective.

First, we should recall that there has been substantial progress by China in achieving a much freer market system of economics, replacing the Soviet model of strict central planning—which had the same disastrous results in China that it has brought to the Soviet Union, Poland, and indeed to every other country that has tried it.

In China hundreds of thousands of farmers have experienced the great benefits of the novel (to them) concept that if you worked harder and were more productive, you could keep more of the profits for your own consumption. In one of the most striking scenes I saw on my first trip to China in 1983, a very old farmer was laboriously pushing an even older cart, but on the cart were cartons containing a Sony television set and a washing machine.

Second, there is substantial opposition within the Chinese government to that move toward a free market.

Third, Zhao Ziyang and, particularly, Deng Xiaoping and others who favored the new economics were familiar from bitter personal experience with the extraordinary, anarchistic Cultural Revolution, under which mobs of rioting youth quite literally cost China a whole generation of growth. The Cultural Revolution punished, in a most degrading and demeaning way, everyone with leadership qualities, apparent intellectual abilities, academic distinction. Deng himself was imprisoned at least twice during that mad period, and his son was thrown from a window by the Red Guards and paralyzed for life.

Again and again the Chinese leaders emphasized to me that the insanity of the Cultural Revolution would never be repeated, and that stability—that word stressed and repeated many times —would be assured in the future under any and all circumstances.

What follows now is admittedly conjecture; but I believe the reason the Chinese government concluded it had to react against the very large student demonstrations was that the leadership feared revival of the Cultural Revolution and determined to prevent it. It is easy for *us* to distinguish between student demonstrators of 1989 crying for "more democracy," and the hordes turned loose on the streets by direct order of Mao with specific instructions to destroy everything they saw. But to men who were the victims of that earlier madness, such distinctions were probably not easy to make. Still, ordering troops to fire into crowds of unarmed people *is* a horrendous crime and a major blunder.

It seems likely that Deng and Zhao, aligned on economic reform, parted when stability seemed threatened. When opponents of economic reform became more vocal and challenged the reforms proposed by the student demonstrators, Zhao probably held out against the use of force too long for his own political survival.

As we properly condemn the atrocities in Tiananmen Square, we should bear in mind how vital it is for us and the Pacific, and indeed for the world, that China not be driven by our condemnation into isolation or again into the arms of the Soviets. Preventing the realization of both of those possibilities will require extraordinarily skilled diplomacy on our part, and President Bush appears to be taking precisely the right tack so far in opposing the normal clamor for more and more punishment of China. In the long run, the latter course would punish us far more.

China is far too important to the United States, and the United States to China, for us to think only of new penalties. We should concentrate instead on trying to convince the Chinese that they need to make major changes that can enable Western democracies to return to the path we had so successfully followed since 1981. It brought the United States so much closer to the relationship we need with a country that is central to the future of the Pacific.

X

The Strategic Defense Initiative

*F*or those whose normal activities do not include attendance at the innumerable conferences on military and security problems around the world, the fierceness of the controversy that erupted when President Reagan proposed his Strategic Defense Initiative (SDI) has always been difficult to grasp.

But to those who traipse from resort to resort reading each other's papers on security and strategy, the idea that any country might try to defend itself against the nuclear missiles of any other country was not only revolutionary, it was sacrilegious.

For many years, before the Anti-Ballistic Missile Treaty was signed in 1972, those so-called experts had been preaching the doctrine of Mutual Assured Destruction (MAD) with all the fervor and conviction of Keynesian economists. Stated at its most elementary level, MAD is the doctrine that countries, or at least the two superpowers, were safe only as long as each knew that the other could destroy it at will. That knowledge, coupled with the capability of actually carrying out the destruction, meant that neither superpower would attack the other because neither would want to be destroyed. There is an arcane sublevel of that strategy; that is to say, there are some proponents of "original MAD." That group believes that our offensive weapons should be aimed at enemy cities. "New MAD" theorists argue that our targets should be enemy military forces and installations.[1]

In his matchless history of World War I, *The World Crisis*, Winston Churchill speaks movingly of watching the long line of British battleships and their attendant cruisers as they steamed past in a naval exercise at Portland shortly before World War I began, and realizing that the safety, the very survival, of Britain depended wholly on those ships.[2] If any combination of enemies

---

1. In an attempt to avoid angry mail from security theoreticians, I hasten to say that our current strategy has as its targets Soviet military forces and installations and other targets of *military* value. The key difference between that and the Old MAD of simply trying to destroy cities is that we need more, and more accurate, nuclear weapons to carry out the actual strategy of New MAD.

The issue of city targets versus military targets is important because it helps explain the differences in negative reactions to SDI. Since it takes only a few hundred warheads to destroy all city targets, the formal MAD advocates (the "academics") said that unless SDI was 99 + % effective in a world of 10,000 + Soviet warheads, we would still have MAD. Conversely, the advocates of targeting military bases (that is, some of the JCS) would accept considerably less effective defenses, but only as a means to defend retaliatory forces. However, the latter group likes defenses only if they are cost effective (How much is it worth to save a continent, or for that matter, a life?); and only if the Soviets do not have any. In practice, their opposition was less emotional than the academics', but every bit as real. What they all could not, or did not, want to see was that President Reagan and I were talking about moving to a new strategy that did *not* rely on missile *retaliation*, regardless of the targets. And thus we were not only concerned with protecting our missiles or installations, but also wanted a defense designed to protect continents and people. Meanwhile, of course, we all agreed that in the absence of an effective defense against missiles, we must modernize and strengthen our retaliatory capability.

2. Winston Churchill, *The World Crisis*, First Edition, Vol. I, pp. 119–20:

. . . I recall vividly my first voyage from Portsmouth to Portland, where the Fleet lay. A gray afternoon was drawing to a close. As I saw the Fleet for the first time drawing out of the haze a friend reminded me of 'that far-off line of storm-beaten ships on which the eyes of the Grand Army had never looked,' but which had in their day 'stood between

were able to destroy them, nothing would remain to block an invader from landing on the British Isles. That long line of ships was perhaps a thin reed on which to rest the survival of the British empire; but then, at least, it was a powerful deterrent. It was a visible, tangible set of mighty engines capable of destroying enemy attackers.

But our security, by contrast, and indeed our whole ability to survive under the Mutual Assured Destruction theory, depends on an assumption—an assumption as to how a little-understood enemy, governed and controlled by men whose values, attitudes and standards are utterly different from ours, would act. The assumption is (and the theory rests only upon that assumption) that on the big issues of nuclear strategy, they would act as we would; they would take no risks we would not. Perhaps the

---

Napoleon and the dominion of the world.' In Portland Harbour the yacht lay surrounded by the great ships; the whole harbour was alive with the goings and comings of launches and small craft of every kind, and as night fell ten thousand lights from sea and shore sprang into being and every masthead twinkled as the ships and squadrons conversed with one another. Who could fail to work for such a service? Who could not when the very darkness seemed loaded with the menace of approaching war?

For consider these ships, so vast in themselves, yet so small, so easily lost to sight on the surface of the waters. Sufficient at the moment, we trusted, for their task, but yet only a score or so. They were all we had. On them, as we conceived, floated the might, majesty, dominion and power of the British Empire. All our long history built up century after century, all our great affairs in every part of the globe, all the means of livelihood and safety of our faithful, industrious, active population depended upon them. Open the sea-cocks and let them sink beneath the surface, as another Fleet was one day to do in another British harbour far to the North, and in a few minutes—half an hour at the most—the whole outlook of the world would be changed. The British Empire would dissolve like a dream; each isolated community struggling forward by itself; the central power of union broken; mighty provinces, whole Empires in themselves, drifting hopelessly out of control, and falling a prey to strangers; and Europe after one sudden convulsion passing in to the iron grip and rule of the Teuton and of all that the Teutonic system meant. There would only be left far off across the Atlantic unarmed, unready, and as yet uninstructed America, to maintain, single-handed, law and freedom among men.

Guard them well, admirals and captains, hardy tars and tall marines; guard them well and guide them true.

---

greatest assumption of all was that the Soviets also subscribed to MAD. Once this curious strategic theory gained general acceptance, its logic argued that we should not have strategic defenses—and that the Soviets would not want them either—because we both understood that mutual vulnerability was a vital precondition to MAD. Thus, according to the syllogism constructed by the strategic experts, both sides would be completely safe, *because* both were completely vulnerable.

In 1972, when the MAD concept was ostensibly codified in the ABM Treaty, it became inviolate in the minds and words of most of our policymakers and virtually all of the "experts." It became, in short, the "conventional wisdom," and woe to anyone who attacks the conventional wisdom!

In his 1886 treatise "What Is Art?" Leo Tolstoy aptly describes the syndrome:

> I know that most men—not only those considered clever, but even those who really are clever and capable of understanding the most difficult scientific, mathematical or philosophic problems—can seldom discern even the simplest and most obvious truth if it be such as obliges them to admit the falsity of conclusions they have formed, perhaps with much difficulty—conclusions of which they are proud, which they have taught to others, and on which they have built their lives.

The ABM treaty is a prime example of a flawed stategic concept designed to enhance nuclear stability between the United States and the Soviet Union. The treaty was based upon at least two assumptions that were not borne out: that there would soon be deep reductions in offensive weapons, and that both parties would give up defenses (except for specifically permitted narrow, and basically not very effective, systems). The Soviets upset both

assumptions. They never stopped their buildup and modernization of nuclear offensive arms and never abandoned defensive
strategies. In fact, immediately after signing the ABM treaty they
began working to develop the same strategic defenses they so
violently object to when we pursue them. They also deployed
and then modernized all defensive systems permitted under the
ABM treaty, and violated the treaty by constructing a huge radar
system at Krasnoyarsk.

These developments threatened the basic strategic concept the
United States brought to the ABM bargaining table in the early
1970s: that defenses were destabilizing because retaliatory missiles must be able to retaliate. Given those assumptions in 1972,
when the treaty was signed, the hope was that the Soviets would
then agree to deep reductions of their offensive missiles, and
would not violate the treaty itself.

The preamble to the ABM treaty stated that its underlying
premise was "that effective measures to limit anti-ballistic missile
systems would be a substantial factor in curbing the race in strategic offensive arms." Moreover, both parties declared "their intention to achieve at the earliest possible date the cessation of the
nuclear arms race and to take effective measures toward reductions in strategic arms, nuclear disarmament and general and complete disarmament." Gerard Smith, then head of the Arms
Control and Disarmament Agency and chief United States negotiator of the ABM treaty, made it clear in a unilateral statement ap-
pended to the treaty that the United States expected progress in
offensive weapons reductions within five years. It was a vain hope.

As the text of the ABM treaty suggests, the important issue—
real reductions in offensive arms—was put off to some future,
unspecified, date. That was perhaps the gravest error the United
States has made over the past two decades.

One of the few people who did not accept automatically the
scarcely comforting formulation that without any defenses we

would be safe, *because* we had *not* constructed any defenses, was Ronald Reagan. Back in the years when he was Governor of California, he had expressed to me the not surprising view that we would be better advised to rest our defenses on military strength, not only of an offensive character, such as the missiles themselves, but also on means of protecting against the missiles of the other side. But there were very few others who either wished to, or dared to, attack the conventional wisdom. As a result, most of the strategic thinkers, conferences and resulting articles concluded that Mutual Assured Destruction was received wisdom; and they devoted themselves to other topics, such as whether we would destroy cities or armies, or what types of offensive weapons we should have or, more frequently, the desirability of arms limitation (no one really talked about arms reduction) treaties.

When the SALT II Treaty was being discussed, between 1972 and 1979, the conventional wisdom was that its terms were the *maximum* limitation the Soviets would agree to, and since we had to have Soviet agreement in order to get a treaty, and since we *had* to have a treaty, we should accept the Soviet desires for "cosmetic agreements" that effectively invited arms expansions rather than reductions. Indeed SALT II, when finally signed, in the fall of 1979, turned out not to call for any reductions at all. Instead, the treaty had almost no effect on the rate of expansion that was anticipated would take place with no treaty at all. We would have had to *add* over 6,000 warheads to reach the SALT missile warhead limits. Not only were the Soviets allowed by the Treaty to increase by some 6,000 nuclear warheads; *they did just that*.[3] That is why the Treaty was correctly defined as a strategic

3. The theoretical limit on the Soviets, with a heavy emphasis on ballistic missiles, was on the order of 18,000 warheads, ALCMS (Air Launched Cruise Missiles) and bombs under SALT II. They had under 5,500 nuclear warheads in 1979. They have about 11,000 warheads today, and continue to add more weapons to their arsenal.

arms *limitation* treaty (that is, one limiting the *expansion*), rather than an arms reduction treaty.

Like the ABM Treaty, SALT II was widely hailed. But unlike the ABM Treaty, SALT II was ultimately rejected—thanks largely to the courageous work of some of the negotiators who could not support the treaty. Negotiators such as General Edward Rowney, one of our most clearheaded, courageous and effective strategists, pointed out to the Senate committees considering ratification that the treaty would worsen the relative position of the United States vis-à-vis the Soviet Union; and that it would not reduce nuclear warheads, but would in fact call for more of them. Still the Treaty was supported by the Carter Administration—until the Soviet invasion of Afghanistan, whereupon as part of the "punishment" we administered to the Soviets for that action, the Carter Administration withdrew the Treaty from consideration by the Senate. It has languished with a flickering half-light ever since.

"Languish" is perhaps not quite the correct term. Many members of Congress and too many in the executive branch of both the Carter and the Reagan administrations seem to regard the Treaty as a standard and a promise to be kept despite its never having been ratified or made part of our law. Very frequently, long after December 1985, when the Treaty itself would have expired (had it been enacted), Treaty supporters spoke witheringly of various proposals as being "a violation of the SALT II Treaty." I was never able to understand how an unenacted Treaty that had expired could be violated. But if an unenacted Treaty could be violated, then, as the President reported to Congress many times, the Soviets had violated it many times, despite the pious rhetoric of their leaders and of some of our own people, that they were adhering rigorously to its unenacted provisions.

During all of the 1970s no one ever really seriously challenged the ABM Treaty, except a small number of people viewed as eccentrics by the Security Establishment; those eccentrics kept talking about the desirability of constructing an actual defense against Soviet missiles. Although we had very limited means of verifying whether or not the Soviet Union was complying with key provisions of the ABM Treaty, from time to time those realists asked what would happen if the Soviets violated the Treaty, since we also lacked any prudent hedge against a so-called ABM breakout by the Soviets.

The principal discussions between the executive branch and the Congress, following the adoption of the ABM Treaty, revolved around whether we should deploy the ground based and largely ineffective antimissile defenses that were actually permitted by the Treaty. Initially, those were to be emplacements for one hundred ground-based ABM intercepter missiles located to protect each nation's capital and one other site. In 1974, that number was confined to a single site. We chose to put our defensive missiles into a site at Grand Forks, North Dakota, as the best allowable means of trying to destroy Soviet missiles coming at Minuteman silos from the north. In short order, however, there was a waning of Congress's appetite and willingness to spend money for even that minor defensive capability permitted by the ABM Treaty; and after investing close to a billion dollars, we abandoned the effort. We thus entered the 1980s with zero defensive systems, in the belief that our strategic nakedness would keep us free from destruction by Soviet missiles.

Meanwhile, what of the Soviets?

They continued deployment of the ground-based defensive systems permitted to them under the ABM Treaty. They also continued intensive research toward a more capable defensive system against intercontinental range ballistic missiles.[4] And they

---

4. Many SDI opponents in the country disputed the U.S. Government's assessment that the Soviets had an SDI program of their own—that is, *until* General Secretary Gorbachev acknowledged in an interview with Tom Brokaw on NBC on November 30, 1987, that: "The Soviet Union is doing all that the United States is doing, and I guess we are engaged

implemented plans, conceived during the Treaty negotiations, to build a nationwide complex of huge radars used as part of the ABM Treaty–forbidden defenses against ballistic missiles. The most insidious of those, near the city of Krasnoyarsk, clearly violates the Treaty's restrictions against defenses, or against installations designed to be used with and as a part of defenses, given its location in the interior of the country.[5]

The Soviet strategic defense work proceeded in the greatest secrecy in the Soviet Union, but *it proceeded*. It was, and is, a massive effort. Many of the classified technologies that we know the Soviets have sought from us and others in recent years were directly related to their strategic defense effort. They were successful in obtaining some of those technologies, by theft and by purchase, from us and our friends. They also were successful in developing some, particularly involving lasers and radio frequency (RF) devices, on their own. As a result, by 1981 they were far ahead in efforts to secure strategic defensive systems, particularly in their work with lasers. Quite apparently they, unlike our conventional-wisdom advocates, had not adopted MAD.

We did little until 1983, contenting ourselves with some minor research designed to try to improve the effectiveness of the 1970s-vintage ground-based Sprint and Spartan defensive missile systems that were deployed briefly in North Dakota. Those systems were permitted to us by the ABM Treaty. Essentially, however, the effort was very minor, and resulted primarily in demonstrating what we already knew.

I learned about many of those Soviet efforts for the first time when I started receiving the briefings from the Defense Department and our intelligence agencies at the end of 1980. I men-

---

in research, basic research, which relates to these aspects which are covered by the SDI of the United States."

5. As the Soviets themselves finally admitted in November 1989.

---

tioned aspects of them to the President from time to time, particularly when he discussed with me his continuing dissatisfaction with the conventional wisdom that a nation defenseless against intercontinental missiles was safe. Our discussions usually concluded with our agreeing that we should try to develop such a system, but recognizing that there would be opposition to it by those who felt their standing as strategic experts would be impaired if their standard approach was violated.

And from time to time, the President talked with me about his understanding of, but not agreement with, the moral and conscientious objections that some of our scientists held toward working on offensive nuclear weapons. He always expressed the belief that they would work far more eagerly on systems that were not really weapons at all, but were the means of destroying nuclear missiles before they could wreak the destruction that would inevitably be part of any nuclear war.

Early in 1981, I had asked for a special briefing on the status of our defensive work and had discussed with some of my staff the makeup of a possible commission or committee that could look into whether effective defensive systems could be developed. Even before Inauguration Day, I had publicly discussed my ideas.

On January 15, 1981, in a meeting with *New York Times* reporters of the Washington Bureau, I said we would consider reviving plans for an ABM defense system and that extension of the ABM Treaty beyond 1982 was not "automatic." I also referred to "ABM with later technology" than that of the missile defense systems developed by the Army.[6]

Then, on October 2, 1981, at a White House press briefing on strategic weapons systems, I emphasized that "there are some broad new things that look quite promising and that we [are] going to be exploring because obviously, if we are able to destroy

6. *New York Times*, January 16, 1982, p. 10 (Section A).

incoming missiles, I don't think it would be destabilizing; I think it would be extremely comforting."

But almost all of our energies were devoted, during the first two years, to regaining offensive deterrent strength—and that meant modernizing and strengthening all three legs of our strategic nuclear triad. The effort required the development and deployment of the B-1 and Stealth bombers to replace the B-52, the MX to replace the Minuteman, and the D-5 submarine launched missile to replace the earlier, less accurate missiles that lacked also the capability of destroying hardened Soviet military targets. That program faced no opposition within the Administration; and generally, with the exception of the MX missile, the modernization effort was supported as well by the Congress.

Congress had varying ideas on how best to modernize the airborne part of the triad, with some wanting to develop the B-1B bomber—an immediate successor to the aging B-52 bomber—while others favored waiting until we developed the new Stealth bomber, then a highly classified program involving new methods of avoiding detection by Soviet air defense radars. That program was prematurely disclosed by the Carter Administration shortly before the 1980 presidential election.

There were also widely differing views with respect to the modernization of the ICBM leg of the triad. Many in the Congress still supported President Carter's "race track" or Multiple Protective System, under which we would construct about 4,600 shelters to hold 200 of the new MX missiles. Those missiles would be moved from silo to silo by special trucks in an attempt to confuse the Soviets and conceal from them the actual location of our missiles. The "race track" concept had always seemed to me to be a heavily flawed system, particularly since, in spite of its vast expense, it would not really give us any additional survivability for our missiles. The Soviets would be quite aware of the exact location of each of the 4,600 shelters, having observed their construction from their spy satellites and presumably having had detailed reports from their agents. For that reason, and not for the alleged environmental objections of some Western Republican senators, the President and I opposed the Carter proposal. I knew that *any* missile deployment site would be violently opposed on environmental grounds, no matter where it was located. (During all the years I was at the Pentagon, I encountered only one person, Paul Etchepare, a noted Wyoming sheep rancher, who favored putting MX on his vast holdings.)

We reviewed a number of different options, and finally concluded that added survivability was indeed desirable—but that the very presence of the new MX missiles in the ground, able to be fired, would be the most effective strengthening of our deterrent that we could bring on line, and the quickest deployed—a very important factor, since the Minuteman missiles of the 1960s did not have the accuracy to destroy newly hardened Soviet targets.[7] I felt a great urgency about the matter, because the Soviets had already developed and deployed, during the time we had been debating the MX, several new systems with very accurate high yield missiles that could easily destroy specific targets in the United States, particularly since none of our targets had been hardened to the extent they were in the Soviet Union.

The question was examined by various commissions, including one I had named in 1981, headed by Dr. Charles Townes, the Nobel Prize winning scientist who had done valuable work in the field of lasers. I urged the Townes Commission to look at every conceivable alternative to land-based deployment of the MX, including airborne and seaborne deployments. The great

---

7. Those targets included hardened command posts and silos, which the Soviets would try to preserve after *their* first strike so that they would have the forces and leadership structure necessary to prevail in a nuclear war. That enormous effort of hardening their vital military installations was yet another piece of evidence that the Soviets believed they could fight and win a nuclear war.

weight of the MX made those alternatives difficult to achieve, although Dr. Townes felt an airborne MX in a slow, continuously airborne patrol plane was practical. I also pushed as hard as possible to speed the deployment of the new D-5 submarine-borne missile, which had both the accuracy and yield to destroy Soviet hardened targets. But we were told that to move up the scheduled deployment of the D-5 from 1989 to 1988 would add another billion dollars, an expenditure I did not find practical.

Another commission, headed by General Brent Scowcroft, appointed in 1982 at the suggestion of the White House staff, looked at the same problem. The Scowcroft group, in a typical compromise, concluded that we should develop and deploy the MX missile with its ten very accurate warheads in existing modified Minuteman silos (as we had recommended), but that we should also develop a new single warhead missile, the so-called Midgetman, which would be shuttled around in a number of different locations in our Southwest, thus increasing survivability. The Midgetman was a favorite missile of the MX opponents—primarily, I always felt, because it was easier for them to support a missile we did not, and would not, have for several years. The Scowcroft Commission also recommended that we proceed with all other aspects of the modernization of our strategic triad, exactly in accordance with the recommendations I had made to the President in October 1981.

All of this took a great deal of time and effort, and it was, of course, not the only item on our agenda. Several crises, major and minor, refused to wait patiently while strategic modernization was being developed and completed. So not until the end of 1982 and early 1983 did we begin serious work to initiate a program for deploying a defensive system that could indeed protect not only our continent, but our allies overseas, from the horrors of Soviet nuclear missiles.

There had been a few vigorous and vocal advocates of our developing a defensive system, including a group called "High Frontier," led by retired Army Lieutenant General Daniel Graham. A very few people in the Department who had never shared the enthusiasm for the ABM Treaty also urged that we do some far more effective and extensive work on strategic defense.

My own feeling is that the issue was finally and completely decided in the President's mind after a meeting in the Cabinet room that he and I had with the Joint Chiefs of Staff on February 11, 1983. At that meeting we discussed the ABM Treaty, my own basic objections to it, and the vulnerable position in which I thought it had left us. My concerns had only grown as we learned more and more about the Soviets' unilateral program to develop very comprehensive strategic defenses—ones that threatened increasingly to render our missiles ineffective.

At that meeting of the Joint Chiefs, Admiral James Watkins and General Jack Vessey, the Chairman, both advised the President of the importance in their eyes of our developing a defensive system. Admiral Watkins, Chief of Naval Operations, and now Secretary of Energy, summed it up in a memorable phrase; I knew from the President's immediate reaction that it would stay in his mind as the ultimate and complete justification for proceeding with such a system.

After discussing the possibilities of our obtaining such a system, Admiral Watkins asked rhetorically, "Would it not be better if we could develop a system that would protect, rather than avenge, our people?"

"Exactly," said the President. I knew then that the President would want us to work intensively to obtain that system. Admiral Watkins's phrase had summed up most succinctly and simply the great hopes that the development of such a system would bring.

And so I increased our own efforts, asking that some of our

research, for which we had very small funding, be devoted to an enterprise far larger and more effective than simply trying to get the most out of Sprint and Spartan.

Very shortly after that, I learned that a small White House staff effort was begun to help develop, not so much the system itself, but the best time, place and method to present the idea and launch the initiative.

The project was treated by those members of the White House staff working on it with the utmost secrecy; only my friendship with two of them, Bill Clark and Ed Meese, enabled me to know what they were working on. The others were, of course, under the impression that no one outside the working group knew, but it was fortunate that I did have a general briefing from time to time from my friends. I wanted to gear our own efforts in Defense so as to be ready to move vigorously and publicly once the presidential decision was announced.

Incidentally, it seems to be the custom of many White House staff people to regard the Cabinet departments as their natural enemy from whom the President must be protected. The White House staff also is always afraid that leaks by the departments will spoil the surprise, or other public relations effect they seek for some of the President's announcements. That posture overlooks the fact that many leaks come from the White House staff itself. And its passion otherwise for secrecy too frequently causes, not unnaturally, such a lack of coordination that many are led to believe the executive branch is quite disorganized. In any event, it was fortunate, in this case, that as a result of the Byzantine efforts that had to be made to keep informed of the clandestine activities in the White House, the Administration did not appear to be quite disorganized.

As it happened, the President decided that he would announce the initiative sooner than originally planned. His historic speech of March 23, 1983, contained the first public decision by an

American administration since 1967 to work on defensive systems—defensive systems far more extensive and sophisticated than any previously thought of.

The President, speaking from the Oval Office, that night said:

> "What if free people could live secure in the knowledge that their security did not rest upon that threat of instant U.S. retaliation to deter a Soviet attack, that we could intercept and destroy strategic ballistic missiles before they reached our own soil or that of our allies?
>
> "I know this is a formidable technical task. . . . But isn't it worth every investment necessary to free the world from the threat of nuclear war?"

On the morning before the President's speech, I received a hurried and surreptitious call from my friends in the White House advising me of the speech coming that night; and I immediately began preparations to ensure that the announcement did not fall on totally astonished NATO ears. I was in Portugal, on March 22 and 23, for one of my regular NATO Nuclear Planning Group (NPG) meetings, and there were many calls, all that day of the twenty-third, back and forth to Washington for further detailed disclosures of what *precisely* the President was going to say.[8]

I knew our NATO allies would be quite disconcerted if, moments after I completed meeting with them, the President announced a massive change in the strategic plans and goals of the United States, about which they had not been briefed.

Unfortunately, a portion of the White House staff, still desiring total surprise, made it difficult for me to get the *full* text of the President's speech, even though I knew that, in general, he was

---

8. I have noted one account to the effect that I was opposed to SDI and tried to block the inclusion of it in the President's speech. It is quite false, and is more of the typical Washington writer's tactic of talking to one source and then writing the story as the writer's previously adopted scenario required.

going to propose that we begin work to determine the feasibility of our developing and deploying a strategic defense that could effectively destroy Soviet missiles at all stages of their trajectories.[9]

Finally, I felt I could wait no longer, and so advised the President, who agreed. I then began telephoning the individual defense ministers around Europe with advance notice of the general nature of the President's historic speech to come that night.

As always when I felt the need to turn to the President directly, rather than going through the various filters established in the National Security Council and White House staff, he immediately perceived the problem and was most helpful. He was this time too, in approving early notification to the NATO defense ministers. As a result, our colleagues had some notice, and at least could not contend that they were totally surprised by their major ally.

My own feeling has always been that it is *far* better to prepare the ground, and advise as many of your friends as possible, as far ahead of time as possible, of any such major announcement as the President was now about to make. By doing so, we gained at least the hope of receiving some favorable and supportive comment from others.

In any event, because we were not able to reach all of the defense ministers before the speech, there were some whose displeasure at not knowing about the initiative ahead of time outweighed their appreciation of the significance of the new proposal. Predictably, at home, most of the specialists—who accepted and adhered to the MAD principle—were both astounded and outraged. The American people, as evidenced by several polls over the years, were also surprised—but surprised, mostly, to learn that *we had no defense* against Soviet or other

---

9. Ironically, the original draft of the President's speech was prepared by my staff. However, the subject originally agreed to was the great progress made in Defense over the previous two years. In fact that *was* the subject of the speech, except for a brief, historic "insert" announcing the creation of what came to be called the Strategic Defense Initiative.

hostile missiles. The people, however, in contrast to the specialists and experts, were—and are—strongly supportive of the idea of our developing effective defenses.

In, to my mind, the most saddening feature of the response to the President's announcement, a very large number of the academic and scientific community, whom we had hoped would give both vocal and scientific support, came out against the idea, even though we were proposing a system designed to *destroy weapons* and not people, and to protect people rather than to avenge them.

The disregard of conventional wisdom embodied in SDI was simply too much for those people to accept; without really considering, much less discussing, that it was not a weapons system at all we were talking about, they immediately had to register their opposition.

Many members of Congress took the same view, and to a considerable extent that was because there had not been early presentation of the President's plan to them. The result was that strong opposition developed immediately, and many considered the proposal something to be derided or killed as quickly as possible. I believe that the excessive, indeed obsessive, desire of a few of the White House staff to keep the President's plan a secret was at least partly to blame for the lack of congressional support for it; but it is also possible that congressional opposition could have killed SDI aborning, if Congress had known of it ahead of time.

Unfortunately, many feel that if they have not been told in advance of the President's plans, those plans are automatically bad and must be opposed. That is the "Had you only consulted me earlier" syndrome.

But to say that there was "opposition" to the plan does not really convey the torrent of fury and scorn that was released by the President's proposal.

Senator Kennedy's staff, after working overtime, came up with the idea that SDI should be subjected to as much scorn as possible—and thus they coined the phrase "Star Wars," as if it were some fantasy that bore no semblance to reality. Indeed, as ears in the Soviet Union picked up the "Star Wars" theme and the owners of those ears began to play it back to our negotiators in Geneva as "space strike arms," Dr. Fred Ikle would sagely observe that "the Soviet Union had been successful in infiltrating the semantics of the West."

The colorful and quite inaccurate title of "Star Wars" was an instant success for the programs' critics. It fitted neatly into head-line writers' allowable space, and provided the convenient label required for those 90- to 120-second television references in the morning and evening news; it also conveyed the proper scorn for the proposal by the Security Establishment. So almost from the beginning, the proponents of what was, and is, the most hopeful strategic concept for at least the last forty years—one that holds out the prospect of freeing the world of part of the threat that has hung over all of us since the development of nuclear weapons—were placed on the defensive, and were hard put to defend the true merits of this imaginative and creative proposal of the President's.

And it *was* the President's proposal. Others who have pur-ported to write some of the history of the development of stra-tegic defense have either said or implied that it was another staff idea about which the President was persuaded. Of course, those people had not been with the President for many years, and had not heard him talking, as I had, first when he was Governor, and later in 1981, about how a defensive system could indeed inhibit, and ultimately operate to prevent, further development of more nuclear weapons. The President, in supporting the idea of de-fensive measures, used to ask, "What if we signed a treaty pre-venting the use of gas masks?"

Never, however, for a moment did the President waver in his conviction that first we had to complete the modernization of our own offensive deterrent system. We all knew that strategic defense might not be found practical or obtainable with the degree of reliability that the President and I wanted. We also knew that if we continued to allow the deterrent capability of our existing offensive nuclear systems to erode, as we had during the 1970s, we would have little or no credibility at any negotiating table to which we might entice the Soviets.

In any event, we in the Defense Department were ready to move quickly after the formal announcement by the President, and we did. In response to a presidential directive to study the technical feasibility and policy implications of ballistic missile defenses, we commissioned two major studies. The technology study, under the direction of James Fletcher, once and future head of NASA, included some of the most able people in the field that we could persuade to serve. The policy study, under the direction of Dr. Fred Ikle, consisted of two independent groups: one composed of outside contractors under Fred Hoffman, of Pan Heuristics—a California based research institute—and another interagency group under Frank Miller of the Department of Defense. While we awaited their reports on the technical feasibility of such a system and its policy implications, I began thinking about the best organization and structure for work on developing the system within the Department of Defense.

There is no doubt that each of our three services would have been eager to be assigned the task; the Air Force, for example, certainly had been pleased to have the responsibility for developing some of our intercontinental range ballistic missiles. There was also no doubt in my mind that some within each service would be less than enthusiastic unless the project *were* assigned to them to run.

Then there would be others, in all the services, who would be very apprehensive that the funds required for the enterprise would be diverted from projects already underway and much closer to their hearts than the development of the new, and (to their minds) possibly unattainable, strategic defense system.

I concluded, after considerable thought, that the best way to insure that we applied every available resource, as quickly as possible, to the development of this major initiative of the President, was to create a new unit within the Department, assign to it full responsibility for the research and development of the project, and reallocate to it all of the resource funding that was available then for defensive work. I placed that new unit directly under me, with its head reporting to me, so that I would know of everything happening on the project, and would be able to block attempts that I knew would be made to divert resources and support from strategic defense, or to slow or dilute the Department's commitment for the Strategic Defense Initiative— or SDI, notwithstanding the media's preference for the term "Star Wars."

My decision, of course, disappointed many who wished to bring SDI under the wing of one of their own existing departmental units; it also was a source of some concern to each of the services and to the Joint Chiefs.

I have never regretted the decision, nor felt that it was other than the right way to proceed. My confidence was partly attributable to our remarkably good fortune in having Lieutenant General James Abrahamson to serve as the first director of the Strategic Defense Initiative Organization (SDIO).

General Abrahamson was just completing work as director of the Space Shuttle program, and had previously been associated with such other great successes as the development of the F-16 fighter plane and the Maverick missile. He was an experienced and decorated combat pilot in the Air Force, and he fully understood and supported both the President's dedication to the development of strategic defense and my own complete determination that we would proceed as vigorously and as rapidly as possible to secure and deploy a system that could destroy Soviet missiles at all stages of their trajectory—no matter how strong the opposition from any quarter, or how numerous the sneers and jokes we encountered along the way.

General Abrahamson was also an expert advocate and briefer on the progress we were making, as well as on the objective of our new strategy embodied in the SDI. His briefings were sufficiently impressive so that both Prime Minister Margaret Thatcher and Prime Minister Rajiv Gandhi of India asked for repeat performances.

After the commissions reported their conclusions that a strategic defense system was technically feasible and that it should be pursued at a pace limited only by technological progress—not funding; and after General Abrahamson became available on completion of his work at the Space Shuttle project, I made his appointment official, and he began rapidly to assemble a staff to undertake this massive and most hopeful project.

Meanwhile, however, as was the case with so many other things that we were trying to do in the Department, it became necessary to mobilize public support behind the project. The President, as always, was magnificent in that effort, and his speeches brought home to many Americans the truth, shocking to them, that we did not have any defenses against Soviet missiles, that we should have, and that it was vital that we work to develop a system to do just that. I too gave many speeches, had many television appearances, and innumerable newspaper interviews, and wrote several articles, during the balance of 1983 and thereafter.

Of course, we first had to persuade the Congress that it should appropriate adequate funding to enable us to start a massive research effort. That was no small task, in view of the deeply entrenched support for the theory of Mutual Assured Destruction, and the congressional feeling that anything that violated MAD had to be bad.

In Fiscal Year 1985 Congress was persuaded to appropriate to the Department of Defense $1.4 billion for SDI ($1.8 billion was requested); in FY 1986, $2.67 billion ($3.75 billion was requested); in FY 1987, $3.27 billion ($4.8 billion was requested); in FY 1988, $3.6 billion ($5.2 was requested); in FY 1989, $3.74 billion ($4.5 billion was requested); and President Reagan's much needed FY 1990 request was $5.6 billion.[10] (Congress appropriated no funds for SDI in FY 1983 or FY 1984. We attempted to reprogram some FY 1984 funds, but were blocked by Congress, so FY 1985 was the first year for which Congress made a specific SDI appropriation.)

All of those sums were, it is fair to say, wrung from the Congress after protracted and highly confrontational hearings.

In the final analysis, the determining factor in our ability to get the funds we did was, I think, the President's continued leadership, and the fact that representatives and senators became aware, from their own polls, how much the people in their constituencies really wanted strategic defense. Those constituencies were attracted to the idea of a system that did not destroy people, but destroyed weapons instead; that public support was growing despite the increasingly frantic efforts of the security and defense experts to convince everyone that the system would not work, would be too expensive and, worst of all, would violate the ABM Treaty.

At every opportunity the Soviets also voiced their opposition to our pursuing ballistic missile defenses, even though they themselves had been working on them for decades. That was a further problem, because all the people who urgently wanted agreements with the Soviets in any endeavor were able to argue that our continued pursuit of strategic defense represented an obstacle to

10. That 1990 request was reduced to $4.6 billion as a result of various compromises with congressional leaders before formal congressional hearings began.

Before Congress went into recess in August, the Senate Armed Services Committee authorized $4.3 billion for SDI and the House Armed Services Committee authorized only $2.8 billion in FY 1990.

This was finally compromised again at $3.6 billion, less than the appropriation for 1989.

such agreements, and that the only way we could get agreements with the Soviets was to remove that obstacle by stopping work on strategic defense. The Soviets themselves contributed by putting various blandishments before the President and the country in the form of agreements they said they might sign, if only we would give up strategic defense.

The Soviets were particularly vehement about space-based defenses. On several occasions in Geneva they made tentative overtures along the lines that they had no real objection to ground-based defenses if we insisted we must deploy some type of strategic defense. Furthermore, they at least hinted that they would let us deploy ground-based defenses if we agreed to ban all weapons from space. Meanwhile they moved vigorously ahead with their own military space activities. The Soviets object not so much to defenses; it is *space*-based defenses they fear. That, of course, is precisely because space-basing alone allows defenses to reach their full potential.

During this time, I had been thinking about ways to broaden the support for strategic defense, and also reap contributions that, I knew, experts in other countries could make to the program during its formative stages. With those aims in view, and bearing in mind the strong pleas made to me at every NATO meeting by my defense minister colleagues to improve the balance of military payments—which simply meant that they wanted us to order more military goods from them—I decided to offer them the opportunity to participate in strategic defense. I did that by letter to all of the NATO defense ministers. Later I sent the letter also to defense ministers of some other countries. I also spoke about SDI at an informal luncheon with all the NATO defense ministers when we met in Luxembourg in March 1985.

Predictably, their reaction was mixed, with many ministers raising questions that showed they had been subjected to all the standard criticisms I have related; others worried that our proceeding with SDI would offend the Soviets. There were many questions after my presentation, but I kept emphasizing American public opinion polls, which showed support for SDI, and kept trying to drive home that novel concept of destroying weapons and not people. And on the strictly economic side, I emphasized that the ministers' countries would benefit because we hoped to allocate contracts for research and development to a number of their manufacturers and scientists.

That last argument proved most telling. Eventually, after long and difficult negotiations, we signed SDI collaboration agreements with England (December 1985), Germany (March 1986), Israel (May 1986), Italy (September 1986), and Japan (July 1987). The agreements provided for eased procedures under which we could award contracts to manufacturers and research specialists in those countries for work on SDI. There was considerable interest in many of the countries over the possible commercial "fallout" for research work done on strategic defense; and of course we reminded our audiences of the very large commercial benefits that had come from our space program and other pioneering defense research efforts.

Many other governments, not directly involved, including France, have substantial industrial involvement that their governments tacitly support. Recently, South Korea has expressed tentative interest in signing an SDI agreement with us. On the other hand, Australia actually *prohibited* its companies from working on it.

One interesting sidelight of the negotiations with other countries involved then-British Defense Minister Michael Heseltine and his eloquent and insistent demands that before the British would sign an agreement to participate in strategic defense, they must be "guaranteed" at least a billion dollars in SDI research and development contracts. We were clearly unable to comply, because we did not know whether there would be successful applicants for amounts in that size from the United Kingdom; and of course, we did not know how much Congress would allocate to us each year for SDI. Ultimately, Michael Heseltine was persuaded to see that the demands he was making were simply untenable. His successor, Defense Minister George Younger, an exceptionally able, intelligent and effective minister, and I worked closely and effectively together in all defense matters. That included carrying out the first of our SDI foreign contracts, which were with England.[11]

It is difficult to convey the strength and, as it seemed then and still seems to me, the irrationality and the fury of the opposition to SDI in our Congress. The very mention of the program seems to bring out exceptionally violent reactions. It must be said that there were a few who were devoted to the program,[12] and there were some who wanted to start on it at once—even though we had not yet achieved results in our research program that would warrant "starting." But there were many more who seemed to feel they had to fight anything connected with strategic defense. Thus, Democrats in the Senate blocked confirmation of the appointment of General Abrahamson, the director of the program, to be a four-star general, simply because he was the leader of the SDI program. That action was an extremely petty and unwarranted abuse of a skilled and deserving officer. Democrats in the Senate also prevented the creation of a federally funded research organization to assist with SDI, even though that pattern had been followed many times in the past, and even though the SDI organization was strongly recommended by a very distinguished group on the advisory committee to the program.

Among the proponents, we had difficulty in fending off those who desired that we start constructing something immediately. My position was that we did not have anything effective to construct, and that we should wait until we had our so-called First

11. Between October 1985 and December 1988, firms and research establishments in the United Kingdom received $55.8 million in contracts and subcontracts.

12. One of the most effective supporters was Senator, now Vice President, Dan Quayle.

Phase of a fully designed program ready to deploy. However, there was strong interest from Lockheed Corporation in getting funding for one or two preliminary pilot-type programs. They looked unpromising to us; and with our resources so limited, and with the strong desire we had not to let the program sink back into a familiar mode of solely ground-based, largely ineffective, defensive systems, we felt it necessary to oppose some of our more ardent supporters on this point.

Meanwhile, however, the research program under General Abrahamson's direction was producing some remarkable results, and by early 1987, we could see clearly the most promising directions we should take.

Of all the SDI research areas that have borne fruit, one of the most exciting is a concept called "Brilliant Pebbles." Under this program, a large number of very small satellites would be placed in space—perhaps several thousand in all. Each of those satellites would hold one small intercepter, probably weighing no more than 20 pounds. On alert, the satellites would open their heat-seeking eyes, locate attacking enemy missiles from thousands of miles away, fire their own rocket motors, and crash into their ballistic missile targets. The current cost estimate of $25 billion for the system would be far less than the $40 billion cost of the proposed Midgetman offensive missile—a weapon system I have always felt to be misconceived.

General Abrahamson's February 9, 1989, "End of Tour" memo on Brilliant Pebbles says:

> Strategic Defense Initiative research progress has been dramatic and will soon yield major new cost reduction possibilities. The most compelling and immediate of the possibilities is the "Brilliant Pebbles" approach to a space-based architecture. For approximately $10B a full deployment of these very capable, space-based interceptors could be achieved. To complete a Phase 1 SDI system that

also replaces our existing Tactical Warning and Attack Assessment (TW-AA) satellites as well as our Command and Control Capability (C^3) would cost an estimated $25B. If limited SDI funds are available, the space-based system should be first priority because it will add defensive deterrence to our offensive capability at less cost than adding new survivability features to a part of our ICBM force. Further, it will provide "extended defensive deterrence" on a global basis to our Allies as well! This system will also provide maximum leverage in arms control negotiations.

This initial system, available in the mid-1990s if adequately funded, could be followed within five to ten years by a constellation of about 25 space-based lasers that would be able to hit and destroy enemy missiles within seconds of their liftoff. It is estimated that such a constellation would cost *$40* billion or less. The space laser system would completely cut off the Soviets from strategies involving the use of intercontinental offensive missiles. Even if the Soviets tried to redesign their missiles, at immense cost, to evade the Brilliant Pebble intercepters, there is no way they can dodge a laser beam traveling at the speed of light.

While it initially seemed that computing requirements beyond our current capability were called for, recent work shows that even our existent computers would be adequate. The "Brilliant Pebbles," described above, have a very capable computer brain. With such "smart" weapons, the central control computer need not be very large. Indeed, the current computers within Cheyenne Mountain in Colorado could do most of what we need.

The *Wall Street Journal* correctly pointed out that Brilliant Pebbles "plays to America's competitive strengths—technology in optics, small computers, guidance systems—instead of trying to match the Soviets at what they do best—rolling out missile after missile without fear of lawsuits from environmentalists or peaceniks. . . . [This] quickly vindicates Ronald Reagan's judgment in launching the SDI program. He understood that science advances in ways we don't expect, that answers would be forthcoming if we unleased U.S. scientists on defense. Mr. Reagan's contribution was moral—releasing those pent-up energies by destroying the perverted notion that defense against nuclear attack was somehow illicit."[13]

Also, in the nature of things, as part of an effective and complete research program, we had to look at various alternative methods of destroying Soviet missiles, both with respect to the platforms from which the destructive force would be launched and the varieties of destructive forces available. That examination, of course, involved a number of experiments to improve the range and reliability of laser beams as well as other directed energy sources.

But during all of this time there was a continual nipping at our heels, or throats, by representatives of the State Department, as well as other opponents of the program, who constantly raised the question of the ABM Treaty, and questioned whether each experiment, or each action that we took, violated or would violate that Treaty. In the first few years, our work was so preliminary that there was general agreement that we were not violating the Treaty. As our research brought in more and more effective and successful results, and as we moved toward testing some of the most promising methods, we appeared to be approaching the boundaries of the Treaty.

Following a comprehensive review of the ABM Treaty negotiating record, the State Department's Legal Advisor, Abraham Sofaer, who was far more open-minded about the program than most of his colleagues, judged that the negotiating records and Treaty allowed for more testing activity than "strict construction"

13. *Wall Street Journal*, editorial, March 30, 1989, p. 14.

would admit. Under Mr. Sofaer's "broad interpretation," the Treaty would allow us to conduct a wide array of tests of such systems that were regarded under the more traditional or "restrictive" interpretation to be illegal. Our newfound freedom, of course, caused immense pain and suffering to the opponents of the program. It also brought to the front a group that might be called the "Pride of the Senate school"—people who felt that the ABM Treaty, when ratified by the Senate many years before, meant what they thought it meant at the time, irrespective of what the Soviets had actually agreed to. According to that school, no one was allowed to have a different interpretation of it.

During all of this arcane legal argument, I took the position that none of it was either relevant or very useful, because it was clear to me that the President wanted us to deploy the system once we developed it. It was also clear that we could not deploy the system without changing the ABM Treaty. Finally, it was equally clear that the ABM Treaty itself provided for either side, when its supreme national interest was involved, to give notice that it was setting aside the Treaty, or that portion of it that forbade deployment of any SDI system. Such notice by us—as provided for by the Treaty itself—would have resolved the so-called legal problems in one sentence. It would not be "violating" the Treaty, as so many of the opponents said with horror, because the Treaty itself provided the means by which the parties to it could take the steps otherwise precluded by the Treaty.

One of the strongest opponents of SDI in the State Department was Ambassador Paul Nitze, one of our arms control negotiators. It seemed to me that his opposition was based to a considerable degree on the fear that by pursuing the SDI program that the Soviets were determined we should give up, we would give the Soviets an excuse not to give us any kind of Strategic Arms Reduction Treaty. Most treaty negotiators feel that their task, and the measure of their success, is to negotiate a treaty—any treaty. Therefore to get a treaty, it would be perfectly acceptable to them to give up SDI. So Ambassador Nitze, in a February 1985 speech in Philadelphia, proposed a formula that would limit our ability to proceed with the SDI program, unless it could be demonstrated that it would be "survivable and cost effective at the margin."

There were varying interpretations of the "cost effective at the margin" formulation, but all of them in Ambassador Nitze's view seemed to add up to stopping SDI—unless we could demonstrate something that could not be demonstrated at that early stage, or indeed until SDI was finished. It was also a formulation that did not need demonstrating, unless one was prepared to say there is a cost to saving mankind that is considered too high, because it is not "cost effective at the margin." Nitze's ploy was picked up and supported by others in the State Department and on Capitol Hill who had opposed SDI all along.

It is ironic that Paul Nitze should have become so taken with what came to be called the "Nitze criteria" as a means to retard or arrest the momentum of the SDI program. In fact, the criteria of military effectiveness, survivability, and cost-effectiveness were originally formulated and articulated to a wide audience—a year prior to the Nitze speech—by two members of my strategic policy staff, Franklin Miller and William Furniss, as general, overlapping criteria for effective ballistic missile defense systems. Those criteria, which were adopted by the Reagan Administration months prior to their articulation by Nitze, routinely are assigned to weapons systems of *any* kind.

Due to a lack of understanding of the nature of defense planning, the staff of the State Department believed that they had stumbled onto a secret Pentagon formula with which they could block deployment. Some were particularly taken by the quasi-economic term "at the margin," in the mistaken belief that its additional qualification posed an even greater hurdle to the deployment of strategic defenses. In fact, the term, to the extent that it means anything at all, is supposed to state that we should not build SDI if the Soviets could build countermeasures that would cost us more to overcome. But that elaborate academic calculation can always be made—by any opponent—to "demonstrate" that we should not build SDI, because they always can give unverifiable estimates of what it would cost to overcome an undeveloped, and veiled, Soviet defense effort. Also, there are some things we *have* to build, such as command and control systems, no matter how easy or inexpensive it may be for the Soviets to destroy them. And it is clear to me that we need SDI as much as we need command and control systems.

But the more the Defense Department tried to point out that "cost effective at the margin" was strategic gibberish, the greater the conviction at the State Department that they had really hit on something clever. The debate went on acrimoniously for over a year, until we concluded that it was more "cost effective" to let the State Department go on making misleading and nonsensical statements on a subject in which it had no formal responsibility or expertise.

The actual National Security Decision Directive's (NSDD) language, which the anti-SDI people considered a great victory, said that although the cost effective criterion is "couched in economic terms, it is more than just an economic concept." By that, the President meant that SDI would also impose severe penalties on the Soviets as they sought to counter our SDI deployments, and that factor too should be counted, in casting up the "cost effective equation," as should other nonmonetary values, such as protecting lives and keeping the peace; which was what I had argued all along.

For example, if the Soviets built "fast-burn" missile-boosters to try to render our space-based weapons in Phase I useless, that effort would force the Soviets to spend billions and billions of rubles on an entirely new strategic force—this *on top of* their already massive investments in nuclear forces during the decade of the 1970s—rubles that could not be spent on other military programs.

In any event, through all of this nipping at our heels by SDI's opponents, the program proceeded, and it proceeded far more rapidly and effectively than anyone could have dreamed in 1983.

One of the severest tests for the survival of SDI came with the Soviet demands to the President at Reykjavík, Iceland, in October 1986, when the Soviets, in a set of preliminary public relations thrusts, held out the prospect of eliminating all nuclear weapons, if he would only give up strategic defense. The President stood magnificently firm, SDI proceeded, the Iceland conference broke up; and the Soviets, now understanding that we were going ahead with SDI under President Reagan no matter what they might try to do, agreed, in November 1987, to sign the INF Treaty without any provision whatever for stopping the SDI program.

Beginning in August 1986, under the direction of Dr. Ikle, Richard Perle, and Lieutenant General Abrahamson, the Department conducted an analysis of the progress on SDI and the likely availability of SDI technology. In the course of some four or five briefings throughout the fall, that analysis became a search for the best route to effective defenses. In meeting after meeting, we considered and rejected options featuring early, off-the-shelf, relatively near-terms technology that offered little improvement over the ground-based point defenses available in the late 1960s. In my view, the early deployment of those ground-based systems would do little more than recapitulate the ABM debate of 1969–72—with the same result. Time and again, I directed General Abrahamson and the staff assistants in OSD Policy to continue to look for the first point from which we could build effective defenses. Since early 1984, it was clear to all in the Department that a defense capable of reaching the President's ultimate goal would have to be deployed in phases. Consequently, we were searching for the first effective, space-based deployment.

Opponents, who had not taken the trouble to learn that our policy had always been to approach the deployment of ballistic missile defenses in phases, asserted that our interest in such a less-than-perfect first phase amounted to "abandoning the President's goal"; that we were seeking only the defense of silos or other points, and not the safety of a continent. Each time I would counter the new canard.

By December we had identified a deployment concept, and I decided to take the briefing to the President. On December 19, I went to the President with Richard Perle, Frank Gaffney, General Abrahamson and JCS Chairman Admiral Crowe. I recommended that the President eschew premature deployment of any program that was not an integral part of an effective, space-based system. I urged that we continue to conduct space-based testing and to make general improvements in our space infrastructure. The President understood immediately the importance of proceeding only with a Phase I that would be an integral and basic part of the full system he wanted. He also agreed that an exclusively ground-based system could not be expected to stand up to Soviet proliferation of offensive missiles and other countermeasures. The President approved the general outlines of our Phase I and follow-on deployment concept, and over the next year we were able to move SDI technologies from the pure research phase into the acquisition process, where they could be demonstrated and validated in rigorous testing.

After securing the President's approval to *reject* early deployment schemes involving the least capable, but more readily available, systems, and instead to pursue a research and development program aimed at developing and deploying effective technologies for a deployment decision in the early 1990s, I was rather surprised to read in the papers some days later that I had *recommended* just such an early deployment approach to the President. The morning press was again trying to tell me what I was thinking and doing. As I found later, opponents of SDI objected to the very idea that the Secretary of Defense would brief the President on the status of this defense program, and had decided to discredit what they thought had occurred by characterizing it as "early deployment."

Other efforts of Ambassador Nitze to block the program revolved around a continuing demand, made by him and others in the State Department, that the United States sign an agreement with the Soviets defining what we would be allowed to do, and what we could not do, in the research program to develop strategic defense. This was Nitze's "prohibited-permitted" plan. It resulted, in early 1986, in constant attempts, by some of our Geneva delegation to the arms reduction talks, to undercut the President's decision that our delegation should *not* offer *any* space control proposals.

Nevertheless, the head of our delegation, Max Kampleman, began discussing with the Soviets "outer space arms control," including possible bans on antisatellite weapons. The Soviets were delighted, believing they could define those matters with some all too willing United States negotiators, to block SDI indirectly, rather than directly—an alternative they soon would try again in Iceland.

I had word of all of this from Colonel Dan Gallington, my representative at the Geneva talks, in time to prevent any change in the instruction to our delegation.

I fought the "prohibited-permitted" plan as vigorously as I could in every meeting in which it was raised; it seemed to me to be precisely the kind of strategy that people who opposed the program would adopt. In any attempt to probe the frontiers of science and technology and beyond—and that is clearly what is required to develop a successful SDI—no one can know in advance what we could safely prohibit ourselves from doing. For people who did not want to deploy strategic defense, "prohibited-permitted" was a clever strategy because it would have involved us in endless discussions and negotiations with the Soviets on each experiment. It would also have enabled them to claim that every experiment we needed to do, whether foreseen or not at the time an agreement was signed, in effect would violate the so-called permitted-prohibited agreement, had it been signed.

Just for one example, opponents of SDI wanted us to sign agreements regulating the permitted intensity, or "brightness," of lasers, and other technical controls, all of which would have prevented us from undertaking the full scope of scientific work required to develop an effective strategic defense.

Again, President Reagan stood extraordinarily firm in his refusals to enter into that kind of negotiation. It was clear to him, as it was to me, that in scientific work needed for SDI you cannot, in advance, agree to prohibit yourself from working on something that (as it might suddenly develop) you needed to work on if indeed you wanted to deploy the system. President Reagan did and does want to deploy an effective strategic defense.

I am convinced that if we could have secured adequate funding from the Congress, we would have been able to deploy the first phase of an effective strategic defense system by 1993. However, it became increasingly difficult to persuade the Congress to vote the amounts required for Defense as a whole; and because SDI was a controversial program at a time of large Government-wide deficits, it was easy to cut. At this writing, Congress in the 1990 Fiscal Year Authorization Bill authorized $3.6 billion. This inadequate amount, of course, delays, unreasonably and unnecessarily, the time when the world could benefit from our defensive system. The future depends on how vigorously the fight will be made to develop and deploy a full strategic defense system.

More and more, the desires of people in Congress and elsewhere to remove controversy and opposition from each issue, so that ultimately everything is compromised, particularly endangers SDI and threatens to water it down to the point where it is little more than research for a refined ground-based, and therefore inherently ineffective, system. The full deployment of a space-based strategic defense system, of the type described by General Abrahamson and envisioned by President Reagan—one with the very real probability of being able to destroy Soviet missiles before they re-enter the Earth's atmosphere—is essential. The goal is to make those Soviet missiles obsolete.

To those who told us we could not guarantee a one hundred percent destruction of Soviet missiles, I responded on December 19, 1984, that "if properly planned, the transitional capabilities would strengthen our present deterrent capability. But this is not our only goal, not the end of our vision." The President, as usual, said it better: "The ultimate goal [is] eliminating the threat posed by strategic missiles."

SDI can contribute to curbing strategic arms competition by nuclear Soviet missiles. And, as the President said on March 14, 1988, SDI is "vital insurance against Soviet cheating." By contrast, the President pointed out, MAD depends on "no slip-ups, no madmen, no unmanageable crisis, no mistakes—forever."

My own feeling is that if we do fund, and have the will to deploy, a complete system, it could destroy a very high percentage of Soviet missiles. The Soviets, seeing the effectiveness of our defenses, would be even more hesitant to launch a first strike attack. Opponents of SDI will always say that if it cannot destroy one hundred percent of all Soviet missiles, then we should not build it. But those are no more than desperate arguments that continue to be used to try to block our working on the whole program.

I conclude this brief history of the SDI program by saying only that I believe it is vital for the United States and for our allies to develop and deploy a defensive system that is as effective as our skill, ingenuity and resources can secure. That strategic defense is not a defense against battlefield nuclear weapons or cruise missiles is certainly not a reason for not building it—as rapidly and effectively as we can. The fact that a shield against intercontinental and intermediate range nuclear missiles would not end war is not a basis for denying ourselves the enormous benefits of defending the United States in a highly effective way from some of the most horrible weapons mankind has yet developed.

In fact, it turns out that "spin-offs" from our work on SDI also will be very effective against other types of nuclear weapons, including battlefield missiles, Third World threats (such as Libyan missiles), and cruise missiles. Here the key is space-based sensors to locate the attacking missiles, and provide the data to ground-based weapons systems so they can perform the task of destroying those short range, low trajectory nuclear weapons. Of particular note, the laser system I mentioned before would provide us with global antiaircraft capabilities: The same lasers that could shoot down missiles could destroy attacking aircraft. It is partly due to such spin-offs, particularly the space-based ones, that the Soviets react with such fear to SDI.

In my opinion, anything other than studying and building and *deploying* is to waste money and destroy the prospects of the single strategic concept that offers the most hope to the world since nuclear weapons were first deployed.

So I think it exceedingly fortunate for all of us that despite all of the attempts to block strategic defense, we have thus far stood firm.

And, of course, we must never forget that throughout all of this period, the Soviets have been working as hard as possible, with no internal opposition or sneers, to try to develop their own space-based strategic defense. That closed society, despite recent talk of "glasnost," prevents us from knowing the full extent of Soviet achievements.

The latest strategics to kill SDI now take the form of appearing to advocate strategic defense by saying that we should pursue a research program and that we should "concentrate on," and "examine carefully" (and similar expressions of weak intent), a program designed only to enable us to destroy one or two missiles that might accidentally be launched by our enemies.

The infuriating aspect of these continuing attempts to do something less than the full program is that they are usually proposed by people who know better. Their sole goal seems to be to support something that has the least possible controversy or opposition to it. The fact that those substitute proposals would deny to America and our allies the possibility and the hope of being freed from the effects of many of the most destructive weapons ever devised by man, should be enough to overcome and defeat these arguments of weakness, indecision, irresolution and fear of opposition.

XI

The Intermediate Nuclear Forces Treaty

A recent, rather startling poll indicated that 71 percent of Republicans and 74 percent of Democrats believe that the United States can trust the General Secretary of the Soviet Union, Mikhail Gorbachev. Trust in what sense?

Trust that Mr. Gorbachev will turn his back on the goals of the Soviet state? Trust that he is becoming more like us in economic values? Trust that the Soviet Union will never violate an agreement with the United States (the historical record notwithstanding)? Trust that Mr. Gorbachev is diametrically opposed to the precepts of the Communist Party that he leads (precepts that are of course diametrically opposed to Western values and principles)?

All of this is highly unlikely. Mr. Gorbachev does appear to be committed to some significant, perhaps even historic, internal economic reforms: his perestroika, or restructuring. Many of those reforms are truly significant in that, taken at their face value, they represent major revisions in Soviet domestic policies. Mr.

Gorbachev is clearly adept at public relations in international politics. There is great danger, however, that his approach will obscure the fundamental and unchanging nature of the Soviet system. The poll results are testimony to the effectiveness of Mr. Gorbachev's courtship of Western public opinion; but that General Secretary Gorbachev wears a smile and dresses fashionably does not mean there is any fundamental change in Soviet goals. To be sure, Mr. Gorbachev is making changes—and most likely does want to buy some time from the West in order to stimulate his country's moribund economy. But perestroika aimed at constructing a more effective socialist regime, which is clearly the General Secretary's goal, does not by any means translate into a move toward Western-style democracy.

A nineteenth century Frenchman who traveled to Russia, the Marquis de Custine (a contemporary of Alexis de Tocqueville), remarked in his journal: "I do not blame the Russians for being what they are, I blame them for pretending to be what we are." That thought is particularly appropriate today.

President Reagan came into office with the explicit intention of restoring our military and political strength, and doing so without apology. The United States has made enormous progress toward that vital goal. One of the primary results of that restoration became a reality with the signing of the Intermediate-range Nuclear Forces (INF) Treaty in December 1987. That restoration of the West's security must not be abandoned to an overoptimistic view of East-West relations.

It is of course necessary, particularly in the nuclear age, to negotiate on arms and to work toward a more constructive and stable relationship with the Soviet Union. This still requires strong defenses. President Reagan was firmly committed to that course, and so is President Bush. It should not be abandoned because of euphoric rhetoric or public opinions polls about the popularity of the current Soviet General Secretary.

There is not a better example of the importance of negotiating from strength than the INF Treaty. That lesson takes on great significance for the discussions between the United States and the Soviet Union to cut strategic nuclear arsenals in half (the Strategic Arms Reduction Talks, or START), as well as for the conventional-arms reduction negotiations. There is not a better argument for President Reagan's defense policies than the INF Treaty, which the President and I proposed in October 1981. At the time, the Soviets held that same proposal—the so-called zero option—up to scorn, knowing that America was weak militarily after a decade of neglect, and believing that we lacked the will to regain our strength.

The INF Treaty shows that the Reagan Administration's policies were correct. It shows negotiations from strength and achieving peace through strength, works. It shows that by sticking with a negotiating position, by refusing to be intimidated by Soviet walkouts, and by not permitting America's goals to be linked to Soviet demands that weaken our strategic defense, we can successfully achieve our security goals in a negotiation.

Verifiable agreements reducing armaments are an integral part of national security, but they are not an end in themselves. That should be self-evident; but it is often overlooked in the pressures of summitry, politics and the desire to achieve results. A START agreement may be within grasp; but as questions about our long-term security surface during this critical period, we must ensure that the mistakes of the 1970s—the "decade of neglect" and of "detente"—are never repeated. Our new relationship with the Soviets presents great opportunities as well as some great hazards. As we confront the new challenges ahead, and the old, underlying conflicts on which they rest, we must draw upon some of the lessons we should have learned from the past.

George Orwell once said: "We have now sunk to a depth at which the restatement of the obvious is the first duty of intelligent men." As we are poised on the eve of a potentially new relationship with the Soviet Union, it is critical that we take stock of the lessons of the last two or three decades. My purpose in this chapter is to recount the history of the INF Treaty and to restate its obvious—and not-so-obvious—lessons for the role of arms reduction agreements as elements of United States national security.

In 1977, the Soviet Union began deploying the SS-20, a three-warheaded, intermediate range nuclear missile, that we believed to be (and later verified to be) sufficiently accurate to destroy hardened military targets, and sufficiently high in yield and long in range to destroy any city in Europe—or indeed any military target in Europe.[1]

The deployment of the SS-20 seriously upset the strategic balance in NATO Europe at a time that the Soviet Union had achieved at least parity in intercontinental strategic systems. We and NATO had no equivalent counter to the SS-20.

NATO saw that imbalance as a politically and militarily threatening change in the nuclear balance in Europe, and debated the matter for close to two years. After a major internal struggle, its members agreed upon the December 12, 1979, Dual Track Resolution.[2]

A great deal was to be heard about that resolution all during the time I was Secretary. In essence, it provided that NATO would deploy the intermediate range Pershing IIs[3] and the ground-launched cruise missiles that we were then developing. The United States would deploy them in countries where they could put at risk Soviet targets. The recipient countries would

---

1. Destroying a city does not require high accuracy.

2. It is a source of some amusement to listen to former Chancellor Helmut Schmidt inveighing on television against "your American missiles on German soil" and to recall that Schmidt was one of the principal supporters of the December 1979 resolution. At that time he correctly called them NATO missiles.

3. The Pershing II is a single warheaded, nonmobile, very accurate, intermediate range nuclear missile. The Soviet SS-20 has three warheads and a slightly longer range, and is a mobile system.

include the United Kingdom, Germany, Italy, Belgium and the Netherlands. That was the first track of the "dual track" 1979 resolution.

By the second track, the United States would open negotiations with the Soviets to seek the reduction, or the removal, of the Soviet SS-20 missiles.

It was that second track that finally induced the most reluctant countries, the Netherlands and Belgium, and then therefore the others, to go along with the deployment of missiles as the first part of the dual track approach.

The whole subject of the Soviet INF missile, the December 1979 dual track decision, and the development and initial deployment of our missiles to counter the SS-20, came up as a major point of discussion at every NATO meeting that I attended from January 1981 through November 1987.

The NATO defense ministers meet four times a year. Two of those meetings are called meetings of the Defense Planning Committee, which considers the broad range of NATO's defense requirements. The remaining two are meetings of the defense ministers, sitting as the so-called Nuclear Planning Group (NPG), which focuses on NATO's nuclear requirements. The NATO Defense Planning Committee always meets in Brussels; defense ministers meet as the Nuclear Planning Group twice a year in whatever country can be persuaded to serve as the host.

In the early 1980s, some governments were so concerned by the antinuclear demonstrations that regularly took place in their countries that they declined to carry out the commitments they had made earlier to serve as hosts for the NPG.

The first time that happened, I volunteered the United States to serve as host, out of turn. Our people at Fort Carson in Colorado Springs did a magnificent job with less than two months to plan and conduct one of the most successful NPG meetings held.

All of the NATO meetings followed a reasonably similar pattern. In Brussels, at the NATO headquarters at Evere, a short distance from the city on the road to the airport, in a complex of buildings that can be most kindly described as "functional," we would gather around an immense oval table. At its open center, the NATO symbol was incised into the floor. The delegations were arranged in alphabetical order, with the Secretary General at the head of the table. The alphabet always brought the United States out at the end; but the end being, like the beginning, next to the Secretary General, we rarely had problems in securing recognition in the debate.

There were two different types of sessions. To the "restricted" sessions, "only" one hundred forty people were admitted, consisting of many working with and serving the individual delegations. The other sessions were even larger. The Secretary of Defense, the American Ambassador to NATO, and the Chairman of the Joint Chiefs usually sat together at the table, with our most expert people in NATO issues, disarmament, technology and weapons systems, ranged behind us.

The United States always plays a leading role in the NATO meetings, so the United States Secretary of Defense is called on to give several reports. He also is expected to intervene on most questions, since the United States is considered, albeit with some reluctance, by some to be the major and indispensable player in NATO. Two reports were required at each of the NPG meetings during this period. One was on the status of development and deployment of the weapons systems called for in the first track of the December 1979 resolution; the other report was about the status of negotiations called for in the second part of the resolution.

At the first NATO meeting I attended in the spring of 1981, and thereafter throughout that year, many of my colleagues spoke in favor of the "zero option," which in effect meant that if the Soviets took out their SS-20s (and their older SS-4s and SS-5s and their newer SS-23s), then we would not deploy the Pershing

IIs or the ground launch cruise missiles. The zero option was supported by a number of antinuclear groups as well as by many others. But it was *opposed* by those who worried that the Soviets would never take out the SS-20s and feared that the calls for a "zero option" would seriously postpone the date when we actually had a deterrent to counter the SS-20s deployed in Europe.

The more I listened to the debates about the zero option, the more it seemed to me to make some sense, if we could be sure of two things. By the first of the two, the Soviets would not only remove the SS-20s, but would actually destroy them. That was important because the SS-20s were mobile; they could be moved back and forth from their present emplacements to places of concealment and back again, all within a few days. The other essential, I felt, to any treaty on any subject with the Soviet Union, was thorough on-site verification. Even that would probably not be a one hundred percent guarantee of their compliance; but it would be far better than anything else we had to date.

Meanwhile, I did not feel we should stop our work on the Pershing IIs or the cruise missiles. I felt that there would be *no* possibility of the Soviets agreeing to take out their SS-20s, unless, and until, they had the kind of inducement that deployment of the Pershing IIs would bring. The Pershing IIs would be able to strike targets in the Soviet Union in less than 12 minutes after launch, and there was no defense against them. Although the Soviets were comfortable deploying their three-warheaded SS-20, whose capabilities were in some ways superior to the Pershing II, they were very uncomfortable with NATO's having any system capable of depriving the Soviet Union of a sanctuary.

But none of those cautions or conditions appealed to those Europeans, or indeed to many Americans, who simply wanted to get rid of nuclear weapons. They were not particularly interested, or so it seemed to me, in either deterrent balance or safeguards against possible Soviet cheating.

Most meetings on the subject of defense in NATO were routinely picketed, and the cause of major demonstrations in many European cities. Later I saw demonstrations of nearly 100,000 people in Hyde Park in London. ("Saw" is perhaps not quite the right term. My wife and I were in London, and we had taken a very circuitous route to return to our hotel after lunch, not because of any fears of the police about the demonstrators, but simply because traffic was effectively blocked for miles by the demonstrators; so, in a sense, we were caught up *in* the demonstration.)

There was considerable evidence too (according to Scotland Yard) that the demonstration had been organized "from the outside." A great many of the demonstrators arrived by bus, with all transportation costs paid by some mysterious sources. At one of the earliest of the NATO meetings I attended, in Bonn, several of the major squares were filled with some 60,000 demonstrators all chanting against nuclear weapons, demanding a nuclear free Europe, nuclear freezes and the other familiar litanies. At no time did I see even a single sign, much less a demonstration, against the SS-20s. The demonstration was always against our proposed counter to the SS-20s—a counter that would give Europe a deterrent capability—a counter that would provide a European-based capability to hold at risk targets in the Soviet Union, and thus strengthen our deterrence.

As more and more of the demonstrations were held, at least partially through arrangements made by the Soviet Union as part of their acknowledged attempts to influence public opinion in the West, more and more defense ministers at the NATO meetings urged, either as their own views or as opinions being presented to their governments, that more be done on the "second track" of the December 1979 resolution. It was becoming clear that to secure an agreement with the Soviet Union on intermediate range missiles, negotiations must widely be seen as being open, active and vigorously conducted, if we were to retain support of the host governments for deployment of the Pershing IIs and the ground launch cruise missiles.

It occurred to me, as I thought about all that at the various meetings, that we might have an opening in the negotiating side of the INF Dual Track Resolution if we were able to persuade the Soviets to sign a verifiable treaty taking out all of their SS-20s. That would save us the expensive and difficult task, politically, militarily and fiscally, of deploying counters to the SS-20s.

Therefore, I discussed with the President, in the fall of 1981, the possibility of our side offering the true "zero option"—that is, to say to the Soviets, If you will take all of yours out, we will not put any of ours in. I also felt that if we could get a Soviet agreement to an acceptable treaty, particularly including very strict verification procedures, that would be a good result in and of itself. It would also be a compelling answer to the growing impression, fostered by all the demonstrations and all the manipulation of Western public opinion by the Soviets, that President Reagan really did not want arms reduction; that he secretly, at least, believed that we could and should fight a nuclear war.

That and similar nonsense was being circulated in all quarters fundamentally opposed to the President's military policy and to his generally conservative beliefs and his several challenges to the conventional wisdom. With that in mind, and being particularly aware how vital it was that we hold NATO support and keep the unity of NATO that is its principal strength, I suggested to the President that he very strongly consider offering the Soviets the zero option in an agreement with suitable safeguards for on-site verification. I emphasized that the good that would result if we could actually secure that dramatic proposal would outweigh the surprise and instinctive disapproval of many.

I had talked to some of our military people and to my principal staff people, including Richard Perle, who was and is a very considerable expert, both in dealing with the Soviets and in comprehending the more arcane aspects of arms reduction and arms control. Perle had been a staff assistant to Senator Henry Jackson (Democrat of Washington) and was thoroughly familiar with American negotiations for the Salt II Treaty, as well as for other agreements. He was also completely up to date on NATO and European politics. We discussed both the political effect and the military results of the plan I had suggested to the President. My memory is that Richard was able to conceal quite well any enthusiasm he may have felt for my idea. Later, however, he supported it loyally and effectively.

There was indeed some surprise expressed that the President and I were proposing and supporting the zero option. In fact, it ran counter to so many myths about my supposedly "hawkish, warlike" image that few, if any, accounts at the time bothered to mention my support of the basic plan that, in 1987, formed the basis of the INF Treaty.

With respect to the military sufficiency of the zero option or any such arms reduction proposal, my feeling has always been that the basic question one should ask in considering *any* arms reduction proposal is: What's left? In this case, I felt there would be enough strength left on our side, assuming we could get a verifiable treaty eliminating all of the Soviet SS-20s and assuming that then we would decide not to put any of our counters in. The What's left? would include, on the strategic level, not only our present submarine missiles, but the new D-5s that we were developing, which would have the accuracy and the yield to destroy Soviet hardened targets; and it would, of course, also include both the existing and the proposed improved ICBMs, as well as the new air launched cruise missiles that we were planning to put on our strategic bombers. On the European theater level, we would still have dual-capable aircraft such as the F-111s based in England, which were nuclear capable, as well as Lance missiles and artillery (which, of course, would need modernization in the early 1990s).

The President liked the idea. During several meetings in the fall of 1981, he told me he liked the boldness of the suggestion, and the surprise and, as he hoped, the relief it would secure. But he also liked the substance of it, because for a long time Ronald Reagan, contrary to virtually all of the popular myths about him (and I know of no one who has engendered more myths than the President) actually was very unhappy with the need to rely on nuclear weapons. He was convinced, and said many times, that a nuclear war could never be won, and therefore must never be fought. He was convinced that both sides had too many nuclear weapons, and that a proposal of this kind might very well lead to a great many other reductions. All of the required briefings, exercises, and the "Doomsday" scenarios new Presidents have to be given, simply reinforced his own beliefs.

So he embraced the zero plan, despite strong opposition from Secretary of State Alexander Haig. Haig felt that it would leave us with too little, that it would start and fuel an antinuclear movement in general, and that it would alienate many in Europe who were supporting the deployment of our counters to the SS-20.

Haig need not have feared, because to the President's disappointment and mine, the immediate reaction was almost *all* negative.

The arms control establishment all derided the proposal, since they said (before the Soviets had even responded), that it was obvious the Soviet Union could not and would not accept it, and therefore it was not a proposal that could lead to an agreement. Therefore it was "not serious," they said, even though it embodied many of the points that many of them individually had recommended.

The Soviets also derided it, I am sure because they saw that we did not yet have any Pershing IIs or ground-launched cruise missiles deployed, and because they were convinced they could block deployment through manipulation of public opinion; and ultimately, they were counting on an American and European faintheartedness to prevail while they maintained their already deployed SS-20s. They saw no *inducement* to take out those SS-20s, whose numbers they were adding to every month.

The President stuck with his proposal, but it became increasingly clear that the Soviets were not interested in any mutual arms reduction agreements. What they wanted was nuclear superiority sufficient to weaken and divide NATO, and they thought they could succeed. They were sure their ability to manipulate Western public opinion could block any NATO deployments. Therefore, from their point of view, why get into serious negotiations or discussion of an agreement that seemed to offer no inducements?

Seeing that, the American opponents of the President's plan to get rid of all longer range intermediate range missiles, East and West, wanted us to scuttle our proposal. Those opponents unfortunately included some in the executive branch, who rather quietly set aside the President's zero option proposal and proceeded to try to negotiate along tracks with which they were familiar. Some of those same people had brought us such "achievements" as the unratified SALT II Treaty, which allowed the Soviets to add some 6,000 nuclear warheads to the stock they had on the signing of the treaty, and the ABM Treaty, under which we gave up defenses while the Soviets aggressively pursued defenses.

The modus operandi of the arms control establishment essentially was to start with the idea that we must, above all, secure an agreement, no matter what it says.

The dictate of such a premise was that any apparent obstacle to that goal, such as Soviet opposition to an American position, required that the American position be modified; because otherwise we could not get an agreement. The idea of sticking with an American position and telling the Soviets that if they themselves would remove their opposition to it, we could have an agreement, seemed never to have occurred to some of our negotiators.

The other tack that is taken, of course, is that of compromise. Compromise, in this case, usually means partially giving up an American position, because as our negotiators put it, we must show our "flexibility," in order to get an agreement. Therefore, we end up with something less than we want, and the Soviets, not feeling any such compulsion to get an agreement, usually end up with far more of what they wanted. All is sacrificed on the altar of an agreement, since "agreement" is the politically popular be-all and end-all of arms control negotiations.

The President changed all that by taking a position that he felt was in the best interest of the United States and NATO, and staying with it. He told the Soviets, in effect, that if they wanted an agreement, they would have to accept our position. Unlike many of his predecessors, he did not worry that the press and other critics would consider any failure to sign an arms control agreement a major disaster. The Soviets, not having any public opinion at home, were not subjected to such pressure, and found it easier, therefore, to wait for us to come around to their position. In fact, the Soviets have a saying that they believe they "can always outwait impatient democracies." Western democracies are indeed impatient. We want results; we want achievements. We want something that can be measured by headlines that report agreement between the Soviets and the United States. We like televised signing ceremonies of agreements, since they demonstrate "an effective President."

The President risked the violation of all of that, and ultimately, by being patient and politically courageous, secured a very good treaty—one in which the Soviets gave up all of their cherished "non-negotiable positions." But that was not until 1987, and we must not get ahead of the story.

After the scornful rejection in 1981 of the President's zero option proposal, various maneuvers of the conventional wisdom school were used to restore the negotiations to a more conventional track. The inevitable "compromise" proposal was not long in coming.

It came in the form of an offer during the famous—or infamous—"walk in the woods" conducted by our negotiator, Ambassador Paul Nitze, and the Soviet negotiator, Yuily Kvitsinsky on July 16, 1982. This was not much of a compromise from our viewpoint, because it gave the Soviets what they wanted most: our agreement never to deploy the Pershing IIs. The Pershing II was the American weapon that the Soviets feared the most, because, as noted before, it could destroy targets in the Soviet Union with a very short flight time—and they had no defense against it.

In return for our staggering concession, the Soviets would agree to take out some (but not all) of their SS-20s.

When Paul Nitze presented the terms of the proposal to a number of us upon his return from that most stunning of his innumerable negotiating meetings, I found it hard put to remain polite. However, I used the required formula by saying that we would examine the proposal carefully from the point of view of military sufficiency, and we would let him know.

I do not know if everyone in the Defense Department and the Joint Chiefs was as horrified by the proposal as I was, but I stated the Department of Defense position as strongly as possible against the "walk in the woods" proposal, and it died aborning when the President agreed that it would not be in our national interest.

Much lamentation broke out in the arms control community, because the two negotiators' agreement was considered the ideal compromise, since the Soviets would probably not only have agreed to it, but indeed most probably instigated the idea. There was the usual "informed" speculation that Kvitsinsky would not be able to "sell" the proposal at home. This of course was designed to whet our appetite for it. But to anyone even remotely familiar

with the Soviet system of government and the way their negotiators operate, it would take an extremely naive person to believe
that Kvitsinsky himself either had proposed *or* had agreed to such
a proposal, on his own and without the most detailed instructions
from the Soviets in Moscow.

Things languished on the negotiating front thereafter, until
we made it unmistakably clear—as meeting after meeting of the
NATO defense ministers endorsed and reendorsed (but usually
not without some reasonably strong argument being required)
the deployment of the Pershing IIs and the ground launch cruise
missiles—that we were indeed going ahead with deployment, in
the absence of an agreement, despite all the best efforts of the
Soviets to stop us.

After we did indeed begin to deploy, the Soviets walked out
of the INF negotiations, on November 23, 1983, vowing not
to return until we had taken out all of our Pershing IIs and
ground launch cruise missiles. Later, they also walked out of the
parallel START negotiations covering the longer range nuclear
missiles.

One would have thought that even the most hardened arms
control establishment people would now be convinced that we
had to continue with the deployment; but many of them took
the position that the Soviet walkout was our fault for not agreeing
to the Soviet position. They cited the "inexperience" of the President and his team, and the fact that the President was not following the advice of their (establishment) band of "trained
professionals" in arms control. Indeed, and fortunately, the President was not.

Despite their continued support for the deployment of the
Pershing IIs and the ground launch cruise missiles, the NATO
defense ministers faced uneasy and sometimes unhappy governments at home. Those governments did not relish the continued
demonstrations and the fierce opposition of their political opponents to deployment.

It was odd that during all that time there was never a demonstration against the SS-20s. Nevertheless, one by one, the NATO countries, which had supported the *idea* of deployment, agreed to actual deployment. England had perhaps the least trouble agreeing, although the demonstrations were no less persistent there than in other countries. And as the deployments were agreed to, we kept to our schedule and sent the missiles in with their crews for training, testing and deployment. I recall that when Belgian Defense Minister Freddie Vreven advised me that his parliament had accepted the deployment schedule, we were able to send the first missiles to him within less than twenty-four hours—meeting our schedule.

Over the years following deployment, I was particularly gratified, not only because our NATO allies had been so courageous in authorizing deployment in the face of all the manipulation and public opinion against them that the Soviets could manage, but also because every one of those courageous governments that deployed was re-elected the next time it faced the voters.

The long, tortuous path of negotiations suddenly reopened when the Soviets saw that they could not block deployment. They saw that the various intimidating gestures they tried (such as placing their submarines off the East Coast of the United States far closer than they had been for many years; such as adding to their forces in East Germany) had also failed to move the West from its position of restoring the nuclear balance at the intermediate range.

There is no need to recount the day-by-day path of those negotiations here. That has been done many times. Suffice it to say that in every forum where the Soviets tried to offer great blandishments to the President, if he would only agree to giving up the strategic defense initiative, or if he would only agree that the Soviets could keep one hundred of their SS-20 missiles in Asia, or if he would only agree that we must count the French and British independent nuclear deterrent, or if he would only agree that we give up our absurd idea of on-site verification, then he could have the kind of treaty that he wanted—in spite of all of these offers, offers that I felt were chimerical, the President stayed firm.[4]

When Ambassador Ed Rowny consulted with Japanese officials, they told him that the Soviet idea of keeping one hundred SS-20 missiles in Asia was unacceptable. The speed and clarity of that response, and the difficulties of verifying other than "global zero," reinforced President Reagan's determination.

Ultimately, by November 1987 the Soviets had given up every one of their cherished "non-negotiable" positions and signed precisely the kind of treaty the President and I had proposed in October of 1981.

I had resigned November 23, 1987, because of my wife's health shortly before the Reagan-Gorbachev Summit in Washington, at which the Treaty was signed. It is ironic indeed that some saw my departure as a protest against the soon-to-be-signed INF Treaty—ironic, because I had proposed the treaty in the first place. Also, many failed to give the President credit for the real achievement that the Treaty represents. I felt that such reluctance simply showed the extremes to which some apologists go when they are determined to ignore the commonsense proposition that successful negotiations *are* concluded when one negotiates from a position of strength and is willing to stay with constructive positions until the other side gives up.

Some attributed the Soviets' caving in to changes in their leadership. But I was never able to accept that belief. My feeling has always been that no general secretary of the Communist Party

4. There were reports that in some of the preliminary sessions at the Reykjavík meeting (with bargaining resembling a poker game and each side raising and doubling the other), the President had given some the impression that he would accept the Soviet demand that they keep one hundred SS-20s in Asia. Fortunately, that was not the result of the Iceland meeting.

of the Soviet Union will be allowed to alter in any fundamental way the basically aggressive nature of Soviet behavior.

Mr. Gorbachev is different in one significant way, aside from all the superficial differences he exhibits. That fundamental difference is that, unlike most of his predecessors, he seeks favorable world opinion. Most of his statements and his promises of proposed reductions are, in my view, designed to secure that favorable world opinion. So great is such a novelty on the part of the Soviet General Secretary that a number of polls and other measurements have shown that people in Western Europe particularly, and indeed many in the United States, believe they can trust him. They place him high on their personal popularity lists.[5]

Despite all of this and despite the great skepticism with which I view Mr. Gorbachev's conversion to Western ideals of democracy, I think we should take advantage of every opportunity that his economic and other policies offer. The INF Treaty, in its final form, was such an offer. Not only did Gorbachev give up all of the Soviet "non-negotiable" demands, but he gave us precisely the kind of treaty that the President had sought for seven years. That act of course does not mean—any more than does the Soviet withdrawal from Afghanistan—that the USSR has given up its long-term aggressive designs.

That withdrawal was simply, in my view, an admission that they could not win, and indeed had lost, in their goal of trying to pacify the Mujaheddin with their own troops, so that their

---

5. See Caspar W. Weinberger, "Arms Reductions and Deterrence," *Foreign Affairs*, Spring 1988, p. 700. I think a large part of this euphoric reaction to Gorbachev in popularity polls arises from the fact that so many people in democracies believe what they want to believe. Most people are delighted with any evidence of easing tensions and are either bored or annoyed by warnings that the Soviet military power not only has not declined, but is still increasing, even though there may be occasional leveling off of their total spending as they complete production runs on some models and must retool before they start their latest series. The important thing to watch is their output, and that continues to outstrip ours each month in virtually all categories.

"puppet government" would be safe. They pump more than $300 million a month to shore up that puppet.

The other bit of evidence that most people use to support the belief that the Soviets have changed is the statement by Mr. Gorbachev that he will take out 500,000 Soviet troops, including some 240,000 along the NATO Central front.[6] To the date of this writing, that has not yet happened; but even if it should, it would still leave the Soviets with an extremely large imbalance in their favor in conventional arms. Nor do we have any idea yet what would be the composition of the 500,000 troops that Mr. Gorbachev *might* withdraw; or, perhaps even more to the point, we do not know whether he will be *allowed* to withdraw them.

A number of security "experts" are worried that Mr. Gorbachev may "gain the public relations upper hand" by all those offers. They advise that we must go Mr. Gorbachev "one better" in offering reductions, so that we can regain the "public relations upper hand."

Our own defense needs require more thought than that entailed in seeking mere public relations advantages. Yet, the constant harping by many commentators that President Bush must "do something" encourages the kind of thoughtless response for which Gorbachev obviously hopes.

There is no better example of the importance of negotiating from strength than the INF Treaty; there is no better argument for President Reagan's defense policies, by which we regained very great military strength since 1981, than the signing of that Treaty. Sadly, the question remains whether America, at least,

---

6. This offer seems to be of the same stripe as Gorbachev's "unilateral" offer of May 1989, that the Soviets take out 500 of their short-range and battle nuclear missiles. Since they possess some 10,600 such missiles, and more than 550 become obsolete each year, the "offer" scarcely seemed to justify the enormous press attention given to it. Also, two days later it became clear it was not really a unilateral offer; it seems it was dependent on NATO concessions after all. But it achieved its public relations goal of further weakening Germany's willingness to modernize our Lance short-range weapons.

has learned those lessons. In the last three years Congress has cut the defense budget in real terms below the previous year's budget. (The 1990 budget "compromise" with the Congress agrees, in advance of any hearings, to another below zero reduction.) Neither the assumption that the deficit is more important than our security, nor the hope that the Soviets have changed (so that we do not need to worry about the threat from their military strength or their unchanging goals) is a legitimate rationalization.[7]

The facts run counter to those favored assumptions that we can safely reduce our hard-won military strength. The Soviets continue to spend very large amounts each year to add to their offensive military strength. They sell their most advanced bombers to Libya; they continue to supply and resupply Cuba, the Sandinistas in Nicaragua and the Salvadoran guerrillas with offensive weapons. Their as yet unrealized offer to reduce their forces by 500,000, and their suggestion that they will stop production of weapons grade nuclear materials in two of their 14 plutonium plants, do not reduce their war-making potential.

The lesson of the INF Treaty is that we can secure our own modest agenda, which is simply peace and freedom, only if we are militarily strong. Further, we must be militarily secure enough to be able to resist Soviet aggression. It can flame into action very quickly.

The INF Treaty should, and I think will, stand as a monument to President Reagan's determination to regain our military strength, and to put his desire for a treaty that is in American

---

7. The Democratic minority report of the National Economic Commission issued in March 1989 expressly states that the Soviet threat is fading and therefore that even the President's request for *zero* real growth for Defense is too much. The subsequent compromise budget plan for 1990 accepts that position, so the matter is no longer debated. The only open question is, How much deeper cuts will be ultimately agreed to?

interests far ahead of the political clamor for a-treaty-whatever-it-says.

We must not forget the fundamental difference between the Soviet Union's political structure and ours. In the Soviet Union, four or five men sitting around a table in the Kremlin (regardless of their highly publicized elections, in which only government approved candidates appeared on the ballot) can, and do, decide how much they will add to defense; what will be their military capabilities and for how many years they will continue to add to them; and when, and whether, they will start new weapons systems. They do all of this by their own decision, without any true "public opinion," without any meaningful votes, without any substantive roll calls, without any "unapproved" editorials,[8] and without any of the normal delays required in a democracy.

On the other hand, we will sometimes agonize eight or ten years over whether to replace a missile that no longer has the effectiveness we need for deterrence. We also, as we have seen, can come very close to signing, or indeed sign very bad agreements simply because public opinion in democracies demands agreements.

None of this is to say that we envy the Soviet system, or that there is anything in it we wish to copy. But it is to say that we should realize what an enormous military advantage such a system can give a country that is perfectly willing to have its citizens, year after year and decade after decade, denied anything like the quality of life that we would require as an essential minimum. The Soviet Union is a country and a system in which the only public opinion and only individual liberties and rights are those that the government allows.

In a world in which there are two superpowers, one of which has the governmental structure and military might of the Soviet

---

8. And if there is an unapproved editorial, the editor is removed.

Union, it is essential for our very survival that we retain the military strength we acquired in the 1980s—the strength that brought us the INF Treaty. That strength is our real and only assurance that we and our allies can indeed remain free and at peace.

XII

Iran and the Hostages

This is the most difficult and disagreeable chapter for me to write, because I feel that the Iran hostage activity was the one serious mistake the Administration made during the seven years I served as Secretary of Defense. It was the one time that the President, misled by some who had full access to him, followed advice that led him away from his sure instincts. To my knowledge, it was the only such instance during his years in the White House; indeed, in my opinion it was the only major serious error of his long career of public service, and that includes his eight years as Governor of California and his eight years as President of the United States. That is an extraordinary record.

The President's motives were the best, and completely understandable for anyone who knew, as I did, his warm and compassionate nature, and the revulsion he felt over Americans' being held against their will by a group of fanatical terrorists. The fact remains, however, that the President was misled and badly served by Robert McFarlane and some of his staff who should never have been appointed to the White House staff, and who were completely unwilling to recognize their own severe limitations of intellect, or moral principles, or any real understanding of history.

The Iran hostage problem has been argued, discussed, debated and heard by so many groups, that I think there is little that can be added; except that I can attempt to convey the personal impressions and the personal viewpoint of one who was present at some of the critical meetings. And I think it is important for the public —particularly those who ask "How could it have happened?"— to understand how the White House and the Presidency operate, or can operate, when people who turn out to be quite inadequate are put in positions where they can use the influence "the White House" always has. But first, some background and a few reminders of past events may be useful.

I was not in office on November 4, 1979, when militant Iranian students seized our Embassy in Teheran, kidnapping sixty-six Americans. (Fifty-two of them were held for 444 days in complete and direct violation of all the rules that govern the conduct of nations that call themselves civilized.)

My feelings about that incident were, I suppose, no stronger than those of most other Americans, but I felt strongly then and do to this day that conduct of the kind Iran exhibited during the seizure of our Embassy completely disqualified it from any civilized intercourse with other nations. I feel that as long as the leadership in Iran remains as it is (and in my opinion it has not changed substantively after Ayatollah Khomeini's death), it is futile to expect that any kind of agreements with such a government would be kept or would be of any value.

From time to time after the January 1981 agreements had been reached under which our hostages in the Embassy were finally freed, voices would be raised at the State Department, and occasionally elsewhere, recalling the strategic importance of Iran's location, and looking back with some nostalgia to the days when the Shah was in command and Iran had been a very good friend.

I of course recalled those days, including meetings I had with the Shah when I served in Washington between 1970 and 1975. I also felt that we had been to some extent responsible for the fall of the Shah and for not supporting him as vigorously as we should have when he most needed help.

The Shah of Iran, prior to his illness and fall, had been a strong supporter of modernization and moves to more democracy in Iran. Obviously he had a long way to go; but in such fields as education, health and women's rights, I felt he was making very real progress in the late 1970s. In various conversations that I and others had with him, he frequently talked of those matters and of his hopes and plans to do more.

New schools, colleges and graduate institutions were being built and staffed; women were encouraged to give up the veil and to attend the new schools, and to enter professions previously barred to them.

Many felt that the Shah's downfall was due not to repressive measures of his government, but to a too rapid westernization in Iran. That was one of the points that the fanatical Khomeini raised repeatedly in his tirades against the Shah.

In any event, it seemed to me that we continually harassed the Shah to move more rapidly toward more and more of our ideas of what a proper democracy should be. In my opinion, the continual demands we made on the Shah to free all prisoners in Iran whom we defined as political prisoners, and the Shah's compliance with our demands, was a leading cause of the speed with which the Khomeini fundamentalists were able to mount their revolution.

After the Shah's fall, I always hoped that somehow we could, as we had done in the past, identify and support some new leadership in Iran with which we could reestablish a similarly productive, cooperative relationship. (Of course, I hoped that leadership would eliminate some of the abuses that had occurred, and that remained after the Shah died.)

Clearly Iran had vital strategic importance to us, and so it was in our interest that we try to reestablish such a relationship when we could.

At the same time, I was always completely convinced, as I am to this day, that it was impossible, unwise and very undesirable to try to secure any kind of relationship with a country led by terrorists, whose principal platform was vitriolic and unreasoning hostility to America and to all the values we honor. I also felt, with some support from the intelligence community, that most of our citizens who had been seized and held as hostages in the Middle East over the years since 1984 had been kidnapped either by direct Iranian action or by the actions of people working for, and under the direction of, Iran.

The plight of those hostages was a continuing deep concern of everyone in our Administration.[1] We discussed many times methods that might be pursued to free the hostages and bring them home. Each time the possibility was discussed, the President always said, "Oh, that is what I most want to do."

Through all such discussions, there was one underlying, unchanging thread of agreement, and that was that we must not bargain for the release of these hostages; we must not pay ransom, or its equivalent, for them. Also we understood—or I thought all did—that any kind of discussions or negotiations with the Ayatollah and his followers were useless, and worse: Their virulent anti-Americanism made agreements impossible, and ransoming our hostages would encourage the Iranian fanatics to

---

1. Terry Anderson, Thomas Sutherland, Frank Reed, Joseph Cicippio, Edward Tracy, Robert Polhill, Alan Steen and Jesse Turner are the Americans still being held hostage today (August 1989). My former Junior Military Assistant, Marine Lt. Colonel William Higgins, while chief of the UN Observer Group in southern Lebanon, was kidnapped and later reported killed by these barbaric fanatics.

believe that all they ever had to do to secure what they wished was to seize an American with the confident expectation that we would pay ransom for his release.

Occasionally an article or a paper would appear by one of the so-called strategic experts who gravitate from one conference to another arguing that we should try to develop "openings" to the Iranian government; that there was hope that they may want a friendlier relationship with the United States; and similar non-sense, as it seemed to me.

There was no doubt that our policy consensus that no country should provide arms to Iran, a policy that we sought to enforce against Iran (through our Operation Staunch), was doing some good—although there were many violations, occasionally by our own companies but more usually by foreign-based companies, that concealed the purpose and destination of their sales to Iran. Nevertheless, we knew that the Iranian Air Force, which consisted almost entirely of American planes sold to the Shah, was in extremely bad shape because of its inability to get spare parts or have any expert repair or maintenance work done. Indeed, the religious fanatics who ran Iran had murdered so many of the Shah's military leaders that Iran would have faced substantial military difficulty in the event of any kind of organized or skilled invasion of that country. Iran was able to hold its own in its war with Iraq only because Iraq had decided that it did not want to commit the substantial resources required for a military victory.

However, Iran had one thing on its side that gave it a military advantage. That was the feeling that the Ayatollah had instilled in so many of Iran's youth that death in battle was a glorious thing. Indeed, death was to be sought, because it provided the keys to Paradise. That type of fanatical militarism was not completely unknown to us. We knew that it meant a long, difficult task for Iraq, a country trying to limit and contain its war with Iran. In fact, repeated assaults by the Iranians had pushed the Iraqis into many dangerous positions. Iraq's defensive strength seemed sufficient, however, to hold its own boundaries. Our official policy was to remain neutral in the conflict; but the Iranian outrages against our people, beginning in 1979, made it difficult for me to remain neutral in any conflict to which Iran was a party. Occasionally we managed to have official United States statements and actions convey that we "tilted" toward Iraq, but for the most part the United States tried not to take sides too publicly.

I could never understand why the Iraqis did not take advantage of the deplorable state of the Iranian Air Force, but their goals were limited. Their hopes seemed to be that if they did not escalate the action themselves, eventually the war would be ended by the exhaustion of the Iranian resources and will.

Ultimately that happened, but not before August 1988. Contributing to the resolution of the war was the fact that Iranian attempts to intimidate and stop Iraqi oil shipments and other legitimate, nonbelligerent commerce in the Gulf were completely frustrated by our forces and those of our allies there, as I detail in the next chapter.

All of that is simply to say that there had never been anything in Iranian behavior, with its continual barrages of anti-American violence, or in its leadership, that should have led anyone to believe there could be any agreement that would be kept by people so led and willing to be so led.

On October 13, 1983, William P. Clark resigned as the President's National Security Adviser to accept appointment as Secretary of the Interior. For the Defense Department that meant a major change for the worse in its relationship with the National Security Council staff. Bill Clark had been and is one of my oldest friends, a skilled, resourceful, and highly effective attorney, later a respected judge, and one of the President's earliest and at all times most important and most loyal friends, from 1966 to this day.

Bill Clark represents the finest part of the American West, with a family going back several generations in California. Their numbers included several sheriffs of frontier communities, and ranchers and horsemen of many generations familiar with frontier conditions and the importance and difficulty of maintaining law and order in those areas.

Bill Clark had a very great deal to do with the success of Ronald Reagan's two terms as Governor of California, and his thinking and that of the President coincided on a great many matters. They were extremely comfortable with each other because of many shared interests, especially including horsemanship and ranching in California. There never was the slightest question of Bill Clark's total loyalty to Ronald Reagan and his devotion to the principles the President had enunciated so fervently and so effectively.

Bill Clark had left his secure seat as a Justice of the Supreme Court of California to come to Washington at the President's request in 1981 to serve as the Deputy Secretary of State under Al Haig. There, he was subjected to criticisms from a press who generally did not recognize his exceptional value because (rightly) they did not see in him any semblance of the familiar "conventional wisdom" foreign policy establishment.

Despite that severe "handicap," Bill Clark, with careful and thorough study, acquainted himself well with many of the difficult and arcane issues with which the State Department deals, and he carried out several assignments in South America, Africa and elsewhere discreetly and effectively.

The President so admired his work that when Richard Allen, the first National Security Adviser, resigned, the President turned to Bill Clark. He was ideal for the role of Security Adviser, insuring that all different viewpoints reached the President on the many matters to be decided and never wavering from his determination that he was there to serve the President and not himself. He knew that he could not serve the President if the President did not hear all viewpoints, and not simply those that coincided with some private agenda of the National Security Adviser.

He shared fully the need that the President and I felt for rebuilding America's defenses, and he understood the problems of maintaining continued congressional and public support for that difficult task.

Unfortunately, all of this drastically changed when Bill Clark resigned on October 13 to take over the Department of the Interior, a Department that deals with matters that were always close to his heart as a Westerner who embodied much of the history of California in his own person.

He told me of his decision by telephone the night I arrived in Tokyo after I had led a delegation to the funeral service for Korean Cabinet ministers murdered in Burma by North Korean terrorists.

I pleaded with him to stay, and I am sure that if I had been successful, the entire Iran arms sale–Contra funding problem would never have happened. If anyone had proposed such a scheme when Bill was in office, he would have rejected it immediately.

Bill Clark's successor as National Security Adviser was Robert McFarlane. "Bud" McFarlane is a strange, indrawn, moody former Marine Lieutenant Colonel who had worked around the fringes of the security field, and been part of Henry Kissinger's staff some years before. He had also worked in the State Department under Haig.

McFarlane is a man of evident limitations. He could not hide them, but he did attempt to conceal them, by an enigmatic manner, featuring heavily measured, pretentious and usually nearly impenetrable prose, and a great desire to be perceived as "better than Henry"—a difficult task at best. It was in pursuit of that vague agenda, I am convinced, that McFarlane, who was almost totally staff-driven, allowed some enthusiastic staff members with equally little judgment to put forth and sponsor a number of proposals and agenda items of their own, when they should simply have been serving to insure that the President had all proper staff work done for him, and the opportunity to review the different options and proposals in the whole complex foreign policy/national security field.

Significantly, the longer McFarlane was in office, the more suspicious and unhappy General Jack Vessey, Chairman of the Joint Chiefs, and the Chiefs themselves became of McFarlane and the "wilder" members of his staff. It was not in any sense the classic case of professional military men chafing under civilian direction. Rather it was the correct appraisal by the Chiefs that McFarlane and many of his staff, some of whom indeed were military people, lacked both judgment and any understanding of a certain very basic fact, which our military had learned all too well in Vietnam: Military actions not fully supported by the American people cannot succeed.

Also the military, and certainly I, felt that McFarlane and a few others, with no responsibility for the safety and well-being of our troops, were always eager to use the military for political or "diplomatic" purposes whenever that fitted their personal agendas.

There was considerable ground for those worries of our military about McFarlane. One of the first of his staff's ideas was that we should encourage Egypt, by offering it "several" (McFarlane was never sure quite how many) American infantry divisions, to invade Libya. Also, on one of his earlier trips to Lebanon as special Lebanon negotiator, he warned Washington that "Beirut was about to fall," because he experienced one of the more or less normal shellings on that capital of anarchism. He demanded that we commit more troops and military resources, presumably to "save" Beirut. Since Beirut had long since "fallen" as far as it could go, that McFarlane cable became known among the military as the "McFarlane's 'sky is falling' " cable.

In early 1984, as members of the National Security Council staff later told the so-called Tower Commission, they were becoming concerned as to what might happen in Iran after Khomeini's death. As a result, on August 31, 1984, McFarlane formally requested "an interagency analysis of American relations with Iran after Khomeini" (NSSD5-84). The detailed study, completed in October of 1984, correctly reported that the United States could do little to establish any influential contacts within the Iranian government, in view of the kind of government and the kind of groups that led Iran.

The NSC staff members and Mr. McFarlane, who had their own agenda, which was to establish contacts with Iran, did not accept that as an answer. It is the habit of government officials with their own agenda, that if they do not get the answer they want on the first try, they try again. This time, as I found out later, they took the tack of "updating" and paraphrasing and rephrasing intelligence estimates for the President, to make sure their estimates demonstrated that the Soviets—but not the United States—could take advantage of any chaos that might develop in Iran.

In any event, on June 17, 1985, McFarlane transmitted a draft National Security Decision Directive (NSDD) to Secretary George Shultz and me. The origins of the exercise were then hazy, but later became clear.[2] In that paper the suggestion was made that we should now explore the possibility of better relationships with Ayatollah Khomeini's Iran. A number of well-known points were made about the strategic and geographical importance of Iran; and the NSDD then discussed the desirability of opening a "dialogue" with Iran, and making an effort to reestablish good working relationships with it—even to the extent

2. See *Report of the Select Committee on Intelligence*, United States Senate, February 26, 1987, p. 2.

of giving Iran arms. Here is the key policy option from that NSDD:

> Encourage Western allies and friends to help Iran meet its import requirements so as to reduce the attractiveness of Soviet assistance and trade offers, while demonstrating the value of correct relations with the West. This includes provision of selected military equipment as determined on a case-by-case basis.

(The irony here is that McFarlane and his associates did not even adhere to the "case-by-case basis" once we began shipping arms. No hostages were returned after the first shipment, yet the NSC staff plunged ahead in spite of its explicit prior promise to put an end to the initiative if no hostages came out.)

Inasmuch as Iran was responsible for the taking and holding of a number of our citizens as hostages, was continuing to pour out the most venomous anti-American, anti-Western propaganda, and had demonstrated its basically barbaric conduct in Lebanon and elsewhere, I felt that this was one of the more absurd proposals yet to be circulated, and so noted in the margin of my copy of the proposed NSDD, adding, with reference to our then current problems with Libya, that this would be similar to "asking Qadaffi over for a cozy lunch."

Later in my formal reply on July 16, 1985, to the McFarlane idea that we should sell arms to Iran, I condemned the proposal, saying:

> Under no circumstances should we now ease our restrictions on arms sales to Iran. [Such a] policy reversal would be seen as inexplicably inconsistent by those nations whom we have urged to refrain from such sales, and would likely lead to increased arms sales by them and a possible alteration of the strategic balance in favor of Iran while Kho-

meini is still the controlling influence. It would adversely affect our newly emerging relationship with Iraq.

George Shultz also told Mr. McFarlane that he objected to the proposals, saying:

> The draft NSDD appears to exaggerate current anti-regime sentiment and Soviet advantages over us in gaining influence. Most importantly, its proposal that we permit or encourage a flow of Western arms to Iran is contrary to our interest both in containing Khomeinism and in ending the excesses of this regime. We should not alter this aspect of our policy when groups with ties to Iran are holding U.S. hostages in Lebanon. I, therefore, disagree with the suggestion that our efforts to reduce arms flow to Iran should be ended.

Nothing more was heard about the matter for several months, and in the press of other business, which continued at its normal pace of sixteen to eighteen hours a day, I paid no further attention to McFarlane's suggestions that there, somewhere in the middle of Teheran, was a "kinder, gentler nation."

Among his other problems, Mr. McFarlane was very secretive and, as I have said, indrawn about his work. He seemed to feel that what he did was too important or classified to be discussed with anyone else. This was of course in total contrast to his predecessor, Bill Clark, who recognized that we were all working for the same things and for the same President, and who talked freely and openly with those who had a need to know about all of the things that came before him. Bill Clark expected and assumed that we would follow the same course in our many discussions with each other.

I did not know then (and I doubt that very many others knew of it), that the entire McFarlane initiative arose from meetings he had been holding with various representatives of Israel, with whom some Iranians were in close contact. The Israelis were trying to secure, in a clandestine way, American approval and participation in a complex scheme to satisfy Iran's great need for spare parts and equipment for Iran's enfeebled air force and army. In return, the Israelis told McFarlane, Iran would *consider* freeing some of the hostages they had kidnapped many months, and in some cases, years, before.

Israel's association with Iran derives, in part, from three factors. First, there is that natural affinity of all religious and ethnic minorities in the Middle East to unite (when at all they unite) against the vast majority—the Arab population. Hence some Jews, Christians, Turks and Persians have long linkages. Second, there is a substantial Jewish population in Iran. And third, Israel had close ties to Iran under the Shah.

Iran knew that we supplied a very large number of weapons of all kinds to Israel; and Israel of course knew that if we learned that it was diverting some of those shipments to Iran for any purpose, we would have to suspend shipments to Israel—as required by the Arms Export Control Act, and as we had done earlier when Israel bombed the Iraqi nuclear power plant.

Israel had long had a running and well understood feud with Iraq, but it also had a close secret association with Iran. The real consideration to Israel for its help in securing United States arms for Iran was to be protection for both the Israelis and the Iranian Jews living in Iran. Iran also wanted antitank and antiaircraft weapons, specifically our Tow and Hawk missile systems, in order to counter Iraq's superiority in armor and air strength.

I learned *much* later that beginning in January 1985, and before McFarlane's efforts to "update" the intelligence estimates concerning Iran and the future, Iranian and Israeli arms dealers had been meeting and discussing whether they could promote either direct arms sales from the United States to Iran or sales from Israel's substantial stocks of American weapons. In early May

1985, McFarlane employed, as a consultant, a Michael Ledeen, to meet with Israeli leaders, and in June Israeli government officials met with McFarlane at the White House to talk about a possible "dialogue" between the United States and Iran, which dialogue, from Israel's point of view, would lead to a sale of weapons to Iran in return for the "protection" of persecuted Iranian Jews in Iran; from Iran's point of view, that arrangement would produce the weapons from the United States and Israel that the Iranians urgently needed in their war with Iraq.

The inducement to the United States, which McFarlane foisted on the President at many of his daily meetings with the him, was to be promises for the return of some of our eight hostages who had been held by the Iranians for many months. Actually, the NSC staff at that time said that they were only trying to peddle the idea that we needed to cultivate a "strategic relationship" with Iran, and we were not actually to get the return of any hostages, but instead promises that Iran would "consider" helping us get the hostages back. It was that murky background that spawned McFarlane's memorandum about the importance of our establishing better relationships with Iran.

In short, McFarlane took the bait and willingly went along with this Israeli-Iranian plot.

McFarlane later "recalled" that he had briefed the President about his meeting with a David Kimche, the Israeli representative and the Director General of the Israeli Foreign Ministry; but McFarlane also "recalled" that he had briefed Secretary Shultz and me on July 13. His "recollection" here exceeds mine on this, as it did on many other points. I recall no such meeting. July 13 was the Saturday the President was operated on for abdominal cancer; and I was going over office papers in the garden at our home in McLean, Virginia, and not being briefed by McFarlane.

To the best of my knowledge, McFarlane kept all those matters as secret as possible, talking only about the possible advantages of a new working relationship with Iran when he discussed his initiatives at all. In any event, he certainly did not refer to the discussions he had had with Kimche or others in the memorandum he circulated in the summer of 1985, wherein he argued we should encourage Western allies and friends to help Iran meet its important requirements, including "provision of selected military equipment."

As I said before, my memorandum of July 16, 1985, responding to these suggestions, objected sharply to the entire proposal, as did the memorandum circulated by Secretary Shultz.

Since Secretary Shultz and I heard nothing more about it, we assumed that the whole proposal had died. But McFarlane continued his secret negotiations with the Israeli and Iranian arms dealers, including one of the most unreliable and untrustworthy people in the international scene, a man named Manucher Ghorbanifar.

The story gets even more cloudy thereafter, because McFarlane claims he cabled a proposal, on July 14, 1985, to Secretary Shultz (but not to me) about allowing a hundred of our Tow missiles to go to Iran from Israel, in return for which seven of the Americans held would be released. The Tower Commission report confirms that account, but says Shultz replied at first "with a tentative show of interest without commitment."[3] Knowing George's feelings on that matter, I strongly doubt that he exhibited any *favorable* interest!

Reports of parts of those shadowy discussions may have been sent, or communicated in some form, to the President, before, during and shortly after he returned from Bethesda Naval Hospital, where he underwent his cancer operation.[4] In the context of his Israeli-induced personal plan of opening a "new dialogue" on United States–Iranian relationships, McFarlane claimed later

3. See *The President's Special Review Board* (Tower Commission Report), February 26, 1987, pp. 1–6.

4. The President was in Bethesda from July 12 to July 20, 1985.

he had met with the President on that proposal to let Israel send our missiles to Iran. The President could not recall any such meeting. That seems to me to be entirely reasonable; because even if McFarlane ever did raise this subject with the President, it would have been when the President was in the hospital, and in the weakened condition familiar to anyone who has had major surgery.

McFarlane would not let the matter die, and on August 2, as I learned later, again met at the White House with the Israeli government representative, David Kimche. Apparently, according to the subsequent investigations, Kimche kept proposing that the hundred Tows missiles should go to Iran without anything in return, as a means of "establishing good faith." No one explained why it was so important to show the Iranians good faith, when they illegally and criminally had played an important role in the seizure and holding of seven American citizens and other innocent persons of other nationalities.

I did not know of any of those proposals for Tows to go from Israel to Iran, or of our furnishing replacements to Israel, but I do recall a meeting on August 6, 1985, with the President upstairs in the White House in which we all (George Shultz, McFarlane, Don Regan, and either Bill Casey or John McMahon, his deputy) sat on the yellow upholstered couches at the end of the long main hall on the second floor of the White House residence quarters. The President was still in his hospital bathrobe.[5] That end of the corridor, overlooking the Old Executive Office Building, is used as a sitting room. The issue came up again and again. Both George Shultz and I argued as forcefully as we possibly could against the whole idea, explaining how it would completely

---

5. I was asked frequently by media reporters during the 1988 Presidential campaign, "What was the role of the Vice President?" He was present at some of the meetings I attended, but he was called out frequently to take phone calls; and he rarely offered the President opinion-based advice in those meetings, preferring, as I understood it, to discuss matters with him when the two were alone.

violate our agreed upon and accepted policy of not ransoming hostages, and that we should most certainly not give Iran arms directly or indirectly when we were pleading with our allies and friends all around the world not to allow any arms shipments of any kind to go to Iran.

I made the further point that there was nothing to indicate any slight change in the virulently anti-Western, anti-American attitude of those in charge of Iran, and that we would never be able to explain ourselves to our friends and allies, nor secure their support for any kind of anti-Iranian arms boycott, if it became known that we were actually dealing with Iran, either directly or through Israel on the side. And by implicating the President in such a secret deal, the Administration's future policy could be subjected to the equivalent of *blackmail* by any of those who knew. It seemed to me clear, although the President did not state so there, that the President agreed that we should not proceed with this matter.

McFarlane, thereafter, apparently took it on himself to advise the Israelis that it was all right for them to sell the weapons we had furnished them to the Iranians, and that we would resupply the Israelis, and we "hoped we could get some hostages out." Reports of later investigations made it clear that the President was "upset at this news," according to Don Regan. As I learned later, McFarlane then said the Israelis had simply "taken it upon themselves to do this."

The President later wrote to the Tower Commission that he could not recall anything "whatsoever about whether I approved an Israeli sale in advance, or whether I approved replenishing of Israeli stocks around August of 1985. My answer therefore and the simple truth is, 'I don't remember—period.' "

I believe the President. He never approved any such plan in my presence, and I do not believe he ever did. Besides being ill, he also was involved in preparations for the Geneva meeting with Gorbachev. Four major presidential events were scheduled on arms control, human rights, regional issues, and the whole subject of United States–USSR relations. The President had to give a major speech to the United Nations, and he met with at least fifteen heads of state in New York or Washington during those months. There were continued battles with Congress over the budget, and on October 7, the *Achille Lauro* cruise ship was seized by terrorist hijackers and an American, Leon Klinghoffer, was killed and thrown overboard. Furthermore, I think it is most likely that McFarlane later tried to "jog the President's memory" to support McFarlane's claims.

The discredited Israeli and Iranian intermediaries with whom McFarlane continued to deal apparently intended that Israel's transfer of a hundred Tows was not conditioned upon a hostage release, but was only designed to show "good faith." For our hostages the Iranians demanded another 400 Tows from Israel, which McFarlane presumably felt we could thereafter also replenish for Israel.

On September 15, 1985, Reverend Benjamin Weir, one of our hostages, was released by his captors. Later I learned that on September 14, 1985, Israel had delivered 408 Tows to Iran. The release of *all* the remaining hostages, predicted by McFarlane, of course did not occur. Nor was any connection established between the Israeli delivery of arms to Iran and Weir's release.

McFarlane, later reports showed, continued to refer to the so-called moderates in Iran with whom he was dealing. The few times I was present, I made the point that in my opinion the only moderates in Iran were long since dead, that the present Iranian leadership was all of a piece, and that it was absurd to be taken in by any suggestion that any of the Iranian arms dealers were in any way sympathetic to the release of any hostages.

McFarlane said later that he told Secretary Shultz about those various plans. Secretary Shultz reported that McFarlane said he had spoken and acted for the President in allowing the Israelis to ship Hawk missiles, which we would replenish for the Israelis. The President did not remember that, and I do not believe McFarlane ever had such a conversation with him, unless it was in Bethesda right after the President's operation.

The Tower Commission, and others who had looked into the matter, indicated that the situation at all times was very cloudy, with many conflicting stories about events through the summer and fall of 1985.

The secret, covert and wholly discreditable way in which the transactions were handled by National Security Council staff members who pursued their own agenda, without discussion with the American government officials responsible for activities in these areas, is emphasized by the fact that the first I ever heard that there had been discussions, including American representation, with the Israelis and the Iranians, was from some puzzling cable traffic that was reported to me in the fall of 1985, in the course of my normal briefings. When I inquired the meaning of some of those oddly phrased messages I was told by our intelligence agencies that they had made a mistake and that they had received instructions *not to let me see* any of those messages.

I had to remind them as forcefully as possible, through my military assistant General Colin Powell, that the National Security Agency was part of the Department of Defense, that I was to see *all* messages that they received, and that no one had any authority to give them any instructions not to let me see the messages. They said that their instructions had come from "the White House." I reminded them again that *buildings* do not give instructions; that I was their immediate superior; that they reported to me; that they would report to me *all* traffic of any kind; and that they would also report to me *any* instructions they received not to let me see anything they received; and that any future attempts to keep us from access to all intelligence would result in changes in the working domiciles of all who took part.

As a result of my finding those cables, which I came upon

quite by accident, I demanded the meetings that were held by the President in the late fall of 1985—long after I thought the entire proposal for closer relationships with Iran, the provision of United States arms to Iran, and negotiations to free our hostages had been killed.

On November 30, 1985, McFarlane resigned. He never made clear why. Most reports said he was "frustrated" and "tired." I later learned that on that same day Lieutenant Colonel North of the NSC staff proposed a new "arms-for-hostages" deal to McFarlane's successor, Admiral Poindexter. That proposal, we found out from the Tower Commission hearings, involved the transfer of 3,300 Israeli Tows and 50 Israeli Hawks in exchange for the release of all the hostages. The delivery of those weapons to Iran was to result in the release of one or two hostages for each installment of weapons, and ultimately all five of our hostages would be freed. By that time one hostage had returned (the Reverend Benjamin Weir), and one had died in captivity (William Buckley).

When that latest proposal was considered by the President on December 7, again Secretary Shultz and I opposed the plan in the strongest possible terms. I reiterated all my old arguments that we would be helping a country that seized Americans and held them hostage; that we had no assurances that they would let the hostages go; that we could not have any kind of relationship with a country like Iran and its viscerally anti-American leaders; that we would lose all credibility with our allies and Iraq if we sold arms to Iran; and that such actions, last but not least, were probably illegal. George Shultz made the same points equally forcefully and probably more effectively.

To my unhappiness, Mr. McFarlane (although he had resigned) had now decided he would go to London to deliver a message to the Iranians, including the notorious Ghorbanifar. His proposed trip was supposed to be discussed at the December 7 meeting. Both George Shultz and I left that December 7 meeting feeling the McFarlane trip had been blocked. Indeed, after the meeting, I told Rich Armitage that the "baby [McFarlane's plan] had been strangled in its cradle." But after the meeting McFarlane, and apparently Admiral Poindexter, then decided McFarlane could go.

To the best of my knowledge, McFarlane had no instructions, nor do we know what he actually had told the Iranians. He "debriefed" some of the December 7 attendees on December 10, but I always felt that McFarlane's "debriefings" were imaginary reports on what he wanted his auditors to hear.

On December 9, Lieutenant Colonel North submitted to Admiral Poindexter a memorandum (of which I learned only much later) proposing *direct* United States deliveries to Iran in exchange for release of the hostages.[6]

The confusion and murkiness of subsequent events continued. But one thing stands out in my mind, and that is that no matter what happened, or what was said at the few meetings which I attended on the subject, I always expressed the most vigorous opposition, as did Secretary Shultz, to the whole plan, including the idea of even having discussions with anyone in the present Iranian government. I called attention to the repeated number of promises that had been made and broken. But during these sessions, the President was always very concerned about the fate of our hostages, and extremely unhappy that apparently nothing could be done to release them.

Later, when people asked how this whole activity could have developed in the face of the opposition of the Secretary of State and Secretary of Defense, the answer seems to me to be simple, clear and most unfortunate. People with hourly access to the President, such as McFarlane, if they had their own agenda, could phrase things to the President in the most favorable terms, report

6. *The President's Special Review Board*, February 26, 1987, p. 10.

to the President all manner of "hopeful indications," and generally lead a busy President, occupied with many other things, including preparations for meetings with the Soviets, arms control negotiations, budgets and so on, to believe that "progress was being made," that the "broader strategic dialogue," so frequently promised, was being established with the Iranians, and that ultimately our hostages would be released.

As McFarlane, his staff, and his successor, John Poindexter, kept pushing various aspects of the plan, and emphasizing the desirability of that promised broader strategic dialogue and the "new friendship with Iran," out of which might come the release of the hostages, the more plausible they made it seem. That was true particularly because they kept reporting to the President more and more "progress" on all aspects, and detailed "agreements" they thought they were making with wholly discredited Iranian representatives and arms dealers. Since they kept nearly everyone else in the dark, and did not encourage meetings with opponents of their plans, including me, no other viewpoints or arguments were presented to the President, except at one or two large, formal meetings.

Add to that their daily access and their earlier indirect and direct presentations to the President, without any opportunity for other views to be presented, and one might rather easily see how the President's "approval" would be assumed, and reported to others, especially by people who urgently wanted it.

The next step was also easy for them to pursue, although very nearly politically fatal to the President: That is, apparently at some stage, unknown to me, someone hatched a plan to "overcharge" the Iranians and turn some of the proceeds for the arms we were selling them over to the Contras in Nicaragua, whose funding Congress had sporadically but repeatedly denied. It seemed like a "neat idea" to North, and to some of the Security Council staff. (North later testified on July 8, 1987, that Ghorbanifar had made the suggestion in a men's room in either Frankfurt, Germany, or London.) Because they knew of the President's strong desire for the Contras to have congressionally authorized funding, it seemed to them a short step to regard this scheme as the way to get it without troubling about Congress's refusal to fund the Contras or the legality of the action, and without bothering to tell the President or anyone else the details, or indeed about the whole alleged scheme itself. I first heard of it on November 21, 1986, the fateful day the Attorney General and the President announced it, and the same day the President dismissed North and Poindexter.

The Contras should have been funded, but there is only one way to secure legal spending by our Government, and that is by vote of the Congress.

Several in the executive branch hoped that other countries would see that it was in their interest also to prevent the establishment of another Soviet base in the Caribbean, and that we should not have to carry the whole burden. But it was quite clear to me that we in the United States could not spend anything unless Congress voted for it in the regular way.

In any event, on January 7, 1986, at a meeting in which we all participated, and although Secretary Shultz and I again argued in the strongest possible terms against the very idea of letting Iran have any arms regardless of how convoluted the plan was, the President gave me the impression that he had approved the idea. Later it was shown that, either that day or the day before, he had signed a draft "intelligence finding" authorizing the transaction. I never saw the signed draft. Much later, I saw a draft that the President was said to have signed, but it did not bear his signature. There was also supposed to have been an earlier, December 5, 1985, "finding," said to have been signed by the President, that John Poindexter testified he tore up and threw away.

After the whole matter was disclosed to the public, I was told that the President had signed a later, revised, copy of the order on January 17. In any event, on that day Admiral Poindexter told me that the President had approved an arrangement under which the Department of Defense was to sell 4,000 Tows to the CIA, and the CIA would then transfer them to Iran.

That had been finally agreed to at a meeting at which neither Secretary Shultz nor I were present, and again emphasizes the way in which those matters could unravel given the almost hourly access of one or two advisers in the White House who had a specific and determined agenda of their own, instead of doing their job, which was to ensure that all viewpoints of the operating departments had been heard.

Neither Secretary Shultz nor I, nor even Don Regan, saw the final, January 17, finding (until it was revealed publicly); it supposedly authorized the transaction and, in effect, provided for the NSC to be the manager of the whole activity. Here is an excerpt from that finding:

> The U.S. Government will act to facilitate efforts made by third parties and third countries to establish contact with moderate elements within and outside the Government of Iran by providing these elements with arms, equipment and related material in order to enhance the credibility of these elements in their efforts to achieve a more pro-U.S. government in Iran by demonstrating their ability to obtain requisite resources to defend their country against Iraq and intervention by the Soviet Union. This support will be discontinued if the U.S. Government learns that these elements have abandoned their goals of moderating their government and appropriated the material for purposes other than that provided by this Finding.

When I was told that the President had approved the sale, I insisted that any weapons transferred from the Department of

Defense go to the CIA only under the terms of the Economy Act,[7] which was a legally permitted mode of transfer requiring that the CIA reimburse us in full for the cost of the weapons, and I avowed that we would have nothing further to do with the transaction thereafter.

I reminded everyone that direct transfer from the Defense Department to Iran would violate the Arms Export Control Act, and said that I would refuse to allow such a transfer. I must record here that I hoped this added objection would at least slow down or possibly even stop the sales.[8] In any event, I felt that if there was to be such a sale, the CIA was the proper agency for the covert transaction. But, as was easily predictable, although the arms ultimately did go to Iran, the hostages were not recovered, and the matter eventually became public.

Mr. McFarlane was still being used by the new National Security Adviser for "consultation" on his contacts with Ghorbanifar and, presumably, with the Israeli representatives. Throughout the spring of 1986, and specifically in May, there were more indications that further shipments of arms in differing detail were being planned for Iran; and as late as May 15, 1986, McFarlane was still planning for his "secret mission to Iran." All of that was done secretly, and without my knowledge. Indeed, although on May 17 Colonel North had strongly urged that Admiral Poindexter include Secretary Shultz and me in a meeting with the President to review McFarlane's proposed trip, Admiral Poindexter responded in a written memorandum, "I don't want a meeting with the President, Shultz and Weinberger."

McFarlane arrived in Iran on May 25 in a plane that carried

---

7. The Economy Act (31 U.S.C. 1535) provides that one government agency may provide goods or services to another agency, but only if the agency providing the goods is fully reimbursed by the receiving agency.

8. The NSC internal computerized notes show that North viewed my objections on this point as just another attempt by me to block the whole sale.

more Hawk spare parts. No hostages were released, and the talks were fruitless, the Iranians demanding additional payments. Nothing happened with respect to release of the hostages, but the Hawk spare parts were released by McFarlane and removed from the aircraft, even though McFarlane achieved nothing on the trip. Three more American hostages were kidnapped in September and October of 1986, and while Father Lawrence Jenko, who had been taken many months before, had been released on July 26, it was not in any way clear that his release had any connection with any of the shadowy figures with whom McFarlane had been dealing—although Admiral Poindexter claimed, while briefing the President, that the release was "undoubtedly" a result of Mr. McFarlane's trip in May.

Even up to October 1986, North and others were meeting with Iranian representatives. It was during McFarlane's May trip to Iran that the United States fell to a depth of absurdity not often seen. That was when Colonel North presented the Iranians with a Bible with a laughable story about what the President said after "praying for a whole weekend." In fact, the President had been persuaded to sign an inscription in the Bible by Admiral Poindexter, who had told him that the passage would help get through to the Iranians. Here is Colonel North's story to the Iranians. Even seeing it in print may not help the reader to believe that anyone would tell such a tale, let alone claim those things had actually happened. Upon presenting the Bible, Colonel North reported that he said:

> We inside our Government had an enormous debate, a very angry debate inside our government over whether or not my president should authorize me to say "We accept the Islamic Revolution of Iran as a fact . . ." He [the President] went off one whole weekend and prayed about what the answer should be and he came back almost a year ago with that passage I gave you that he wrote in

front of the Bible I gave you. And he said to me, "This is a promise that God gave to Abraham. Who am I to say that we should not do this?"[9]

Even worse, at some time during the course of those convoluted, shadowy and discreditable discussions, some of the American representatives, McFarlane and/or his staff, without the slightest authority or agreement by the President, gave the Iranians *military intelligence* concerning the Iraqis and their defensive dispositions at the exact time when we were trying our best to insure that at the very least Iran would not prevail over Iraq— and when it was becoming increasingly clear to many of us that we should be tilting in a more significant way toward Iraq rather than doing anything to support the barbaric and fanatical government of Iran. Some of that intelligence, which should never have left the country, was deadly accurate, and helped the Iranians inflict additional losses on Iraq. McFarlane later tried to excuse that act on the ground that it was necessary to show the Iranians our "good faith."

It also seemed clear that White House representatives, presumably Colonel North and others, even though they had no authority to do so, were notifying the Iranian representatives that the United States had agreed to various other arms sales.

On November 2, 1986, another hostage, David Jacobsen, was released, but there was no way of determining whether there had been any connection between that and the negotiations. Then, on November 3, the story of the McFarlane mission came out in a pro-Syrian Beirut magazine. On the following day, the Speaker of the Iranian Parliament, Hashemi Rafsanjani,[10] publicly

---

9. *The President's Special Review Board*, February 26, 1987, p. 18.

10. This is the same Rafsanjani who was "elected" President of Iran in August 1989, and who was frequently named by McFarlane as "friendly to the U.S." and an Iranian "moderate."

acknowledged and denounced the mission, and once again called the United States "the Great Satan," demonstrating one more time that the so-called pro-Western moderate feelings that McFarlane always professed to see in him were without warrant or foundation.

The near-tragic result of the entire affair was that the confidence of the American people in the President and the Administration as a whole was shaken very badly. For the first time, a sizable majority of the public lost faith in the President and said they did not believe his explanations, nor did they agree that negotiating for the release of the hostages under those circumstances was the proper thing to do. It took many months, indeed over a year, for the public to regain its confidence in the President; but fortunately it did, starting with Admiral John Poindexter's dramatic testimony, before the Congressional Select Committees, on July 15, 1987 that:

> The buck stops here with me. I made the decision [to divert profits from the Iran arms sale to aid the contras]. I felt that I had the authority to do it . . . I was convinced the president would in the end think it was a good idea. But I did not want him associated with the decision.

Admiral Poindexter's revelation that President Reagan had not known of the diversion of funds to the Contras was headline news. Congressional Committee members and counsels took to the airwaves, offering a profusion of commentaries and insights. One such "insight" came as a shock to me: that the committees had received that critically important information from John Poindexter fully ten weeks earlier, in an unpublished deposition before those Committees.[11]

11. In his May 2, 1987, deposition before the combined Committee, classified TOP

Committee members, stung by repeated criticisms throughout the hearings that Congress could not be trusted to keep a secret, had kept this one absolutely airtight, and some of them virtually gloated about it after Admiral Poindexter's televised testimony. Reflecting on the loss of public faith in the President, which could have been restored more than two months earlier, I could not help wondering, with more than a little dismay, why the Congress could not have chosen some other important fact to safeguard in order to demonstrate its powers of self-discipline.

For the most part, however, the Select Committees, under the fair and able Co-Chairmanship of Democratic Senator Dan Inouye and Democratic Representative Lee Hamilton, did their work professionally and effectively. Appearing before any congressional committee is, as I have said earlier, not an experience to take lightly, and certainly I felt that way in anticipation of my appearance before this combined Committee, which was to take place July 31, 1987.

I spent many hours going over all the records in the Department of my attendance at the various White House meetings, my own rather meager notes, and the few memoranda that had been circulated to me.

And because the events had taken place two years and more before the hearings and much of the detail of one meeting had merged in my memory into other gatherings, or phone conver-

---

SECRET at the time but declassified as soon as Admiral Poindexter testified on television, he said:

"I felt that I had the authority to approve Colonel North's request. I also felt that it was, as I said, consistent with the President's policy, and that if I asked him, I felt confident that he would approve it.

But because it was controversial, and I obviously knew that it would cause a ruckus if it were exposed, I decided to insulate the President from the decision and give him some deniability; and so I decided—told Colonel North in that meeting, after thinking about it for several minutes, to go ahead and proceed ahead with it, that it was a method of essentially providing bridge financing to the democratic resistance until we could get the legislation passed, and I decided at that point not to tell the President."

sations, I asked several others in the Department to go over the events in their proper sequence with me many times before the actual testimony. Also, I had been interviewed by the Committee Counsel some months before my actual testimony, and I had also testified to the Tower Commission many months before.

So I spent a very great deal of time in preparation, and in the final days before July 31, I met with Will Taft; Larry Garrett, the General Counsel of the Department; Ed Shapiro, an Assistant General Counsel; Rich Armitage and his Special Assistant, Linc Bloomfield. I asked them to grill me in the most unfair and dishonest way they could dream up, to throw the wildest accusations at me, based on any outrageous leaps of logic they could construct from any documents that had figured in the matter or the Committee hearings to date.

They did, and were very skillful, which is to say they were extraordinarily irritating and provoking. This went on for several hours each day for nearly a week.

The Committee hearings, on July 31 and August 3, were not mild, but they were certainly not as bad as those conducted by the tormenters I myself had appointed. It was very like the most realistic military maneuvers in the jungles and swamps which, in some cases, were worse than combat.

Nevertheless, the two days of hearings were not easy ones, with the annoying eye of the television cameras staring at one every second, and some 26 congressmen and senators watching one, plus assorted counsel rising in two semicircular banks around the witness.

For me the best comment came near the end when Senator Warren Rudman of New Hampshire, a particularly tough questioner at all hearings, quoted a statement the day before by Rafsanjani, one of McFarlane's Iranian "moderates," to the effect that Iran must avenge its losses in the Persian Gulf (actions related to which were going on all through the period of the hearings) by "uprooting Saudi rulers from the region." If Rafsanjani was a "moderate," Senator Rudman asked me, would I mind defining an "extremist" for the Committee?

I was grateful for the rhetorical question, and replied that it was simply another example why we could not deal with people like that.

The President was characteristically selfless and exhibited great political and personal courage in admitting publicly that he had made a mistake. He agreed that it was not possible to negotiate or do business with the Iranians, and that there were no moderate factions there, and that the advice he had been given by Mc-Farlane and others was not only wrong but dangerously wrong. I think that the President, because of his innate loyalty toward people who worked with him, was far milder in his statements than he actually felt. Also, I believe his kindness was due to his desire not to hurt people like McFarlane, whose inadequacies and errors were so glaringly exposed by the whole episode.

The President was badly hurt by people whom he had trusted. He felt, correctly, that they had not only imposed on that trust, but directly and indirectly misled him into believing that progress was being achieved when it was not, and into feeling that those actions could result in a better relationship with Iran—when it was painfully apparent to anyone who did not have a Mc-Farlanesque personal agenda that it was not possible to deal with the Iranian anti-American fanatics, and that we could not trust them to do any of the things they promised.

For my part, when I was told by Admiral Poindexter that the President had approved the actual transfer from the Department of Defense to the CIA of Tows and Hawk parts so that the CIA could send them to Iran, I seriously contemplated resignation.

Initially, I was greatly attracted to the idea, because I was totally opposed to the policy and because I knew it could never work. It took no great gift of prophecy to know that it could only bring great harm and damage to the President and America.

The longer I thought about the prospect, however, the less it seemed to me that I could accomplish by resigning. At that time, the entire matter was still totally unknown to the public and to our allies, and so I would not, through resigning, have been able to make any kind of a statement that would be effective in stopping the operation. Nor could I accomplish anything by resigning even after the first shipment had gone, to mitigate or reverse what seemed to me to be a dangerously wrong policy. In any event, I finally concluded that I would stay on, saddened though I was by this major error, but hoping that in some way we could reverse the dangerously failed policy initiated by McFarlane. It was a policy he secretly and wrongly initiated largely because of his desire to be in command of what he hoped would be a spectacular success, instead of simply concentrating on the less glamorous task of trying to assemble and present to the President all views and options with respect to pending actions.

Several careers were shattered as a result of his choice. American hostages are still held, Iran obtained arms that it should not have had, and Iraq's faith in us, and indeed our credibility with all of our allies, was severely shaken by the knowledge that we were ourselves doing what we repeatedly pleaded with them not to do.

In the end, however, the President fortunately emerged from this whole episode undiminished after an extremely unhappy period of seven months. He has regained the trust and faith that the American people always had in him, and he finished his second term with his popularity higher than it had ever been. America again is in a position in which we have achieved and earned substantial respect from our allies, our friends and our opponents. It is in many ways the most remarkable tribute of all that have been rightly accorded the President that the American people in overwhelming numbers kept such deep respect and affection for their President. And it is a happy thing for America that he served as our President for eight critical years.

One must find it a saddening and unhappy thought, however,

to realize how badly served he was by several of the National Security Council staff in whom he placed his trust and his confidence. For it is very clear that confidence and trust were misplaced. It is equally clear that the phrase "The White House wants . . ." was misused by those people in a way that could have wrought untold damage to the United States—and did, in the view of many. I hope that lesson has been learned now. I doubt that any National Security Council or other staff would again so abuse the apparent authority given them to speak and act on behalf of the President. If that lesson has indeed been learned, and if it will long be remembered, then it is possible to find some small shred of comfort in this whole misbegotten affair.

XIII

The Persian Gulf Success Story

*K*uwait is a small, sparsely populated, immensely oil rich nation that sits on the northeastern border of Saudi Arabia, facing the Persian Gulf. On January 13, 1987, Kuwait formally asked the United States to assist in the convoy of its oil tankers through the Persian Gulf, expressing the fear that Iran's open attacks on Kuwaiti and other shipping in the Gulf posed a major danger to the freedom of the seas. Specifically, Kuwait said it was uncertain whether oil shipments could continue to get through the Gulf unassisted. By September of 1986 it had become increasingly clear to U.S. Defense Intelligence officials that Iran had singled out Kuwait as the focal point of the pressure it elected to use against the Gulf Arab states. Iran was launching naval attacks against shipping of all nations bound to and from Kuwaiti ports in an effort to intimidate that small country and its neighbors, and dissuade them from providing political and financial support to Iraq. Besides the naval attacks, lethal Iranian or Iranian-sponsored activities against Kuwait during 1986 included three bombing raids on Kuwaiti territory, mining of Kuwaiti shipping channels, deployment of Chinese Silkworm surface-to-surface missiles aimed at Kuwait and located on the captured Iraqi peninsula of Al Faw, and terrorist attacks on Kuwaiti oil facilities. Adding to tensions in the Gulf shipping war were increased small-boat attacks by the naval arm of Iran's Islamic Revolutionary Guard Corps (IRGC), a paramilitary organization more fanatical and more ideologically "pure" than the regular military. Many of the latter had been trained by the United States some years before.

The Kuwaiti decision to seek U.S. help had been made only after a major debate within the Kuwaiti government. It came to us with its request even though it had already approached the Soviets, in December 1986, and had received their favorable response.

Kuwait had been perhaps the friendliest of all of the moderate countries of the Middle East toward the Soviet Union, having established relations with it in 1962, soon after achieving independence from the British. The Kuwaitis were more distant toward us than toward the Soviets because of our refusal to sell them certain military equipment—which the Soviets were only too willing to provide—and because of the difficulties always present in the Congress when the Kuwaitis wanted to buy any weapons from us. But the vital importance of getting their tankers through the Gulf on a regular basis overrode their normal objections to requesting United States military help, or to appearing to be close to the United States. In November 1986, Kuwait also had taken its concerns to the Gulf Cooperation Council; and while none of the members was enthralled with the idea of asking support from the superpowers, most of them urged Kuwait to ask the United States over the Soviet Union.

My immediate reaction, as well as my conclusion after further study, was that we should agree to the Kuwaiti request. It seemed to me that if we failed to do so, and if, as the Kuwaitis feared,

Iran's continued attacks could slow or even stop the flow of oil out of the Gulf, we would be accepting Iran's right to close the international waters of the Gulf, and block nonbelligerent and extremely important commerce from moving in those waters. It was also quite clear that if we did not assist in the movement of the oil shipments through the Gulf, the Soviet Union would be more than happy to become the sole guarantor of the security of the small Gulf states. In fact, I knew that Kuwait had gone to the Soviets first, and they knew we knew.

Kuwait had asked the Soviets first for two very obvious reasons, even though, as a Muslim nation, it would clearly not want to establish close ties to the USSR. First, the Kuwaitis knew that the USSR would not have to do any significant "consulting," and would respond relatively promptly. Second, they also knew that their request to the USSR would not appear on the front page of *Izvestia* within 24 hours of the initial proposal, but that similar discussions with the United States were quite likely to be reported in full.

Later, many would claim that we were "played" against the Soviets by the Kuwaitis; that somehow we were taken in. That theory ignores some basic facts of life. The importance to us of the Persian Gulf and its energy resources has been acknowledged by every administration since President Eisenhower's. Furthermore, the Soviet Union has long sought to increase its presence in the Gulf as a counter to our considerable influence in the region. I knew that the Soviet government had already told Kuwait it would help; and I was, and still am, convinced that it was not in our interest for Soviet forces to move into an area so vital to us. That was a major point in my calculus. We in the West need the Gulf's oil resources; the Soviets are more than self-sufficient in oil. Their position in the Gulf, should they achieve a vital presence there, could only be one of denial toward us. They would gain a tremendous strategic advantage that I did not want them to have.

When I testified before various Senate and House committees, briefing them on our Administration's ultimate policy decision to help Kuwait, I heard the usual objections. Some committee members were fond of saying that it did not matter what we did, because the Soviets could go anywhere they chose. On the surface that assertion seemed true, but it ignored some very real constraints to Soviet mobility. The Soviets are free to send their entire Pacific fleet into the open waters of the Persian Gulf, but they would have real problems sustaining that fleet without basing and logistic support from the local governments. We are able to maintain our Middle East Force in the Gulf and the North Arabian Sea partly, at least, because the Arab Gulf states allow us access to port facilities and provide us with needed logistic services. In fact, Kuwait was the primary source of contract fuel for all of our naval aircraft and ships in the region during the actual escort operations. The government of Kuwait also partially absorbed the cost of fuel for our ships and aircraft involved in escorting the American-flagged Kuwaiti oil tankers.

The Soviets do not enjoy that level of support, and did not even during their escort of three Kuwaiti chartered tankers.[1] The closest source of significant air and naval support for Soviet forces is Cam Ranh Bay in Vietnam, although the Soviets do have a small base at Aden.

From the outset I was quite sure that if we did not respond positively to the Kuwaitis, the USSR would quickly fill the vacuum, and that the Gulf states, already concerned for a number of reasons about American reliability, would not be able to deny basing and port facilities to their new protectors. Then we would indeed see a large Soviet naval presence in the Gulf.

Many argued that we would be drawn further into the Gulf war; that we had enough oil, and it was comparatively unim-

---

1. Soon reduced to two tankers, because one of the three had an unfortunate contact with a mine.

portant to us whether oil shipments moved in the Gulf, so long as we ourselves were not adversely affected; that our saying yes to Kuwait would set us on a collision course with the Soviet Union; and that Kuwait was not a reliable friend.

The argument that this was not our worry because it was not our oil we were protecting ignored two important facts. The first is that oil is a fungible commodity: Once it leaves port it can end up anywhere, and you cannot distinguish Kuwaiti oil from American oil. So, any loss of oil intended for European and Japanese markets would affect our own oil supply because then we would all be competing for our supplies from a smaller "pool." Second, a very large percentage of the oil in the Gulf is lifted, shipped and refined by American oil companies. Thus, closure of the Strait of Hormuz would directly affect American companies that pay United States corporate taxes and employ United States citizens. There is one market for oil: a global market.

The complaint that Kuwait was not a reliable friend ignored the fact that Kuwait had some reason for not considering the United States a reliable friend. How could the United States be considered a reliable friend if it did not live up to its commitments to the region, made on many occasions by all our Presidents from President Eisenhower to President Reagan? Actually, Kuwait has been reasonably steadfast in its diplomatic relations with the United States, despite contradictory signals sent by past American policy decisions.

Then too, I heard many times the comment that we agreed to protect Kuwait's tankers on the spur of the moment, without thoroughly looking at the options and consequences—the old "you have no strategy" canard. The truth is that I saw the Kuwaiti request not as a problem but as an opportunity for us. My staff and I were well aware of the negative image we had in the region as a result of some past history. There was, of course, the old worry of many Middle Eastern countries that we seemed to want only one friend in the area. And perhaps the most damaging charge against us was our failure to support the Shah when Iran was in turmoil. That failure was not lost on our friends on the other side of the Gulf, which was partly why Kuwait had seemed to hold us at arm's length.

For years Kuwaitis had seen us give training and assistance to the Shah and his military; and they heard us talk about Iran's importance to our policy of containing Soviet aggression; and they knew we had supported the Shah's modernization of Iran. But then they watched as we abandoned the Shah during his worst crisis. Our abandonment was followed by the rise of the Ayatollah Ruhollah Khomeini and, in short order, by Iranian militants' criminal seizure of our embassy and its diplomatic personnel. Our people were held hostage for 444 days, in direct contravention of the laws of all civilized nations. The fiasco of the Desert One rescue attempt did nothing to restore confidence in America as an effective ally. Adding to the damage, all the other Gulf Arab states now faced similar internal threats. Most have significant populations of Shiite Muslims, many of whom revere the Ayatollah Khomeini, worship the memory of him, and would gladly assist the installation of similar fanatical and barbarous regimes throughout the region.

Prior to the war between Iran and Iraq, Kuwait had a significant population of Iranian workers, who crossed the Gulf seeking employment in the oil rich sheikhdom. Bahrain, a small island country in the Gulf, just off Saudi Arabia, is constantly in danger of internal turmoil from local Shiite dissidents who are directly sponsored by the Iranian government. The eastern province of Saudi Arabia has a large Shiite population, elements of which have been supported in their destabilizing, antiregime activities by Iran. Saudi Arabia, Kuwait and Bahrain alike suffered terrorist activity fomented by fanatics in power in Teheran.

Bahrain was particularly vulnerable. It had been claimed by the government of Iran, which funds, trains and supports Shiite dissidents there. Those dissidents have made several attempts to destabilize Bahrain's ruling al-Khalifa family. The Amir of Bahrain, Sheikh Isa bin Sulman al-Khalifa, is a particularly good friend of the United States. For years his government has supported the U.S. Navy Middle East Force, which consists of a command ship and a number of combatants at the Bahrainian port of Mina Sulman. In fact, the U.S. Navy has had a presence in the region, lending it stability, since 1949; and at least one commander of our Middle East Force, a Navy admiral, was more influential in the Gulf than many of our ambassadors there have been.

In 1983 when the Amir of Bahrain made his first trip to the United States, I became very much aware of the value of our naval presence to both sides. I had invited Sheikh Isa to lunch at the Pentagon. We both had a number of senior military and state officials in attendance; and on my side of the table sat Vice Admiral Tom Bigley, who was then Director, Strategic Plans and Policy, on the Joint Staff, but had previously served as Commander of the Middle East Force. He was a personal friend of the Amir. In fact, Tom was there because the Amir wanted to see him. In the course of some brief remarks made during the lunch, Sheikh Isa referred to the past and present Middle East Force commanders as "my admirals." While I have found all Gulf Arab officials very friendly toward Americans, I knew that a relationship as strong as the one between the Amir and "his" admirals was very difficult to achieve and very valuable.

I also know that to betray such friendship through inaction in the face of danger would set back U.S. relations in the region for as many decades as it had taken to build them.

When Gulf Arab governments saw us abandon the Shah after years of close relations, they wondered how valid our commitment was to them. The message they read in our treatment of the Shah was: "You can't trust the United States to help in any crisis." That we found their assessment unfair was not nearly so important as another truth—that it *was* their perspective, right or wrong.

So I also saw the present request by Kuwait as an opportunity to dispel that perception, and to take actions very much in our own interest. None of the objections raised against our support of Kuwait seemed to me to balance the harm that would come of our declining to help. I was sure that if we did turn down the Kuwaiti request, we would be demonstrating once again to our friends, and to potential adversaries in the Middle East and elsewhere, that we were not a reliable, strong, or useful friend in any crisis.

There was another interesting aspect of Iran's attacks against Kuwaiti shipping: Iran claimed it was attacking shipping that was supporting the Iraqi war machine; but that was hardly true. The Iranians primarily attacked nonbelligerent oil tankers bound to and from Kuwaiti ports. None of those ships carried a single item of arms contraband. Furthermore, the Iranians usually made no attempt to board and search the ships to discover whether they were carrying contraband. The main carriers of arms contraband, that is, weapons destined for Iraq, were the Soviets, and the Iranians knew that. Only once to my knowledge did Iranians board a Soviet arms carrier that was carrying a cargo of weapons destined for Iraq. Those Iranians led the carrier toward the port of Bandar Abbas, in southern Iran. As soon as the Soviets heard that their ship had been boarded and confiscated, they sent an Alligator Landing Ship Tank with troops escorted by several warships from Aden toward Bandar Abbas. At the same time, a representative of the Soviet government visited officials in Teheran and ordered Iran to release the ship. It was immediately released to proceed on its way north, its cargo hold full of weapons destined for Iraq.

Under international law, a belligerent may claim as a prize of war any ship it finds carrying a cargo more than fifty percent contraband. In this case, Iran could have claimed the Soviet merchant as a prize of war, but the facts of life regarding the Soviets persuaded Iran to behave meekly. They did not treat helpless merchant ships with such deference.

Clearly a factor that caused us great concern was the Iranian acquisition of the Silkworm surface-to-surface antiship missile. Iran got the missile from the People's Republic of China, and it was a very destabilizing weapon. Up to this point, neither Iran nor Iraq had a weapon with the explosive power to sink a large tanker. Now Iran had a large warhead weapon that could conceivably close the Strait of Hormuz. Intelligence had discovered a number of potential and actual Silkworm sites in Iran along the coast, both east and north on the Strait, that were ideally suited for targeting any ship in the Strait; and in February 1987 we had detected a test flight of the Silkworm from the Iranian island of Qishm, at the north end of the Strait. We served notice through our European friends who still maintained embassies in Tehran that we considered the installation of those missiles to be threatening, and would take appropriate measures to protect our ships.

When Kuwait first inquired whether it could place its ships under the American flag for protection ("reflagging"), I thought our initial response was too weak. The State Department's draft cable to the Kuwaitis said that reflagging would take at least six months under United States law, and that we only had a few ships available to help them. On the margin of the draft cable, I commented that our response was too weak for me, but at least it offered Kuwait some hope. I knew that getting the cable redrafted by State and reapproved by all concerned would take too long.

Shortly, though, the arguments took a new turn. Kuwait, satisfied by Defense's informed advice to them that we could reflag much sooner than six months, changed its request, and now sought to have six of its tankers put under the protection not just of American convoys, but of the American flag, with the remaining five of its tankers going under the Soviet flag and Soviet protection. I felt that our first response, lukewarm, had encouraged the factions in the Kuwaiti government supporting and seeking Soviet protection; that Kuwait had revised its proposal to satisfy heightened worries in the sheikhdom about placing so much reliance on the United States. Kuwait's stated reason for changing its request was that the Soviets had indicated that virtually all the USSR required for reflagging was that the Kuwait Oil Tanker Company haul down the Kuwaiti flag and raise the Hammer and Sickle. On the other hand, from our tepid response and their preliminary discussions with our Coast Guard, Kuwait felt that it would take six months or more for its tankers to come into compliance with U.S. safety regulations. So I felt that in order to be responsive, we would have to agree to protect all eleven of the KOTC ships, regardless of whether they were flagged in Kuwait or the U.S. and to speed reflagging if they wished.

One evening early in March, Sandy Charles, Director for Near Eastern and South Asian Affairs, reporting to DOD Assistant Secretary Rich Armitage, and Commander Skip Miner, the Persian Gulf desk officer, had received a message from Ambassador Tony Quinton in Kuwait advising us of the proposed five–six split.[2] Realizing the impact of that message, Sandy and Skip quickly drafted a short note to me for my weekly breakfast meeting with other Cabinet members, scheduled for the following day. The note advised me of the continued interagency dispute on reflagging (DOD and NSC for reflagging, State against) and our options, and recommended that I consider offering Kuwait

2. Sandy Charles was an experienced Middle East hand who had risen through the ranks of that office to become a director, and I knew of her effective work from previous Middle East policy actions. Her desk officer, Skip Miner, had previously spent a number of years in the Middle East/Africa Division of the Joint Staff's Plans and Policy Directorate. Both had the great privilege of serving under Rich Armitage.

American protection for all eleven tankers regardless of flag, Kuwaiti or American. After extensive but sterile and fruitless debates with the other members at the breakfast meeting—particularly with George Shultz, who did not share my enthusiasm for this mission—I made one of my few calls to the President, urging that we tell the Kuwaitis we would protect *all* of their tankers, either under their own flag or under our flag.

I recognized that the option of American flagging would be politically more difficult to fulfill, but the basic effect was the same. No difference in our naval forces would be required to protect the shipping; and it seemed immaterial to me whether the Kuwaiti ships were reflagged or not. To my mind the main thing was for us to protect the right of innocent, nonbelligerent and extremely important commerce to move freely in international open waters—and, by our offering that protection, to avoid conceding the mission to the Soviets.

Frank Carlucci, as National Security Advisor, understood fully the vital importance of our agreeing to Kuwait's request, and worked to the limit to assure that we got a satisfactory resolution to the problem of the Kuwaiti tankers.

The President agreed that we should protect all the Kuwaiti shipping, and I conveyed that policy decision to the government of Kuwait in early March. Kuwait was a little surprised that we would agree to protect Kuwaiti-flagged ships, but responded in early April that it preferred to put all eleven tankers under the American flag.

Reregistering and reflagging foreign ships with the American flag is a comparatively simple procedure, fully covered by our statutes.[3] For the most part the process had been used the other way: Many owners of American ships prefer to have them registered under the flag of another country, to avoid United States

3. Act of December 27, 1950, C.1155, 64 Stat. 1120.

taxation and safety regulations. In any event, the Coast Guard was very helpful; and where I could, I issued waivers of some rules that enabled us to start our protection sooner.

We had looked at this mission in past discussions with the Commander in Chief, U.S. Central Command (USCINC-CENT), General George Crist, USMC, because we had been concerned for some time about the nature of the attacks against ships in the Gulf. Prudent military planning demanded that we consider the range of options available to us if we should be required to protect all American-flagged vessels in the Gulf. As a result, we already had a reasonably good framework for this mission, including the size of forces needed to provide an acceptable level of protection.

Initially, though, the Navy was far from enthusiastic about this operation, fearing that it would divert a large number of its forces from existing, long-term commitments; that it would be expensive, taking funds from projects the Navy cherished; and that it might result in some loss of life and ships.

I told them that it was vital we protect this critical commerce; that our forces were ready; and that the course we and the Kuwaitis had chosen was one of the best ways of preventing a far more arduous and risky task later, should the Gulf indeed be closed by the Iranian intimidations and attacks.

Various other objections continued to issue from the Navy even after the President's decision, particularly as to the scope of the forces that I felt must be marshalled for the task. This was hardly the first time I had augmented service recommendations made by others when we required forces. I always remembered the fate of those who did too little, too late!

Also, in an attempt to respond preemptively to what I knew would be congressional and other demands for our allies to share the burden, I suggested that we sound out Britain and other naval members of NATO to see if they would be prepared to assist in the convoying operations.

And I strongly advocated, in conjunction with our military approach, a diplomatic initiative through whatever channels were available to persuade Iran to negotiate a cease-fire with Iraq. In addition, I urged that pressure be put on Iran to adopt the principles of UN Security Council Resolution 598, then being debated, and later passed in the summer of 1987. It called for, among other things, an Iran-Iraq cease-fire, a return of all forces to their own international boundaries, the exchange of prisoners, and the organization of an international body to determine the causes of the war. With each step, we tried to use what little influence we enjoyed to encourage Iran to accept the UN resolution, and to get countries with more influence to join us in that effort. Iraq had immediately accepted the resolution, but Iran continued to demand the death of Iraqi President Saddam Hussein, the installation of an Islamic government in Iraq, billions of dollars of reparations from the government of Iraq, and other impossible nonsense in keeping with the usual practice of Iran under Khomeini.

The reflagging procedures under American law require approval of other agencies such as the Coast Guard and the Maritime Administration, and Kuwait was now advised that it should begin those procedures; it did so. The first large tanker was to be registered and equipped with an American flag in July. Our plan was to have American Navy ships, fore and aft, piloting and guarding the Kuwaiti tankers all the way from below the Strait of Hormuz, the narrow chokepoint at the southern end of the Gulf, on past Iranian naval bases, and up to safe harbor in Kuwait City. But soon congressional committees were out in full cry, although we had briefed them many times about the operation and about why we felt it was essential that we accept the Kuwaiti request and try our best to carry it out.

Oddly enough, the hue and cry raised by Congress had not reached anything close to full force in March, when we initially announced our intention to reflag the tankers. In fact, congressional reaction initially ranged from positive to indifferent. One member of the Senate Foreign Relations Committee still even offered to change reflagging laws to speed up the process. We in Defense made many attempts to brief the appropriate Senate and House committees, but usually they did not have time for my briefers. They were too involved at that time in putting together a congressional committee to investigate the Iran-Contra affair.

Some of the most insistent congressional demands were that the President send notices according to the War Powers Resolution that our forces were being sent into situations of "imminent hostilities." Issue of those notices would trigger the authority of Congress to stop the action at any time it wished.

The President did not feel that our cooperation with Kuwait was a situation of the type described in the War Powers Resolution; he shared the belief of all of our prior five Presidents that the War Powers Resolution is unconstitutional; and he agreed that any such restraints on the power of the President would be not only unwise but extremely risky for our forces. Further, we did not believe that our convoying American flagged ships in international waters was what Congress envisioned as a triggering event when it passed the War Powers Resolution in 1973.[4]

As we developed our policy in the Gulf, I saw the War Powers Resolution as a political tool that could very easily result in needless death for many of our military personnel. The mission itself, protecting American-flagged shipping and keeping open the international sea lanes of commerce, was clearly crucial to the United States. And until recently, the U.S. Navy was actually

---

4. The Founders, including both Jefferson and Hamilton, had no doubt that the President had supremacy in international affairs. Jefferson, who was always ready to oppose a too powerful executive branch, wrote to President Washington in 1790 saying that the transaction of business with foreign nations is "Executive altogether." See Caspar W. Weinberger, "Dangerous Constraints on the President's War Power," in *The Fettered Presidency: Legal Constraints on the Executive Branch*, L. Gordon Cronitz and Jeremy A. Rohkin, eds. (Washington, D.C.: American Enterprise Institute for Public Policy Research, 1989), p. 97.

required by statute to do just that. In more modern times, the statute was reduced to a standing Executive Order. However, any effort to impede our Gulf policy by congressional interference could only jeopardize our military forces, because subjecting them to a fixed withdrawal date established by Congress—a key requirement of the War Powers Resolution—could only help Iran. Additionally, it would confirm our lack of resolve both to the Iranians and to our Arab friends. Such intervention by Congress would signal defeat of the mission before the first convoy began.

We viewed the War Powers Resolution as inapplicable also because commerce *was* moving through the Gulf, even though a state of war existed between Iran and Iraq. Hundreds of ships and aircraft were conducting business every day. An element of danger existed because of the proximity of the war and the irresponsible behavior of the Iranian government, but the commercial world did not feel the situation threatening enough to cease activity. We were protecting legitimate United States commerce. In the absence of direct action by Iran, which had clearly demonstrated in the past a decided intent to avoid American warships, we were confident that we were not subjecting our forces to imminent hostilities; so, again, we felt the War Powers Resolution did not apply.

It was gratifying that when, after 110 members of Congress sued the President, trying to force a judicial ruling requiring us to be bound by the War Powers Resolution, the courts dismissed the suit out of hand.

But another objection was voiced in a July memo to me by the newly appointed Navy Secretary, James Webb. He wrote that we would never be able to know when "we had won." His main point was that we had no clear objectives and, as result, would not be able to achieve or sustain public support, nor could we expect support from allies or friends. He also argued that I was violating my own prerequisites for combat, which I had set out in a November 1984 speech to the National Press Club. In that speech, I proposed six "tests" governing my definition of a situation requiring us to commit our forces to "combat."[5] Those six tests, in brief, are:

1. Our vital interests must be at stake.
2. The issues involved are so important for the future of the United States and our allies that we are prepared to commit enough forces to win.
3. We have clearly defined political and military objectives, which we must secure.
4. We have sized our forces to achieve our objectives.
5. We have some reasonable assurance of the support of the American people.
6. U.S. forces are committed to combat only as a last resort.

Thus, the answer to Jim Webb's charge seemed to me to be clear and simple. I said we would consider that we had achieved our objective, or "won," each time a commercial ship with non-belligerent commerce went back and forth in the international waters of the Gulf without being subjected to attack, indiscriminate or otherwise, from Iran. I also told Jim that the free movement of important commerce on international waters was vital to our security; that that freedom had been one of the cardinal principles we had supported since our foundation as a nation. Finally, I told him that we were not now engaged in "combat," but ultimately we might be, if we did not protect the right to move freely in international waters.

Secretary Webb, incidentally, was my personal choice to be Secretary of the Navy. He is a Naval Academy graduate, and had a superb combat record as a Marine in Vietnam, displaying con-

---

5. See "Uses of Military Power" speech in full, in Appendix.

spicuous bravery on many occasions and great leadership at all times. He is also a brilliant novelist and author. I admired him deeply, and was sorry indeed when, in early 1988, severe budget cuts led him to conclude that he should resign.

There arose another factor complicating our mission in the Gulf. On May 17, 1987, Iraq made its mistaken missile attack on one of our destroyers, the USS *Stark*. Tragically, thirty-seven American lives were lost; and there was substantial damage to our ship. The ship was saved through the exertions, skill, and courage of her officers and men, but nothing could repair the loss of life. Iraq most certainly had made a serious mistake, but that did not and could not change our interest and that of our allies in keeping the Gulf waters open.

Iraq was clearly concerned that we understand the tragedy was an accident. Its government issued an immediate apology and condolences to families of the victims for the fearful error, and offered to pay damages and appropriate compensation. In addition, Iraq asked us to establish military-to-military meetings to work out safeguards against future problems between our forces in the Gulf. We agreed to hold meetings in Baghdad for that sole purpose. Those meetings were in no way intended to indicate that we had taken sides in the war or would assist Iraq in the war. We were merely trying to ensure that both of us avoid the danger of an accidental confrontation.

More importantly, although we did not actually change the Rules of Engagement, I told General Crist to make it abundantly clear to each of our ship commanders that each was fully supported by the chain of command in taking all reasonable steps necessary to protect his ship and the lives of his men. That included permission to shoot first (and not wait until fired upon) if the commander felt such action was required to protect his ship.

Incidentally, the *Stark* episode underlines for me the dangers of believing fully "first" reports. The first report to me on the

Stark was that the ship had been hit but that there were only a few minor casualties. "Never act on first reports" is a good Pentagon rule I learned from General Vessey.

Now, congressional opposition to our whole Gulf operation flared, and many briefings were demanded and given. The President stood completely firm, raising the issue with his summit partners in Venice on June 11, and refusing to bow to objections raised again on June 30 by some congressional leaders. Such attempts to block the reflagging and even stop all our Gulf defense activities continued until July 15, when Senate Democrats became entangled in a monumental parliamentary thicket of their own making, and at last dropped all of their proposals to block the reflagging.

On July 21, our first convoy began. Unfortunately, the reflagged Kuwaiti tanker we were escorting, the *Bridgeton*, struck a mine and suffered damage; but it was able to reach Kuwait.

Iran claimed, as it did whenever it used covert or third-party terrorist activity, that "the hand of God" had caused the damage. We considered retaliation, but decided to show restraint, particularly since the damage was limited and no personal injury or loss of life had occurred.

Congressional fury was vented again, but I knew we could not stop then. We added quickly to our minesweeping capabilities, drawing ships from home and calling on our friends abroad. For this first convoy we had used Saudi minesweepers, Kuwaiti helicoptors, and American divers to clear a channel to Kuwait waters; but Iran, denying it all the time, had planted more mines after our first sweep. While we were waiting for our own minesweeping equipment to arrive, Admiral Hal Bernsen, Commander of the Middle East Force, used two tugs provided by Kuwait and a length of cable connecting them to clear moored mines wherever they were found or suspected of endangering American shipping. That Yankee expedient worked quite well, and we continued to use it even after our other minesweeping ships and aircraft arrived in the Gulf.

We knew that mining would be one of the ways Iran would probably choose to attack us, but its capability was rudimentary and depended upon luck as much as skill and equipment. In fact, Rear Admiral Tom Brooks, the DIA Deputy responsible for intelligence support for Admiral Crowe, in June 1987 established a special task force to provide around-the-clock intelligence support to our defense agencies involved in the Persian Gulf escort operations. The ad hoc organization, known as the Persian Gulf Working Group (PGWG), or "Pig Wig" to its friends and members, had accurately predicted that mining was a real but limited danger. From July 1987 to September 1988 the PGWG provided invaluable intelligence assistance to the Gulf effort.

In late May, as part of the earlier Senate attempts to block our Gulf actions, Senator Robert C. Byrd (Democrat of West Virginia) had initiated a resolution demanding a report to Congress as a prerequisite for protecting Kuwaiti ships. We provided that report on June 15, before the *Bridgeton* incident; and that generated another fracas based on apparently conflicting assessments within the intelligence community of conditions in the Gulf. Congressman Les Aspin (Democrat of Wisconsin) felt that the CIA had a much gloomier picture than the DIA, and that the CIA had not been given the opportunity to comment. Neither of his fears was based in reality. The CIA contributed to the report, but the paper itself was reflective more of the immediate military threats we saw than of the long-term political threats— which would persist whether or not we protected Kuwaiti tankers. Of particular concern to Congress was the threat of increased terrorism reported by the CIA. Defense agreed with the CIA, but we also felt that threat was not new. The U.S. had been facing terrorism from Iran since the fall of the Shah; and failing to defend our own interests in the Gulf was a sure way to guarantee further blackmail by terrorism when we again ran afoul of the Ayatollah, as we surely would.

In July, frustration and fury now fueled congressional demands that we stop helping Kuwait. They said that our ships might strike more mines; that we were derelict in not having more minesweepers; and that in any event that single mine proved that the President must invoke the War Powers Resolution.

We knew from the beginning that we would need some support from the neighboring Gulf countries. The first thing we required was substantial improvement in our warning time of possible Iranian attacks—and that could come only from American and Saudi AWACS aircraft. We had sold some of those early-warning planes to Saudi Arabia some years before, after the defeat of a fierce congressional effort to block the sale. Initially we relied upon observation and intelligence gathering flights from our own carrier based planes, but it became increasingly clear that the AWACS would be a most valuable part of our early warning capability.

We had been operating our own AWACS aircraft from Saudi Arabia since the outbreak of the Iran-Iraq War in September 1980; but that activity provided only coverage of the northern Gulf and early warning of possible Iranian air threats to the Saudi oil fields. It did not protect United States shipping in the Gulf. What we needed now was to expand our coverage to include the lower Gulf, which required Saudi use of its own AWACS to complement ours in support of our escort regime.[6]

A complex series of negotiations to secure that assistance began

---

6. Carrier based aircraft, such as A-6s, A-7s, F-14s and P-3s, flying from Diego Garcia, received early warning from the carrier's E-2 Hawkeye when air cover for escort operations in the southern Gulf was deemed necessary. But Saudi-based AWACS was needed to cover the central Gulf; the aircraft housing that system had longer endurance than Hawkeye, and could see much farther. The same assistance by AWACS was provided also for American ships inside the Gulf.

in June 1987. They were difficult negotiations because, despite the interest the Gulf states have in freedom of navigation in the Gulf, there was and is a continuing reluctance among even the friendliest of the Arab nations to be seen as having a very close military association with the United States.

I made every effort to secure Saudi agreement to use their AWACS to help us, since that cooperation could extend, by several valuable minutes, the warning time we would have of the takeoff and route of approach of any Iranian planes.

Saudi agreement finally came on June 4, when I met in France with Prince Sultan, the Defense Minister of Saudi Arabia and the father of the Saudi Ambassador to the United States, Prince Bandar. As we flew in to Nice from London, I was provided a very detailed briefing by my Assistant Secretary Rich Armitage, on whose skilled advice and great friendship I had long relied, and by Dick Murphy, an exceptionally able career foreign service officer, experienced in Middle Eastern affairs, a former U.S. Ambassador to Saudi Arabia whose expertise in Arabic and whose affinity with and knowledge of the area and its people stood us in good stead then and in many previous meetings I had had with Arab leaders; and by my desk officer for Saudi Arabia, Mike MacMurray, a retired naval officer and an experienced Middle East hand.

Our meeting took place in Prince Sultan's extremely comfortable villa on the French Mediterranean. We had a long day of general talks, and detailed translations were required; Prince Bandar acted as a skilled interpreter and translator for his father and for me. I realized the vital necessity of our mission and the need for various steps we must take to secure use of the AWACS and other help. I also knew that the sovereignty of the Kingdom could not be in any way weakened. Eventually, piece by piece, the agreement was reached. We were delighted with it. Saudi-based aircraft would now help us in our venture, and give us the most valuable thing we could have: additional time and knowledge of Iranian intentions and actions in the lower Gulf, particularly the Strait of Hormuz.

Prince Sultan's villa at Nice was an odd place to be discussing martial matters such as warfighting capabilities, clearing the Persian Gulf of Iranian intruders, early warning aircraft. The villa, originally owned by the Aga Khan III, was large to start with, and the Prince had made it larger. It looks out on the Mediterranean, which, on that sunny day, sparkled in all of its legendary and breathtaking blue. We met in the library at a very long table. The handsome room featured tapestry, paintings, marble floors and the mixture of Middle Eastern modern and classical French that is frequently seen in the Saudi palaces. Lunch, an immense feast with all of the traditional Middle Eastern dishes, was in the dining room, a long gallery encircling a large, ornamental indoor pool; the brilliant Mediterranean lapped at the edge of the house on the other side of the table.

The Saudi delegation and Prince Sultan were particularly cordial, but the negotiations took all day, with Prince Bandar translating fluently and tirelessly. At the end of the day, we had agreement on the things most vital to the success of our mission. The Saudis made substantial concessions, agreeing to engage in our operations, including the AWACS patrols, more directly than had been their custom in the past; successfully escorted convoys subsequently demonstrated the value of that agreement.

The Saudis agreed at once to help us with medical facilities for any of our people who might need them; that took no negotiating. In fact they had already made all medical facilities available to us without any prior agreement, when the USS *Stark* was hit.

Such long and vital discussions as the ones we had concluded are very draining. Not until they are over, the farewells have been said and you are back on your plane, headed to the next destination, do you feel you are offstage and can relax. On that flight back from Nice, I barely had time to watch the glories of the southern coast of France disappear into the sunset before I fell asleep.

Earlier, we also had negotiated understandings with Bahrain that enabled us to use bases and other facilities in that country for the urgently needed shore-based activities of our growing fleet in the Gulf.

Further valuable Saudi Arabian contributions to the Gulf effort included their permitting us to berth large barges (lent cost free by Kuwait) to house our Army helicopters and Navy and Marine Corps crews off the coast of Saudi Arabia. The helicopters complemented the AWACS in searching out Iranian naval craft, giving us not only early warning of Iranian air and naval activities and intentions, but also increased capabilities of attack should an Iranian threat require that resort. The barges also served as storehouses for vitally needed naval supplies. We moved the barges out to sea after they had been properly fitted out by Kuwait, at no small cost to itself. Besides housing Army attack helicopters, those barges were homes for Marines and Navy Special Operations personnel often known by their acronym, SEALs (Sea, Air, Land), denoting their multidimensional capability. The barges virtually ended Iranian small-boat activity in the northern Gulf.

I must record that most of the Navy (Admiral Crowe, Chairman of the Joint Chiefs, excepted), did not like those barges. In fact, some Navy officers were openly hostile to them; they were large, ungainly, and distinctly unattractive in appearance. But they represented to me all the advantages of vitally needed shore bases, and I had eagerly accepted the Kuwaiti offer of them. I have always been glad we did so.

Throughout the Persian Gulf escort endeavor, some members of Congress made the entire operation more difficult than it had to be.

Just before the first convoy of reflagged ships, we decided to brief the leadership of Congress on the specifics of our first escort plan. National Security Advisor Carlucci, Admiral Crowe and I, late on the afternoon of July 14, 1987, personally briefed the leaders of both houses and the chairmen and ranking members of our oversight committees.

Representative Les Aspin, Chairman of the House Armed Services Committee, was one of the more active questioners. At the start of the meeting, Admiral Crowe had specifically stated that the information to be briefed was extremely sensitive and should be treated accordingly. But immediately following the briefing, in the hallways of the Capitol, Aspin held a press conference divulging the exact details of the convoy: when and where it would start, the number of ships participating, and more. The next day, the specific details of our escort operation appeared across the front pages of the *Washington Post*, along with specifics of some rather delicate negotiations between some of our Gulf allies. Ten days later, the lead ship in the first convoy, the *Bridgeton*, struck a mine that had been laid in its path only hours before by the Iranians.

I do not know if the information of the convoy's position presented by Aspin to the media was a contributing factor. Probably not; but I do know that had any member of the Defense Department, in the political leadership or on the military staff, leaked the same information to the press, that person would have been punished or dismissed.

The only outcry to Mr. Aspin's indiscretion came from the military members of my staff, who resurrected the old World War II slogan, Loose lips sink ships, and modified it for the occasion. Around the Pentagon for the next several days, the tongue twister Les's lips sink ships was pronounced repeatedly in honor of the loose-lipped chairman of the House Armed Services Committee.

Not only had a member of Congress released specific details of a sensitive military operation, but he also told the press that the United States had been granted certain overflight privileges for its AWACS early warning aircraft. His breach of confidence went beyond violating our frequent statements that we would not need the Saudis' help: Our *secret* use of an airborne early warning aircraft over the southern portion of the Gulf was an element we deemed basic to our escort missions. We had established an orbit pattern near the Gulf Emirates only through extensive negotiations with the ruler of one of the Emirates and with a head of state of another Gulf country; their agreeing to our request entailed an exchange of personal promises between the two of them. We of course promised those two Gulf leaders that we would keep the security air patrols confidential. In most cases their concern and need for secrecy arose from internal pressures from their own population; many of the governments cooperated much more than all but a few people were aware. To many of the Gulf leaders, a gentlemen's agreement should remain a gentlemen's agreement—it simply did not need to be advertised.

But Representative Aspin and his impromptu press conference did just that. He spoke openly of the overflight agreement, insuring that the agreement with the two Gulf leaders was spread across every major newspaper. As a result, we lost the southern AWACS orbit and had to try to renegotiate it; the safety of a military operation and of the Americans executing it was carelessly jeopardized; a close Gulf ally who negotiated on behalf of the United States was embarrassed. All this for some self-indulgent press coverage.

The Persian Gulf operations also were an excellent example of Congress's attempts generally to manage the smallest details of our military, rather than concentrating on setting broad policies and leaving the execution of those policies to the Department of Defense.

The high interest shown by Congress in our Gulf military mission was reflected in the greatly increased number of congressional visits to the area. From July 1987 through January 1988,

at the height of operations, more than thirty-five members of
Congress insisted on personally visiting the Gulf. To the task of
accommodating them I assigned one of my staff officers, who
ended up spending more than one day in every five in the Persian
Gulf region during the six months involved. And then there was
the amount of time that the force commander and his staff, and
the ship and aircraft officers and men, spent away from their
primary responsibilities in order to brief, rebrief and brief yet
again their congressional visitors.

Yet although the visits were difficult for our forces engaged in
operations, I felt that the benefits in most cases far outweighed
the inconveniences. Most of the visiting members of Congress,
even those who originally did not support the Administration,
returned home fully convinced of the level of support and friendship being shown us by the Gulf allies. Even some of the more
skeptical members became totally supportive upon experiencing
firsthand the sincerity of those allies, and became strong advocates.

But again, for all the good that came from the face-to-face
interaction, problems arose. One member of Congress, while
visiting Oman, was so offended that he would not be meeting
Sultan Qabus ibn Said, the head of state, that he waited until
after midnight to cancel his early morning meeting with one of
Oman's deputy ministers. That particular senator evidently believed that he should be afforded the courtesies of a head of state;
after all he was a well-known senator. When he was not given
the personal attention of the Sultan, he decided a little dose of
"ugly American" rudeness would show his hosts just how important he was. The U.S. Embassy staff reportedly spent most
of the early morning hours smoothing the ruffled feathers of the
host nation's ministry. A mid-morning meeting with the deputy
minister was finally agreed upon. But the Omanis, not to be
outdone, returned a diplomatic "shot across the bow." According
to the embassy, the Omanis let the distinguished senator cool

his heels for about twenty minutes before the deputy minister finally met with him.

The very next group of congressmen to visit Oman were forced to spend about an hour clearing customs upon arrival at the international airport. Previously the congressional delegations had been "expedited." The new policy was explained by the State Department as the Omani government's way of letting us know they did not appreciate the rudeness of one of our distinguished legislators. As a result, not only did subsequent congressional delegations suffer; for several months it became more difficult to expedite other official visitors. There were too many other such incidents, all of which, I tried to explain to our foreign friends, were caused by our having two governments in Washington— one executive, the other legislative.

Now back to the operation itself.

In the course of the early summer, Iranian attacks against shipping increased and a number of mining incidents led to increased cooperation among our European and Gulf friends. In May and June 1987 the merchant vessels *Ethnic* (Greek), *Marshall Chuykov* (Soviet), *Primrose* and *Stena Explorer* (both Liberian, American owned) struck mines near Kuwait. And as related earlier, the USS *Stark* was mistakenly attacked by Iraq. It was against that background that the American-Kuwaiti-Saudi Arabian mine-sweeping operation began in July, and continued until the Iranians gave up their attacks in 1988.

In August 1987 the *Texaco Caribbean* (Panamanian flagged, and not an escorted ship), carrying a load of Iranian oil, struck a mine at an anchorage off Khor Fakkan, in the Gulf of Oman. That incident was followed a short time later by the loss of a service ship and five of its crew. Khor Fakkan is a United Arab Emirates (UAE) port facility where merchant ships would anchor while awaiting company orders to proceed into the Gulf. It was also close to our marshalling point for beginning escort voyages north to Kuwait.

The mining was an obvious escalation by Iran, but by conducting intelligence efforts we were able to determine, with fair confidence, which Iranian ships were doing the mining. The increased mining prompted the UAE to request European assistance. And ultimately minesweepers were provided to our joint efforts from the United Kingdom and France. Italy, Belgium and the Netherlands followed a month later.

Also in August, we witnessed Iran's unofficial Revolutionary Guard Corps navy conducting its exercise "Martyrdom," which included simulated small-boat attacks, a claimed missile firing, and a minisubmarine launching. Clearly we were seeing Iranian threats, but we were also getting a good insight into Iranian strategy.

During one of my trips to Europe, where I discussed the need for mutual assistance against Iranian activity in the Gulf, I received help from an unexpected quarter. On September 2, 1987, Iran attacked the Italian merchant ship *Jolly Rubino* while the Italian government was debating its involvement in the Gulf and what level of support it should provide us. Following that attack, Iranian forces conducted a singularly vicious attack on the UK merchant ship *Gentle Breeze*. Thus Iran solidified both Italian and British support for our activities in the Gulf.

On September 21, our helicopters came upon a converted Iranian troop ship, the *Iran Ajar*, which had been laying mines (all such enterprise denied by the Iranians) in the path of the convoyed oil tankers. That we caught the ship was no accident. As I stated earlier, we had been using our night surveillance helicopters based on the barges to monitor Iranian activity coming from the Iranian Exclusion Zone (a warning area, declared by Iran, that bisected the Gulf). By very rapid, effective, and skilled actions our helicopters attacked the Iranian mine-layer, and left it dead in the water. Later our men boarded the *Iran Ajar*, seized the ship and took the crew prisoner, before the Iranians had any opportunity to destroy the clear evidence that they had been lying about their mine laying activities.[7] Since we were not at war with Iran, but had acted in self-defense, I ordered the captured Iranians repatriated. The Omani government was good enough to act as an intermediary for us in that effort.

I was in the Gulf shortly afterward, visiting our forces. They were performing so well, but coming under increasing criticism from the Congress—as was our whole role in the Gulf at that time—that I thought a visit by me might be helpful to our forces.

I always hesitated before indulging my desire to meet with the men and women who perform all those difficult and dangerous tasks for all of us all over the world. I always recalled, from Army days in New Guinea and the Philippines in World War II, how much of a nuisance visiting firemen can be for the troops.

But I was assured most earnestly by senior officers how much of a help it is for the morale of our people in distant places to be visited by the Secretary of Defense. Certainly the warmth of the welcome I received on all those visits, and the seriousness and value of the questions our men and women asked me in the question and answer sessions I always held with them, made it seem that the Joint Chiefs and others were right in encouraging me to visit.

I knew, at first hand, something of the extreme heat, difficult conditions and dangers our forces were encountering in the Gulf. On every count, I wanted to let them know personally how deeply grateful the American people were for their skills and their courage; and I wanted to show the importance of their mission, so that people at home too would be aware of their sacrifice.

One of the first things I saw during the rather hectic September

---

7. In April 1989, then Speaker Hashemi Rafsanjani, apparently to bolster his credentials for ardent anti-Americanism, absurdly claimed that the *Iran Ajar* had been sunk because its location was given to us by spies in the Iranian Navy. This was, of course, the usual absurd Iranian lie. We found the ship on one of our routine air patrols, and caught it in the act of laying mines. This matter is notable only because Rasfanjani was one of the Iranians McFarlane had told us was a "moderate" with whom we could negotiate!

25 tour of four of our ships and four of our facilities in Bahrain, Saudi Arabia, and the Gulf itself was the captured Iranian mine-layer. Our crews had brought the *Iran Ajar* alongside our large barge bases. Our men, quite properly, took enormous pride in their achievement, but described it in the most modest terms. They showed me the racks on the deck where the mines had been positioned; they displayed the holes made by our shelling, which brought about the Iranian surrender of the ship.

By then we had acquired all the intelligence we could from the ship and its crew members. Incidentally, the fear we had felt that Iranian sailors would scuttle their ship and die with it rather than let themselves be captured and interrogated was quite unfounded. They clearly preferred to live as prisoners of the U.S. Navy rather than to die for the Ayatollah; in the event, they had to do neither because we repatriated them.

The press asked me what we would do with the ship itself. I was surprised by the question. I thought it would be quite clear that we should sink it, after we had learned all we could from examining the ship and the crew, and I said so. I had given orders earlier for the ship to be taken out into the Gulf, away from any navigable shipping routes, and blown up that evening. That was done, and some rather muted criticism issued from home to the effect that this was a provocative act that would widen the war; that it was an escalation that was not justified; and that we should have given the mine-layer back to Iran (presumably so the Iranians could continue to use it to lay additional mines designed to sink American ships). While the debate continued, the Iranian mine-layer lay at the bottom of the Gulf.

That trip to the Gulf, which turned out to be one of my last official trips as Secretary, was unusually hectic even by the standards we set with most of our travel.

We had left Andrews Air Force Base on September 23, and after a long flight (with refueling at Shannon, in Ireland) we landed at Dhahran, in the eastern province of Saudi Arabia near

Bahrain. We stayed overnight at the Dhahran Gulf Royal Palace and visited the ships the next morning. On each of the visits to the four ships I made that day, I talked with as many sailors and airmen as possible—starting in the engine room, because conditions there were the worst of all. The surface temperature was about 110 degrees Fahrenheit; but in the engine room it regularly ran around 125 degrees, and in no time at all, it seemed, not only were you soaked through, you even felt your hair very hot against your scalp. All the sailors seemed to appreciate being talked to individually, and on most of the ships I requested an opportunity for a question period, usually in the mess deck or well deck of the ship, or in whatever larger space we could find. These were always very well attended, and I found them extremely helpful to determining what was worrying our men and what we could do about it.

Some policy was also made at those meetings. When I called for questions on one of the ships, a very large sailor who was in charge of one of the engine room crews rose slowly, and asked whether or not there was going to be a medal for their work in this zone. My immediate reaction was, Of course; but then I was stopped by the thought that bestowing decorations might give some credence to the congressional voices arguing that this was a combat zone. I was hardly eager to give ammunition to those who asked to invoke the War Powers Resolution. Nevertheless. I also recalled that we had previously issued service medals and campaign ribbons for duty within the continental United States—and so I felt no hesitancy in responding that I thought it was an excellent idea, and would see to it when I returned. I did, and there are now 75,000 soldiers, sailors and airmen eligible for this expeditionary campaign ribbon as a result of their Persian Gulf activities.

Nowhere was the skill and bravery of our young Navy men more evident than in the pilots and crews of HC-2, the aviation detachment that flew the helicopters taking me and my party to the ships out in the Gulf. Resupply of ships at sea by helicopter is routine in the fleet, but is still very dangerous work, especially in a hostile environment.

Later in the trip, I saw the T-shirts that some members of the party had purchased in Bahrain. On the front side was a cartoonlike drawing of a helicopter and the "Desert Duck" that was the symbol of HC-2; but on the back was an American flag and, below it, lettering that read "These colors don't run." Nothing could come closer to symbolizing the President's policies and the spirit of our brave young men and women in those difficult days. The President may have been criticized by some in Congress, but his policies were understood and supported with pride in the fleet.

Iranian activity picked up after my return to the States. Another incident, on October 8, further proved the value of the helicopters and barges. Three Iranian small boats fired on an observation helicopter checking out radar contacts. The copter called for assistance; and the three Iranian small boats, a Boghammer and two whaler-type boats, were damaged or destroyed by helicopter gunship fire. In recovering the wreckage, we found a battery from a Stinger missile launcher. The find confirmed our suspicion that the Iranians had been able to obtain a small quantity of those missiles, probably from a shipment they had seized on the way to the Afghan Mujahadin.

Throughout the Gulf war, we observed two distinct Iranian naval organizations with differing command structures and styles of attack: the regular navy, called the Islamic Republic Iranian Navy (IRIN), and the previously mentioned IRGC. The IRIN had been trained by the United States under the Shah and had such combatants as frigates, destroyers, and fast patrol boats. The IRIN used conventional tactics when conducting attacks, and generally was much more conservative than the IRGC. The IRGC was an irregular force that conducted hit-and-run tactics using small speedboats converted for naval attack, primarily

Swedish Boghammers and whaler-type boats. (I got into trouble with the American manufacturer of Boston Whalers for calling those Iranian speedboats Boston Whalers. In fact they were of a generic design; my intelligence people only referred to them, for convenience, as Boston Whalers. The American company most certainly was not supplying Iran with boats, and we hastily dropped the misnomer.)

The attack on the helicopter was followed with a Silkworm strike from the Iranian-held Al Faw peninsula. The Silkworm was a surface-to-surface missile with a large warhead and a self-contained radar used for terminal guidance. It was a Chinese version of a Soviet missile, sold by the People's Republic of China (PRC) to *both* the Iranians and the Iraqis. The Iraqis had also acquired an air launched version with the purchase of Badger bombers from the PRC.

Since December 1986 Iran had been firing Silkworm missiles at Kuwait, and one had struck Kuwaiti territory. On October 15, 1987, a Silkworm hit the Liberian-flagged, American-owned tanker *Sungari*, at the sea island terminal off the coast of Kuwait. It was an oil terminal, built by Kuwait Petroleum Company to load tankers for the outbound leg. The next day, the American-flagged Kuwaiti tanker *Sea Isle City* was hit by a Silkworm at the sea island terminal. The *Sea Isle City* was supposed to sail up the east coast into Minaal Ahmadi, in Kuwait, but the skipper decided to steam directly north to *take pictures* of the *Sungari* before going into port. He was at the wrong place at the wrong time. The terminal itself was struck on October 22.

This time I felt we had no choice but to respond, and the President fully agreed. I felt that it was important for us to deny the Iranian forces some measure of capability, and to impress upon them that we were not going to yield the Gulf to them. After some internal debate about the proper target, we selected the oil platform Rashadat, in the central Gulf. It was a good target for several reasons. It had been used as a staging area for small-boat and helicopter attacks against American-flagged and other shipping, and as a forward "listening post" to collect intelligence on our ship movements in the Gulf. It was not providing oil, so any people on board the platform were there for military purposes only.

Three ships were selected from the Middle East Joint Task Force to conduct the operation. After providing a warning to the platform personnel, and upon determining that the Rashadat had been abandoned, the ships shelled the platform. Over a thousand shells were expended, and the press seemed to take delight in criticizing our Navy's marksmanship. In fact, the Navy was quite accurate. What its critics did not realize, and what I had learned from officials of the oil company that had once owned the platform, was that such rigs are made from extremely strong steel girders and sheet metal. Therefore, either the artillery shell is going to hit something very hard, such as a steel girder, or it is going to hit sheet metal, which has all the stopping power of cake frosting. Unfortunately, radar cannot "see" the difference.

One effect that proved most spectacular was the failure of the "down hole," or safety cap, used to plug the oil wells on the platform. When it failed, the resulting emissions caught fire and fueled a large plume. My staff began referring to it as "the Ayatollah's eternal flame," and it was seen for miles in the Gulf for some months thereafter.

Because of the continuing Silkworm attacks against Kuwait (of which there were many from December 1986 through December 1987), the Naval Research Lab was tasked with helping the Kuwaitis develop a defense against the missiles. With Kuwaiti funding and mutual cooperation, we produced several radar reflector barges designed to present an inviting radar picture to Silkworm missiles looking for targets. The success of those barges was clearly evident on December 7, 1987, when a Silkworm missile hit one of the reflector barges instead of the Sea Island oil terminal, the intended target.

Two days later, in the Strait of Hormuz, IRGC small boats attacked and sank the *Norman Atlantic*, carrying naphtha. It was the first sinking of a merchant vessel as a result of small-boat attacks. The pictures on television were dramatic indeed. The IRGC was now often using incendiary rounds to set fires on ships. Such attacks were particularly vicious, because they targeted crew quarters for maximum injury and loss of life.

By this time we were getting very substantial help for our activities in the Gulf. All our allies benefited. We received several ships from the British, the Dutch, the Belgians, the Italians, and offers from the Germans. Also, Japan, although prevented from sending any combat vessels—its constitution provides for defensive activities only—agreed to provide a valuable and much needed navigational system to help our minesweepers as they methodically went about clearing the Gulf waters of Iranian mines. The system is now installed in Kuwait. During November 1987, in cooperation with the Saudis, Belgian, Dutch, British, Italians and French, we found nineteen Iranian mines in various locations throughout the Gulf.

To those who insisted that the Allies were not sharing enough of the burden: Each of our European friends were contributing a larger percentage of their naval forces directly to Gulf activities than was the United States, and there were more allied naval ships than American in the Gulf action. In fact, the British escorted hundreds more British-flagged and British-titled vessels than we did American-flagged ships. We also had very substantial support from Oman and Bahrain, the Saudi AWACS, as previously described; a variety of assistance from Kuwait; and access to ports in the UAE.

We were taking other approaches as well toward discouraging Iranian activity in the Gulf. By no means insignificant was Operation Staunch, our effort to stop the flow of weapons to the Ayatollah's military and terrorist forces.

We faced a very basic problem in executing this effort: how

to stop the sale or transfer of weapons to Iran from another country without revealing our sources of information. It was the old problem faced by intelligence and policy officials: The policy makers want to execute the President's objectives and use information obtained by the intelligence community; the intelligence community is concerned, and rightly, with protecting its information sources, some of which sources are human.

To resolve this very real dilemma that had emerged in our Gulf activities, we established a weekly meeting at the State Department. State had the lead in Operation Staunch because the program involved so many other countries. The new weekly regimen enabled working level officials from the policy side of the concerned agencies to meet in confidence with the intelligence community and work out emergent problems, case by delicate case. Whenever the intelligence community uncovered arms sales to Iran originating in a specific country, it provided that information to members of the Staunch committee. From there the group used the weekly meeting to find ways of approaching the country in question without divulging specific intelligence sources. Sometimes it was agreed that the information was too valuable or too tenuous to risk exposure. At any rate, this Staunch committee proved itself an excellent means for slowing the flood of weapons to Iran to a more tolerable level.

It would be most disingenuous of me to say that our own sales of arms to Iran in 1986 did not hurt that effort. Beyond my other objections was the damage I knew it would do not only to the Staunch program but also to our credibility with the moderate Arab states, particularly in the Gulf. After all, they were the nations most directly affected by the Iran-Iraq War.

And then there was the damage it did our credibility with our allies. There we were—persuading, cajoling and sometimes harassing them to forgo lucrative weapons contracts with Iran and stand fast with us in denying weapons to that vicious regime, but secretly we were selling arms to Iran.

That sad error was made public in October 1986. My Middle East staff was besieged with phone calls from local embassy officials, colleagues in government, and the media. One staff member acquired a number of pin-on buttons declaring ARMS TO IRAN—I DIDN'T KNOW. The entire supply was gone in a matter of hours. Whenever anyone came to the Pentagon to be briefed on the unhappy story, those buttons were worn by many people—who indeed had not known.

However misguided the Iran arms sale policy was, it was an aberration. We quickly tried to recoup, and salvage as much as we could of the Staunch program. Slowly our efforts began to pay off, and the effectiveness of Operation Staunch became evident in the tactics we observed the Iranians using.[8]

One of the obvious problems we faced was determining serious arms sales from the many false offers being made by individuals trying to deceive the Iranian government. In the early days of the war, a number of fake arms merchants were able to bilk the Iranians. After a few such experiences, Iran learned to demand a performance bond from companies claiming to sell weapons. We soon discovered a pattern to the traffic. Whenever we heard of a large sale of hi-tech, exotic weapons, we could be fairly confident it was someone's attempt at a sting. But if the transaction involved the standard fodder of war, such goods as artillery

---

8. For example, in the early days of the ship strikes in the Gulf we saw a number of F-4 attacks using Maverick missiles sold to the Shah. As time went on, those attacks dwindled to nothing as the shelf life on the missiles expired and made them unreliable. The Iranians switched to ship attacks using a relatively short range French AS-12 antitank missile on helicopters. But those too became unreliable, and they switched to more reliance on small-boat attacks using rockets and machine guns. The naval combatants used gunfire, and also had one success using the Standard missile in its surface-to-surface mode.

In the air-to-air battle they found the Phoenix missiles to be experiencing problems due to lack of trained people to work on them, lack of spare parts, and an inability to acquire replacement stock. At one point in the war the Iranians were test-firing Hawk (surface-to-air) missiles from aircraft, and several times tried the Standard missile in an air-to-surface role. That worked once in 1985 and then never again. The Hawk effort failed.

rounds, guns, spare parts, then it was probably "legitimate." We would track it down and try to stop it.

Another problem we discovered was the willingness of the Israeli government to permit arms merchants in Israel to supply the Ayatollah with arms. Israel claimed that by 1987–88 it was no longer selling arms to Iran, but our intelligence agencies had doubts. First, the Israeli government considered Iraq to be an incorrigible enemy, and viewed the Iran-Iraq War as a blessing. Second, Israel used the sale of arms as a means of aiding its beleaguered economy, and was always striving to increase its global market share. Finally, there was its encouragement of and involvement in the arms sale in the Iran-Contra affair. Israel officially denied involvement, probably because of the negative reaction it experienced in the United States when its part in that arms sale was first alleged. Also, Israelis might lawfully continue to deal in arms as private citizens, beyond the supervision of their government.

In the end, Operation Staunch, though weakened for several months after news of our sales to Iran became public, grew stronger and more effective: We best demonstrated our resolve when Iran became more vicious in its attacks on nonbelligerent shipping. The regained vigor of Staunch hurt Iran's ability to acquire sophisticated weapons and ammunition for the continued prosecution of its war with Iraq; and in August 1988 Iran accepted UN Security Resolution 598.

I left office on November 23, 1987, content that our forces and our friends had performed so well and would continue to do so. I left convinced that we would never bow to any future Iranian intimidations.

After my departure, our military operations continued methodically, with more and more convoys passing north and south.[9]

---

9. Except for a few incidents, the early days of 1988 were relatively calm in the Gulf; but the land war began to heat up. On February 27 Iraq hit the Rey refinery in Teheran, and on the following day Iran renewed the "war of the cities" with a Scud attack on

Finally, on August 15, 1988, the Iranians gave up. Khomeini
said it was like swallowing bitter poison; but he agreed to comply

Baghdad. On the 29th Iraq hit Teheran with a medium range missile: It was the first
time Iraq had been able to reach the Iranian capital with missiles fired from Iraq. During
the next five months their exchanges proceeded in favor of Iraq by about four to one
and greatly demoralized the Iranian population.

However, a major turning point in the war occurred during April 1988. On April 14,
the USS *Roberts*, a guided missile frigate proceeding south in the central Gulf, having
just completed a convoy north, struck a mine that injured ten and seriously damaged the
ship. Once it was determined that the ship was safe, my successor, Frank Carlucci, set
about determining the nature of the attack. The Commander of the Joint Task Force,
Rear Admiral Tony Less, concluded for two reasons that the mines had been newly laid.
The USS *Roberts* had covered the same water going north with a convoy, without incident;
and pictures of the unexploded mines were free of marine growth and other indications
of age. Armed with that information, we selected an appropriate response from a number
of options. To deprive Iran of a significant portion of its naval capability, United States
forces attacked the oil platforms in the Sassan and Siri fields on the morning of April
18. The American Government had also planned to eliminate the FFG *Sabalan*. That
ship was selected because its skipper had been singularly aggressive in attacking unarmed
merchant ships. He was frequently heard to challenge merchants on bridge-to-bridge
radio, asking them about the nature of their business, and then wishing them a "good
day" as they sailed on, apparently safe. Once they had moved off, he would attack them
with guns or missiles. Unfortunately, the *Sabalan* was in Bandar Abbas at the time the
American operation began.

During the attack on the Sassan and Siri oil platforms, IRGC small boats attacked a
United States-owned rig in a UAE oil field, a United States-flagged tug and a UK tanker.
At the time, the United States had air cover up, and sent two A-6 bombers as soon as
it discovered the attack was in progress. The A-6 bombers sank one small boat and drove
off the attackers. In the meantime, the Iranian Patrol gunboat *Joshan* challenged the three
U.S. warships in the Siri oil field. The patrol boat fired a Harpoon missile against the
force, after being told to leave or be destroyed. The American combatants responded
and sunk the *Joshan*.

Shortly thereafter a sister ship of the *Sabalan*, the Iranian frigate *Sahand*, steaming in
the vicinity of Bandar Abbas toward three United States combatants, fired on two carrier-
based A-6 Intruders. The A-6s and A-7s attacked the combatant with missiles and bombs,
and the *Sahand* was finished off by a Navy surface combatant. Almost immediately
afterward, the *Sabalan* attacked an A-6; it responded with a bomb attack, leaving the
ship crippled. With that Iran was permitted to withdraw, and the two forces disengaged.

Thus on a single day nearly half the Iranian Navy was destroyed. The other half never
emerged to fight.

By an odd coincidence, on April 16–17 Iraq launched a swift, murderous attack against
the Iranian occupying forces in Al Faw, and recaptured that peninsula. It had been held
by Iran for over a year. The successful recapture of Al Faw ended the land-based Silkworm
missile threat to Kuwait and set Iraq on a course of successful military campaigns that
led to Iran's giving up and asking for a cease-fire.

However, on July 3, 1988, in a final incident prior to the end of the Gulf war, the USS with UN Resolution 598, and to accept a cease-fire with the Iraqis. It was then that the lengthy negotiations looking for the final settlement of the Iran-Iraq war began—and then that we could answer the Navy Secretary's question.

When would we know we had won? Jim Webb had asked. We had now clearly won. We had achieved our objective of making sure that nonbelligerent and crucial commerce could and would flow freely in the open international waters of the Gulf without being subjected to mining or other attacks by Iran.

However, I am not entirely convinced that we have seen the end of the issue. Many of Iran's performances of the more recent past indicate that it has not changed its attitude toward us, and the incident in which Khomeini ordered the execution of the novelist Salman Rushdie merely reinforces that belief. I have met many Muslims both on a professional and personal level, and my understanding of Islam as they have explained it to me bears no resemblance to the "religion" practiced by the late Ayatollah Khomeini. His megalomania and fanaticism would not permit him to change. He was like his ship's captain who "cleared" innocent merchant ships, and then fired on them.

It is not unlikely that Khomeini was trying to use the UN truce to sell oil and replenish his weapons stores so that he could

---

Vincennes, the most modern guided missile cruiser in the fleet, equipped with our Aegis system, engaged and shot down an Iranian civilian airlines plane enroute from Bandar Abbas to Dubai. It was a tragic accident.

Much has been made in the press of the Aegis's "inability to determine the size of the radar target" by measuring radar cross sections. But that function had never been the purpose of that radar; nor is it a particularly useful capability. Too many factors can present false data when the need is to determine aircraft size. The purpose of the Aegis system is primarily detection and tracking in a combat environment. That, it does very well indeed.

The tragic event underscores the risk that Iran was running by trying to conduct business as usual when it was engaged in hostile activities throughout the Gulf.

In this particular incident, its small boats were engaged in a running fight with our naval ships even as its civilian aircraft was overflying our warships. Captain Will Rogers of the *Vincennes* made efforts to identify the aircraft and only fired when warnings went unheeded. In my view, he was fully justified in his actions.

---

resume his fight with Iraq. The only way he was discouraged was by our maintaining the support of our Gulf friends.

We have been successful to date, but we must continue to be vigilant. It sadly seems clear in December 1989 that the new leadership in Iran required by Khomeini's death will not change anything. Thus far the only new factor is that Gorbachev has seized the opportunity to expand the strategic reach of the USSR by trying to curry favor with Iran's Speaker Hashemi Rafsanjani, since "elected" President.

The Gulf escort action and our role in it seems to me to be another proud chapter in the history of our military.

We worked with many of our allies in a well-conducted activity in an area of high strategic importance. We kept the Soviets out, despite their historic ambition for a larger role and a port in the Gulf region. In so doing we reconfirmed our own forty year role in the Gulf.

We helped our Gulf Arab friends to survive, and to see the possibility of a brighter future with Khomeini dead and the war over. Most important of all, we demonstrated to our Arab friends that they could indeed rely on a strong, resolute and effective America.

At the end of the operation, when we were able to reduce substantially the number of our naval vessels in the Gulf, the waves of criticism that had rolled over the operation since it began were stilled. We instead heard occasional words of praise from members of Congress; and even more remarkably, a favorable editorial or two appeared.

We learned a most valuable lesson from all this. If after careful consideration, it is determined that a particular course of action must be followed to safeguard our present and future security, then it is vital that we follow that course of action coolly and resolutely, and not be deterred or swayed by criticism, no matter how intense or how fevered, nor by setbacks, no matter how severe they may appear.

In many ways this was the classic battle between the legislative and executive branches of our government. The President had to decide whether to agree to Kuwait's plea for protection of its ships; and once having agreed, then the President had to keep his commitments to help, and keep the Gulf open for nonbelligerent commerce despite mounting congressional opposition and continued attempts to fetter the President and reverse his decisions. But the President stood firm, our troops performed magnificently, our Allies joined in the effort and gave vital support, the Congress finally gave up trying to block the President, and we accomplished everything we set out to do.

The principal difference between this operation and some of the others we had to engage in during my years at the Pentagon, such as Libya and Grenada, was that the Gulf operation lasted for many months. That meant that it required more patience, more firmness, and more strength—all of which our service men and women, and our President, contributed in full measure. Recalling the long weeks and months of superb service that our forces gave, I was (somewhat sardonically, I fear) amused by one particular manifestation, post-Grenada, of faint praise: "Well, anything we can do quickly, such as Libya and Grenada, we do reasonably well, but we have no staying power."

We had enough staying power in the Gulf to win, and to insure that "Freedom of the Seas" is more than a slogan.

CONCLUSION

*T*he fight for peace is never over, unlike some of the wars in which we have engaged. Certainly we will have to fight another of those wars in the future, unless we keep ourselves strong, and unless we really are willing to fight for peace in peacetime.

But maintaining that readiness and that resolve is difficult, and is widely viewed as an unpopular and a largely unrewarding task. It involves persuading people in freedom-loving democracies that they should follow a course instinctively repugnant to them. It also requires large and continuous investments to keep our military strong, modern and ready, so that no country, or combination of countries, can ever feel they can make a successful attack upon us.

Clearly, no nation is strong enough alone to keep its own freedom. Every nation requires alliances, friendships or associations of one kind or another with other countries who share its goals and ideals. That truth certainly applies to the United States. So we must make major efforts to secure those alliances, and to keep strong friendships with many nations, some of which may not always follow precisely the path that we would wish them to follow.

Keeping our peace also requires that we fight the tendency to believe what we want to believe, on the basis of some hopeful or soothing rhetoric, and that we be willing not to follow the popular path of reducing our military investment simply because the world's strategic climate temporarily may appear to be better.

We must never forget that Mr. Gorbachev, for example, even assuming he is sincere and trustworthy, could have a very limited term of political leadership if he continues to displease the Soviet military or the majority of the Soviet leadership. We should recall that another Soviet General Secretary, Mr. Khrushchev, preached and tried many of the same reforms and was ousted. Khrushchev was deposed not because of his personal problems and his boorish behavior, but because the Soviet leadership felt it could not tolerate changes of the same kind Mr. Gorbachev is now talking about and for which advocacy he is securing wide public support all over the world.

Our survival will ever depend upon how much importance we attach to peace and to our freedoms, and upon whether, in the interest of keeping them, we are willing to submerge those instincts that Alexis de Tocqueville summarized more than one hundred fifty years ago.

> The ever-increasing numbers of men of property who are lovers of peace, the growth of personal wealth which war so rapidly consumes, the mildness of manners, the gentleness of heart, those tendencies to pity which are produced by the equality of conditions, that coolness of understanding which renders men comparatively insensible to the

violent and poetical excitement of arms, all of these causes
concur to quench the military spirit [in a democracy].[1]

We need not change our personality as a nation, nor any of
the qualities that make democracy so enormously valuable and
the people who live in a democracy the most fortunate on the
earth. But we must understand how critically important it is, if
we want to keep our democracy, our peace, and our freedom,
that we be willing to make sacrifices—sacrifices often difficult,
expensive, and unpopular. Wise and resolute investment in our
military strength is not only quite consistent with all of the blessings of democracy; it is the only course that will let us keep our
democracy, our peace and our freedom.

If we want peace, we must be willing and able to fight for it.

---

1. Alexis de Tocqueville, *Democracy in America*, trans. Henry Reeve (New York: Vintage,
1945), p. 279.

AFTERMATH

*T*he last event chronicled in *Fighting for Peace* is the successful action we took in the Persian Gulf, culminating in the surrender of the Iranians and their admission on July 20, 1989, that they must "swallow the bitter poisoned cup of defeat." So much has happened since then that my publisher, quite properly, suggested an epilogue, or coda, would be in order for this paperback edition.

In a very real sense, however, the book itself could be viewed as the Prologue, and this brief new chapter, as the *real* story.

The pace and dynamism of events since 1989 seem likely to continue to the point that virtually every attempt to record them are apt to be out of date the next week.

This Aftermath will attempt to reflect some of that pace and dynamism, and relate it to the events and policies chronicled in the earlier chapters.

I should say at the outset that having left office in November 1987, I had no personal involvement in these exciting and momentous events. I did serve for a year or so on the President's Foreign Intelligence Advisory Board and on the National Economic Commission, both by appointment of President Reagan. The full responsibility for defense and day-to-day activities were held and run by my good friends Frank Carlucci and Colin Powell[1] until the inauguration of President Bush.

---

1. My extremely high estimate of both of these skilled leaders is in the book. A further

Therefore the original plan of the book, that is, writing of the major security actions of my seven years as Defense Secretary as a personal narrative, necessarily has to be changed for this Aftermath.

It seems to me the best way to continue the history is to summarize, briefly and chronologically, the breathtaking changes in Eastern Europe and how those nations began the difficult process of liberating themselves after more than four decades of harsh Soviet domination and repression.

Simultaneously, other equally exciting events were happening elsewhere in the world. Japan, China, Taiwan, Nicaragua, Panama, and of course the eternal disputes and hatreds of the Middle East, all posed challenges and opportunities, and required difficult and decisive decisions during this whole period.

The continued desire of the Congress to increase domestic spending and cut defenses, and the success of some of the President's men in persuading him to accept tax increases, despite his long-stated opposition to those increases, ensured that uncertainties and instability would also be a part of our domestic policy.

But now to the events that began shortly after *Fighting for Peace* ended in August of 1988:

On October 1, 1988, Mikhail Gorbachev was named President of the Supreme Soviet of the USSR succeeding Andrei Gromyko. The Supreme Soviet also made several other changes interpreted as consolidating Gorbachev's hold. This might well be called the high-water mark of Gorbachev's power. His great enemy, Boris Yeltsin, was removed from the Politburo in February and had previously lost his post as head of the Communist party in Moscow because he had criticized the slow pace of Gorbachev's reforms.

In mid-October the Czechoslovakian Cabinet was replaced because it too wanted more reform faster.

estimate of Colin, which I wrote as a column for *Forbes* magazine on January 22, 1990, appears as an appendix to this Aftermath (see page 460).

But by November the pendulum began its swing in the opposite direction. Estonia, one of the three Baltic nations whose annexation by the Soviets we had never recognized, declared it could and would ignore any Soviet law it felt infringed on Estonia's authority. Later that month, Hungary appointed a new prime minister and economic minister who advocated economic "change."

Earlier Gorbachev had moved tentatively toward policies that sounded more like capitalism than Marxism, but this proposed "restructuring" was too tentative for many, as was his glasnost, or openness, which permitted some, but not much, public dissent from the increasingly murky Soviet party line.

But there was nothing tentative about the pace of change in 1989. In January, Hungary allowed pluralistic political parties and open demonstrations, and Estonia made its language the official language, as did Lithuania.

In February, the Communist government of Czechoslovakia jailed a dissident named Vaclav Havel and others for participating in rallies opposed to the Communist regime. In March, the Soviet people, in the first national election since 1917, overwhelmingly defeated several high-ranking official Communist candidates, and Boris Yeltsin, Gorbachev's leading opponent, won by a landslide.

In April at least twenty were killed in Tbilisi, Georgia, when Gorbachev's government suppressed peaceful unarmed demonstrations by using bullets and poison gas.

In May, martial law was imposed in Beijing, China, because of the continuing student hunger strike in Tiananmen Square; and Gorbachev was elected to the new post of President of the Soviet Union by his (largely handpicked) Congress of the Peoples Deputies. This group also denied Yeltsin a place on the Supreme Soviet, but later recanted when there was a public outcry.

In June, watched by millions on television, China's military crushed the student demonstrations in Tiananmen Square using tanks and guns. In July Soviet miners went out on strike in Siberia and the Ukraine.

In August Lithuania declared its independence from the USSR, and Poland formally named a Solidarity leader, Tadeusz Mazowiecki, Prime Minister.

In September the most dramatic events of the decade began when East Germans poured into Hungary, which allowed them to stay or to seek the promise of capitalism and a better life in West Germany.

In October President Manuel Noriega of Panama survived a coup. Erich Honecker, Communist leader of East Germany for eighteen years, was ousted, and over 300,000 East Germans demonstrated for democracy. In November the East German government resigned, all restrictions on travel were lifted, and crowds surged through the Berlin Wall day and night, headed for the West and freedom. Also that month, Gorbachev began his vacillations, which continue to this day: He announced that there would be no private ownership of property or competing political parties allowed. The country was not ready for this, he said. A little over a week later, the Czechoslovakian government resigned after huge demonstrations continued for eight days, demanding democracy. Next, Hungarians voted in their first free election in 42 years, and the Soviets denounced Lithuanian statements of independence. Harsh Soviet measures of repression began: Tanks were used to intimidate the Lithuanian parliament, and the Soviets broke promises of oil and energy shipments to Lithuania. These Soviet attempts failed.

December brought East Germany's decision to have free elections, Havel's election to President of Czechoslovakia, and the overthrow and execution of Nicolae Ceauşescu in Romania. East Germany ceased to be a separate Communist nation, and the newly unified Germany entered the new decade with a basically conservative government under Chancellor Helmut Kohl. On December 20 we responded to Noriega's unilateral declaration of war against the U.S. by sending troops into Panama. By the end of the year Noriega was out and shortly thereafter our combat troops left Panama, their mission accomplished.

* * *

Meanwhile, economic conditions in the USSR worsened every day. While Gorbachev promised troop and military reductions, the Soviets continued development of newer and better nuclear systems, and they continued work on their own strategic defense systems.

In 1990 the opposition to Gorbachev in the Soviet Union deepened almost in inverse ratio to the adulation he received abroad. This reached a climax in November when he was both awarded the Nobel Peace Prize and greeted by stony silence from his own Soviet parliament after a seventy-minute defense of his policies. These policies had become ever more confused as time went on. He refused to adopt the major and drastic economic shifts to market economics and capitalism proposed by his own appointee, Dr. Stanislav Shatalin, as a remedy for the desperate condition of the Soviet economy. Boris Yeltsin had no such hesitancy. He had become head of the Russian Republic, largest of the fifteen Soviet Socialist republics, and had been turning it into a separate and sovereign country as quickly as possible. Having firmly and unequivocally rejected Communism and Socialist economics, Yeltsin adopted the Shatalin plan, and in the 500 days allowed by that proposal, he plans to move a long way toward capitalism. Gorbachev flatly refused to do this. He not only insisted that he would not renounce Communism and Socialist economics, but in fact repeatedly stated his support for both and his determination not to let any of the fifteen Soviet republics experience the freedoms he had earlier promised them and Eastern Europe.

In keeping with his tactics of trying to please all sides, he tried to merge the Shatalin plan with a plan that would keep power for himself and his central government. Yeltsin contemptuously called that an attempt to "mate a hedgehog with a snake."

Gorbachev's continued attempts to keep and extend the power of the central government are quite inconsistent with the wishes of the majority of the people of the fifteen republics and certainly the Baltic nations, which have repeatedly shown that they want their own freedom and their own sovereignty. Indeed the spirit of revolt and the demands for independence and sovereignty are growing daily in each of the fifteen republics. The USSR central government and Gorbachev appear to be more irrelevant as time goes on, and the shortages, rationing, food lines and general misery of the majority of Soviets increased. Gorbachev still insists that he will not support anything that eliminates Communism or Socialist economics. And he has now taken from his largely self-appointed Supreme Soviet the standard powers possessed by dictators everywhere, to rule by directives, not laws. His first use of these directives was to insist that the dissident and hungry republics continue to send their fruit and produce to Moscow, and to stop tearing down statues of Lenin.

He is also desperately seeking loans, credit and economic help of all kinds from Germany, France, ourselves, and anyone who will listen. In late November 1990, Gorbachev proposed yet another plan keeping for himself as President all of the real power over the military, the police and the KGB, and, probably, foreign policy, and "sharing" what is left with a new Federation Council of the leaders of the fifteen republics. "Presidential Representatives" (the new political commissars) will enforce the President's orders. The desperate shortages of food are to be addressed "later." The three Baltic republics and Georgia promptly announced that they would not join in this scheme, which they said was "only to decorate an all-powerful presidency." Boris Yeltsin announced that the Russian Republic, the largest and most powerful in the USSR, also rejected the plan, saying it was simply a proposal to "strengthen the center," meaning the Central Soviet government and Gorbachev himself.

Not surprisingly all of this has caused Gorbachev's other large group of opponents, the military and the high-ranking bureaucracy, the so-called Nomenclatura, to demand a return to the days of their happier memories, the days of Stalinism. Gorbachev is acceding to their demands as he adds to the power of the KGB.

Indeed, at the end of January he followed, as the *New York Times* correspondent Serge Schmemann said, "the bloody crackdown in the Baltic republics with the chilling announcement that armed soldiers will patrol the street with the police and with a decree authorizing the KGB to search any business, ostensibly to uncover economic crimes that deprive the citizenry of goods." He also restored censorship of the Soviet national television and, according to the *Wall Street Journal*, "shelved all efforts to introduce market forces into the economy." The "economic crimes" that the KGB now has complete freedom to stamp out take us most of the way back to the era of Stalinist totalitarian rule.

Underlining all of this are the increasingly harsh measures he is taking to forbid the Baltic republics from exercising the freedom of choice he told everyone (when he was seeking political and economic favors from the West) they would have.

With the continuing political disintegration of the Soviet Union, contributing to bad morale in the Soviet military, desertions, and draft dodging, and the virtual disintegration of the Warsaw Pact, many in our Congress and elsewhere have concluded that the Soviet Union no longer presents a military threat to the United States. From this they argue that we can make drastic cuts in our defense investment, including deep cutbacks in our commitments to NATO, and apply the "savings" to more politically popular domestic programs. Sadly, until the brutal events of January, many seemed to ignore the possibility that the current crumbling of the Soviet Union could end in a full return to a Stalinist dictatorship, with their military again being used as instruments to try to secure Soviet foreign policy goals of world domination by intimidation and terror.

The theory that we no longer need to be concerned with maintaining a strong defense because there are no more threats to freedom was rudely exploded on August 2, 1990, when Saddam Hussein, one of the world's most brutal and aggressive threats to peace, suddenly invaded Kuwait and began to carry out the rest of his plans to conquer Saudi Arabia and the Emirates, and thereby gain control of about 70 percent of the world's known oil reserves.

Fortunately for the world, the United States had the military capabilities, the leadership, and the will to block this aggression and to organize a very powerful coalition of Arab, Asian, and European nations fully capable of acting with the United States to destroy Saddam Hussein.

President Bush deserves the utmost praise for his immediate and decisive actions, which blocked Saddam Hussein's planned advance and saved both Saudi Arabia and the Emirates. That was the first objective, but the major, long-range goal is to establish the rule of law on a global basis—to make it unmistakably clear that aggression and the use of brute force will not be tolerated nor allowed to succeed.

As I write, the outcome is not yet decided. What is clear is that the remarkable coalition of nations and the United Nations have imposed a very effective set of economic sanctions against Iraq, enforced by an air and sea blockade. It became increasingly apparent, however, that because the blockade specifically excluded foods and medicines, Saddam Hussein's iron grip on the country enabled him to interpret these vital exceptions, originally designed for children, as he wished and to channel whatever he could get to his military. The sanctions could not, in any reasonable time, force Saddam Hussein out of Kuwait. It was also apparent that his continued occupancy of Kuwait was causing increasing hardships and misery not only to Kuwaiti citizens but to thousands of workers and refugees who fled Kuwait.

The President tried every possible diplomatic move. But when Saddam Hussein forbade his representative even to receive the President's letter, I concluded, as I am sure many others who had hoped that sanctions could work to achieve our goals, that the force authorized by virtually unanimous UN resolutions, and later by our Congress in a close but decisive vote, must be exercised. On January 16, the Allied forces unleashed air strikes of unparalleled intensity against Iraq, and made it clear that these attacks would continue and would be followed by ground action, which will ultimately be necessary to free Kuwait.

In addition to the strength of our military action, the sanctions and boycott are continuing and are doing great harm to Iraq, a nation that imports about 75 to 80 percent of its food and nearly 100 percent of a vast number of other items needed for its war machine. There is also a substantial and justified unhappiness within Iraq with the brutal minority Ba'ath party rule in Iraq. This unhappiness, particularly among the Iraqi military, might well lead to the overthrow of Saddam Hussein and his replacement with a government that would recognize that it neither can nor should try to stand alone against the major nations of the world, to keep a country it has stolen.

There are, however, some danger signs primarily arising from the continued capability of the Soviet Union to cause mischief.

It has become so fashionable to praise Gorbachev and to accept the conventional wisdom that we must do everything we can to keep him in power, that we are prone to ignore the possibility that he just might not be either the freedom-loving friend of the West or our continued strong supporter in the Gulf. Thus far the principal Soviet contribution to our actions in the Gulf has been not to oppose the UN's actions and our strong moves against Iraq's aggression. The great bulk of Iraqi weapons, including the Scud missiles, came from the Soviet Union, and their instructors and advisers are still in Iraq. It is possible that even the Soviet verbal support of what we are doing is very fragile. When outrage in our public opinion caused by Gorbachev's brutal moves in the Baltics became apparent and we postponed the February summit, in something less than the biting terms called for by Gorbachev's actions, their new Foreign Minister, Aleksandr Bessmertnykh, immediately began expressing doubts as to our conduct of the war and a "fear" that we might plan to do more than simply expel Saddam Hussein from Kuwait, thus "exceeding" the UN mandate.

It is quite apparent that whatever the words of the UN resolutions, their intent is clear: Saddam Hussein must not only be expelled from Kuwait and the legitimate Al Sabah government restored, but Iraq cannot be left with a military capability and a leadership that could enable them to reinvade Kuwait a few weeks after they were expelled. That is one danger. Another is that America's patience could wear thin. Also, other nations may be unwilling to maintain their forces for very long, and voices will undoubtedly be raised urging that more food and medicine be allowed to enter Iraq. That would gravely weaken effective sanctions. All of this could result in a desire to seek or accept an unworthy compromise designed to "let Saddam Hussein save face," or let him keep "half of Kuwait," or similar "solutions."

But at the end of January 1991, there is very real reason to hope that we and our allies can achieve our objectives before too much longer, although the difficulties of the military task should never be underestimated.

In any event, we have already accomplished far more than anyone who watched the unpunished and similarly brutal aggression by the Soviet Union against Afghanistan in 1979 could have guessed. The reason for the difference is clear. In the 1980s we regained both the military capability and the resolve to use it if necessary, which we lacked in 1979.

Another major event at the end of 1990 that would have seemed impossible at the date I completed *Fighting for Peace* was the signing of the conventional arms reduction treaty, which many hailed as marking the end of the Cold War. The Soviets agreed to major asymmetrical reductions of their huge conventional arsenals in Eastern Europe, bringing them down to NATO arsenal levels in the West. It may be viewed as churlish to point out that shortly before the treaty was signed the Soviets moved some 20,000 of their newest tanks and 30,000 artillery pieces east of the Urals so that they would not be caught by the treaty limitations. I mention it only to show it could be dangerously naive to believe that the signing of the treaty eliminates the need for a continued strong U.S. military capability. In any event, the treaty still gives the Soviets until 1994 to make the required reductions and it does not require reductions in troop levels.

The postponed February summit also delays the signing of a Strategic Forces Treaty. With the current chaotic situation in the Soviet Union, however, any treaty signed by their disintegrating central government would be of doubtful value. Indeed the critical question is not whether the central government would keep any promises it made, but who in fact would control the Soviet military in the coming months. That alone should be enough, quite independent of anything that happens in the Gulf, to persuade America and the freedom-loving nations to keep their military strong and ready.

I am sure this viewpoint will be regarded as a tiresome, boring reiteration of old themes, outmoded by new conditions. But before we dismiss it, we might want to recall that it was when and because we regained our military in the 1980s, after our disastrous decade of neglect in the seventies, that all the happy events and portents of the nineties became possible. That is why I regard much of the past, as recorded in *Fighting for Peace*, to be but a prologue for a bright future.

It seems entirely appropriate and just to pay tribute to another gallant fighter for freedom and peace—Margaret Thatcher, who resigned as Prime Minister of the United Kingdom on Thanksgiving Day 1990. She always stood with America, and her relationship with me and with President Reagan was a vital part of our newly regained strength. I am proud to count her as a personal friend. Working with her was a delight and I hope she will return soon to the world stage. Characteristically, her last act as Prime Minister was to add another 12,000 British troops to the large contingent she had previously sent to support us in the Gulf.

Advocates of peace at any price, deep cuts in defense appropriations, and compromises as a first and last resort will dispute this. They believe that all the welcome changes in Eastern Europe occurred because of Mr. Gorbachev. My own view is that he is not all that dissimilar to his predecessors, but that he has used different and far more sophisticated and clever tactics. I believe he recognized that with our regained military strength he could no longer use the old tactics of threats and attempts to intimidate, based on their vast conventional military capabilities, and their very modern, lethal and accurate nuclear weapons. He recognized that he would have to try to enlist the support of the West to help him out of the disasters into which Communism and Socialist economics had led his country. To win the West over he saw that he would have to demonstrate to them that he had changed, and that the Soviet Union no longer presented a threat. That required both soothing rhetoric and the granting of some freedoms that the West favored.

The rhetoric that he employed greatly impressed the Western media and some officials, but my own feeling is that the few freedoms he granted unleashed forces—generated by forty years of hated Communist domination in Eastern Europe and the USSR itself—that were too strong for Gorbachev or anyone to control. Now in his desire to retain power, he has abandoned the forces he helped unleash and has returned to the views of his earlier years when he loyally served the Communist dictatorship with its implacable opposition to the West, and to peace and freedom.

From all of this I conclude that the lessons I attempted to point out in *Fighting for Peace* were and are still valid, that we should continue to base our policies on a determined, never-ending search for peace, and that this quest will elude us unless we keep strong militarily and are ready and willing to fight for peace. If we are, we can and will achieve peace.

Mt. Desert, Maine
January 31, 1991

APPENDIX

Text of Remarks by Secretary of Defense
Caspar W. Weinberger
to the National Press Club
— November 28, 1984 —

"THE USES OF MILITARY POWER"

Thank you for inviting me to be here today with the members of the National Press Club, a group most important to our national security. I say that because a major point I intend to make in my remarks today is that the single-most critical element of a successful democracy is a strong consensus of support and agreement for our basic purposes. Policies formed without a clear understanding of what we hope to achieve will never work. And you help to build that understanding among our citizens.

Of all the many policies our citizens deserve—and need—to understand, none is so important as those related to our topic today—the uses of military power. Deterrence will work only if the Soviets understand our firm commitment to keeping the peace . . . and only from a well-informed public can we expect to have that national will and commitment.

So today, I want to discuss with you perhaps the most important question concerning keeping the peace. Under what circumstances, and by what means, does a great democracy such as ours reach the painful decision that the use of military force is necessary to protect our interests or to carry out our national policy?

National power has many components, some tangible—like economic wealth, technical preeminence. Other components are intangible—such as moral force, or strong national will. Military forces, when they are strong and ready and modern, are a credible—and tangible—addition to a nation's power. When both the intangible national will and those forces are forged into one instrument, national power becomes effective.

In today's world, the line between peace and war is less clearly drawn than at any time in our history. When George Washington, in his farewell address, warned us, as a new democracy, to avoid foreign entanglements, Europe then lay 2–3 months by sea over the horizon. The United States was protected by the width of the oceans. Now in this nuclear age, we measure time in minutes rather than months.

Aware of the consequences of any misstep, yet convinced of the precious worth of the freedom we enjoy, we seek to avoid conflict, while maintaining strong defenses. Our policy has always been to work hard for peace, but to be prepared if war comes. Yet, so blurred have the lines become between open conflict and half-hidden hostile acts that we cannot confidently predict where, or when, or how, or from what direction aggression may arrive. We must be prepared, at any moment, to meet threats ranging in intensity from isolated terrorist acts, to guerrilla action, to full-scale military confrontation.

Alexander Hamilton, writing in the *Federalist Papers*, said that "it is impossible to foresee or define the extent and variety of national exigencies, or the correspondent extent and variety of the means which may be necessary to satisfy them." If it was true then, how much more true it is today, when we must remain ready to consider the means to meet such serious indirect challenges to the peace as proxy wars and individual terrorist action. And how much more important is it now, considering the consequences of failing to deter conflict at the lowest level possible. While the use of military force to defend territory has never been questioned when a democracy has been attacked and its very survival threatened, most democracies have rejected the unilateral aggressive use of force to invade, conquer or subjugate other nations. The extent to which the use of force *is* acceptable remains unresolved for the host of other situations which fall between these extremes of defensive and aggressive use of force.

We find ourselves, then, face to face with a modern paradox: The most likely challenge to the peace—the gray area conflicts—are precisely the most difficult challenges to which a democracy must respond. Yet, while the source and nature of today's challenges are uncertain, our response must be clear and understandable. Unless we are certain that force is essential, we run the risk of inadequate national will to apply the resources needed.

Because we face a spectrum of threats—from covert aggression, terrorism, and subversion, to overt intimidation, to use of brute force—choosing the appropriate level of our response is difficult. Flexible response does not mean just any response is appropriate. But once a decision to employ some degree of force has been made, and the purpose clarified, our government must have the clear mandate to carry out, and continue to carry out, that decision until the purpose has been achieved. That, too, has been difficult to accomplish.

The issue of which branch of government has authority to define that mandate and make decisions on using force is now being strongly contended. Beginning in the 1970s Congress demanded, and assumed, a far more active role in the making of foreign policy and in the decision-making process for the employment of military forces abroad than had been thought appropriate and practical before. As a result, the centrality of decision-making authority in the executive branch has been compromised by the legislative branch to an extent that actively interferes with that process. At the same time, there has not been a corresponding acceptance of responsibility by Congress for the outcome of decisions concerning the employment of military forces.

Yet the outcome of decisions on whether—and when—and to what degree—to use combat forces abroad has never been more *important* than it is today. While we do not seek to deter or settle all the world's conflicts, we must recognize that, as a major power, our responsibilities and interests are now of such scope that there are few troubled areas we can afford to ignore. So we must be prepared to deal with a range of possibilities, a spectrum of crises, from local insurgency to global conflict. We prefer, of course, to *limit* any conflict in its early stages, to contain and control it—but to do that our military forces must be deployed in a *timely* manner, and be fully supported and prepared *before* they are engaged, because many of those difficult decisions must be made extremely quickly.

Some on the national scene think they can always avoid making tough decisions. Some reject entirely the question of whether any force can ever be used abroad. They want to avoid grappling with a complex issue because, despite clever rhetoric disguising their purpose, these people are in fact advocating a return to post-World War I isolationism. While they may maintain in principle that military force has a role in foreign policy, they are never willing to name the circumstance or the place where it would apply.

On the other side, some theorists argue that military force can be brought to bear in any crisis. Some of these proponents of force are eager to advocate its use even in limited amounts simply because they believe that if there are American forces of *any* size present they will somehow solve the problem.

Neither of these two extremes offers us any lasting or satisfactory solutions. The first—undue reserve—would lead us ultimately to withdraw from international events that require free nations to defend their interests from the aggressive use of force. We would be abdicating our responsibilities as the leader of the free world—responsibilities more or less thrust upon us in the aftermath of World War II—a war incidentally that isolationism did nothing to deter. These are responsibilities we must fulfill unless we desire the Soviet Union to keep expanding its influence unchecked throughout the world. In an international system based on mutual interdependence among nations, and alliances between friends, stark isolationism quickly would lead to a far more dangerous situation for the United States: We would be without allies and faced by many hostile or indifferent nations.

The second alternative—employing our forces almost indiscriminately and as a regular and customary part of our diplomatic efforts—would surely plunge us headlong into the sort of domestic turmoil we experienced during the Vietnam War, without accomplishing the goal for which we committed our forces. Such policies might very well tear at the fabric of our society, endangering the *single*-most critical element of a successful democracy: *a strong consensus of support and agreement for our basic purposes.*

Policies formed without a clear understanding of what we hope to achieve would also earn us the scorn of our troops, who would have an understandable opposition to being *used*—in every sense of the word—casually and without intent to support them fully. Ultimately this course would reduce their morale and their effectiveness for engagements we *must* win. And if the military were to distrust its civilian leadership, recruitment would fall off and I fear an end to the all-volunteer system would be upon us, requiring a return to a draft, sowing the seeds of riot and discontent that so wracked the country in the '60s.

We have now restored high morale and pride in the uniform

throughout the services. The all-volunteer system is working spectacularly well. Are we willing to forfeit what we have fought so hard to regain?

In maintaining our progress in strengthening America's military deterrent, we face difficult challenges. For we have entered an era where the dividing lines between peace and war are less clearly drawn, the identity of the foe is much less clear. In World Wars I and II, we not only knew who our enemies were, but we shared a clear sense of *why* the principles espoused by our enemies were unworthy.

Since these two wars threatened our very survival as a free nation and the survival of our allies, they were total wars, involving every aspect of our society. All our means of production, all our resources were devoted to winning. Our policies had the unqualified support of the great majority of our people. Indeed, World Wars I and II ended with the unconditional surrender of our enemies . . . the only acceptable ending when the alternative was the loss of our freedom.

But in the aftermath of the Second World War, we encountered a more subtle form of warfare—warfare in which, more often than not, the face of the enemy was masked. Territorial expansionism could be carried out indirectly by proxy powers, using surrogate forces aided and advised from afar. Some conflicts occurred under the name of "national liberation," but far more frequently ideology or religion provided the spark to the tinder.

Our adversaries can also take advantage of our open society, and our freedom of speech and opinion to use alarming rhetoric and disinformation to divide and disrupt our unity of purpose. While they would never dare to allow such freedoms to their own people, they are quick to exploit ours by conducting simultaneous military and propaganda campaigns to achieve their ends.

They realize that if they can divide our national will at home, it will not be necessary to defeat our forces abroad. So by presenting issues in bellicose terms, they aim to intimidate Western leaders and citizens, encouraging us to adopt conciliatory positions to their advantage. Meanwhile *they* remain sheltered from the force of public opinion in their countries, because public opinion there is simply prohibited and does not exist.

Our freedom presents both a challenge and an opportunity. It is true that until democratic nations have the support of the people, they are inevitably at a disadvantage in a conflict. But when they *do* have that support they cannot be defeated. For democracies have the power to send a compelling message to friend and foe alike by the vote of their citizens. And the American people have sent such a signal by re-electing a strong chief executive. They know that President Reagan is willing to accept the responsibility for his actions and is able to lead us through these complex times by insisting that we regain *both* our military and our economic strength.

In today's world where minutes count, such decisive leadership is more important than ever before. Regardless of whether conflicts are limited, or threats are ill-defined, we *must* be capable of quickly determining that the threats and conflicts either *do* or *do not* affect the vital interests of the United States and our allies . . . and then responding appropriately.

Those threats may not entail an immediate, direct attack on our territory, and our response may not necessarily require the immediate or direct defense of our homeland. But when our vital national interests and those of our allies *are* at stake, we cannot ignore our safety, or forsake our allies.

At the same time, recent history has proven that we cannot assume unilaterally the role of the world's defender. We have learned that there are limits to how much of our spirit and blood and treasure we can afford to forfeit in meeting our responsibility to keep peace and freedom. So while we may and should offer substantial amounts of economic and military assistance to our allies in their time of need, and help them maintain forces to deter attacks against them—usually we cannot substitute our troops or our will for theirs.

We should only engage *our* troops if we must do so as a matter of our *own* vital national interest. We cannot assume for other sovereign nations the responsibility to defend *their* territory—without their strong invitation—when our own freedom is not threatened.

On the other hand, there have been recent cases where the United States has seen the need to join forces with other nations to try to preserve the peace by helping with negotiations, and by separating warring parties, and thus enabling those warring nations to withdraw from hostilities safely. In the Middle East, which has been torn by conflict for millennia, we have sent our troops in recent years both to the Sinai and to Lebanon, for just such a peacekeeping mission. But we did not configure or equip those forces for combat—they were armed only for their self-defense. Their mission required them to be—and to be recognized as—peacekeepers. We knew that if conditions deteriorated so they were in danger, or if because of the actions of the warring nations, their peace keeping mission could not be realized, then it would be necessary either to add sufficiently to the number and arms of our troops—in short to equip them for combat . . . or to withdraw them. And so in Lebanon, when we faced just such a choice, because the warring nations did not enter into withdrawal or peace agreements, the President properly withdrew forces equipped only for peacekeeping.

In those cases where our national interests require us to commit combat forces, we must never let there be doubt of our resolution. When it is necessary for our troops to be committed to combat, we *must* commit them, in sufficient numbers and we *must* support them, as effectively and resolutely as our strength permits. When we commit our troops to combat we must do so with the sole object of winning.

Once it is clear our troops are required, because our vital interests are at stake, then we must have the firm national resolve to commit every ounce of strength necessary to win the fight to achieve our objectives. In Grenada we did just that.

Just as clearly, there are other situations where United States combat forces should *not* be used. I believe the postwar period has taught us several lessons, and from them I have developed *six* major tests to be applied when we are weighing the use of U.S. combat forces abroad. Let me now share them with you:

(1) *First*, the United States should not commit forces to *combat* overseas unless the particular engagement or occasion is deemed vital to our national interest or that of our allies. That emphatically does not mean that we should *declare* beforehand, as we did with Korea in 1950, that a particular area is outside our strategic perimeter.

(2) *Second*, if we decide it *is* necessary to put *combat* troops into a given situation, we should do so wholeheartedly, and with the clear intention of winning. If we are *un*willing to commit the forces or resources necessary to achieve our objectives, we should not commit them at all. Of course if the particular situation requires only limited force to win our objectives, then we should not hesitate to commit forces sized accordingly. When Hitler broke treaties and remilitarized the Rhineland, small combat forces then could perhaps have prevented the holocaust of World War II.

(3) *Third*, if we *do* decide to commit forces to combat overseas, we should have clearly defined political and military objectives. And we should know precisely how our forces can accomplish those clearly defined objectives. And we should have and send the forces needed to do just that. As Clausewitz wrote, "No one starts a war—or rather, no one in his senses ought to do so—without first being clear in his mind what he intends to achieve by that war, and how he intends to conduct it."

War may be different today than in Clausewitz's time, but the need for well-defined objectives and a consistent strategy is still essential. If we determine that a combat mission has become necessary for our vital national interests, then we must send forces capable to do the job—and not assign a combat mission to a force configured for peacekeeping.

(4) *Fourth*, the relationship between our objectives and the forces we have committed—their size, composition and disposition—must be continually reassessed and adjusted if necessary. Conditions and objectives invariably change during the course of a conflict. When they do change, then so must our combat requirements. We must continuously keep as a beacon light before us the basic questions: *"Is this conflict in our national interest?"* "Does our national interest require us to fight, to use force of arms?" If the answers are "yes," then we *must* win. If the answers are "no," then we should not be in combat.

(5) *Fifth*, before the U.S. commits combat forces abroad, there must be some reasonable assurance we will have the support of the American people and their elected representatives in Congress. This support cannot be achieved unless we are candid in making clear the threats we face; the support cannot be sustained without continuing and close consultation. We cannot fight a battle with the Congress at home while asking our troops to win a war overseas or, as in the case of Vietnam, in effect asking our troops *not* to win, but just to be there.

(6) *Finally*, the commitment of U.S. forces to combat should be a last resort.

I believe that these tests can be helpful in deciding whether or not we should commit our troops to combat in the months and years ahead. The point we must all keep uppermost in our minds is that if we ever decide to commit forces to combat, we must support those forces to the *fullest* extent of our national will for as long as it takes to win. So we must have in mind objectives that are clearly defined and understood and supported by the widest possible number of our citizens. And those objectives must be vital to our survival as a free nation and to the fulfillment of our responsibilities as a world power. We must also be farsighted enough to sense when immediate and strong reactions to apparently small events can prevent lion-like responses that may be required later. We must never forget those isolationists in Europe who shrugged that "Danzig is not worth a war," and "why should we fight to keep the Rhineland demilitarized?"

These tests I have just mentioned have been phrased negatively for a purpose—they are intended to sound a note of caution—caution that we must observe prior to commiting forces to combat overseas. When we ask our military forces to risk their very lives in such situations, a note of caution is not only prudent, it is morally required.

In many situations we may apply these tests and conclude that a combatant role is not appropriate. Yet no one should interpret what I am saying here today as an abdication of America's responsibilities—either to its own citizens or to its allies. Nor should these remarks be misread as a signal that this country, or this Administration, is unwilling to commit forces to combat overseas.

We have demonstrated in the past that, when our vital interests or those of our allies are threatened, we are ready to use force, and use it decisively, to protect those interests. Let no one entertain any illusions—if our vital interests are involved, we are prepared to fight. And we are resolved that if we *must* fight, we *must* win.

So, while these tests are drawn from lessons we have learned from the past, they also can—and should—be applied to the future. For example, the problems confronting us in Central America today are difficult. The possibility of more extensive Soviet and Soviet-proxy penetration into this hemisphere in months ahead is something we should recognize. If this happens we will clearly need more economic and military assistance and training to help those who want democracy.

The President will not allow our military forces to creep—or be drawn gradually—into a combat role in Central America or any other place in the world. And indeed our policy is designed to prevent the need for direct American involvement. This means we will need sustained congressional support to back and give confidence to our friends in the region.

I believe that the tests I have enunciated here today can, if applied carefully, avoid the danger of this gradualist incremental approach which almost always means the use of insufficient force. These tests can help us to avoid being drawn inexorably into an endless morass, where it is not vital to our national interest to fight.

But policies and principles such as these require decisive leadership in both the executive and legislative branches of government—and they also require strong and sustained public support. Most of all, these policies require national unity of purpose. I believe the United States now possesses the policies and leadership to gain that public support and unity. And I believe that the future will show we have the strength of character to protect peace with freedom.

In summary, we should all remember these are the policies— indeed the *only* policies—that can preserve for ourselves, our friends, and our posterity, peace with freedom.

I believe we *can* continue to deter the Soviet Union and other potential adversaries from pursuing their designs around the world. We *can* enable our friends in Central America to defeat aggression and gain the breathing room to nurture democratic reforms. We *can* meet the challenge posed by the unfolding complexity of the 1980s.

We will then be poised to begin the last decade of this century amid a peace tempered by realism, and secured by firmness and strength. And it will be a peace that will enable all of us— ourselves at home, and our friends abroad—to achieve a quality of life, both spiritually and materially, far higher than man has even dared to dream.

November 5, 1987

Dear Cap:

It is with the deepest regret that I accept your resignation
as Secretary of Defense, effective upon the appointment and
qualification of your successor.

Nearly 20 years ago, I had the good fortune to have you serve
as my Director of Finance for the State of California. Your
exceptional performance in that post as well as in subsequent
positions with the Federal Government -- among them, Chairman
of the Federal Trade Commission, Director of the Office of
Management and Budget, and Secretary of Health, Education,
and Welfare -- left me no doubt that you would make an
outstanding Secretary of Defense. Not only was I correct in
my judgment, but I am confident that you will be remembered
as the most distinguished and effective Secretary of Defense
in our Nation's history.

For the past seven years, you have worked tirelessly to help
restore both America's military strength and its self-confidence.
You have always recognized that the mantle of liberty carries
with it responsibility and leadership. You've been indispensable in upgrading our military preparedness by promoting the
B-1 bomber, overseeing expansion of our Navy to 600 ships,
and eloquently advocating the Strategic Defense Initiative -- the
most important technological breakthrough in defense strategy
in our lifetime. You have successfully enhanced the quality of
our military personnel and improved morale, so that today the
percentage of high school graduates among enlistees in our
armed services is the highest in our Nation's history. You
have also set an example in cracking down on waste and abuse
in Pentagon spending, ensuring American taxpayers that their
hard-earned monies are being properly and efficiently utilized.

I know well that you are an ardent admirer of Winston Churchill and an astute observer of history. As Secretary of Defense, you have demonstrated time and again the vision, the passion, the sound judgment, and the ability to inspire which Churchill possessed in such full measure. You recognize, as he did, that we live in a dangerous time when the survival and triumph of freedom are not self-evident. If freedom is to endure and expand, it will only be because we understand the lessons of history and the nature of the implacable enemy that confronts us globally. Having immersed yourself in these issues, you have helped this Nation apply these lessons to the many crises that we have faced together. As a result, the United States has been able to conduct itself in the 1980s in a way befitting a great Nation and the leader of the free world.

Cap, you have my heartfelt gratitude for your incomparable service to our Nation. I know that as you return to the private sector, you will continue to champion the public policies that have kept our Nation strong, prosperous, and free.

Nancy joins me in offering you and Jane, and your loved ones, our warm best wishes for every future happiness. May God bless and keep you.

Sincerely,

Ronald Reagan

The Honorable Caspar Willard Weinberger
Secretary of Defense
Washington, D.C. 20301

Letter from President Reagan to Secretary Weinberger, accepting his resignation, November 5, 1987. (private collection)

Commentary
on Events at Home and Abroad
By Caspar W. Weinberger, Publisher

GENERAL COLIN POWELL—AN INSIDE VIEW

No matter how accurate newspaper writers may be and no matter how well-intentioned they are about conveying accurate word portraits of people in the news, it is well-nigh impossible for anyone who does not have deep personal knowledge of his subject to do the job properly.

General Colin L. Powell is much in the news now as Chairman of the Joint Chiefs of Staff, the highest post in our military service, and the principal architect of our Panama operation. It seems certain he will continue to be one of our most important and written about leaders. So I think it appropriate to share my knowledge of General Powell, based on my nearly 20 years of personal friendship and close professional relationships with him.

General Powell and Defense Secretary Cheney at press briefing on Panama

First, he is a superb soldier whose greatest ambition has been to command troops in the field. He has done that many times, including tours in Vietnam, where he was wounded. But his other talents have attracted Presidents and cabinet members whose urgent pleas for his services he has heeded regardless of his own preferences.

Second, he is a great patriot in the best and truest sense of the word. He is not blind to America's faults. He has suffered under them—fighting a war in Vietnam we never intended to win; and his wife and family, while he was away fighting that war, living in the miserable conditions that prevailed in parts of Alabama in the Sixties. None of that embittered him nor did anything but convince him that he should fight harder to correct those faults, which he has consistently done.

Third, he has a truly global, nonparochial view of the world and the leadership role we must play in it. His work as chief military assistant to the Secretary of Defense and as National Security Advisor to the President uniquely qualifies him to know the extent and vital necessity of our commitments, and leaders, civilian and military, with whom he will be working.

He is also a particularly effective administrator-manager who anticipates and prepares for the various twists and turns events can take.

He is a born leader with whom and for whom people in all walks of life like to work. He has both staying power and the flexibility to change quickly and decisively when necessary. That comes from being a skilled infantry commander of troops.

Colin Powell is a man of high moral standards, with a model family to whom he is devoted.

He will never take us unprepared into any kind of situation that our civilian leadership requires. He will not hesitate to advise the President of his true opinions, whether they are popular or not.

In Panama he knew well in advance of the actual decision to intervene that in all likelihood we would have to do just that. That is why, within a few hours, we were able to deploy very strong forces that were able to achieve all their important objectives in a few days, and to turn a criminal dictator into an impotent fugitive within a few hours.

Carping will be, and has been, heard, as is always the case whenever the U.S. does anything—in Grenada, or Libya, or anywhere. But I have expressed these thoughts because I believe it is essential that we really know the person we have in charge when it is necessary to call on our armed forces.

And to those who may say, "Oh well, you are hopelessly prejudiced, having known and worked with him for 20 years," I would only respond that, if you have worked closely with a person for 20 years, and you are indeed hopelessly prejudiced in his favor, that, too, tells you something about him.

Copyright by *Forbes* magazine, January 1990. Reprinted with permission.

INDEX

CASPAR WEINBERGER has served in Cabinet positions for three presidents, including seven years as Secretary of Defense for the Reagan Administration. He is a decorated veteran of infantry conflicts in the Pacific theater during World War II, a Phi Beta Kappa, magna cum laude graduate of Harvard College and Harvard Law School. Currently, he is publisher of *Forbes* magazine and practicing law at the prominent Washington firm of Rogers & Wells.